THE SOPRANOS

Born under a Bad Sign

Often hailed as one of the greatest television series of all time, *The Sopranos* is a product of its era, firmly embedded in the problems of post-industrial, post-ethnic America. In *The Sopranos: Born under a Bad Sign*, Franco Ricci examines the groundbreaking HBO series and its impact as a cultural phenomenon.

Ricci demonstrates an encyclopedic knowledge of the series, the genre, and the show's social context in his analysis of its complex themes and characters. He explores *The Sopranos'* deep engagement with problems of race, class, gender, and identity, specifically in its portrayal of the Italian-American experience, consumer- and media-driven society, and contemporary psychosocial issues. The series' protagonist, Mafia boss and patriarch Tony Soprano, in many ways embodies the anxieties of our age. Focusing on Tony Soprano's internal struggles and interactions with his therapist, family, and associates, Ricci traces this archetypal character's existential conflicts and sheds light on his search for self, connection, and meaning.

Comprehensive in scope and sophisticated in approach, *The Sopranos: Born under a Bad Sign* is richly rewarding reading for anyone with an interest in the popular television drama, both as entertainment and as social commentary.

FRANCO RICCI is a professor of Italian studies at the University of Ottawa.

FRANCO RICCI

THE SOPRANOS

Born under a Bad Sign

UNIVERSITY OF TORONTO PRESS
Toronto Buffalo London

© University of Toronto Press 2014
Toronto Buffalo London
www.utppublishing.com

ISBN 978-1-4426-4764-0 (cloth)
ISBN 978-1-4426-1571-7 (paper)

Library and Archives Canada Cataloguing in Publication

Ricci, Franco, 1953–, author
    The Sopranos : born under a bad sign / Franco Ricci.

(Toronto Italian studies)
Includes bibliographical references and index.
ISBN 978-1-4426-4764-0 (bound).   ISBN 978-1-4426-1571-7 (pbk.)

1. Sopranos (Television program).   2. Social interaction on television.
    I. Title.   II. Series: Toronto Italian studies

PN1992.77.S66R53 2014   791.45'72   C2014-900827-9

University of Toronto Press and Franco Ricci acknowledge the generous support for the publication of this book from the Faculty of Arts, University of Ottawa.

University of Toronto Press acknowledges the financial assistance to its publishing program of the Canada Council for the Arts and the Ontario Arts Council.

 Canada Council   Conseil des Arts
for the Arts   du Canada

University of Toronto Press acknowledges the financial support of the Government of Canada through the Canada Book Fund for its publishing activities.

For Alessandro ... My first reader ... Il mio primo lettore

... that's the good thing about being halved; that one understands the sorrow of every person and thing in the world at its own incompleteness.
Italo Calvino, The Cloven Viscount

Contents

Acknowledgments	ix
Introduction: "Coming Heavy": Revisiting, Rereading, Rethinking *The Sopranos*	3
Revisiting the Television Phenomenon	3
Rereading the Narrative	11
Rethinking Visual Traces	18
1 Inner Sanctums	**22**
Opening Shots	28
Dr. Melfi's Office Anteroom	32
Dr. Melfi's Office	42
The Soprano Home	52
The Bada Bing	60
Tony's Inner Sanctum of Darkness	66
2 When I Grow Up I Want to Be an American	**77**
Ethnic Prologue	77
Ethnicity: Business or Nostalgia?	80
What Melting Pot?	91
To Be or Not to Be a Mobster	105
3 God Help the Beast in Me	**120**
Act Like a Man	120
Made Men	125
Mad Sons	132
The Brotherhood of Prodigal Sons	143

4 Two Tonys: Drawing Conclusions from Mediated Mob Images	160
World Construction	160
Duplicity or Deceit?	169
Word and Image	178
A Blacker Shade of Pale	187
5 An Appendix of Verbal Bits and Visual Bytes	196
Introduction	196
Paintings	203
Posters	205
Photographs	209
Verbal Subtexts	212
Newspapers	220
Books	223
Carmela and Books	229
Television on TV	234
Statues	256
6 Conclusion	260
Notes	267
Suggested Readings	295
Episodes Index	305
Name Index	309
Subject Index	317
Title Index	321

Acknowledgments

Many conversations with colleagues and students have found their way into these pages. Lively and stimulating discussions conducted in my Italian Heritage in North America course helped shape the notions. I am indebted, however, to the doctors and nurses of the Bone and Marrow Transplant Program of the Ottawa Hospital for their unflagging tenacity and indomitable determination to help me carry my Soprano project to its end. In particular, Dr. Lothar Huebsch, Dr. David Allan, Dr. Harold Atkins, Dr. Isabelle Bence-Bruckler, Dr. Carolyn Faught, Dr. Mitchell Sabloff, and Dr. Jason Tay. A special thanks to my BMT Liaison Nurse Katie Lucas and all the nurses on the Fifth Floor Cancer Ward of the Ottawa General Hospital for their patience, their smiles, and their honest care. They are truly angels in comfortable shoes. Never an appointment passed without a doctor's query regarding the status of this manuscript; never a salutation without an enheartened discussion of some current theoretical concern of mine. I have learned in various ways from them to adroitly move from under a bad sign.

***

Le revisioni finali del testo sono state rese piacevoli e alleggerite dall'inestimabile sostegno morale di Domenico e Antonella Santacroce. Hanno reso il loro albergo, il Santacroce Meeting, una mia reggia personale. Li ringrazio di cuore per l'indescrivibile ospitalità e illimitata generosità. Il loro impegno quotidiano è un armonioso insieme di lavoro assiduo, attenzione alle persone, cura dei dettagli e quella saggia speranza contadina che si fondono per formare amicizie vere e durature.

Un saluto allo staff alberghiero: Nicolina Antuzzi, Concetta Gianpietro, Samantha Mancini, e Ruth Lucariello. Apprezzerò sempre i loro sorrisi, la loro operosità, la perenne disponibilità ... e gli ottimi cappuccini mattutini.

Per lo staff culinario serbo uno speciale ringraziamento per momenti di impegno in cucina che hanno reso la mia permanenza a Sulmona un'esperienza indimenticabile di lavoro-vacanza-studio, che spero possa ripetersi.

Allo Chef Franco Ranallo un sentito abbraccio per le sue lezioni di cultura culinaria e professionalita'. Di Leonardo Santacroce e Deyan Miatovich conservo memoria di alternati momenti di serieta' e svago. Ancora un grazie e un dolce sorriso per Antonella Santacroce che ripropone i nostri dolci tradizionali con inesauribile passione e ispirazione.

E infine al Master Chef Domenico Santacroce un caloroso abbraccio per avermi consentito l'umile e generoso abbandono ai sapori più genuini.

***

The death of actor James Gandolfini of a heart attack while in Rome on 19 June 2013 was particularly painful since I have spent the better part of the past ten years mulling his most infamous character, Tony Soprano. Gandolfini was immensely excited to be in Italy. On this rare Italian sojourn, he was on his way to the Taormina Film Festival in Sicily where he was to have hosted a Master Class along with Gabriele Muccino. He was also scheduled to receive the Taormina City Prize alongside actress Marisa Tomei. Instead, a moving retrospective of his multifaceted career served as a sad tribute that brought the spell-bound gallery to tears.

There was an innate, deep, and special goodness to the man that shone through his gut-wrenching performances because, as David Chase eulogized James, "The feeling was real. The feeling was real. The feeling was real. I can't say that enough." That feeling shone through the cracks of the performative facade and drew audiences to love him, no matter how despicable the character he portrayed. Gandolfini, in other words, was genuine. I hope to have lent some insight into his extraordinarily gripping performance as Tony Soprano, a character born under a bad sign that was played by a likeable, loveable, powerfully humane actor's actor. I thank him for Tony.

THE SOPRANOS

Born under a Bad Sign

Introduction

"Coming Heavy": Revisiting, Rereading, Rethinking *The Sopranos*

> It is the ambition of the authors of *The Public Enemy* to honestly depict an environment that exists today in a certain strata of American life, rather than glorify the hoodlum or the criminal. While the story of *The Public Enemy* is essentially a true story, all names and characters appearing herein, are purely fictional.
>
> Foreword, *The Public Enemy*, Warner Bros.

> One immunizes the contents of the collective imagination by means of a small inoculation of acknowledged evil; one thus protects it against the risk of a generalized subversion.
>
> Roland Barthes, *Mythologies*

Revisiting the Television Phenomenon

The very question "What is TV?" has been given different answers since its inception and non-stop proliferation. Does it entertain? Does it educate? Does it or can it do both? When a premium cable TV network triumphantly declares "It's not TV, it's HBO," a relevant question would be "Why?" A much more pertinent question, to my mind, is "How?" If you have picked up this text you have inquisitively, rather than passively, watched and thought about *The Sopranos*. You have been bombarded from countless sources – TV advertisements, HBO merchandising, DVD box sets, popular books, blogs – that have given you a simplified impression of the series, a simplified image that is more mythical than real, more commercial than actual. Any ardent viewer will have fashioned impressions, good and bad, based on the functional criteria that, after all, this is just a television series. As such, one may interpret the basic storyline figuratively, allowing oneself the pleasurable liberty of vagary by suspending belief for the benefit of enjoyment. Or one may view the series as a literalist thereby insisting upon logical outcomes of plot, perhaps eventually ruminating notions of elitist or populist conspiracy when expected outcomes are not gratified. In either instance, the interested viewer eventually develops a personal repertoire of character traits, themes, possible scenarios and situations that has allowed one to make relative connotations about the social political cultural and pop significance of the series vis-à-vis Italian-Americans (hereafter I-Ams), the existence or non-existence of the Mafia, television programming in general, and the larger American social context. Ultimately, one may simply dismiss the entire interpretative enterprise and prefer to view the series as just another television pulp fiction that is incidentally based on an entertaining plausible context that sells and has a storyline that is both popular and profitable. Nothing that is really deep, as any superficial interpretation would eventually ascertain; it's just entertainment. But we were promised that "it's not TV," the implication being that this program somehow offers something *more*.

In this study, the reader is encouraged to discover the compelling, sometimes controversial, but always enticing more that has shaped, moulded, engendered, animated, and driven the television classic *The Sopranos*. The reader will be asked to question basic notions of identity within a current American context by confronting the images portrayed in the series with real life America. As *The Sopranos* narrative unfolds, we will note the social influences that generate our stereotypical views of others. We will test the limits of convention by examining those issues that has made the series so controversial and appealing and understand why *The Sopranos* is as much about the viewer's experiences and reactions while watching the series as it is about David Chase's heartfelt inspiration and superbly inspired writing. This text thus attempts to present an intimate, and hopefully unique, perspective on the series by allowing this modern classic to dictate, as Allan Bloom stated in *The Closing of the American Mind*, "what the questions are and the method of approaching them."[1] This sort of critical reading/ viewing requires moments of perspective adjustment, of wider context, of more refined and prolonged instances of reflection that playfully associate the multiple with the contradictory, the heretofore assumed with the expectedly impossible. Such lateral thinking strategies present a challenge in these days of slim LED screens and an instantly fleeting historical perspective. It takes courage to question the values and ideas one has harboured and wilfully accepted as given; to give intellectual depth to the flat dimension images that parade before us on the myriad of screens that surround us daily. In this study, the reader is encouraged to discover subjective critical authority while examining important critical, political, social, and aesthetic issues raised by *The Sopranos*.

I wish to remain above the petty politics and ethnic controversy and instead use the more pertinent issues raised by the series itself to examine the various story motifs. My method is systematic, analytical, and cohesive. I will build a story from the narrative outline of *The Sopranos* that provides insight to those leitmotifs that subtend the weekly storylines and create an evolving personality for the characters. I will thus examine not the function of the story vis-à-vis uncomfortable I-Am stereotypes or trans-historical immigrant assumptions but instead search for those cardinal moments that transform the television event into an emblematic statement of present-day I-Am character identity and place in contemporary American society.

The Sopranos is the perfect contemporary television narrative to accomplish this task because unlike much mediated ethnic imagery often embodied by predictable characters and fueled by worn clichés, *The Sopranos* does not get caught in the trap of fighting the I-Am stereotype but reverses the traditional palimpsest of exclusion, segregation, and discrimination. The series generates its own demystifying questions regarding ethnicity, invites informed discussion about contemporary American mores, and provides a visual artefact of a particular time in I-Am history that does not shun controversy but instead welcomes close readings, accepts amateurish assumptions, fuels erudite musings. The series has been criticized and ostracized by I-Am anti-defamation groups, marginalized by politically correct viewers for its non-appeal to the WASP imagination, but never minimalized. The show's impact was immediate, its legacy ongoing and enduring. More than a story, it is a pageant of riveting wiseguy violence wrapped in the seductive fiction of a contemporary I-Am family of ill repute trying to make it in America. Moving beyond controversy, the series explores stereotypes without exploiting them. For what it's worth, *The Sopranos* has been hyper-hyped and hyper-analysed, often in haste by pop commentators and serious academics quick to cash-in on the run-away phenomenon, exploited for its commercial caché, ransacked for sound bites, but never reduced to a naive sitcom.

Though I began this book thinking I would write about a popular mob series, I soon realized that my attention was constantly drawn to issues of identity. Despite the intricate embroidery of the myriad themes and motifs that resonate through the arc of the story, questions of divided and unstable identity are the subtending template that clarifies the many complex currents that would otherwise have remained murky. From the very first episode, characters are in search of a stable sense of place in a consumer- and media-driven society. More specifically, they crave a public identity of salacious visual consumerism. From Tony Soprano to Paulie "Walnuts" Gualtieri, Carmela Soprano to Janice Soprano to Dr. Melfi, to the panoply of goomahs, capos, aunts and uncles, thugs and wanna-be wiseguys, all dispend significant energy seeking to create a public personality that finalizes their often feeble sense of personal worth and popular celebrity. Christopher Moltisanti is one of the most taxed of characters, for example, because he realizes that he has no public face, or at least the notoriety he so desperately pretends to deserve. In an age of cell phones and social networking, Christopher bemoans his invisibility to the point of envying gangster rappers: "The moolies, they got it goin' on. And they're on TV. The Soprano crew is always secret this, omertà that; fuckin' gets on my nerves" ("A Hit Is a Hit" I.10). Times they are indeed a-changin' as questions of private self-worth are juggled with visions of public celebrity, a torment for all the characters. Hence Christopher's inextricable tendency to fancy both an ideal and popular spiritual self through writing while simultaneously destroying his real mobster-infested body with drugs and alcohol.

Uncle Corrado "Junior" Soprano (referred to as Uncle Junior or Corrado), on the other hand, is so dependent upon the monolithic facade of his secretive mob image that he terminates a profound love relationship with a lifelong partner lest he be publicly harpooned as weak by his insensitive cohorts for a perceived sexual proclivity. Dementia eventually robs him of his constructed masculine identity. Mamma Livia Soprano's feigning of the loss of her polarized identity momentarily gains her the family's indemnity while conveniently providing her troubled self a viable excuse for attempted filicide. Both Carmela Soprano and Dr. Jennifer Melfi question the resolve of their career choices. One attempts to save her tainted soul from the fires of hell with episodic forays into her Catholic catechism. The other wades through the open wounds of her pained ethnicity armed with the intellectually appealing canon of psychiatry. Both seek uneasy comfort in their oft-chafing skin. Carmela may imperiously (though sarcastically cognizant and impotent) quip to flighty sister-in-law Janice: "A woman has to keep her sense of identity" ("Toodle-Fucking-oo" II.3), but in this murky world of shadowy ethnic origins, everyone's identity is at risk, everyone's name is susceptible to the erroneous stroke of a distracted clerk's (or fate's) pen. The corruption of one's name is an aberration suffered by Phil Leotardo whose family name, he despondently reveals to his grandchildren, is really Leonardo ("Stage 5" VI.2). In Sopranoland, genetic endowments are often corrupted for public consumption by a chronic lack of cultural certainty and the deforming forces of social convention, overbearing prejudice, and geographical happenstance.

But schizophrenic identities are not relegated solely to the I-Am main characters. Cannoli I-Ams (hard-shelled on the outside, soft on the inside), Uncle Tom Blacks, opportunistic Eastern Europeans, money-crazed Russians, overzealous Hasidic Jews, even morally conflicted FBI agents abound. All appear confused, compromised, their questionable social success priced with the fear of engulfment, implosion, and mistaken identity. For those I-Ams like Silvio Dante who maintain a protracted and false identification with the equally false ethnic myths of America, the public derision by Native Americans of Christopher Columbus in "Christopher" IV.3 speaks eloquently about the charade of popular image culture and the renewed reliance upon self and independent selfhood. FBI Agent Dwight Harris's overseas assignments may broadcast him to the Middle Eastern Terrorist Squad but his heart strings remain pulled by a Satriale panino, preferably eaten next to the mob perpetrators he once hunted but whose lifestyle he envies and, at least when it comes to adultery, he lustfully emulates ("Made in America" VI.21). The ultimate loss of identity in this parallelepiped realm is death. This fate is reserved for those whose betrayal of group association condemns the perpetrator to exclusion and tribal retribution. There is. indeed, a morbid narrative logic to this protracted voyage of personal growth that is muddied by the competitive impossibility of realizing one's true nature in an I-Am and/or other ethnic American landscape that is not tinged with corruption and greed.

The main focus of this volatilized identity quest is Tony Soprano. As a father he may impatiently bluster to his wife (when she reminds him that his children need a father not a dead man) that "the kids got one … me, Tony Soprano, and all that comes with it" ("Isabella" I.12). In the forum of society, however, he is a rogue thug, a self-admitted "fat fuckin' crook from New Jersey" ("Calling All Cars" IV.11). Within the fellowship of the goodfellas he rules he is an overly rapacious and ruthless boss who, following Dr. Melfi's advice to allow his underlings to "see only what you allow them to see" ("Mr. and Mrs. John Sacrimoni Request" VI.5) stops at nothing, even risking death by opening a fresh stomach wound by fighting Perry Annunziata, the youngest stud of his crew, to prove his mettle and reassert his public authority ("Live Free or Die" VI.6). In all contexts he is surprisingly svelte, reverently impertinent, unfailingly impatient, serenely indifferent, and imperiously egotistic. Embossed with both the reprehensibility of his chosen trade and the vulnerability of his psychological temerity, any threat to his sense of self is immediately refashioned into incandescent schizophrenia. At series end, these (dis)abling features have been mellowed, deepened, embossed with repulsive life experiences and couched in the prejudiced glow of psychoanalytic growth. His dreams contribute to the imagined notion that he is not simply of this time and place but someone very special. Any threat to his precarious identity is volatilized by the different personalities, from infant coddled in a loving mother's arms ("Isabella" I.12) to successful, though doubt-ridden, optics salesman ("Join the Club" VI.2; "Mayham" VI.III), that inform his growth and encapsulate his emerging competence as an effective, remorseless, vicious, unconscionable, and ultimately defiant mob boss.[2]

Beyond the *Slate Magazine* psychological deconstruction of each character and episode that occurred on a weekly basis,[3] the weekly newspaper reviews,[4] the spontaneous viewer blogs, the many articles written by professional critics in public forums and scholars in learned journals, I have attempted to read the series the old-fashioned way – by suspending belief and wondering where the ride would take me; an almost impossible task given the jaded multimedic nature of our contemporary condition, but nevertheless a pleasurable adventure. *The Sopranos* was popular because it attempted, according to David Chase, to introduce intelligent storytelling in television programs. As the media landscape changed dramatically around the turn of the century, new delivery systems, online Internet streaming, on-demand services, big-screen TVs, DVDs, DVRs, all contributed to the notion that serial television was at the edge of a technical and artistic revolution. To be sure, *The Sopranos* enjoyed cutting-edge marketing and an impressively expanding production budget. But with its big-picture feel and privileging of cinematic production values, Chase created compelling drama that filled the burgeoning space of television. The medium may have been the messenger, but the story is the tenacious draw and the seductive hook of *The Sopranos*.

The series owes much to the gangster film genre. Intertextual references, the mimicking of well-known scenes from classic mobster films, the blatant intercalations of film footage into the narrative raised the series from the mundane to the sublime. In "Proshai, Livushka" III.2, for example, we see an image of the dead Salvatore "Big Pussy" Bonpensiero in Tony's hall mirror. The vision calls to mind the final scene of Bernardo Bertolucci's esoteric *Last Tango in Paris* (1972) where a ghostly image of the main character's dead mother appears in the balcony window. In the same episode, Tony, along with the viewer, watches the movie *The Public Enemy* (1931) on TV. Subsequent episodes are peppered with scenes from *High Noon* (1952), *Rio Bravo* (1959), among others, and the ubiquitous The History Channel is regularly intercalated into the action of the series and acts as background information to augment the plotline. Characters routinely repeat dialogue from mobster movies, car horns are tuned to blare the first bars of *The Godfather* theme (1972), while lighting, tone, and scene texture often replicate scenes from Martin Scorsese's *Goodfellas* (1990). Christopher Moltisanti even reprises a scene from this film by shooting a petulant bakery clerk in the foot, a nod to the role he played in *Goodfellas* when his character "Spider" was shot in the foot, and eventually shot to death, by an impatient Tommy De Meo played by Joe Pesci. These playful references are obvious allusions to a cinematic world *out there* that is very comfortable with the television fiction *in here*. They are intended for the cognoscenti who wilfully accept the challenge since it is the cognoscenti who accept the challenge of taking these inferential walks outside the text. But the references do not end with gangster films. *The Sopranos* is a series that, indeed, to quote Uncle Junior, "comes heavy." It is saturated with intertextual echoes to mainstream Hollywood movies, classic westerns, television programs, contemporary literature, erudite artworks, popular culture, and newspaper and magazine articles. Whatever their origin, these moments appeal to the viewer's sensibilities and foster an evolving and active interface with whatever occurs on screen. These postmodern self-referential cues are meticulously structured performances, powerful signifiers that extend the series into the viewer's home and by weaving personal impressions into an extended and original hypertext. In today's media-saturated world, the sole boundaries of interpretation are the viewer's insatiable appetite for conspicuous visual, verbal, and pleasurable gratification.

David Chase's images are potently ideologically and rely precisely upon the viewer's willingness to collaborate in the inexhaustibility of the series' layered dimensions. His purpose in *The Sopranos* is neither to glorify I-Ams, as has been suggested, nor by consequence deride his many myopic detractors. He wished, instead, to simply write an intelligent adult drama:

> HBO at the time ... we didn't know they were the HBO they were going to become. But I realized, however it had happened, I had been given a great opportunity to do something different. And I didn't think it would succeed. And I didn't care. I was so fed up with TV at that time, and so frustrated with my lack of success at getting into features that I didn't care. I just wanted to make the best TV pilot I possibly could. And so I had license in terms of language and action and story development and flow and pace, and I thought, "Just go for it."[5]

The Sopranos wilfully challenged its audience. It never catered to lowbrow conjecture and was unapologetic for its edgy portrayal of life as Chase saw it. In retrospect, he vociferously responded to his critics. And yes, in this age of electronic immediacy, he was able to rebut written criticism and political comment on the uncomfortable issues that arose around his series with quick, frank, often brutish on-screen retort. In this he is no different from the canonical authors revered in literature who responded in kind to their critics with caustic commentary, vitriolic poetry, and unbridled literary imagination. Indeed, the nineteenth-century serialized novel is an apt analogue for the ongoing conversation Chase pursued with his viewers. But the fact remains that *The Sopranos* is an unquestionable contemporary television classic that forever altered moth-eaten notions of television and engaged an increasingly fragmented American audience driven to fill its ennui with self-absorbing premium cable, endless gaming, video on demand, and ubiquitous Internet. The series ushered in a new era that intercalated perfectly with the hyper-conscious media generation that demanded blockbuster programming by their evolving media suppliers on ever bigger (and ever smaller) visual monitors. As the boundaries between big-screen Hollywood and small-screen television blurred, *The Sopranos* provided the requisite spark that jump-started the televised revolution.

I wish to draw attention to the brilliant aesthetic subtleties that animate the hermetic world of this New Jersey mob. Instead of catering to the many critical samples of socio-political disapproval or academic approbation, I will examine the artistic integrity that accompanies the cathartic repartee, the flummoxed shenanigans, and the unmitigated savagery of these compelling and enduring characters. I will not isolate the series from its context but rather draw attention to the aesthetic representation of this reality by discussing those relatively few issues that, to my mind, drive the storylines and produce the action. In other words, and at the very least, I am inviting the reader/viewer to consider *The Sopranos* as an autonomous artwork rather than possible mirror of some exterior ethnic reality that has been exploited for stereotypical content. At the most, the reader is invited to examine the series following modes of interpretation that include the historical, cultural, psychoanalytical, structural, and technical; approaches that produce valid and stimulating, often surprising, interpretative possibilities and readings.

Rereading the Narrative

Given the complexity of its characters, it might surprise that *The Sopranos* was an instant phenomenon. Just as Paramount Studios was saved by the operatic multi-generational crime saga *The Godfather* (1972), the series was responsible for the emergence and financial redemption of a fledgling home box office network known as HBO and for subsequently spawning a network of innovative miniseries and premium pay-per-view shows that revitalized a dormant segment of television. It is a product not just of a single individual but of a whole collective American culture. As such, it articulates the latent desires and overt contradictions of its time. As any project is guided by a proposed vision, Chase's stated intention was to write a story about a middle-aged gangster in therapy grounded in the dysfunctional relationship between a son and his mother. It soon became, however, a crucible that percolated humanism, nihilism, racism, honesty, cruelty, predation, identity, redemption, all coloured with the infamy of the Mafia and tinged with the heart of darkness captured in the character Tony Soprano. Tony embodies the uncomfortable reflex that the underpinnings of the American Dream may be yoked to criminality; its nexus is the uneasy marriage of respectability and reprehensibility. It is a sprawling story reminiscent in its style of encyclopedic nineteenth-century narratives and thoroughly engaged with the events, circumstances, and attitudes of the times, the culturally defining Big American Novels of the 1960s, the art house cinema of the 1970s, and the sociocultural malaise of the end of the millennium.

Television programs, by their very nature of entering the average home, are traditionally constructed to be friendly, cosy, intimate artefacts that can be viewed and reviewed at leisure. They have the ability to become part of the family, weekly instalments of cathartic release or comedic entertainment; an amusing pastime, nothing to be taken seriously. The generic nature of many television programs renders them caricatural as they wilfully exploit volatile tastes and fleeting consumer tendencies. The networks air what the public craves. TV is, after all, a popular cultural medium churning out products of a homogenized ideology (or game-winning style) able to reach as wide an audience as possible. Most programs are forgettable. Routinization keeps the costs of production down and minimizes risks often at the price of sacrificing quality. Conventionality is thus both the boon and death knell of most television programs. As conventionalism incorporates even cutting-edge programming into the corporate ideology, quality is lost and representation becomes trivial. Furthermore, any presumed artistic merit is often conditioned by a dominant ideological process that diffuses individual expression by robbing it of its potentially destabilizing discourse preferring instead a milk-toast approach that satisfies ratings. Though a dominant cultural institution of modern society, television is also a thriving industry concerned with production, distribution, and reception and whose investors are ultimately concerned with immediate profit. Problems arising from ledger issues are usually solved by reducing production costs, choosing well-worn stories, catering to dependable, and programmable, public taste. Critical artistic reception is almost never a measure of success but is often only incidental when discussing a program's commercial footprint. When television programs become popular, therefore, it follows that they subscribe (or are subjugated) to the dominant value system, and that the programs serve the predictable desires of their anticipated viewers. Discussions of popularity are often reduced to just such formulas, despite arguments that decry the lowest common denominator as a controlling socio-economic paradigm.

    This all changed with David Chase. A longtime writer for television, yet an ardent detractor of lowest-common-denominator television programming, Chase's seeds of discontent arose from his experiences inside the industry itself. While producing and writing episodes for *Kolchak: The Night Stalker* (1974–5), *The Rockford Files* (1974–80), *I'll Fly Away* (1991–3), and *Northern Exposure* (1990–5), Chase felt straitjacketed by production schedules, repetitive situational story arcs, and the lack of intelligent dialogue. He once stated, "Network television is all talk. I think there should be visuals on a show, some sense of mystery to it, connections that don't add up. I think there should be dreams and music and dead air and stuff that goes nowhere. There should be, God forgive me, a little bit of poetry."[6] He thus came to "loathe and despise"[7] network television shows. He considered most programs as mundane projects that reflected the consensus of viewers' preferences and that had been gathered, analysed, projected, shaped, and finally "Nielsened" by the powers that finance and control television programming. But was there room in the crowded television universe for a program that extolled technical innovation and thematic idiosyncrasy, that revelled in stylish artistry? And was the television art he envisioned to be autonomous art for art's sake, or art that was relevant and popular?

Chase's response was to engage viewers in an enriching artistic experience, one that countered the experience that the dominant structures of television media had controlled, repressed, or mercilessly rehashed and trivialized. He reclaimed aesthetic representation and correctness of historical vision; he hired resourceful writers that wrote captivating plots, developed multifaceted characters, demanded technical precision and progressive themes; and then he wrapped it all into popular cultural form. He moved beyond the prism of conflict between innovative story and corporate profit. *The Sopranos*, in other words, was popular because it was a damn good story; it was profitable because it was finely wrought storytelling. Chase admitted to his proclivities, "I came up in the late '60s/early '70s when European and Japanese film was very popular. They were much more oblique in their storytelling. You could go to a Fellini movie and say, 'Wow, I loved that! Now what was it about?' And I loved that feeling."[8] He cut his teeth on the art films of Jean-Luc Goddard, Federico Fellini, and Stanley Kubrick, and admits to having had a revelation after viewing Roman Polanski's *Cul-de-Sac* (1966): "Before, I thought films just arrived from the factory, like they were Chevys of Fords. Leaving that theater, I remember thinking, 'these films are personal, they're made by a person.' It crystallized for me that it was something one could do."[9] The trope of ambiguity rides a fine line between high culture that elucidates the masses and the culture of profit that satiates commercial interest. If we consider Aristotle's parameters for the successful delivery of an artistic message – the logos, the content and quality of the argument as expressed in words; the ethos, the quality of the artist that produces the argument; and the pathos, the emotions the message stirs in the listener – then it is quite evident that Chase was supremely concerned with the truth value of his product and the impact the message would have on its audience.

An entire century of archetypal Hollywood gangster films and ethnic stereotyping of I-Ams had engendered an ethnic sensibility to the unwanted mobster mantle many felt was being arrogantly placed upon their upwardly mobile and uncontaminated shoulders. These individuals viewed the transposition of alleged criminal history onto the poetical plane of cinema as an affront to their carefully managed identities as reservoirs of an unsoiled and empowering Italian culture. For them, the dialogues and events in *The Sopranos* acquired the status of factual credentials that overpowered and displaced the real events in the history and culture of I-Ams. The series' reduction of everyday family reality to commonplace mom and pop actuality played on the home television screen brought these untenable arguments closer to the real. Discomfort and discomfiture quickly blossomed. Many I-Am groups felt the series demeaned their ancestry.[10] Others decried the gratuitous violence.[11] Those bemoaning their dented public image were spurred by an overly self-conscious ethnic- and gender-conscious culture, while others were beset by the broader unsettling paradox of caring for fictional characters one would normally loathe in real life. *The Sopranos*, in other words, inspired sympathy for the Devil.[12]

But while the series is set in the bosom of an I-Am family, and Chase's striving for verisimilitude renders the situational and character portrayals strikingly realistic and recognizable by many I-Ams, it is not about issues experienced only by this ethnic group or I-Am family. The panoply of characters and the richness of their physical and psychological descriptions remind the audience of the dangers of witnessing reality from an exclusionary point of view. For example, early Italian immigrants compelled themselves to adapt to the changes of an expanding nation and people. Through their labour and sweat they forged communities that both reflected and advanced humanist features of civility and inbred cultural mores. Italians, indeed, were part of the New Frontier: law-abiding, ambitious, adventurous individuals who toiled indefatigably to create social, political, and economic prosperity. But they were also something more. When Tony Soprano laments "coming in at the end" in the pilot episode, he is decrying the loss of this tumultuous and seemingly limitless frontier. That historical moment was pregnant with opportunities, which permitted all forms of complicity to be born and flourish. But alongside the foundations of honesty, modesty, toil, and labour grew the egregious sins of chicanery, sloth, and illegal activity. That same vital energy that forged the good American spawned the nefarious forces that permitted men, and not only men of Italian origin, to freely generate an ethos of personal profit through greed and violence. They represented the villainous dark side of the American Dream. It is not our purpose to follow the development of Organized Crime as it built and then followed the rich economic watershed that spread across the American frontier. Nevertheless, the series must be viewed as a literalization of the unbridled beast of capitalism that hunkers within the benevolent, socially progressive, and morally inspired nation that America has always foisted as its image. It is this coming of age, or historical reckoning, that Tony, as contemporary representative of that alternative moral centre, simultaneously bemoans and craves. It is the ability to live beyond culpability, unconcerned with the politics of ethics and redeeming values, that he inherently feels and ultimately fears to understand, but towards which he is drawn with unrelenting urgency and pride.

Where advancement at the limen of the burgeoning frontier once meant a steady movement away from the social collective in favour of the steady growth of individual independence and wealth, the ever-retreating frontier stalled unrestrained growth on all fronts, marring even the most perfect of families, and foisting non-traditional patterns on reticent individuals. Tony resists. He is, in essence, the last cowboy. Braving the moaning ghosts that haunt his every gesture, he is still convinced of his invincibility but unsettled about the tenure of his mob enterprise. And herein lies the alleged paradox. The movies Tony loved as a boy taught him that the true cowboy was a hero; that he lived by vital codes, not societal rules. Cowboys slept in their hat and boots and died in the saddle. But so did the urban public enemy who hit the mattresses, took the bullet, and died in the gutter. Both were, in other words, "good soldiers" – a description of himself to Dr. Melfi in "D-Girl" II.7 – a euphemism for the outlaw that understood the lay of the land:

> The twisted and demented psychos ... the Hitlers, the Pol Pots, those are the evil fucks that deserve to die ... We're soldiers. Soldiers don't go to hell. It's war. Soldiers, they kill other soldiers. We're in a situation where everybody involved knows the stakes. And if you're gonna accept those stakes, you gotta do certain things ... soldiers, we follow codes, orders ...

As such they are blameless victims of a historical context that blurred moral polarities. Tony's turn to villainy was a natural extension of the American Dream. He easily identified with his childhood cowboy heroes who often displayed tortured selves that struggled with life choices and circumstances that placed them in the crevice between right and wrong. The Virginian, suffering protagonist of the movie *The Virginian* (1929) and the eponymous 1902 novel *The Virginian: A Horseman of the Plains*, wore black, the colour traditionally symbolizing evil and turpitude. So had another admired hero, Marshall Will Kane, in the movie *High Noon* (1952). Both roles had been played by Gary Cooper. Tony admires these characters' selfless dedication to an ideal, whatever its shade and personal ramifications. He especially reveres Cooper's elegant silence, his rugged strength, his constancy of purpose. He understands Cooper's grave self-consciousness as his characters internalize the same heavy heart and internal conflicts as himself but never vary from their destinies. This sort of public ruggedness shields a private and soft inner layer that is especially appealing since it reminds him of his own divided nature. To these toughened external accouterments Tony grafts the ebullient and kinetic personality excesses of James Cagney's character in *The Public Enemy* (1931). The attraction to these opposite poles belies his tortured duplicity. On the one hand, he is the unrestrained killer, a boisterous public image of unfettered evil who is bent on exploiting the unraveling fabric of society, corrupt, vile to the core. On the other, he exemplifies the loving father, the private guarantor of stolid family heritage, silent patriarchal law, and symbolic order. The fragility of the cleft installs a sado-masochistic relationship with the self that is fraught with social pretense, moral equivocation, and personal hypocrisy. Like the heroes he admires, Tony lives in a world of defined extremes where public resolution lies in the suffered private solutions that form the gist of *The Sopranos*.

The same words, then, used to discuss Tony the lonely avenging hero may be used to discuss the mobster-father. While living inside the anticipated patterns of career and family, he chooses to corrupt the norm by routinely infecting it with money, power, and sex. He is a self-made man who conforms perfectly to the archetype of his commitments; dedicated to the preservation of its many irreconcilable positions. Like his heroes, his life constitutes the fundamental drama of American society: the pursuit of lonely, hard-boiled individualism that, although rooted in the local group culture, lives at the limen of public legitimacy. This marginality is the strength that shapes his actions. Accordingly, the tension inherent in the contradictions that shape Tony is the heart of *The Sopranos* enterprise and is at the root of its public appeal. As a family man, he serves and protects. As reticent loner, he plunders and devastates. Both personae are purveyors of an American cultural ambivalence that marries the law of the *lupara* (shotgun) to that of the hearth. The ambiguities of individualism as projected in the series are thus frighteningly revealed as cultural and social niceties that privilege money and private lifestyle at the cost of upending public welfare and security. What is truly appealing about the program is this portrayal of the devolution of American society, of its culture, its aspirations, its meaning. Tony and crew, for all their devotion to unbending codes, secret rituals, romantic notions of loyalty and solidarity, are in the cutthroat business of end-of-millennium survival. They have chosen the big easy way out, the road most travelled; an American Dream that has become ever more elusive and jaded, commandeered by a minority notion (be it business or crime) of what dreams should be in twenty-first-century America.[13]

The Sopranos has been called everything from a murderous melodrama to a morality play; a sophisticated contemporary existential statement playing to effete middle-age academics; a manipulative self-serving mob parody that caters to the violent instincts of bloodthirsty and violence-saturated viewers. In reality, the program merely flirts with social issues, teases the cultural canon, plays with intertextual gangster references and offers violence as a means towards an end. What makes the series so compelling is the pristine dialogue, the novel story complications, the superb characterization, the meticulous attention to cinematic production values. Like the most sublime of art, *The Sopranos* makes us care because every moment reflects upon a piece of our collective soul. Clearly combining elements of a modern and postmodern aesthetic, it is an exceptional product of its particular cultural moment. It both absorbs the lessons of its ethnic origins and extends their validity into a contemporary and controversial American context. Though I do not quibble whether truths or meanings or lessons can or should be garnered from the many messages, malevolent or not, that emanated from the series, *The Sopranos* has left its cultural mark as an ersatz, urbane, hip, upscale, playful, and ultimately pleasurable viewing activity.

It's simply a good story told well. It never lost its focus and, much akin to the serial novels of Charles Dickens, Anthony Trollope, and George Eliot, stayed in contact with the audience's responses, invited criticisms, and proposed intertextual motifs that lured the serious narrative hound. While vibrant dialogue, intrigue, and violence entice and tease the viewer, the open-ended twists and turns are plentiful and always powerful. Plot lines unfold with a mission, while diverging character foibles implacably broach uncomfortable psychological barriers. Watching *The Sopranos* is to be caught-up in the dragnet of enjoying the chase for the passion of the hunt. What makes the story so compelling are the myriad connections that the sophisticated viewer is encouraged to ponder, the visual and verbal constructs that generate a long-term memory encyclopedia that draws the viewer into an ever-more inquisitive posture. From opening sequence, fast cuts, riveting juxtaposition, quick takes, and biting dialogue, the series eats and spits in its own plate.

The Sopranos is a touchstone for today's bankrupt values, its popularity a measuring stick of the depth of our current sociocultural malaise. Its reality is our message. Tony Soprano essentially reflects the superficial, maladjusted, dysfunctional, and irrepressibly money-driven society we have become. And that deserves some degree of continued scrutiny and pondered revisitation and rereading.

Rethinking Visual Traces

This book is a history of many pleasurable viewings and visual readings of *The Sopranos*. It is a chronicle of inquisitive starts and stops that when pieced together lead to sometimes surprising but always cogent narrative twists and thematic turns. Vicariously whispered around private watering holes, shamelessly scourged in public commentary, few television programs have enjoyed such public success and equally vitriolic diatribe as *The Sopranos*. Even fewer are as aesthetically inspired (drawing upon European art-house modernist and postmodern cinematic traditions, including Frank Capra, Federico Fellini, and Roman Polanski, all the while reinventing this same tradition for television using irony, mock-tragedy, psychoanalysis, and sexuality) and intellectually provocative (chock-full of metatextual gaps and subversive invocations of Francis Coppola and Martin Scorsese). The series was innovative and repetitive, burdening and emancipative. It was naturally oppositional: public law and order versus lawlessness and private codes, speech versus silence, strength versus weakness, family versus business, them versus us, masculine versus feminine. Essentially, these paradigms can be summed as a quest for manhood in a sea of feminine territorial irredentism. Given the territory, these oppositions are driven by an innate pop cultural appreciation of Freudian psychology that allows the categories to wilfully bleed into one another. Ultimately, the series is a touchstone of the gender and political correctness of social relations in America today, built upon the fears and conceited stereotypes of yesteryear.

My reading is a search for the bar codes hidden inside this special incarnation of knife-edge performances, biting dialogue, and captivating narrative. It represents both a synthesis of my research on semiotics, word and image studies, ethnicity, and my own interpretation of these issues as they appear in the series. It is the result of numerous cultural studies courses and lectures that have allowed me to think long and deeply about contemporary society's appetite for a public identity of visual consumerism.

Chapter 1, "Inner Sanctums," situates the psychological drama of the story within specific and recurring semantic havens that include Dr. Melfi's office, the Bada Bing, the Soprano home. We assay the decor and relevant objects placed in these settings and determine the encoding capacity of background paraphernalia, including paintings, posters, photographs, statues, and signage. Never incidental, these purposefully positioned items present an undeniable aesthetic reality that is never sterile but always constructed in accordance with definite form and function. These objects often reflect the evolving emotional state of the characters, and sometimes they affect a complementary impact on the storyline.

Chapter 2, "When I Grow Up I Want to Be an American," aims the spotlight on the problematic issue of ethnicity and the representation of Italian-Americans in modern post-ethnic America. This is a contentious issue and the series offers equally controversial notions of individuality, social responsibility, and citizenship for twenty-first-century America. The question "Who am I?" that burdens each character is eventually punctuated by the Delphic command to "Know thyself," a resounding theme in the series that overrides traditional melting-pot collectivity.

Chapter 3, "God Help the Beast in Me," examines issues of self-identity informed with the quest for genuine manhood. Courage is seen as a human act, an elusive ethical concept that is often conditioned by relative theatres of action. The soul has to hold its ground against hostile forces, but the battle is often sideswiped by facile capitulations to expected and unshakable norms of comportment. If the goal of an individual is authenticity and completeness whatever the cost, then one must measure the capacity of the individual to satisfy this quest against notions of self-hood vis-à-vis culturally imposed restrictions.

Chapter 4, "Two Tonys: Drawing Conclusions from Mediated Mob Images," delves into the persona of Tony Soprano. His character lives on the limen and as such provides a threshold of possibilities for those around him. The divided self is the existential state he inhabits and it is precisely where his authenticity resides. Beyond ritualistic restrictions, psychological self-inquiry, and conflicting family responsibilities, Tony is a schizoid being with many parts and exhibits a full cast of conflicting personalities. Masking is essential to his logic of survival. A single identity for Tony is an illusion if not an impossibility. The series is ultimately premised upon the self-affirmation, self-scrutiny, and self-consciousness of Tony Soprano, the apex, nadir, and nexus of his nefarious world. The subaltern image he comes to project at series' end merely empowers an individual who is finally cognizant of the dramatic fiction he must live in order to maintain the conventions of his opprobrious personal code.

Chapter 5, "An Appendix of Verbal Bits and Visual Bytes," formally addresses issues of visual consumerism that permeates the series. It is an inventory of super-informed series moments and scenes ("beats" as they are termed in the trade) that display deep structures produced for explicit purposes of secondary communication. Similar to heart beats, these series beats often go unnoticed, save for those moments that invade the television screen with an obvious camera angle or close-up shot. By paying close attention to these visual/verbal pegs, the viewer can enter into a multiple set of correlations that become the expression of a variety of contents that ultimately formulate *The Sopranos* experience. Towards this end I make references to visual markers in the series that include posters, artwork, statuary, and book covers to both create and subtend my arguments. For example, in the following sample, I examine Chase's use of a real television program inserted into the series:

In "The Blue Comet" VI.21, Chase takes one last well-aimed shot at the television industry by inserting an episode from the television classic *The Twilight Zone* (1959–1964) by Rod Serling. Tony and his crew watch the program while "hitting the mattresses" in their safe house. The viewer is allowed to watch and hear *The Twilight Zone* episode along with Tony as an anxious screenplay writer begs a haughty television executive for an opportunity to write a television series. The dialogue drips with bitingly superb irony: "Give me a chance. Give me first dibs at this television series thing, whatever it is. Let me do the pilot, please." To which the executive replies: "… the television industry today is looking for talent, they're looking for quality. They're preoccupied with talent and quality and the writer is a major commodity." An irreverent Tony Soprano unintentionally comments upon the situation played on television when he blurts, "Well the situation ain't all bad," he cheerily chimes. Tony's "it ain't all bad" is really a response to one of his men commenting on their steady diet of pizza and take-out food. He is actually referring to their culinary bonus of not having to eat green vegetables. But the retort, timed to coincide with *The Twilight Zone* conversation the viewer is hearing from the small television screen, is classic David Chase cheekiness à la Soprano.

As the informed viewer of the series is aware, network television had rejected Chase's pilot for *The Sopranos* before his move to the premium cable television network HBO. *The Sopranos* pilot had made the rounds at CBS, Fox, NBC, ABC, and back to CBS, and had been refused by all. According to Brett Martin,

> Years later, at the height of his success, Chase delighted bitterly in naming the executive [from Fox] who had neglected to call and deliver the news; he would relate a chance meeting at a Television Critics Association event at which the poor fellow (who surely suffered more than his share of sleepless nights) came up to him to say, "Well, it all worked out for the best!"[14]

Having been rebuffed by television executives, Chase revels in his success by delivering a lusciously frank jab at those executives that had rejected his pilot and therefore his talent as a writer. The fact that he does so through Tony – the most successful and memorable television character on the highest-quality television program in the history of television that featured the best writing the medium had ever entertained – turned the moment into a brilliant saucy punch line. End of story, indeed![15]

But yet another added layer of meaning is also surreptitiously imbedded into the scene by the director. The inclusion of an episode from the original *The Twilight Zone* at the official end and final episode of *The Sopranos* is also a playful nod to the feature film Chase was in the midst of developing entitled *Twylight Zones*. The film opened the 2012 New York Film Festival with the new name *Not Fade Away*.

A note to readers: I had intended to include illustrations, screengrabs as they are termed in the trade, from the series to illuminate moments in the text that make reference to posters, artworks, and statuary used in the series. Permission to use these screengrabs was denied by HBO Programs as they do not fall into the category of promotion and review as HBO defines those terms.

Chapter One

Inner Sanctums

Time and Space are Real Beings, a Male and a Female. Time is a Man, space is a Woman.

William Blake

Painting should call out to the viewer ... and the surprised viewer should go to it, as if entering a conversation.

Roger de Piles, Cours de peinture par principes, 1676

The painting ... it's a trick picture out there ... the barn and the old tree all rotted out inside ... it's a special made psychological picture like that waddyacallit test ... the Korsack.

Tony Soprano, "Meadowlands" I.4

The abundance of artworks and artistic artefacts in *The Sopranos* is what lends the series its ironic bite and sardonic wit. The peppering of the sets with pop posters, commercial reproductions of art, kitsch murals, best-selling book covers, and modern statuary brews an interesting minestrone of intertextual quips and citations that explore a deeper understanding of the series and outlins life in twenty-first-century America. They enhance the decorum of the individual scenes and situate the story in a definitive temporal space that resides outside the series. These strategically placed images of artworks and artefacts subtly suggest that there is more to the action than what is taking place on screen. As metaphorical backdrops, they open up a comparative space that serves to reinforce, if not sometimes reveal, the thoughts of the characters and help to explain their actions. In other words, these visual paraphernalia perform the function of ordering both the geographic and mental spaces of the series in an exhilarating and unbound temporal/spatial flow that deepens the tension and extends meaning beyond the individual scenes. As the story ravels and is unravelled, a subaltern storyline emerges that follows the developing plot and creates a concurrent visual commentary that subtends the narrative. The juxtaposing of the main characters before these sorts of backdrops is what constitutes the subliminal drama that augments the depth of the series. Rather than being toss-out visual tokens or set dressings of no particular importance, the image of Tony reminiscing before stained glass in his old Newark Italian neighbourhood, the posters in the backroom of the Bada Bing, the ethnic regalia of Satriale's Pork Store (which was Centanni's Meat Market in the pilot episode), the artwork and statues in Dr. Melfi's office, and so on, speak of the complex inspiration that marks the entire arc of the series' storyline. Using these visuals as markers of the series' sublime writing style and meticulous attention to detail, David Chase surrounds his characters' moves with these mise-en-abîme signature moments of writer/viewer complicity that enhance aesthetic pleasure in a dance of creative communion.

Watching actors act on a television screen and viewing artworks as they are displayed on a television screen produce two different sensorial experiences in the viewer. Though the two television scenarios are diverse, both are meant to be seen, watched, and understood. In one instance actors speak, move, and interact. Artworks on screen, on the other hand, are normally seen as decor, as immobile and silent additions to the background. A hanging poster is always still while characters are usually animated. Yet both actors and artworks are iconic and reveal spoken and unspoken meanings. The stilled figures one sees in paintings or posters are tantamount to fixing in time a snapshot of an on-screen decorative presence that the casual viewer merely espies, a common tendency, but that the vigilant spectator works to decipher. Moving actors in action pictures, on the other hand, present a complex transcodified reality that, though never still, is readily depicted as a constant fixture (a character with determined traits, for instance) by the casual viewer. The juxtaposing of these two contrasting features creates a matrix of meanings or imaginative *intreccio* (the Italian word for a narrative plot line, which implies a twisting or braiding of elements) that privileges the creation of an evolving overarching structure of complimentary paraphernalia that moves beyond the usual pathways normally associated with watching television.

Seen within the context of this series, the setting decor that accompanies *The Sopranos* forms a subsidiary narrative design that ideally augments spectator involvement and pleasure both visually and intellectually. Similar to the musical soundtrack that augments the story dynamic, the artworks move the viewer beyond the television screen and directly into the recesses of personal experience. The viewer of *The Sopranos* is enlisted to play an important and active role as the appointed ideal viewer,[1] the possible model recipient who director and writer David Chase hopes will understand the visual accouterments and totally embrace the viewing experience by moving beyond the surface images on screen and into the world of *The Sopranos*. In other words, while an ideal viewer does not allow the empirical director/writer's vision to completely condition one's viewing, he/she takes full pleasure in fully interacting with the work and wilfully participating with the director/writer in the creation of a potentially novel and more complete narrative space.

It is precisely this virtual narrative space of the series and its studied setting appointments that give rise to the series' dynamic nature. Chase is constantly testing the viewer's personal memories, intertextual television and cinema competence, general cultural knowledge, and specific visual acuity. The viewer must take into account not only the actual on-screen text but also the surrounding visual text by responding to its purposefully placed peripheral cues. The resulting metatextual grid is not a homogeneous television realm but a potential, multidimensional, and heterogeneous narrative terrain that includes movies seen and not seen, posters familiar and unfamiliar, books read and not read, artworks recognized and not recognized. The mnemonic patterns that are generated affect the manner in which the viewer disambiguates character movement and actions, the developing storyline, directorial intention, real-life settings, and interconnected scenes. The common denominator of this open-ended text is its inherent ability to elicit an almost inexhaustible variety of equally valid polymorphous responses on the part of the audience. In contradiction with traditional television programs where the original intention of the writer had to be approximated as closely as possible, *The Sopranos* offers a field of interpretative possibilities and unfinished story sketches that expect completion from the creative participation of the audience at large. Chase deplored the notion of giving the viewers the certainty of resolution and closure. He demurred from expected endings "because," according to Chase, "I felt it was more interesting that they didn't. I like mystery. I like allusion.

A lot of times, I prefer that to knowing what happened."[2] This ever-expanding contingency constructs an extended story that becomes a pleasurable and participatory event; something to spur lively discussion in front of the office water cooler or, more likely, in online chat groups.

The viewer's personal impressions are thus embedded into the open-ended encyclopedia of the series and are ideally stored for future reference. The competent viewer recalls them from this semantic warehouse when required by the text and extrapolates a possible meaning. This ongoing process of interpretation, actualization, and assemblage privileges multiple viewings of the episodes and stimulates those inferential walks that move beyond and behind the onscreen action and potentializes *The Sopranos* text as an open-ended work. As we shall see, at times the artworks and graphic images present typical notions of stereotypical encoding. This is most evident when considering the narrative's basic story stuff: statues of Murano glass, Uncle Ben's signature image on parboiled rice boxes, and kitschy neighbourhood restaurant murals help enforce assumed social stereotypes. These icons offer a complementary backdrop to the action that occurs before them: Bada Bing strip calendars, I-Am photos of boxers, beer logos, and Frank Sinatra's infamous (and only) mug shot[3] all seem naturally placed if not expected given the blue nature of the series. Most often, though, these set decorations enhance spectator pleasure by stirring an aesthetic response and generating those personal impressions that move beyond the setting and produce the rich interpretative patterns that over the arc of the series have become the tempo, timbre, tension, tone, and visual signature of David Chase. Books, posters, and artworks are visual cues that offer a subtle nod to the ideal viewer that Chase so ably cultivates.

Without exploring theoretical notions of interart analogies or comparisons,[4] suffice it to say that Chase uses his settings, but especially the location of artwork and related objects within the scenes, as extensions of the storyline in time and space. By placing action against a backdrop of readily identifiable images that come from real pop culture, real life, and the world of art, the television program extends beyond the two dimensional limits of the television screen. In this sense, the paintings, statues, movies, book covers, and music generate an alternative semiotic codified system that adds considerable communicative depth to the visual activity that occurs before, within, or around the artworks. Just as Chase's most immediate mentors, Francis Ford Coppola and Martin Scorsese, are careful to pose their scenes before meticulously reconstructed and musically appointed settings, Chase's attention to visual and aural detail places the series in the hallowed aura of art house cinema.

By re-presenting artworks as static and visual counterbalances to the action on-screen, Chase not only gives a nod to the series as self-conscious art but also legitimizes the series' idiosyncratic relevance to the inbred world of mobsters who often use misinterpretations of their public surroundings, including art and cinema, to justify their actions. At the least, the empowerment of competent viewers who have been nurtured on popular TV, film, and iconic poster images creates a dense weave of meta-pictures that form a collective pop identity easily manipulated by the series' writers towards their deliberate ends. These intentions move from the kitschy: the life-size pig on the roof at the front of Satriale's Pork Store, the William Wegman poster of two dogs dressed in trench coats in the hotel room where Tony meets his goomah Valentina, and the mural of the Bay of Naples in Artie Bucco's I-Am restaurant Vesuvio; to the weighty: the stained-glass windows of the church in Tony's old neighbourhood; to the sublime: the artwork in the Brooklyn Museum, the original Pablo Picasso prints at Devon's mansion. Some are humorous: old neighbourhood signs that layer images of Italian sausage, fresh pork chops, chicken parts, and espresso ostentatiously contour Tony's lifestyle and animate his plebian realm. For example, in "House Arrest" II.11, Tony and the gang enjoy an afternoon seated in front of Satriale's Pork Store. As the naïf-style pigs painted on the store's front walls look on from behind Tony's shoulders, the local government "pig," FBI Agent Dwight Harris, strolls the same streets and enjoys the same neighbourhood sights. He stops to talk about the Nets and Knicks with "the guys." The sign Suckling Pigs, Any Size takes on new and significant nuances as the FBI and the mob are conflated into a singular porker icon. Some of the visual imagery is deadly serious: the photo wall in FBI headquarters, the photographs of dead mobsters, the original framed poster of *Dr. Strangelove* (1964) used as a lethal weapon by Christopher when he smashes it over the head of his payment-delinquent friend in "In Camelot" V.7.

When one examines these settings, it is possible to construct possible connections between the artworks on the walls and the subject of the scene in terms of structural analogies, colour, framing, and meaning-creation. This holistic approach permits a more complete appreciation of the aesthetic moment. As the viewer pieces together the elements presented in a scene, a linkage is created that permits these visual systems to effectively dovetail, thus composing a design that comments upon itself in often illuminating ways. One could ask the following questions: How do the artworks and their different styles influence the viewer's expectations? Are there underlying suppositions that favour the choice of one artwork over another? How does the viewer's stance correspond to the aesthetic perspective that Writer Chase introduces to the series? Given the assumption that everything within camera range in any scene is judiciously placed by Director Chase, what are the connections between what is placed to be seen and its relevance to the scene? These and other questions are both a means of eliciting specific responses and of opening the viewer's response towards a more critical visual analysis and intellectual appreciation of the series. The result is a suppression of the usual subjective-objective distance normal to television programs and the emergence of a new aesthetic space that deepens the way the audience performs and experiences *The Sopranos*.

On the other hand, even though the protagonists of the series are normally surrounded by the artistic constructs that the audience views, they often misinterpret or simply do not see the features that surround them. This gives rise to a masterful structural metaphor of their limited vision of the world since each character defines his/her reality by reducing the infinitely possible aspects of "being" into manageable survival packets that eschew their surroundings in favour of a contrived reality. At times they may momentarily contemplate, but simply never truly understand (similar to many of their viewers), the possible import of their surroundings and the objects that inform their lives. Reality thus becomes an uncomfortable space, so much so that many live in abject confusion and constant fear – Tony in particular. Though he is critically aware of his own Jungian shadow archetype (his dark side) he is nevertheless drawn to a Zen-like energy that intimates a vaster ethical space that unites the natural world around him. The eclectic artworks, book covers, movies, and posters that adorn his world are windows into the space of his soul. Those relatively few moments he spends contemplating what he actually sees become mise-en-abîme moments that reveal the premonitions of his inner self to the viewer while consolidating the distance between his true inner self and the deep-seated fear of losing his own humanity. If he could only truly understand what he sees, perhaps he could reify a new and redemptive reality. But he won't allow himself, nor will he permit others to stray from their ordained mobster code and vision. "Forget Hollywood screenplays, forget those distractions ... we've got work to do," he admonishes his nephew Christopher in the closing scene of the pilot episode. The chauvinist tone is hammered and set in stone. Fury and action will triumph over words and images, reality over fantasy, left-brain linearity over right-brain holism, the reality of the mob world over the symbolism of art. Tony's plight throughout the series will be resisting the migration towards a softer position that contradicts this dictum. To truly appreciate its aesthetic and existential implications would undermine his monolithic mobster masculinity. Misunderstanding and false readings of the world he inhabits will eventually sanction his role as hardened, soulless mob boss. By liberally salting his episodes with recognizable artwork and contemporary pop culture artefacts, Chase subtly challenges Tony, as well as the viewer, to engender a new kind of dialectical relationship between the work, its performer, and its audience. Tony, and with him the viewer, thus becomes the active centre of an inexhaustible network of possible relationships that is determined solely by the amalgam of limitations that he himself so consciously enforces for fear of losing his essential fixity of perspective. It is an irrational space that lies somewhere between his mob reality and the fiction of his therapy sessions, his incoherent thoughts and heartfelt expression. His gratuitous violence is simply the sum of the impossibility of redemption.

Opening Shots

Consider the visual barrage with the opening credits: plastic pork insignia, swarthy lumberjacks, pizzeria logos, admonitions to Drive Safely on holding tanks, the New York skyline reflected on a hubcap, highway exit signs, the program's logo with the R of Soprano replaced by a gun, all contribute to situate the action within a definite New Jersey context and the viewer within a real and identifiable landscape.[5] As if to signal their integrity to the series, the credits never change but remain a constant in this dolly shot construction of cultural landscaping. By dramatizing the New Jersey geoscape, Chase lends an artistic aura to ordinary objects, the kind Walter Benjamin discussed as a by-product of electronic reproduction through film.[6]

Often Chase uses carefully placed backdrops to encode the private ethos of the characters deployed before them. These images provide understanding and reflection, and they help induce memories. The viewer perceives these scenes as a composite, watching the action on-screen while noting the images that decorate the actions. Sometimes the two are self-referential with the background art reflecting the action.

For example, troublesome characters are always posed before abstract paintings. Tony's dalliances with his goomahs typically occur in hotel rooms, which are adorned with cheap abstract prints that reflect their flighty dialogues and confused emotions. The maintenance of kept women is an increasingly grey area for Tony given the mounting intolerance of a formerly complicit Carmela. What was once an occupational perk sanctioned by old-school tradition has become the bane of their matrimonial bliss. Irina Peltsin, Tony's young and desultory mistress, will cause havoc in Tony's marriage by falling outside the conventional role she is expected to maintain. Subsequently, whenever we see her, she is flanked by abstract paintings. Her incoherent vision of life is thus mirrored in the seemingly random artworks that surround her and that witness her alcohol-drenched rants. In "Whitecaps" IV.13, she unbridles the same chaos the viewer espies in the abstract painting behind her when she informs Carmela of Tony's dalliance with her cousin Svetlana Kirilenko. Her violent verbal imagery precipitates the destruction of Carmela's nostalgia-ridden and staid visual proto-image of the Soprano family portrait. Irina's cousin Svetlana, for her part, is a retro-image of a stereotypical platinum blond Marilyn Monroe figure charged with Russian proletarian ideology. Her one-legged presence is both an enabling symbol of personal fortitude and a curious Francis Bacon-like portrait of disabled womanhood.[7] As such, she is a visual and moral counterbalance to the strippers at the Bada Bing, cherished for their busts and the svelte-legged imagery that invests the ravenously amoral club. The imagocentric eye-candy and painterly quality of these women is summed up in Valentina La Paz, a brief sex partner Tony steals from Ralph Cifaretto. She is an art dealer. As such she is the harbinger of a vast whole of misunderstood symbols that promote a holistic conception of the world. She promotes art and beauty. She is the catalyst for the portrait of the thoroughbred horse Pie-O-My (prized for its slim body and long legs) that will gain significance as a confessional mirror for Tony in a later episode.

An exception to this imagist pattern is Gloria Trillo, Tony's image of his dream woman. Gloria transcends the correlated crystallization that references Tony's sexual dalliances because she not only reflects Tony's ideal imagery of woman but also possesses attractive male qualities: public strength, financial independence, sexual potency. The spirit of their attraction is emboldened in visual attitudes that reinforce their respective strengths while simultaneously masking their mutually destructive proclivities towards manic depression. The same idiosyncrasies that empower their boundless lust subliminally harbour their gravest dangers and fears. While Tony's initial relation with her is empowering and fulfilling, their mutual neurotic anxieties can only breed pathology. Their surroundings glaringly echo their innermost feelings. Their most sublime moment occurs beneath a canonical painting of a Venetian canal, that most timeless of romantic places for lovers. Their flirtations in the snake pit at the zoo posit a paradisiacal archetype that places Tony and Gloria in a postmodern Eden replete with images of the Fall that include a sibilant serpent, mounting sexual tension, and carnal knowledge. Their eventual demise as a couple occurs in a chiaroscuro setting of malice and hate. Appropriately, there are no artworks on the walls of Gloria's home. Her life is an empty canvas coloured only by the blackness of her suicidal mission. A solitary statue of Buddha signals a cry for a life of wholeness, a means to decorate life with the spiritual splendor of a coloured palette. But it doesn't. Her obsessive neediness only implodes the emotions of any willing sexual partner.

Confused visual patterns are reserved for characters that are equally confused and normally despised by Tony. One such character is Tony's nemesis Ralph Cifaretto. In "University" III.6, we see him watching TV in his home. Behind him hangs a painting that is a splatter of colour, a nebula of emotive turbulence that ably reflects his volatility if not his demonic character. The same colours and abstract patterning is seen in "The Army of One" III.13 when a pathologically anxious Ralph consoles Rosalie Aprile after the death of her son, a death he himself has privately ordered and now publicly suffers with mock compassion. The painted blotches forebode violence. The dominant swatches of red foreshadow the widening splash of red blood that will encircle his dead body as he lies on the kitchen floor in "Pie-O-My" IV.5 after an indignant Tony bludgeons the vile villain for killing the race horse for insurance money.

Often the art reveals unspoken truths and, much like a Greek chorus, expresses what the audience already intuits. The image now becomes theatre, a site for a possible performance that extends the action that takes place before it. An example is found in the hospital scene in "Isabella" I.12. Tony is in the hospital as a result of an unsuccessful mob hit staged by his mother Livia Soprano and his Uncle Junior. FBI Agent Dwight Harris is at Tony's bedside and has just offered him immunity and a new life in the Witness Protection Program. A visually distraught and emotionally assertive Carmela is pushing for the move. As Tony derails her arguments with visions of living in the desert, selling Indian relics curbside ("maybe start a rattlesnake ranch"), and eating tasteless tomatoes, he rebuts her lamentations that their children need a more conventional father. He blurts that "the kids do have a father, this one, me, Tony Soprano, and all that comes with it." The children are waiting in the hospital waiting area. As son A.J. murmurs, "I don't believe it was a carjacking," sister Meadow places an arm around her younger brother providing comfort and safety. Her earlier comment, "God, self-involved much?" refers to A.J.'s lamentations of missing a school dance because of his father's shooting. But the comment also refers to her father's self-aggrandizing braggadocio. As Tony's "the kids do have a father" rings in his hospital room, children Meadow and A.J. wait quietly in the hospital ward, the poster behind them eavesdrops on their muddled emotional confusion and publicly reverberates a deep-set private longing: Safe Families: Everybody Needs One. The viewer can only exclaim: Safe family, indeed! The only safe thing about the Soprano household is that it lives in a perpetual state of willed blindness that permits it to mask its perfidious desires, or any other thing family members may be thinking or feeling, in order to maintain a confirmatory perceptual model of their mobster reality. The scene quickly cuts from Meadow and A.J. to Livia's apartment in the seniors' residence and a close-up camera shot of a framed photo of Tony as a babe proudly held by his young mother Livia in a *safe* family portrait of yesteryear. In the background, Livia and Uncle Junior watch a television newscaster announce news of a "gangland execution gone awry" on northern New Jersey mob figure Tony Soprano. The camera slowly tracks backward from the black-and-white photograph of Tony and is replaced by the televised colour news footage of a wounded Tony being transported on a hospital gurney. Livia and Uncle Junior, architects of the botched attempt, are visibly disturbed and increasingly wary. Livia's frantic "How could this happen?" is fatefully ambiguous. How could what happen? The fact that Tony has been shot or that he has survived? Her supplication to an agitated Uncle Junior, "My son got shot ... and he got away" clearly places the dilemma on a razor's edge. Uncle Junior's equivocation, "What do we do now, Livia?" is coldly dismissed by the increasingly aloof and malevolent Medea figure: "We go see 'em." Then, in a veil of tears that evince her mendacity she tearfully blabbers, "He's my only son." Concerned for their own safety, given the inevitable and expected reprisal from Tony, they decide to visit him, again reiterating, reinforcing, and contemptuously enabling skewed Soprano *safe family* values.

A similar appositional message is staged while daughter Janice Soprano visits her ostentatiously unbearable mother Livia at the Green Grove Retirement Residence ("Guy Walks into a Psychiatrist's Office" II.1). Janice guardedly broaches the topic of her inheritance money with Livia. As the mother masterfully rebuts Janice's poorly veiled entreaties with biting sarcasm, the camera angle follows Janice's line of sight to an In Case of Fire, Use Stairs sign that looms behind Livia. It features a stylized silhouette of a male figure running down the stairs. At obvious loggerheads and frustrated with her mother's disarming subterfuge, Janice imagines Livia as the figure tumbling down the stairs. Though Livia may indeed be wicked in her wily posturing, Janice is equally disarming in her visual treachery. Safe family, indeed! Recklessness, bravado, and purposeful deceit are the touchstones of the Soprano family.

Dr. Melfi's Office Anteroom

The opening shot of *The Sopranos* places the viewer in Dr. Melfi's anteroom. The room is similar in colour and tone to the inner office. The area is graced with two paintings and a large green statue. Magazines provide the usual time killer for waiting patients. As the episode begins, the camera lingers for a seemingly inordinate and uncomfortable length of time on the figure of a dumbfounded man (who we come to know as Tony Soprano) sitting in this waiting room. The large green statue (a Gustav Klimt reproduction) dominates the frame, while the camera's crotch shot captures Tony sitting firmly ensconced within the thighs of this brazen nude female sculpture. In a later episode, Carmela is positioned in this identical setting and pose (but appears considerably less befuddled than Tony), and she expresses her own immediate reading of the statue's threatening message to Dr. Melfi: "... that statue is not my favorite" ("Second Opinion" III.7). Carmela rejects the statue's public display of willed feminine energy because it negates the private paradigm of her own submissive posture and her willed delegation of self to Soprano family values. If we collapse Carmela's defensive viewpoint with Tony's confounded stance, we note that while she outright refuses the statue's unabashed feminine message, Tony is definitely bewildered and hapless. This opening image adumbrates the issues Tony will confront during the psychiatric sojourn he is about to begin. The green statue (and anteroom paintings as we shall see) visually extemporize Tony's most intimate and pressing fears both towards women and the still-undefined feminine *anima* he carries within.

The image of the green statue is so integrated into the opening scene of the series that it is hard to unthink. Instead of representing a simple set decoration, its central position in the room, as well as its overpowering and all-encompassing possession of the entire screen, installs a potent feminine dialogue that is both visually oppressive and semantically inhibiting. Its upward thrust and naked strength threaten semiotic upheaval in a realm that is intrinsically masculine and repressively staid. The view of mob boss Tony Soprano framed within the triangle formed by the statue's legs is equally novel and visually appealing (especially since between a women's leg is one of his favourite places). But we may uncover an ulterior, possibly an unintentional elucidation to this projected symbolic Ur image[8] of Tony. The statue merits an equal amount of the viewer's attention because it sets the interpretative mood of the entire series. In the first place, just as Tony is beginning his voyage through therapy, the viewer, too, is commencing a viewing experience replete with characters, symbols, views, and situations that will need interpretation. Both the viewer and Tony, at this initial stage, are equally confused. Tony ponders, as does the viewer, where these sessions will lead and, ultimately, wonders what he is doing there. He, with the viewer alongside, will be posed before the statue at significant junctures of his therapy and we may assume that he probably contemplates its contours every time he enters Dr. Melfi's anteroom. Eventually, a smaller replica of the statue will appear at Dr. Melfi's side during several sessions, further suggesting the willed inclusion of the statue's message into the rhetoric of patient Tony's narrative. Our shared protracted voyage through his self-cognizance, as it is played during the arc of the series, will disclose a rhetorical pattern of visual iconoclasm, deep-set fears about imagery coupled with a distrust of figurative language that eventually reveals an antipathy for race, gender, even class. A neophyte to psychiatric care, he fears the revelation of his inner self, just as he subliminally fears the statue's message, for it will overwhelm him with unwanted guilt.

We may thus hypothesize a latent, confessional content in the image of a contrite Tony seated before the statue. This first visual impression of Tony verifies our reading and the basic premise of the series, namely, that he is a man trapped within the vice of feminine ascendency and power. Tony, we come to know, fears emasculation and is fraught with the idea that he is losing his family. He has wilfully succumbed to the repressed aggressivity of his bipolar mother and the annoying intrusive nature of his uncle. The result is a lack of an inner sense of a solid foundation, which is reflected in the early stages of the series through the fragility of his public and private masculine identity. To prevent the appearance of any chink in his armour, he invents a rigorously abrasive and callous relativism that regards the world of signs and cultural systems with scepticism and ruthless scorn. He deludes himself by constructing a false sense of self that is dominated by appearance and corroborated by his mob peers and his family. In essence, his latent fear of private and public emulation is grounded in both the muteness of this opening scene set before a dominant virago figure and the subsequent fear of public and private castration. This threat is re-echoed in the series and, in this scene, augurs the potential and perhaps expected transformation of Tony from dominant male to doxy puppet, a mere feminine plaything that willingly reveals his feelings behind closed doors. Again and again he will be placed in situations that reveal his self-serving rhetoric of masculine iconoclasm. This voyage through therapy will uncover deeply entrenched fears about female imagery, figurative language, interracial relations, gender, even class. Question is, will Tony follow a traditional arc of introspection, moral change, and redemption or will masculinity and recidivism mark his ascendency as mob boss?

The statue is a definitive icon threatening his world view, a possible harbinger of wilfully shrouded memories of childhood, of past and future anxieties both with his mother, which have yet to play themselves out, and with the other females in his life, which he has heretofore repressed if not completely neglected. It is a symbolic structure where personal and public meanings interpenetrate. Interestingly, Fran Felstein, Tony's father's goomah that he meets in "In Camelot" V.7, describes his mother Livia Soprano as "statuesque," an intentional and slyly placed connection to the menacing green female statue in the anteroom. In that episode's flashback sequence, Livia has just suffered a miscarriage and is in the hospital. After spending the night with Fran instead of with his ailing wife, Giovanni Francis "Johnny Boy" Soprano visits Livia early the next morning. He lies to her about his whereabouts the night before, claiming he spent the night at his brother's house because of a flat tire. Tony, the teenage son, awkwardly corroborates his father's blatant flagrancy. He lies to his mother; but his plaintiff face displays the same confusion and disquieting guilt the viewer notes as he ponders the green statue in the opening scene of the series. Even in her weakened state, Livia Soprano displays strength as she berates her son for his dishonesty. Even now, years later, the man cowers before the statue, a symbol of the latent imperiousness of his mother, as if he were still a boy.

The statue before him displays the same autonomous strength of character that, much like his mother's, usurps the norm usually associated with what, at least in Tony's chauvinist world, is presumed to be the weaker sex. His apparent discomfort with the unblushing virago intimates the possible cracks in his father's legacy as he will confess to Dr. Melfi of his mother "wearing his father down to a nub" ("The Sopranos" I.1). The real message of the statue thus lies in its ability to bring to the surface deeply entrenched childhood memories and wilfully repressed truths that would destroy the carapace that he has so carefully constructed. The image of Tony as a grovelling male signals the reflective awareness that is about to begin and that will expose memories of his father, his mother, and his childhood as false fragmented systems of self-preservation. Tony's relationships with his women and with his male peers will not allow overbearing or more powerful partners. But this sort of personal and public egocentricity is about to be painfully questioned. The menacing Medusa figure[9] that flaunts her wares before him may symbolically engulf him within her legs, but her mockingly virile stance physically troubles and spiritually taunts him as she reaches into the innermost fibres of his being.

Interestingly, legs and images of legs figure prominently in the initial three scenes of the pilot episode. The green limbs of the statue in the opening shot morph into the crossed legs of Dr. Melfi in the first shot of her seated in her office. The centred and low-angle shot of her alluring legs are reduplicated in the statuesque gams of the Bada Bing pole dancers that come into view in the very next scene following this first session. The profusion of leg imagery at this point in the series is mirrored in the action of this episode. Anyone that is hurt, interestingly enough, is wounded in the legs. The broken leg of the recalcitrant gambler that Tony smashes to the ground with Christopher Moltisanti's Mercedes in front of his HMO insurance office intimates Tony's fateful limping through the series, always shifting from one leg to another, seemingly never on stable psychological ground. A limping Gennaro "Little Pussy" Malanga in shorts is marked to be wacked by Uncle Junior. The shorts-wearing image of the man returns to haunt Tony years later in "Members Only" VI.1 as a demented Uncle Junior yells out his name before shooting his nephew Tony in the stomach. The final image of the pilot episode is a reverse shot of Tony in shorts, an inappropriate juvenile image of his postponed manhood that will receive commentary in a subsequent episode titled "For All Debts Public and Private" IV.1. During a routine tête-à-tête, Carmine Lupertazzi, an elder New York boss, will reprimand Tony, reminding him that "A Don doesn't wear shorts." Such connotations do not materialize accidentally but reverberate throughout the series. In "Do Not Resuscitate" II.2, Richie Aprile will run over a disrespectful Peter "Beansie" Gaeta with his car. The consequences of not walking right with Ritchie render "Beansie" a paraplegic without the use of his legs and condemned to a wheelchair. A more permanent cruelty is reserved for the thoroughbred horse Pie-O-My whose spindly legs lead to her brutal demise at the hands of Ralph Cifaretto in "Whoever Did This" IV.9.

The paradigm of *seeing/being seen*, of public display and private respect that is initiated with this initial imagery of legs is a significant and potent leitmotif that is carried throughout the entire arc of the series. But, as we have noted, it begins in the opening scene as Tony gazes at the statue and the statue, because of its position, gazes back. The act of seeing is a purposeful and deliberate stance. Being seen, on the other hand, implies passivity. In any visual exchange, both objects of reciprocal observation become icons of resemblance and foreignness. When Tony sits in the anteroom woefully framed and apparently contemplating the possible significance and subtending implied feminine authority, imparted by the statue before him, the viewer sees him not as a person but as a self-effacing objectified Other in apparent lack of a sustaining personal discourse. As his passively impotent gaze is returned by the threateningly dark and deep-set eye sockets of the unflinching and intimidating female statue, his man-centred authority is stilled; his influence and bluster as mob boss have no draw here. This combination of the experience of meaninglessness (the introverted passive eye) and the courage to be oneself (the extroverted active eye) is the key to the entire series, and it is at the heart of Tony's growth as a mob boss. In essence, in order to be healed, the speaking and seeing subject must be eschewed in favour of the purest form of objectivity. The statue's Medusa stare initiates this rehabilitating process. It is an apotropaic image, a vexing object meant to paralyze Tony in a sedentary stance that promises the unleashing of his latent visceral fears and eventual freedom. But as the object of psychiatric observation, Tony will be presented to himself first and foremost as active gazer of his own troubled and multifaceted self. He will discover the raging "beast" that consumes his soul and conditions his relations; the timorous and inarticulate "sad clown" that persecutes his susceptibility; the recalcitrant and fractious "boss" who promotes self-confidence and political indifference as managerial qualities. In all these instances, Tony is posed as an active-passive recorder, an ever vulnerable and shifting palimpsest that traces the myriad involutions of himself as actor-subject, as both the seer and the seen.

This fearful and apprehensive stance is apparent in his willed disregard for the statue throughout the remainder of the series. Although he spends considerable time in Dr. Melfi's anteroom, we never again see him framed within the statue's legs. Indeed, it is best to bar the statue from consideration; drive it from consciousness. One is safer without its menacing undertones. As if to diminish its central presence in the story and debunk its ramifications in his life, Tony never questions the statue's place in the narrative. This would draw attention to its crucial and pivotal role in his subliminal trauma. Instead, he thwarts its inevitable impact by adroitly deflecting his (and the viewer's) attention by moving his gaze to a painting in the anteroom ("Meadowlands" I.4). This permits him to momentarily, at least at this initial stage, negate his visual fixation with the imposing statue by focusing on a traditionally representative painting; something, in other words, he thinks he can handle. He stares, as does the viewer, at the painting of a red barn. As the viewer is allowed to perceive the painting through Tony's visual saccades, the camera focuses on the barn door and the blackness beyond its threshold. The viewer contemplates, along with Tony, the quiescent darkness within the barn. During the therapy session that follows, a disquiet Tony goads Dr. Melfi smugly: "The painting ... it's a trick picture out there ... the barn and the old tree all rotted out inside."

But the viewer realizes, because privy to the same vision of the painting, that there is no rotting tree. Instead, a healthy leaf-bearing oak dominates the serenity of the scene. Tony has fabricated a false image and has projected his own anxieties and latent fears onto the painting. Attempting to familiarize and simultaneously deflect the uncomfortable ambience of the office space, he calls the painting a "special made psychological picture like that waddyacallit test ... the Korsack."[10] Despite Dr. Melfi's claims to the painting's rural innocence and her own unprogrammed intentions in its casual purchase at a county fair, Tony remains sceptical. He feels manipulated; not quite up to specs. He fears implosion and dreads becoming a patsy in Dr. Melfi's evolving psychological game of unmasking candid identity. The painting, the office, and even the good doctor, according to his inner voice, cry out mockingly: "Hey asshole, we're from Harvard and what do you think of this spooky depressing barn and this tree we put here?" Visibly disturbed, he responds to Dr. Melfi's innocent, though paradoxical, opening query "How are things?" with a sarcastic retort: "Good, had a real good week ..." The emotional outburst and rants about the painting, however, prove otherwise. He is uncharacteristically distraught. While there is no woman, no green virago in the pastoral scene, the statue's gender inferences affect a sense of loss and foreboding. This feeling is all the more heightened by the recent death of his friend and mentor, De Meo family boss Jackie Aprile. Dr. Melfi's questioning triggers a defensive outburst. He is overwhelmed by a pertinaciously distressing sense of mounting ineptitude. At his next session, trees once again return to mind. He asks: "What happens to a tree when it is rotted out?" The same thing, we discover, that happens to a man with cancer: it dies. Tony has made the mighty oak a symbol of his friend Jackie Aprile's robust life, now withering and rotted out by cancer. The barn door leads to Tonys' subconscious unease. Whether it will also lead to an inevitable death remains an open question that will eventually evaporate into a similarly ambiguous darkness.[11]

Open doorways and enigmatic passages return in the very next scene while Tony cavorts with Irina, his Russian girlfriend. Two paintings hang on the bedroom wall. One is a modern abstract: colourful arrows, fleeting lines, geometric figures, a Paul Klee-like drawing of a head, a bull's-eye fill the thin frame. The other is an eccentric beach scene. The viewer stares with Tony at the empty director's chairs (possibly symbolic of the lack of direction in Tony's leaderless crew since the death of Jackie Aprile) placed in front of two sliding doors. Two shadowy silhouettes are discernible within the right frame of the glass. One silhouette is the shape of a tree; the other is of a seated woman. The tree is a mnemonic link to the barnyard painting in Dr. Melfi's anteroom. But is the image really in the painting or simply part of Tony's imagination, and, through Tony, the viewer's imagination? The seated figure cleverly foreshadows images of Tony's mother that appear later in the series. Her seated presence here signals an impending physical or symbolic death. In either case, she is a constant presence in Tony's embattled psyche. He asks his mistress Irina: "What's that paintin' mean to you?" She replies with laconic indifference: "Nothing, it just reminds me of David Hockey." (Actually, the artist is David Hockney, an expressionist pop artist.)

Tony's therapy and Jackie Aprile's impending death lead him to ponder, for the first time in the series, questions that become an exemplifying leitmotif for him: Why am I here? Where am I going? Later on, when he's back in therapy during the same episode, Dr. Melfi asks him, "Do you feel like Frankenstein, lacking humanity?" The analogy foretells an event in "The Test Dream" V.11 when a crowd of characters from *The Sopranos* chase him through the streets and suddenly morph into a similar chase scene from the 1931 classic film *Frankenstein*, replete with barking dogs, lederhosen-clad peasants, and burning torches. Tony remains silent to Dr. Melfi's query. His slumped sitting position, however, mimics that of an enormous listless puppet, his arms and legs resemble dismembered appendages, his head sags like an oversized drooping globe. The image is a compelling allusion to the pieced-together demon monster created by Mary Shelley in 1818. The silence of the session is broken by choral music. As if to posit a surrogate answer to Dr. Melfi's unanswered question, Chase superimposes music from Meadow's school recital into Tony's session. It overlays the scene and bridges the audience's attention as the scene slowly shifts from a slumping and lifeless Tony in Dr. Melfi's office to a school auditorium stage where his daughter Meadow is singing in the school choir. The camera lingers upon a crucifix that hangs above the choir and lends an air of religious solemnity to their words. Tony eventually enters the auditorium and sits beside a despondent Carmela who refuses to lend the emotional security of her hand. Tony, both in Dr. Melfi's office and here it would seem, is on his own. As the choir intones lyrics of peace, gentility, and merciful repose, two deaths are musically framed with *The Godfather*-like timing, religious tone, and criminal precision.[12] One death is metaphorical: the irreverent Christopher Moltisanti is taken to the New Jersey shore and is shot in a ritual mock execution ("Denial, Anger, Acceptance" I.3). From his soiled remains (he defecates into his pants from fear), a newly dedicated, born-again family soldier will resurrect. The other event is a literal death: "Bragging Brandon" Filone is silenced, shot to death while in his bathtub by Uncle Junior's minion Mikey Palmice ("Meadowlands" I.4). Tony the father, meanwhile, has found solace and renewed faith in the sobering lyrics of his daughter's hymn. As the words waft over him like a summer breeze, he recharges his emotions, regains a momentary faith in his own miserable and pieced-together humanity, and is able once again to look at trees and himself and make it, as the song rings, "All through the night."[13]

Yet even this brief token of liberation hides ontological consequences that may disrupt his troubled sense of peace. The paintings Chase has juxtaposed at this early stage in the series present two salubrious but paradigmatically distinct worlds: land and forest, sand and water. The dichotomy is a fundamental global geologic feature of the planet.

Beyond overt comparisons of dry and wet, staid and fluid, and the classical symbology of the elements that characterize all phenomena, these two antithetical dimensions reinforce the melodramatic natural rhythms of *The Sopranos'* ecumenical criminality.

Water is by far the most recurring image in both the life and the paintings that surround Tony from the outset. From the shallownees of his backyard pool replete with the angst-provoking ducks to the nightmarish scape of the Atlantic City Boardwalk, from the breaking waves of the fathomless wet cemetery of the Atlantic Ocean to Whitecaps, the beach house that symbolizes his marriage breakup – water, a natural symbol of life and renewal, does not placate and appease the existential torment that pervades Tony. Being waterside is never restful. He dreams of losing his penis while poolside. Nevertheless, the pool remains his personal respite and watery island of solace amid the cement-clad terrain of emotional anguish. He returns to its borders but doesn't always find peaceful solitude. His reunion with his sister Janice Soprano, for instance, occurs near the soothing water of his pool in the episode "Guy Walks into a Psychiatrist's Office" II.1; but her presence only renewsTony's long-held rancour towards her slimy demeanour. Interestingly, a slithering vacuum hose seen at the bottom of the pool reminds Tony, and forewarns the viewer, of her underhanded and scummy nature. Mother Livia Soprano will snidely refer to Janice as a snake in the same episode. And what better way to disrespect Tony than to profane his pool by urinating in it, an option Pasquale "Patsy" Parisi chooses in "Mr. Ruggierio's Neighborhood" III.1. Tony will imperiously claim his unalienable right to the pool after having been ejected from home by Carmela in Season V, while the couple's most violent argument occurs in the backyard poolhouse in "Whitecaps" IV.13. The Whitecaps beach house was to be an inheritance property for the children, an isolated and peaceful ocean oasis for the troubled Soprano clan. Instead, it comes to represent the disintegration of their family. Tony's most painful memory emerges as he sits in a desolate backyard and contemplates his covered pool in "Long-Term Parking" V.12. His mind returns to riverside romps as a teen with his cousin Tony B., a relationship he must tortuously conclude. From whatever angle, water is an entrapping, isolating, and sinister presence that envelops Tony's existence and erects perplexing perimeters within which he moves and swims as a beastly automaton.

These watery entrapments are presented in contrast to the sanctioned murders that normally occur in wooded areas: Mikey Palmice shot by Christopher Moltisanti and Paulie "Walnuts" Gualtieri while jogging in the woods in "I Dream of Jeannie Cusamano" I.13; Christopher and Paulie futilely attempt to execute a belligerent Russian thug while in the Pine Barrens, a dark, secluded wood in southeastern New Jersey in "Pine Barrens" III.11; Adriana La Cerva is mercilessly liquidated amidst the rustle of autumn leaves in "Long Term Parking" V.12; chopped-up corpses are normally buried in the woods by Tony's men. Tony's onscreen murders also occur in the countryside: Fabian "Febby" Petrullio is dispatched in the wilds of New England in "College" I.5; Matthew Bevilaqua is shot to death in Hucklebarney State Park in "From Where to Eternity" II.9; and Christopher Moltisanti is horribly suffocated along a lonesome stretch of highway wilderness in "Kennedy and Heidi" VI.18. The seaside and water also play a role in Tony's tales of murder and loss. The ocean is the ultimate burial ground for former friends turned traitors. Their ultimate treachery merits the most extreme banishment. Such cases also demand his personal attention: Chucky Signori in "I Dream of Jeannie Cusamano" I.13; Salvatore "Big Pussy" Bonpensiero in "Funhouse" II.13.

Though the woods and verdune landscapes, blue seas and watery haunts occupy a significant portion of screen time in the first seasons of *The Sopranos*, as the series moves towards its ultimate resolution the natural imagery that accompanies Tony becomes more arid and, seen from a gendered perspective, even less reputedly soothing and more masculine and cruel. Expansive oceans become forest-bound lakes, the backyard pool is emptied to reveal a rectangular grave-like hole; wetness overcome by the dryness of the desert, the holistic life force of water by cold soil and death. If Tony were capable of accurately understanding the vital and aesthetic qualities of the reality that surrounds him, he could probably move beyond life's often puzzling imagery and discover a possible redeeming import. But he cannot. Tony's life is vowed to preserve and cultivate a parallel world of maleficent onus and savage accountability. Tony's real world is founded upon delusion and subterfuge. He sees trees, but he thinks rotting graves. He may go fishing, but he angles for cadavers. This is also the reason that he interprets the paintings he sees either as threats to his self or as perplexing oddities. Painted images stymie him in the same way that Dr. Melfi's psychoanalytic proscriptions engulf him in implosive revelatory experiences that have the potential of creating a transcendent self but that repeatedly resuscitate innocent and natural yearnings that are best squelched. Yet these painful memories and daily symbols are undeniably present. His prudent words, studied responses, and rehearsed gestures therefore serve to sanction a remote-control distancing of uncomfortable sensory experience. This may produce an initial calm, but ultimately feelings of unease and enmity heighten his detached inertia. The resultant cerebral and always violent responses to his crises preclude escape and subsequently any real healing. But he cannot act towards a positive resolution of his existential dilemma for this would present a threat to his life as a gangster. He has been ordained to a life of conflicting, yet self-preserving, conformities. Images of tranquillity, of barns and beaches do not bring solace to Tony. He must instead live his willed and protracted life illusion by coniving his own well-wrought deceptions, by distorting the images (painted or otherwise) he flippantly regards, or by simply ignoring them (the green statue). He must evoke evasion rather than verisimilitude, and he must somehow protect his lamentably sequestered state in the hope that he maintain the game not for the ironic pleasure of ratiocinative play but for the survival and sanctioning of his own increasingly malevolent image.

Dr. Melfi's Office

Dr. Melfi's office is similar in colour and tone to her office anteroom. We may therefore assume that the conversations held in her office are synonymous and contiguous with the unresolved paradoxes exposed to Tony in the anteroom. In this inner haven of silent, painful meditation and prescribed medication, the exterior world falls silent, receding from immediate comprehension yet ever dangerous and beckoning. Reality becomes less an unreadable rebus, like a dream, and more a readable narrative, like a text. It is a realm of concealment that both resists and fascinates as dazzling improvisational juxtapositions are conjured by the two interlocutors, Dr. Melfi and patient Tony. Visual cuing is crucial within this haven of programmed psychological respite. The topology of the office is designed for comfort, for constructive ratiocinative interplay and heightened self-reference. It communicates only itself and its own organization. Its visual layout is that of a womb, an elongated sphere that resembles an ovule or an egg shape. This is a primitive collision of shapes that evinces dynamism while preserving memory. This internal space is evidence of the fluidity of life and of the complementarity of body and mind, reason and sensuality, of embryonic male and female principles. The potential signifiers this system might spawn are many and depend entirely upon its dialogists.

Meaning, however, is firmly grounded in the fundamental precepts of transference and counter-transference, distance and empathy, confession and forgiveness that the space enkindles and Dr. Melfi's professionalism promotes. The absence of corners and shadowed recesses privilege openness and honesty, qualities alien to the secretive duality of Tony's normal surroundings. Even the windows, potential thresholds to an external familiar ground, are never open, dressed in vertical blinds reminiscent of prison bars. A suite of four paintings of a tree in different stages of natural development grace the wall behind Dr. Melfi's desk. While the individual frames represent the four seasons, when taken as a series the sketches allude to the real work of this fluidly oval space: growth, change, and maturation. The inability to control the semantics of this alien and visually feminine inner sanctum is painfully apparent to Tony. The statuary, the paintings, the books create a nutritive synergism that remains beyond his threshold of articulation. University degrees and a diploma from Tufts College loom ominously over his head, a reminder of personal aspirations never realized. They are a visual testament to a fellow I-Am's tenacity and honest success. The canonical books behind Tony are another tribute to an intellectual's work ethic and posit topics that he might boast to understand (after all he has attended one semester of college) but never truly fathom.

Just as the green statue and the paintings illuminate the anteroom by activating reflections in the viewer that lead to a deeper understanding of the plight of the characters who broach these walls, the artwork and books in Dr. Melfi's office subtend the existential and psychological state of Tony as he moves through therapy. These background accoutrements not only decorate the office but witness the verbal drama of his life narrative. Their presence echo his words, the meaning of which are essentially transposed onto a visual palette, creating a sort of frame-tale or accompanying text that illuminates the evolving dilemma of Tony Soprano.

The statues that grace the office window sills are Robert Graham originals, which were on loan for the series. They become conspicuous to the viewer because both the selection and their placement on the shelves changes throughout the series. As our story begins, the window ledges in Dr. Melfi's office are bare. There are no statues visible. If we assume that this statuary somehow augments or reflects the dialogue of the characters before them, the visual palette is still clean. Tony has yet to tell his tale. We know nothing of his life. As his psychological narrative unfolds, however, statues appear and are constantly changed, moved, positioned in ways that suggest more than casual placement.

The first statue to materialize on Dr. Melfi's window ledge is that of an armless and legless torso in "Big Girls Don't Cry" II.5. The statue may allude to the plight of Peter "Beansie" Gaeta, now a paraplegic. In "The Happy Wanderer" II.6, two statues on the far ledge mimic the sitting positions of Dr. Melfi and Tony. One is the recurring statue of a reclining figure, legs crossed, attentive. The other is the appendageless torso that, when seen from a distance, resembles the sitting blob-like figure of Tony. The two figures will move from far ledge to the ledge directly behind Dr. Melfi and back again throughout the series. Of all the statuary, they best represent the reportorial dynamic that Tony and Dr. Melfi will foster during the series, that is, the taciturn and reticent monolithic patient versus the communicative and intellectually lithe doctor. But this dynamic remains in constant flux. In "Down Neck" 1.7, for instance, the kinetics of the sessions dramatically heighten when Dr. Melfi broaches the topic of Tony's father for the first time in the series. "Let's talk about your father," she innocently begins.

This is a potentially revelatory, and possibly explosive, moment with very significant consequences for one of the most difficult ethical problems facing the patient: the relation of self-affirmation and love towards others but especially the male parent. We note that the window ledge behind her is no longer barren of statuary. A statue of an upright man, apparently singing, has appeared and can be seen directly behind Dr. Melfi. Tony is about to reveal secreted memories of his troubled youth. As he narrates (or sings in mob slang) his account of seeing his father, "Johnny Boy" Soprano, brutalize a delinquent gambling client on a neighbourhood street, he is animated by filial pride. In this world of double entendre and innuendo, where the word Mafia is euphemized as "waste management," everything carries a double, usually sinister, valence. The statue carries the double gravity of mimicking the vicious dance between "Johnny Boy" Soprano and his unfortunate victim and also the courageous attempt by Tony to begin his emotional healing by singing his painful memories in therapy. Behind Tony's right shoulder the viewer espies a strategically placed book that further adumbrates his fractious upbringing. It is entitled *Future Youth*, a subtle allusion to Tony's troubled, perhaps unwanted, role as his father's heir. Both items are present only in this episode. Is this happenstance? Or are the changes in the positioning and selection of statuary on Dr. Melfi's shelves a deliberate ploy to follow Tony's intensifying sessions? Is it possible, in other words, to map the changes in the geography of the statuary and room accoutrements as a silent commentary upon the psychological drama that unfolds before them?

The viewer may only interpret what is seen, but it is nevertheless interesting that subsequent additions of statuary and their changing placement on the two window ledges of Dr. Melfi's office suggest that the movement of statuary is not arbitrary. Statues are added, removed, replaced, and often reappear in a semantic merry-go-round that shadows the circularity of Tony's revelations. They may also reflect the actions of characters that trouble Tony during any given episode. For example, Peter "Beansie" Gaeta's unfortunate loss of the use of his legs returns as an ongoing problem in "Full Leather Jacket" II.8 and is echoed in the replacement of the armless and legless torso already seen in "Big Girls Don't Cry" II.5. In "Proshai, Livushka" III.2 this armless legless bust has been replaced by the dancing figure we originally saw in "Down Neck" I.7. But the statue now assumes a graver presence. Whereas the dancing figure of a clown ably defines Tony proudly singing about his father, in this particular episode Tony must deal with the death of his mother. The subject matter lends the statue a Charles Chaplin–like presence, both sad clown and lightsome hoofer. The statue broadcasts Tony's true feelings surrounding his mother's death. He prefers to dance around the emotional shrapnel imbedded within his soul and remain a swaggering clown, eternally fixed, like the statue, in gay posture. In this session one would expect Tony to reveal unspoken and painful feelings about his mother. But he cannot. Instead, he dances a soft-shoe shuffle around the issue by lamenting the stereotypical duties of sonhood and the vital necessity of being a good son.[14] He is truly confused, irrevocably cloven between the rigorous duties of a model son, represented by the appearance of a statue of a figure frozen in an obedient soldier's stance on the far ledge, and the lightness of the dancing clown before him. Behind Dr. Melfi the viewer also notes a familiar statue of a person in a sitting posture. Its constant placement in the scene over the first two seasons of the series allows one to interpret its presence as a stable feature of the office. It represents Dr. Melfi. Her stance is gracefully poised, silent yet perceptive, acquiescent yet ready to listen, especially at this delicate critical juncture.

If we assume that the statuary in the series comes to represent the intellectual and emotional posturing of Dr. Melfi and Tony during their sessions together, something must change with the death of the mother figure. The positions they have consolidated over the first two seasons of the series no longer hold sway. The death of Livia Soprano, the malevolent mother and reason for Tony walking into a psychiatrist's office, is gone. Her physical absence will continue to affect the series, as it must veer into new areas of conflict and therapy for patient Tony. Her psychological residue in Tony will condition many of his future choices. One should expect changes in the statuary. The primary characters, Tony and Dr. Melfi, cannot remain in the static poses of Seasons I and II (of inveterate dancer and professional listener) but must become flexible, thereby developing a truly healing narrative by further examining the mother–son relationship in all its past, present, and future ramifications.[15] But the moment has not yet ripened. Tony's panic attacks have momentarily ceased, he sees no reason to continue therapy. Ready to dispatch the death of his mother as his primary motive for therapy, he asks, "So we're probably done here, right? She's dead." Before he pronounces these words the camera pulls back for a long shot of the office. Dr. Melfi and Tony sit on either side of a round glass table. The four windows on the far wall appear as a postmodern mirror of the four-panelled suite of trees on the wall behind the analyst's desk. Chase has created a scene within a scene with the far scene literally replicating the scene before it. Three pieces of statuary sit on the far window ledge convincingly mimicking the doctor and patient seated directly before them. The series, and the therapy, is at a crossroads. Tony and Dr. Melfi will either remain petrified in their positions, just like the statues on the far ledge, or will become reanimated and fathom new ontological territory. The therapy, and subsequently the series, must reinvent itself.

Not surprisingly, in the very next episode, "Fortunate Son" III.3, and for the second time in the series, there are no statues behind Dr. Melfi. Once again the viewer is presented a clean visual palette. The subject matter of the episode provides a clue. Tony is about to relive in memory his first panic attack. The visual landscape of the office moves the audience back in time, back to Tony's childhood and to the moment when he suffers his first panic attack. The title of the episode, "Fortunate Son," is an ironic marker that signals a return to Tony in his role as son, a boy divested of any semblance of future mob boss. In essence, the series is recommencing, beginning anew with a fresh perspective on its main character. In this episode Dr. Melfi will help him disambiguate the mitigating factors that led to his current pathology. All subsequent episodes will help further his growth as a mob boss, thereby moving him farther from his indenture to perennial sonhood and indebted to his mother. After having contemplated ending therapy, thereby effectively ending the series, the series may begin anew. The statues have been removed because Tony and Dr. Melfi finally delve into the root cause of his panic attacks. They are no longer static players in a mutual stand-off. The statue of the reclining listener has therefore been removed. Its absence signals the active role that Dr. Melfi is finally able to assume in therapy. At the end of this session she may verbalize a possible source for Tony's existential malaise and approvingly state, "Good work, real progress." The semantically charged dancing figure has also been removed because it no longer suits a psychologically rejuvenated Tony. He, too, will change posture as he is finally taking an active role in his therapy. As the two explore this newly unearthed and fertile emotional territory, images of an aroused father, red meat, recalcitrant mother, implied sex, and verbal violence converge to brew the churning stew of anxiety at the root of Tony's fainting spells.

Yet, in "Employee of the Month" III.4, the figure of the reclining statue has suddenly returned; the dancer is also back in its customary place. It seems that any fissure of hope Dr. Melfi espied in Tony's therapy, just one session earlier, was momentary and facetious. Both may only dance around the issues because of Tony's obdurate resistance to therapy. These two statues remain in these positions until "Pine Barrens" III.11. In this episode, a small replica of the nude green statue in the anteroom has been placed next to Dr. Melfi. Its head proudly aright, upwardly outstretched arms, chest out, nipples brazenly erect. This expression of volatile determination and bravado contrasts with the statue of the reclining listener positioned directly behind Dr. Melfi. If we assume that Dr. Melfi is both active therapist and receptive listener, then the statues fit her double profile. The addition of the statue of the virago reinforces her stance as an indivisible, unavoidable, and inevitable presence in Tony's life. This self-affirmation contrasts sharply with the hesitancy and threat of the nothingness we sense in Tony. Tellingly, there is no statue to mirror Tony's perturbed state of being. Though he appears calm, serene, and confident, he is simply manifesting the false self the viewer has come to know. The doctor's chiding in this episode reminds the viewer that while Tony is still her patient, he is in the same old ontological cul de sac.

As if to signal the increasing petrification of Tony's stance, the very next episode, "Amour Fou" III.12, opens with life-size statues of contorted figures. They are bent, furrowed, frozen in poses of pain; pensive, despairing. The same music that closed the last episode, Celia Bartoli's rendition of the aria *Sposa son disprezzata* (I am wife and I am scorned) by Geminiano Giacomelli, bridges into this episode and connects this gallery artwork to the statuary last seen in Dr. Melfi's office. Carmela and daughter Meadow are visiting the Museum of Modern Art.[16] Simultaneously inspired and depressed for reasons yet to be revealed, Carmela cries while admiring Giuseppe de Rivera's *The Mystical Marriage of St. Catherine*. In the painting, St. Catherine consecrates her virginity to the Christ Child. To Meadows' juvenile comment "She's marrying a baby?" Carmela sarcastically confesses that all women marry babies. It seems the sophisticated innocence and reverent tranquillity the painting inspires is sorely missing in her life. The image of the child lovingly held between the two women in Rivera's painting could have inspired Tony's final longing and childish query to Dr. Melfi that closes the previous episode: "I do right by my family ... does it count for anything?" The two episodes thus merge to extemporize the supposed values that the Soprano family enshrines – family, responsibility, loyalty, personal redemption – but that in reality they are hard pressed to actualize. The series has reached another critical juncture. Episode thirty-eight is the near midpoint of what became a six-year, eighty-six episode series. Like an inveterate Dantesque voyager, an unsuspecting Tony is midway through his journey, finally answering the pertinent questions required by therapy. By this episode's end he will understand that he must play the hand he has been dealt and grow within his contemporary history by individuating those relativistic points of orientation that answer his queries of existential relevance. In other words, he must unquestioningly ground his Ur narrative of mob boss on his own subject-centred perspective.

It is telling that statuary and paintings again assume primary importance in this particular episode. To begin with, there is new statuary in Dr. Melfi's office. A long shot reveals that the statues of the dancer and the reclining listener are no longer behind her but once again have been placed on the ledge of the window farthest from her. As if to signal the shifting therapeutic paradigm, there are two new heretofore unseen statues behind Dr. Melfi. Both resemble Japanese Samurai warriors; one kneels reverently, one stands stoically. The introduction of an Asian motif is revelatory. Tony may still quote Niccolò Machiavelli to Christopher in this episode ("You don't gotta love me, but you will respect me") but the more practical *Art of War* by Sun Tzu (cited by Tony in his discussion with Dr. Melfi) insinuates a new line of reasoning and mode of action.[17] He may compare Gloria Trillo's dark eyes to those of "a Spanish princess in one of those paintings by Goyam" but he is now more judicious, having been alerted to the realization that those eyes are a "bottomless black hole."[18] The hole is equal in depth and traumatic profundity as the dark barn door in the pastoral painting in Dr. Melfi's anteroom, where he first met the ill-fated Gloria.

These seemingly occasional inferences are a sign that Tony is steadily achieving cognizance. In this process he no longer remains conspicuously silent during his sessions nor does he shy away from confronting taxing issues in his familial relations. From here on the viewer will note both a more ruthless gangster and a more conventional if not cynical husband, and an infinitely more attentive father. As we have deduced, he has indeed achieved a turning point. He accepts the existential paradoxes of his life choices and remains firm to his chosen vocation, much like the samurai warriors on the ledge before him. He questions the system and he may even ponder (we will see) alternative life paths, but he acquiesces to, indeed approves of, his violent vocation. By accepting his vital state as the logical consequence of a social routine, that is neither better nor worse than any other, he escapes self-recrimination. In essence, Tony is no longer frozen in psychological time but has accepted the physical posture his time demands. Unfortunately, much like the statues of this episode's opening scene, he is ensnared within a false-self system that masks his schizoid delusions as the only possible life trajectory.

His wife Carmela is beginning to reveal the same moral equivocations. The visual and aural collating of the MoMA gallery statues with the statues on Dr. Melfi's window ledge place Carmela squarely within the existential reach of the figures' artistic dialectic. Her marriage is predicated on deceit and immorality. She has wilfully chosen to nurture her family on the rotten stock of illegality (Tony's other family). Is it any wonder that her tormented psyche is also manifested in the contorted statues? Is it any wonder that a morally destitute Carmela finds both solace and pain in the unspoiled innocence of the naked Christ Child? She is still reeling as she deliberates the total rejection of Tony's blood money (a chastisement given to her by an unforgiving Jewish psychiatrist in "Second Opinion" III.7) against the self-serving Catholic philosophy of living for the goodness in Tony (advice offered by an accommodating New Age priest in "Amour Fou" III.12). She is still searching for that one redemptive act that will move her beyond her own distorted posturing and back to the innocence of the Christ Child. Like Tony, Carmela is entrenched in an uncommunicative solitude that is in sharp counterpoint with any expiative and salutary discourse the vision of the painting should initiate.

The artworks that punctuate this particular episode clearly allow the viewer to contrast the private subconscious verbal text of Tony and Carmela with the public visual images that extend the drama of these characters into broader social issues. The MoMA paintings, Gloria Trillo and Tony's intense love sessions before tranquil scenes of painted Venetian canals, Tony and Christopher's unusually hostile argument before an equally dramatic painting of two sneering tigers, the pizzeria's trivial reminders of a mythical Italy among backward hanging Italian flags, the statuary of Dr. Melfi's office – all of these visual cues heighten the sense of detached inertia that now permeates the series' fabric and portends the debilitating consequences of Tony's deepening cynicism and Carmela's evolving personal growth. It is as if the world and its raw contours have been stilled on canvas for all to see, but no one is really looking. The "incessant self-regard" that Dr. Melfi declaims in this episode has become the external non-regard of surrounding images and artworks that foretell the inevitable worsening of Tony's, Carmela's, and other characters' existential condition.

The impossibility of any stabilizing interior or validating exterior vision enacts the breakdown of heretofore apparently stable relationships in the series. As the unresponsive, impervious, or simply indifferent Other induces a sense of emptiness and impotence in the main characters, destructive fantasies triumph, and an attitude of perpetual frustration poisons long-held myths of gratification in many of the characters. In "Everybody Hurts" IV.6 the hurt escalates to acts of ontic negation. Though suicide can liberate one from an ill-sorted fate, it cannot lessen the anxiety of private guilt and public condemnation. In this episode, Artie Bucco attempts suicide while Gloria Trillo's hopeless death is revealed to an unsuspecting Tony. As a consequence, two new statues appear on the far window ledge of Dr. Melfi's office. Both are of women. One reaches up to the heavens in a gesture of possible liberation from earthly tribulation, perhaps as a crying-out for salvation. Artie's aborted suicide and unwanted surrender to his weaker irrational impulses is mirrored in this gesture. He acts to assuage the angst-driven awareness of his own newly discovered non-being. He will emerge from this act having fully experienced the despair of condemnation. But it will take time before he will supplant the meaninglessness he feels his life has assumed with a newfound faith in his culinary craft (more on this point later). The other statue is of a woman cleaved in half, a possible allusion to Gloria Trillo's recent suicide by hanging. The analogy is reinforced in this episode's dream sequence in which a radiant Gloria sarcastically asks Tony which cloven part of her he wishes to regard: the cleft of her vagina or the open wound of her neck.

Carmela's rejection of Tony at the end of Season IV in "Whitecaps" IV.13 unleashes similar inarticulate desires in him that sorely compensate for the woeful intellectual and social inferiority he feels with respect to Dr. Melfi. Appropriately, new and formerly unseen statues grace the window ledges. All have an African flavour and give the setting an air of primitive primal desire. Behind Dr. Melfi stands the statue of a happy dancer stepping lightly, best foot forward, possibly signifying Carmela's new beginnings, new journeys, her "New shoulders to cry on/ New back seats to lie on." Nils Lofgren's imploring lyrics from the song "Black Books," originally heard in "Second Opinion" III.7, resonate anew as Carmela once again proves that she, as the song intones, "always gets her way." On the far window ledge, however, we also note two statues; one a graceful dancer, the other, a reclining figure, hands and feet firmly rooted to the ground. The statues complement each other in their appositional placement and form a triptych when considered with the carefree statue representing Carmela. These two statues' postures are echoed in the scene played out before them. Tony has come to ask Dr. Melfi to take their relationship to a new and astonishing, for Dr. Melfi, amorous (libidinous and thus primitive) level. The long camera shot places him between the two statues on the far ledge. His slouching posture and size apes the statue seen directly beyond him, while Dr. Melfi's crossed legs and pointed toe mirror the dancer's limber gait. Similarly, their conversation unveils contradictions and contrasts that highlight the differing perspectives of their relationship. Tony is upset and bewildered, resolved yet hesitant. His unleashed passions are irrational but in form since he is merely articulating a conditioned framework of erotic desire. Dr. Melfi, on the other hand, is resolute and firm. Her professionalism may only beget a standard, though visibly pained, rejection of her patient's entreaties. In this, their most private and intense moment to date, they look to each other for comfort and solace as Carmela, represented by the happy dancer statue, watches.

But Dr. Melfi cannot allow their mutual primal desire to bloom. If their relationship as doctor and patient is to survive they must maintain their familiar postures. They must remain like statues, frozen in their stances. They cannot dance like the prancing statue of a newly liberated

Carmela behind Dr. Melfi but must remain reclining, seated, fettered to solid ground like the statues on the far ledge. Between them the tissue box holds an erect tissue that intimates the form of a penis. Tony has yearnings (a Jones in Soprano slang)[19] for Dr. Melfi and he reveals his feelings to her for the first time. As Tony continues his entreaties in the office vestibule, a more blatant white tissue peeks out of the box set directly behind them. But Dr. Melfi continues to reject his amorous advances. He despondently returns home to his chosen soul mate, to the only woman that has accepted his derogations. We see Carmela polishing an apple, a traditional symbol in Renaissance paintings on "the Fall of Adam and Eve." The apple is green, a visual link to the green statue that subtends the gendered subtleties of the series. The episode has seen Tony cast out from his spiritual haven (Dr. Melfi's office) and from his earthly domain (Carmela's home). The episode ends with Tony sitting outside his house, alone, forlorn, and disconsolate. As the scene fades to black, he becomes a non-descript silhouette in the deepening darkness. His hunched molten mass again resembles the statue the viewer has just seen on Dr. Melfi's office ledge. Needing to reaffirm a wounded masculinity, he lights a long plump cigar and wields a menacing rifle pointed to the heavens. One is a turgid, the other an erect, phallic symbol. Both are displayed with menacing readiness. But, since both Dr. Melfi (spirit) and Carmela (body) have repudiated him, he can only hope that the green apple ripens to red and that he is eventually readmitted into Dr. Melfi's office and into his home, both former, and irreverently lost, Earthly Paradises.

The Soprano Home

While Dr. Melfi's office can be considered a psychological inner sanctum, Tony's other safe havens, his home and mob offices, provide writer David Chase the opportunity to flesh-out his character profile by using a visual thesaurus of easily recognizable and recurring popular icons. The Soprano house, for instance, became a model for viewers who wished to build a similar home for themselves. Online blueprints provided the structural plan of the house while Carmela's decorative touches inspired housewives to recreate the Soprano look in their homes.[20] Further exploitation of the brand spawned a wave of tie-in products that included gangster chic garbage bags, calendars, food products, a *The Sopranos Family Cookbook* featuring instructions to viewers on "how to cook like an Italian Mama and how to eat like a wiseguy," and a faux clan history titled *The Sopranos: A Family History* replete with personal biographical tidbits, childhood photos, FBI intercepted emails, and the letter of recommendation that Joan Cusamano wrote for Meadow's admission to Georgetown University.[21] The house, its accoutrements, and the surrounding neighbourhood spawned a new cultural geography that became a commercial hook for the viewer and attracted fans to Sopranoland. *The Sopranos* aficionados paid more attention to the settings and backgrounds than other general television audiences because the links between the video images and familiar locations added another level of meaning to the program. These were Chase's ideal viewers and, similar to deriving pleasure by recognizing artwork in the series, this personalizing effect allowed everyday settings and recognizable locations to became a shared experience. The viewer became an insider, part of a common ontological adventure and aesthetic experience that opened the series onto a boundless homogeneous space. The Sopranos family became an esthetically extended virtual family that lived in an artistically conceived virtual space.

Yet, while *The Sopranos* put the Garden State squarely within the cultural sites of America bestowing upon it a visibility that sat in stark opposition to the hyper-reality of silence, obfuscation, and secrecy real mobsters demand, these ethnically charged and stereotypical marketing strategies contrast sharply with the on-screen reality of the Soprano home. Unlike his childhood home, Tony's house is void of ethnic mementos and markers. While Livia Soprano's second generation I-Am home displays the requisite portraits of Pope John XXIII and President John F. Kennedy along with faded images of "the old country," the third-generation Soprano home is devoid of what can be termed ethnic basement culture. As immigrant families assimilated and became more affluent, material legacies of their peasant roots typically found their way to the seclusion (secrecy) of the lower level. Not so with the Sopranos. As a means of distancing the Soprano family from its cultural roots, thus rendering them more realistic I-Ams, Chase gives the home an unfinished basement with no ethnic regalia whatsoever. The viewer easily defines Tony on familiar turf. A modern kitchen with large refrigerator, pleasantly appointed entertainment areas, pastels and earth tone colours speak more of Carmela's flair for spending his money on contemporary decorators than her need for a more traditional sense of place. Any stereotypical I-Am affinities are reserved for the backroom offices at the Bada Bing and Satriale's Pork Store. The Soprano home thus conveys a strong cultural confirming image of the contemporary

American family that mirrors a decentred, discontinuous, and indistinct space – not the urban village of ethnic lore. More than a mobster's home, it is just a huge house in an overpriced, automobile-friendly, yet meticulously green landscaped and gated community in America. While life in the suburbs breeds just this sort of assimilation, the trappings of Tony's sustaining personal culture can be found in the most secluded area of his family haven, the master bedroom. If the kitchen is the public space where the Sopranos feed family and friends, where the children are disciplined and counselled, and where the materiality of household life is publicly expressed, the private space of the master bedroom is a preternatural safe zone, an area of the home where husband and wife can truly manifest their most intimate and innate personalities.

The Soprano master bedroom boasts a faux roman pedestal for the television set, a reproduction of an Italian Renaissance painting on the dresser, a large Mannerist mural above the headboard. Several other non-descript reproductions grace the bedroom walls. In "From Where to Eternity" II.9, the camera focuses on porcelain Fontanini angels on the night stand. They seem to eavesdrop on the bedroom gossip. As Carmela places her watch in a gold-gilded plate on the nightstand, three angels, hands clasped in prayer, hold vigil over Carmela's often long, sleepless, and restless nights. At the end of this episode the angelic figures are different; now there are four. Their hands are no longer clasped in reverent prayer but are instead held outright in an apparent show of approval, if not amazement. The angels seem to look on jubilantly as Carmela, no longer alone, receives amorous attention from husband Tony. This is the first time the viewer is allowed to witness this apparently rare sexual encounter. The viewer will be allowed entry to this bedroom space whenever it is necessary to restate or realign the intimate parameters between the couple.

Whenever the viewer normally enters the master bedroom, he/she finds the couple either lying motionless in bed or moving about the large room. Accordingly, the bedroom decorations usually remain in the background, receiving scant attention while Tony and Carmela share their frequent verbal altercations but infrequent sexual intimacy. On another occasion as above, however, the viewer enters the Soprano master bedroom from a different perspective. In "Proshai, Livushka" III.2, the viewer is at first unaware that he/she is in the bedroom at all. The scene opens with an extreme close-up of two painted figures. The camera slowly pans down the imposing life-size figures in the mural, allowing the viewer to fully appreciate the mural's size and imposing presence. The painting is a reproduction of Jacopo Carrucci's (also known as Pontormo) *La visitazione* or *The Visitation of the Virgin and St. Elizabeth*. It is a Renaissance-style representation of four women.[22] Two are seen from the side view as they stand face to face. The commanding central figure, right shoulder towards the viewer, wears a gown of regal lapis lazuli blue (a Renaissance style-mark for the Virgin Mary, Queen of Heaven) and a red kerchief (a colour normally reserved for Christ, the Word made flesh, the male God incarnate). The de facto leader of the group, the central figure's right hand rests upon the left shoulder of the woman confronting her as they gaze intently into each other's eyes. This depicted scene is not an a-causal moment; it is instead a pregnant instant wrapped in arresting and inarticulate performance. It is evident that a secret has been shared, or is about to be whispered. Incisive eyes meet with foreboding intent. Bridging their gaze is the stolid, unflinching stare of a member of the sisterhood standing directly behind and between them; another woman stoically covers the central figure's back and peers out from behind her shoulders. Their deep-set dark eyes countersign the foreboding knowledge of secular rites and rituals. The presence of these two women is a formal familial necessity. Their stoic demeanour bestows theatricality to a scene that reflects the encrypted (and in this case painted) reality of the worldly codes they represent. They are the silent ministers and witnesses of their master's mission, determination, expectation, and destiny. They are the avatars of purpose. Technically, we are viewing a visual-verbal composite form. The characters have just finished speaking, or are speaking in gestures, or are about to speak. This is apparent in the arrested moment in time or stilled action affect that the artist has chosen to depict. Yet, paradoxically, there is also a silent anti-linguistic grid at work within the composition. The central interlocutors may not be speaking at all but merely acknowledging a taciturn understanding between them. In this respect, they mimic a world of conspicuous *omertà'* and silent social subterfuge; something which the Soprano family holds vital to its very survival.

The placement of the mural in this precise moment of the Soprano narrative renders it a purposeful heraldic emblem. The allegorical image of these staunchly resolute and divinely chosen women has always accompanied the psychological silhouette of Tony Soprano and, by extension, all his men. But now this delicate imagery becomes the narrative gloss of the series and portends a deeper understanding of its underlying theme. The mural visually extemporizes and simultaneously negates the series' most vital and sustaining premise, that of masculine *omertà*. This feminine presence at the heart of Sopranoland insinuates that Tony's problem, as we shall see, is his inability to come to terms with this vital reality: at the heart of all his decisions and actions, at the base of his chicanery and chauvinism, is his unwillingness to accept his feminine psychological self. With the death of his mother, the dynamite of this inner friction will finally explode. The therapy sessions with Dr. Melfi purposefully assume the tortuous road of recognizing this very conflict. The painting that resides at the heart of the Soprano family's confidentiality must be read as a female version of the Sopranos' secret world order. The masculine grammar that is imposed upon the silent non-verbal tale of the painting intimates a visual narrative of fixed female gestures and images that is anything but masculine. While the teleological framework projects the private language of cries, gestures, touching, body stance, all feminine qualities, it is nevertheless predicated on masculine qualities of tradition, ritual, fealty, lineage, and, above all, *omertà*.

These gestures are repeated and amplified in the public and masculine realm of the mob. In short, the stoic public male brotherhood of Tony Soprano is surreptitiously premised on the expressive and nonlogical holistic qualities of female sisterhood. In the mob world there are no intrusive societal sanctions but instead there are dictums that generationally descend from *la famiglia*. These inherited mores are explicitly masculine in its public display but decidedly and implicitly feminine and private, wilfully hidden in its psychological dimension.[23] In short, this painting is a master text of Tony's inheritance. It is the heraldic emblem, a crest that must be recognized and reckoned with, even by those who wish to resist its possibly debilitating message. Its depiction as the mobster's operative mode is indisputable. Just as Tony is flanked by the male minions Silvio Dante (the brain) and Paulie "Walnuts" Gualtieri (the muscle) during business negotiations, the supporting female duo in the painting provides similar physical security, historical legitimacy, cultural safeguards, and loyalty to the coded honour that has been sworn to the two central figures of heavenly power and saintly respect. The painting is thus a reverse negative print of the male world of Tony Soprano. It is a collusive document of a clandestine mob culture that insists on being seen as a legitimate and parallel social frame, not as a mere illegal supplement. It is the dubious purity of these individuals' will to silence that sanctions their project while it necessarily evacuates their language of any redeeming social value.

We recall that the painting is located directly behind the matrimonial headboard. As the camera slowly pans down the folds and colours of the women's robes and meanders along the gestures in the painting and onto the equally visually suggestive bodies of Tony and Carmela as they lie amidst the bedspread folds, the viewer intuits a visual confluence between the two figures in bed and the main characters in the painting. The narrative importance of the moment is a signpost in the evolving Soprano dynamic. Tony's mother has just died. The female icon of family strength, malevolence, and treachery has passed the torch to her son. As Tony lies beneath the painted icon of private trust, mob power, family fidelity, and nefarious secrecy, Tony and Carmela not only exchange their most intimate verbal and sexual intercourse, but Tony vouchsafes and confirms his miscreant birthright. This directorial acknowledging by David Chase of the painting's presence in the Soprano master bedroom by allowing the viewer to linger long on its figures is not an arbitrary moment. At this juncture in the series the painting is an ideological superstructure that resonates with emblematic symbolism and timeless recursive symmetry. The ultimate implication of this heraldic crest in the life of Tony Soprano is still to be unravelled. But not until Tony fully accepts his full inheritance, not until he comprehends the true psychological impact of carrying this feminine side within will the lessons imparted by his mother and the protomeaning of the painting truly resonate to forge his full character. The same will be true eventually, as we shall see, for family heir apparent Anthony Junior.

While the images in the painting are spatially fixed and unchanging, the vision of Tony and Carmela lying in bed beneath its empowering splendour is somehow ephemeral. Their bedtime narrative, like the rest of their lives, sometimes strongly suggests chance or whim. Their true family portrait has not yet been officially painted and will not be until series' end. But Tony knows that he cannot compromise bedrock family values, the feminine beast that he carries within and that is displayed before him nightly. He cannot betray the founding principles of his profession. He cannot permit chaos in the domestic or workplace sphere because all his past and future choices are conditioned by the blood weight of his nuclear family counterpointed by the bloody reality of his inherited profession even if he does not yet fully comprehend them. Accordingly, a restless and visibly troubled Tony removes himself from the heavily charged scene and moves into the TV room where he comes to rest before another artistic icon, this time male, of the honoured society, the figure of James Cagney in the motion picture *The Public Enemy*.[24] He cries. Perhaps he longs for the unconditional affection of the cheerful mother he sees on the television screen and which he never knew in his own stony-hearted mother. But perhaps he feels his own vulnerability, caught between an ever-present and private core narrative of matriarchy that he carries within and an all-encompassing seductive public patriarchy that promises salvation but is fraught with the crest of hypocrisy and secrecy.

Surrounding this heraldic emblem of Soprano family mores are the bedrooms of teenage daughter Meadow and adolescent son Anthony Junior. They are the still-unconscious progeny of its heraldry, not yet attracted by its lore, rebellious to its silent connotations. Whether father Tony is foolish or simply wilfully innocent when he lectures to pampered daughter Meadow that outside the home it may be the 1990s but inside it's the 1950s in "Nobody Knows Anything" I.11, both parents already know that the two juvenile bedrooms of the Soprano household are beyond their control. Tony and Carmela have shielded their children from knowledge of the family business as zealously as they have prohibited them from entering their bedroom. Secrecy regarding the reality of Dad's waste management business is practised to maintain the conditions for healthy and ordered growth. According to Neil Postman, "If it is hypocrisy to hide from children the 'facts' of adult violence and moral ineptitude, it is nonetheless wise to do so. Surely, hypocrisy in the cause of strengthening child growth is no vice."[25]

The bedrooms of Meadow and A.J. originally appear as enlightened oases, youthful sanctums of developing idiosyncrasies that have little to share with the inconceivable vision portrayed in the Soprano bedroom mural. They are havens in which to sulk in youthful emotions, rant at parental prerogatives, and experiment with teen subculture. The rooms lend visual coherence to their dispersive, and often rebellious, youth. The walls are painted in bright hues; the rooms are well-lit and spacious. A.J.'s room is adorned with band posters and action figures of ball players. Older sister Meadow's room has apparently replaced earlier band posters with the more feminine posters of poetic adages. A large butterfly graces her wall, a visual image of her imminent transformation into a woman ("The Sopranos" I.1). But despite their father's admonition that their home is a haven for the 1950s, it is indeed the 1990s, and just as social conduct has changed in the outside world, so too bedroom computers reveal even the best kept secrets. For Meadow and A.J. nothing is mysterious, nothing of their family pedigree remains hidden. Though the bedrooms begin as havens of childhood, having access to the hidden fruit of adult information quickly changes the inhabitants from innocent youth to informed child-adults. The bedrooms thus quickly evolve in time along with their youthful inhabitants. In Meadow's room, the girlish colours give way to subtle hues that intimate an awakening femininity. The passing of time and the updating of posters give little reason, however, to assume that the ordained underpinnings of her childhood will change. Her pained decision to become a criminal lawyer instead of a pediatrician, as her parents had hoped, is the result of the raw material of youth that projects her into her future profession as her father's protector. Not a surprise decision given her proximity, both physically and metaphorically, to the family crest. The public and private secrecy that permeate the walls of her home have conditioned her to accept the true nature of her character. "You're all me," her father assures her in a particularly touching scene. "Nothing gets by you" ("Bust Out" II.10).

A.J.'s maturation appears less structured and is decidedly more problematic. His progression from innocent pop posters to images of dark gothic bands takes place in successive twisted stages that overlap and redouble in intensity. Our first impressions of him can be defined by a simple character outline: he's mouthy and spoiled, a media-driven kid attracted to wildness and video games. His adolescent reign of terror is condoned by his father who more than likely embodied similar traits as a boy. Self-restraint is still a challenge to Tony; to expect it from his son would be rhetorical fallacy. His pessimistic misgivings about his son are sanguine: "A.J., in my business? Forget it. He'd never make it," he affirms to Dr. Melfi in "The Army of One" III.13. When his plan to correct his son's increasing hostility and bouts of delinquency by sending him to military school is scuttled because of A.J.'s sudden onslaught of panic attacks, Tony becomes characteristically despondent, then genuinely forlorn when he realizes that he has bequeathed his "putrid, rotten, fuckin' Soprano gene" to his offspring. He woefully confesses to Dr. Melfi, "We can't send him to this place." Then painfully implores, "How are we gonna save this kid?"

A.J.'s uncertain rebelliousness, replete with grunge music and clothes, eventually mutates into a more somber and insidious existential menace. He focuses his despondency onto computer sites that spew forth propaganda images from the Al Jazeera TV network, deliver violent scenarios of American soldiers at war, and blaspheme American imperialism. His bedroom becomes a symbolic arena where the vulnerability of his befuddled young life converges with the perils of eminent global destruction. But these progressively more detailed layers that encrust his character do not change our impressions of him as a troubled child. On the contrary, as his room, clothes, and demeanour darken, so does that of the viewer. A.J.'s immaturity and insecurities, we may speculate, reflect Tony's teenage years and, as such, the total picture of A.J. has been in clear view all along. It simply takes time to construct its features and connect all the experiences that eventually form the young adult who will follow, at series' end, the path already trodden by his father. Though A.J., we will see, does not have the spirit to become a hardened thug like his father, he will become a low-level purveyor of pornographic images. He will not be required to exact violent retribution from his enemies because he is so dreadfully maladroit, but he will harness the beast within and create a public masculine facade of composure and calm. He will remain in the family business and, once he has appropriated his genetic heritage, will be well on his way to truly understanding the polarizing complexities of living within the Soprano inner sanctum.

The Bada Bing

The television show *Harvey Birdman* (The Cartoon Network) once ran an episode in which cartoon character Fred Flintstone was played as if he were Tony Soprano. Instead of the Water Buffalo Lodge where Fred and Barney Rubble spent time with the guys, the Soprano version of Fred arrives at the local strip club, a Bada Bing replica for cavemen replete with poles, strippers, and prehistoric hard guys. In many respects, the braggadocio of the cartoon version of Tony as Fred Flintstone and the Bada Bing as primitive sex lair ironically reflect the true nature of business conducted at the Bing. On the surface, at least, the males in the series are allowed to assert their dominant narrative positions while psychologically, and often physically, brutalized women accept their fates as generic accessories. Similar to Satriale's Pork Store, the Bada Bing's "backroom office space" provides Tony and the boys with an inner sanctum where they may flaunt their malevolent nature without fear of ambiguity or repercussion. There is no profound equivocal morality at the strip joint, no politics at Satriale's; just business. No wrenching feminist discourse in either locale; just patriarchy. While these havens may witness personal exploitation and social paradox, resolution is always linear, straightforward, and dreadfully predictable.

If Tony's home is his castle, his backroom offices are his fiefdom. Different from the privacy of home where the public never gains entry, these spaces are private rooms set in public places regularly frequented by his cohorts. They provide the venue for his activity, the stage where morality is suspended and sexual affectation reigns. The backroom of the Bing is Tony's theatre of operations. It is much richer in traditional ethnic texture than the Soprano home and flaunts its gangster subtext with the reality of real-life gangsterism. Besides the requisite commercial beer logos, calendars and posters featuring girls in various stages of undress, the backroom is a haven for pictures of I-Am boxers, worn postcards of Italy, dirty money waiting to be laundered. The struggle to negotiate one's pecking order on the street begins here. It's a men-only club; the topless dancers never enter this haven of masculine hyper-virility; real customers never gain entry to the rear of the shop. Very little changes within these walls; comfort resides in familiarity and layers of well-worn memories steeped in petulant attitude. Shabby desks, worn chairs, a safe chock-full of money, a battered fridge, and a pool table set the dreary minimalist tone. It's the characters that move through its interior that set the mood in these niches of moldy manhood. Several visual additions made through the series are notable. A poster of a young Frank Sinatra in a police mug shot appears in Season V. In "Moe and Joe" VI.10, Vito Spatafore's homosexuality is alluded to in new posters and calendars featuring images of body builders. An interesting intercalation of signage into the narrative occurs in "Mr. Ruggierio's Neighborhood" III.1 duringTony's conversation with Pasquale "Patsy" Parisi. Though time has passed, Patsy remains distraught over the killing of his identical twin, Phillip "Philly Spoons" Parisi, by what he knows to be Tony's direct orders. Tony employs considerable pressure to force Patsy to verbally admit that he has buried his misgivings. He is relentless in his insistence that Patsy repeat the words that he has forgiven and forgotten. The consequences of refusal are cogently displayed by the words on the Hamburger Patties sign that rests on the wall directly behind Tony. As if to dissuade any possible misinterpretation of Tony's intentions, the sign is visually cropped to read Hamburger Pat, a bald allusion to Patsy's becoming minced meat if he does not comply with Tony's aural wishes. Dr. Melfi alludes to a similar end when she asks Tony, "Would makin' hamburger out of me make you feel better?" in "The Happy Wanderer" II.6.

Interestingly, Tony's inner sanctum at the Bada Bing has walls of hammered stained glass, an anomaly of sorts, given the Bing's business and the usual use of stained glass in churches. The glass visually displays the dichotomy between the illicit and flighty sexual content of the Bing and the stolid heavenly veracity of places of worship. The walls of glass lend an air of solemn gravity to the place and remind this viewer of the more opulent stained glass of Tony's old neighbourhood church. During his visit to this church with Meadow in "The Sopranos" I.1, Tony waxes proudly about her great-grandfather and her uncle Frank who were immigrant masons and who had helped build the neighbourhood church. Beyond the obvious religious symbolism and subliminal cultural pride that the colourful vision exudes, the stained glass images frames our perception of the place. Tony and Meadow sit before scenes that represent seminal moments in the life of Christ: "Jesus and the Elders" and "The Presentation of the Baby Jesus." The camera then slowly pans the main altar and its imagery of "The Last Supper." Behind the altar are large paintings of the Birth, Crucifixion, and Resurrection of Christ. These church images represent the traditional bedrock stories of Christianity in blocks of time and space that have been colourfully forged together. Their timeless message, created, ironically, by men like Tony's ancestors, offsets the transitoriness of Tony's sinful presence. Their refracted coloured light imbues the scene with religious solemnity while the marble statuary and alter frontispiece offer imputable certainty. If we compare these windows and the altarpiece to the stained glass and altar that decorate the church of Father Phil Intintola in "I Dream of Jeannie Cusamano" I.13, we note that there are no biblical stories depicted in his sanctuary. Instead, we find abstract splotches of colour that are absent, much in character with the vacuous priest, of any redeeming message.

Tony's offices share a symbolic potential that set them apart from their visual counterparts of Dr. Melfi's office and neighbourhood churches. Whereas these latter inner sanctums can indeed be considered hallowed ground of emotional self-knowledge in the first instance and spiritual growth in the latter, his private offices can only be termed sacristies of slime. They are filled with illegal money, hidden guns, and sexual indecency, and they are harbingers of illicit behaviour. The Bada Bing is the beginning and end of all of Tony's unethical associations and lustful escapades. The *business* that is Tony Soprano is publicly displayed at the Bada Bing. Its outdoor commercial sign features the public consumption of naked women and the promise of related illegal pleasures. The *man* that is Tony Soprano is privately revealed in backroom dealings that enforce the manipulative patriarchy that shapes the controlled hostility that is the hallmark of the Bada Bing. Tony uses these sanctuaries as black confessionals, havens of momentary respite that assuage and abet his contorted soul. One such moment transpires the night Tony must dispose of the corpse of Ralph Cifaretto. Tony has just murdered Ralph and, with Christopher Moltisanti's help, has chopped and buried the body. Rather than returning home, they go to the Bada Bing for expunging drinks and a cleansing shower. After these ablutions that rid the body not of the sin but of the blood stains, they change clothes and fall asleep. Tony awakens the next morning only to find he is alone. Christopher has long departed.

Sullied and confused by the darkness of the place, Tony realizes that the night and the booze have not erased the lingering essence of the now-dead Ralph. As Tony is waking up, the camera focuses on a poster of Tessa (read Tony) the Tease that hangs on the wall behind him. The caption reads She'll Bring You to Hell. Topless Tessa holds a long black silk scarf behind her in a provocative dance pose. One end of the scarf hangs lower than the other. The scarf's balled end resembles that of a head and calls to mind the severed head of Ralph held by Christopher as he placed it into a bowling bag. An adjacent poster features a kneeling stripper clad in white. She is bent and viewed from the rear. Only her legs and posterior are visible as she bends over, her tail end raised alluringly, a visual reference to Ralph's latent sexual proclivity for being sodomized by his female partners. Ralph Cifaretto may be dead, but the memory, unconsciously for Tony but visually for the viewer, is embedded in the darkened rooms of the Bada Bing. Similarly, Christopher's postmortem photograph at the Bada Bing will attract a cat that Paulie "Walnuts" Gualtieri believes is Christopher's reincarnated malevolent spirit ("Made in America" VI.21). While forlorn Paulie's vision of the Virgin Mary floating above the stripper's stage of the Bada Bing in "The Ride" VI.9 may momentarily reconfigure the vulgar space as hallowed ground, it does little to heal the devilish karma that occupies the darkened rooms and emanates for the posters of the Bada Bing.

We spend considerably less time in the backroom of Satriale's Pork Store. The room's décor is a loose collection of pictures and postcards pinned to the walls. A bit like Carmine Lupertazzi's New York backroom hangout, the art is traditional and old; the posters are serial and usually represent commercial images of the Italian peninsula: an Italia travel poster of a hilltop town, a poster of the Duomo of Orvieto, along with the postcards taped to brown panelled and sepia coloured stucco walls. One interesting poster that dates the possible age of the locale is a representation of the allegorical figure of Italia marching with a monarchist Italian flag. The room is darker, smaller, and probably smellier than the Bada Bing's given it is located behind a butcher shop. Tony's meetings are usually conducted in front of the store, where the crew sit at small round tables and sip coffees purchased from the adjacent café. The viewer is introduced to Satriale's Pork Store as a backdrop, a place that would identify I-Ams with their food culture but that also serves as a centre for racketeering. The business, after all, deals in real meat: sausage, veal, suckling pig. But it is also the hub of mob business. "It's a front," A J.'s friends remind him, "like Genco Oil in *The Godfather*" ("Everybody Hurts" IV.6). Unfortunately, unlike Genco Oil, this front masquerades the brutal dismembering and mincing of the meat of human victims on the premises.

We have spoken of the tendency in the series to place specific backdrop images that reflect or echo the on-screen action. This potpourri of wall coverings visually extends into the narrative and vicariously creates what Nelson Goodman calls "symbol systems," that is, a language that provides an entry point for interpretation.[26] This trend begins amidst the hanging pig heads and hams of Centanni's Meat Market in the pilot episode. Christopher Moltisanti is about to kill Emil Kolar, a Czech-American who dared compete with Barone Sanitation (run by the Soprano crew). As he waits for Emil's arrival, he strikes Kung Fu poses, imagining himself an action screen star. His cockiness is reinforced by the music overlay of Bo Diddley's "I'm a Man." Behind him hangs a collage of publicity photos of American film stars who, we eventually come to know, he wishes to emulate. In his DVD commentary on the episode, Chase admits to having found the collage already hanging in the meat shop. Realizing that somehow "it worked," he deliberately moved it into the shot. While the photographs are reminiscent of the Wall of Fame that hangs in Sal's Famous Pizzeria in Spike Lee's controversial 1989 film *Do the Right Thing*, it differs from Sal's wall on two counts. First, Sal privileged an "Italian Only" policy. We recall that when Buggin' Out provocatively asks Sal, "How come you got no brothers up on the wall here?" Sal impatiently replies: "You want brothers on the wall, get your own place. You can do what you want. You can put your brothers and uncles and nieces and nephews and stepfather and stepmother whoever you want. But this is my pizzeria. American Italians on the wall only." Instead, the Satriale wall is multicultural. Interestingly, in *The Sopranos*, Black brothers get their wall of fame in "A Hit Is a Hit" I.10. Unfortunately, the wall is private property. It belongs to the Soprano family's adviser Hesh Rabkin and it's a photo gallery of Black pop singers from the 1950s and 1960s. The photographs are his Mafia trophies, memories of Black performers he sponsored and swindled. The fact that the black-and-white glossies are displayed in the colourful Jewish mobster's home that bilked them of their rightful earnings is poetic irony.

Second, the collage represents a piece of American film history randomly nestled away in the backroom of a New Jersey butcher shop, not a public display of ethnic pride in the volatile Bedford Stuyvesant section of Brooklyn. Again, it is another private gallery of public figures to be secretly admired and remembered for their cultural influence on America. The camera lingers long enough to allow the viewer to recognize the figures of well-known screen stars that include, among others, W.C. Fields, The Three Stooges, Begniamino Gigli, Telly Savalas, Laural and Hardy, Fred Astaire, Ginger Rogers, Edward G. Robinson, Don Rickles, Marilyn Monroe, Sammy Davis Jr., Frank Sinatra, John Wayne, and James Cagney. Christopher's remark about mixing cultures (in reference to learning from Emil that even the Czechoslovakians eat sausage) is relevant as it is reflected in the post-ethnic sobriety of the collage. Like the meat in sausage, these photos are minced and clipped together like so much ground beef and sinew to form a novel American mosaic. The message that Christopher learns from the images, however, is skewed by his own myopia. Christopher admits to Emil that he is ignorant about sausages that are not Italian or Jimmy Dean. His remark punctuates the stereotypical messages that permeate the thin veneer of what passes for knowledge not only in his circumscribed mob world but also in the information age.

But these representations are more than a backdrop for inane quips among these young punks. They are instead realistic portrayals of the thinly veiled public images of popular culture as perceived and acted-out by members of the New Age mob. These film snippets are real to Christopher, even if they are dreadfully misunderstood. The power these images hold is manifest in the formal juxtaposing of the staring eyes of Humphrey Bogart, Dean Martin, and E.G. Robinson with the unflinching eyes of the pig heads and the glazed eyes of Emil's lifeless body as he is murdered by Christopher. These sightlines establish a triangular perspective between the viewer's eye, the framed actors' eyes in the scene, and Christopher's eyes. Photographs and bullets collide in this first scene to simultaneously erase and enforce each other's influence. A seductive game of perverted visual pathology has begun between the viewer and the viewed.

The essential characteristic of the main character here is his puppet-like behaviour and submission to the impact of the visual images displayed in the fantasy world of the collage. The viewer is warned that this visual map is distorted in its descriptions and representations. It foregrounds now the actions, now the power, now the glamour, now the lure of the mob. The series is a convex mirror that perverts the overall global structure of social relations and only foregrounds specific parts according to mob sensitivity. The resultant text is an artistically transcendent and brutally dramatic mobilization of what the viewer is to expect throughout the series. He/she will be a voyeur of private blood spectacles, and a willing participant who is granted privileged access to the marrow of mob truth as it is played out in these corrupt inner sanctums.

Tony's Inner Sanctum of Darkness

Seeing/being seen is a dominant rhetorical paradigm of the series. Its semiosis typifies the visual meta-languages of artworks inserted as backdrop and temporalizes the episodic structure of family history, personal memory, and sensory actuality. The dichotomy is indicative of the mobster's paradoxical dilemma of remaining incognito and anonymous while gaining notoriety and fame. In its most general and in this case criminal terms, being visible with a public identity is a biological risk, while invisibility, the embracing of a traditionally furtive posture, is a basic biological defence.

The series is premised upon Tony Soprano walking into a therapist's office. Therapy implies scrutiny of self in scenarios that are real, imagined, or remembered. Whether using real eyes or the mind's eye, everything grows from this central image of Tony as patient, as primary viewer of himself and the corollary of becoming an object of the viewers' gaze. Tony's actions, his impetuous reactions, his measured reflections subtend and colour the series; they consume and condition every moment of *The Sopranos*. However paradoxical or problematic the foregrounding of his self as primary experience may be, it is the subjectification/objectification of this inner self that creates the visual and dialectical intercourse of fear and anxiety that motivates the series. It is the fear of non-being that sparks Tony's anxiety. The fear of "coming in at the end," along with all the other dreads of his existence, provokes the most compelling episodes of unharnessed rage and caustic anger. Fear and anxiety have the same ontological root, although they are expressed as distinct outward manifestations. Tony fears negation (invisibility expressed as loss of family and/or incompetence as mob boss) and over compensates by exerting a forceful presence (visibility marked as a panic attack, violence, rage) through anger. This preternatural trait determines the story while the attempted cure, the therapy for his anxiety, moves the plot. Both are premised, however, on scrutiny; that is, on the subjective/objective play of seeing or being seen.

When Dr. Melfi tells Tony that depression is "rage turned inwards," she extemporizes one of the fundamental psychological assertions about the nature of human frailty. Any ontology of being necessarily includes an ontology of anxiety and the complimentary gesture of anger. Anxiety and anger are two emotions that are not antonymous. They are instead defensive mechanisms that sort abstract feelings from concrete actions. Both are equated with material existence, with notions, again, of scrutiny and difference, of seeing or being seen. Essentially, everything in the series is perceived and interpreted, seen, in other words, by Tony who is also the exclusive object of the viewer's and of his own gaze. The portals to this ultimate inner sanctum are Tony's eyes. After the prefatory opening scenes that introduce the viewer to the two main characters of the series, Tony and Dr. Melfi, the story effectively starts when Tony begins to tell his tale. As he speaks, the viewer is presented a David Lynchian cropped close-up of Tony's right eye. As the camera pulls away we realize that he is in bed staring at the ceiling. Simply put, the story that will unfold for six seasons will be told from Tony's perspective and may be extended into a self-serving metaphor. Tony will comprehend only the most immediate problems or the most distant abstractions remaining oblivious to the rest of the world. Tony's eyes become a magnetic line of force, bending and curving around and through objects in a game of what Leo Steinberg terms "deflected seeing."[27]

This game effectively ends with the opening scene of the last episode of the series with a view of a prone Tony seen from above in a counterbalancing perspective of the close-up of Tony's eye in the very first episode. As the camera pulls away, the viewer once again sees a close-up of Tony's eyes. The viewer realizes that he is lying in bed. Importantly, and as if to accentuate the dominance of visual codes in the series predicated by Tony's singular world view, his eyes are the last thing we see in the very last scene of the series before all goes black as he looks towards the restaurant door in anticipation of seeing daughter Meadow enter Holsten's Diner. Though the incidents may seem occasional, they nevertheless punctuate the pre-eminence of a visual matrix premised upon Tony's personal perspective. The viewer is permitted to view the world through the maelstrom of this ultimate inner sanctum.

The importance of eyes in the world of Tony cannot be minimized. Differing points of view, gaps, fissures, ruptures, eyes that regard are his greatest nemesis. Dense woods hide his home, darkness shields his covert activities, and false witnesses vouchsafe his integrity. Tony's world is full of potential optic recognition. Eyes are everywhere and cyclophobia (a fear of eyes) is justifiably rampant in his profession. Vision is not a one-way street in a mobster's life of constant surveillance. Tangled as he is in a web of seeing and being seen, the very notion of self becomes a desperate fiction of invented stories to family members, alibis to law enforcement agents, the bending of truth to judges by lawyers. When Tony sees himself as a fictional character on television in "The Test Dream" V.11, he confesses to Carmela, "It's more interesting than life." "Are you kidding?" she replies. "It is your life." Jacques Lacan posited the notion that the very idea of a unified self was preposterous given the fact that our image of ourselves, combined with the vision of others, is pure fiction,[28] something that must be constantly reinforced in the wanted (or unwanted in this case) gaze of others. To see is to be seen. Objects collect Tony's gaze but stare back, sending his gaze back to the margins of his own suspicious thoughts. The public observes his actions, but he bets on their ability to know when not to look. That's a way of not seeing, of aborting public interpretation in order to vouchsafe the fiction of his private existence. Tony may not comprehend his mother's aversion to answering the phone after dark (a visual thing he calls it), but he fully understands the legal resonances of the FBI's perpetual and unblinking stare of stakeouts. The first perspective of the seer is that of the hunter: sure-stepped, calculated, and concentrated on self-preservation. The other of the hunted: an object discerned amidst a tangle of leaves and flickering lights, always wary, never serene.

Throughout the series, Tony attempts to keep these distinctions clear. He wishes to make personal experience an impersonal event, to turn a subjective dilemma into an objective problem, and to speak of business and expediency in lieu of morality and family. More than physical apparatuses for processing light, his eyes not only see but also effectively transform what is seen. Objects and events molt and alter in accord with what he wishes to perceive. Tony's eyes can lend an overreaching logic to the events of the world and corroborate the idea that what is seen is a phenomenological proof. Or he may choose to disfigure reality's contours in order to produce a redemptive confusion.

Tony's adroit vision ably complements his intuition while his astute observations move him beyond his colleagues' musings about living life as if they were imitating Hollywood gangsters. But many times his impressions of the world become a paralyzing trap. At these moments, we usually find him struggling to find himself, to see himself with different eyes, usually in a mirror. Throughout the series, Tony is prone to penetrate his own eyes when gazing in the mirror in search for elusive inner clarity and a sense of self. Though it may seem that this gazing at the self is as close to pure seeing that Tony gets, it's probably closer to blindness. What, indeed, does he see? If mirrors are like eyes, they are a special kind of visual cleft in space; empty and blind until one peers into its reflective surface. The act of looking into a mirror is a gesture of self-reflection, an act that symbolizes reassessment of the self, even confession. The mirror reflects an image of the self that is twice removed. The face in the mirror is either a self-portrait that can mask reality or initiate an act of introspection. The "other" in the mirror opens a catalogue of forward/retro possibilities that can either please or torment.[29]

Tony passes considerable time scrutinizing his eyes in mirrors. His subjective stare gazes back at an objectivized self. This self appears as a mask that both witnesses who we are but at the same time reveals something very different.[30] It is in these moments that reality seems a waking dream, another of those alternate realities where he becomes the ultimate object of scrutiny, where the dream grows into a smothering claustrophobia, when everything and everyone seems to be watching. Some things are too frightening to see, charged with wrenching emotion, present every time he peers at himself in a mirror. On one occasion, a Prozac-induced delirium transports him beyond the looking glass and into the arms of a loving and nurturing mother in "Isabella" I.12. Drugs and alcohol often provoke the stupor that accompanies his morning sojourn before the bathroom mirror. But we cannot refrain from thinking that behind the eyes he sees in the mirror resides the figure of a castrating mother that lurks in his unconscious; a mother ready to render him blind, to "stick a fork in his eye" as he coolly remembers in "Down Neck" I.7.

Beyond the agonizing and probing self-scrutiny of his own reflections of his soul, his eyes persecute his waking and sleeping hours. Though invisibility is the watermark of his clandestine profession, he is compelled to ostentatiously display the success of his illegal activities. Yet he cannot escape the images of watching eyes that condition his existence, of which there are many. These eyes extend the voyeuristic drive of the seires and pursue Tony throughout. For example, a painted eye advertising Madame Marie, Reader and Adviser surveys the Atlantic City Boardwalk in the dream sequences of "Funhouse" II.13. This eye foretells Tony's difficult epiphany regarding the furtive spying of FBI informant Salvatore "Big Pussy" Bonpensiero. While on the boardwalk Tony speaks to "Big Pussy" who has taken the form of an iced flounder. As "Big Pussy" confesses to Tony that "you know I'm working with the government, right Tone," Tony stares into the dispassionate eyes of his once pal-now-fish and ruminates the task of relegating him to sleep with the fishes. When Tony and his boys are counting the collected money, the all-seeing eye, an ancient symbol for divinity within the pyramid capstone that hovers above the unfinished pyramid, stares out from the back of the ubiquitous dollar bills. President Andrew Jackson's eyes look directly at the viewer on the $20 banknote that Christopher Moltisanti tacks to the refrigerator door at his drunken mother's house. Eyes peer into the Soprano world from television newscasters probing for a story, FBI agents lurking in parked cars, hidden bugs that see furtive meetings and hear secret discussions, nosey neighbours with deprecating glances, and pervasive, inquisitive onlookers. Dark ominous eyes stare into the Soprano master bedroom from the mural on the wall behind the headboard; ancestral eyes probe Tony's soul from family photographs; Gloria Trillo's "goyam" eyes, as he calls them, seduce him as do Adriana La Cerva's heavily made-up cat eyes (she even dresses in sexy animal prints). Uncle Junior's Mr. Magoo glasses magnify his eyes but do not help him see anything clearly, and thereby maliciously embroil Tony in unwanted subterfuge; his mother's teary eyes beget loathing; Carmela's eyes beg suffering reprobation. Only Dr. Melfi's professionally inquisitive and sometimes indulgently affectionate gaze, it seems, offer Tony the unrequited possibility of true emotional insight and salvation.

Eyes that see too much are punished. The list of unfortunate witnesses is lengthy. When Adriana La Cerva's eyes are reluctantly recruited by the FBI, her first notion is to remain invisible, to close her eyes thereby averting expected consequences. The improbable scheme fails and, after being heavily pumped by the FBI to provide more information on Tony, she feigns illness in order to miss Sunday dinner at the Soprano home and to avoid seeing, or being seen by Tony in "All Happy Families" V.4. When Tony innocently exclaims "The horse is sick!" to Carmela in the same episode in reference to the thoroughbred horse Pie-O-My, his words dovetail to the next scene where Adriana, sitting alone in her bedroom, injects herself with heroine, known as horse in street rap. Unbeknownst to Tony at this juncture, Christopher's fiancé is as sick as Pie-O-My. When a staring FBI hidden camera, essentially a monocular eye, is positioned to spy on Adriana's nightclub, The Crazy Horse, everyone's eyes are opened to the threat she poses. She has become an untrustworthy family member that will eventually be put down, like a horse, because she has seen too much and, as a consequence, so has the FBI.

Tony's fascination with horses is not surprising. Horses, horse tracks, and gambling are the life blood of mob figures. The Crazy Horse is an extension of his mob holdings and a dispensary for drugs. Tony's infatuation with the thoroughbred horse Pie-O-My, however, is of another nature and brings to the fore a panoply of pent-up emotions ("Pie-O-My" IV.5). He is obsessed by the animal's unadulterated beauty, its earning power, and his childhood memory of wanting to be a cowboy. More importantly, the horse foregrounds a curious unfettered empathy for animals, an emotion he finds difficult to bestow on humans. This antisocial personality disorder is eventually highlighted in the academic essay on sociopaths Dr. Melfi reads in bed in "The Blue Comet" VI.20. The grandiose sense of self, glib indifference for the welfare of others, pathological lying, and manipulative promiscuity can be extended to the coterie of male agents that populate Tony's mob world. Horse symbolism is often used by them to forestall the emotional vacuum of real experience.

In "University" III.6, for example, Silvio Dante refers to Tracee, one of the Bada Bing sexiest strippers, as a "thoroughbred." Ralph Cifaretto intentionally beats the defenceless and pregnant Tracee to death as if he were terminating a rabid animal. The scene is particularly disturbing. Tony's response is equally callous, though visually cathartic. He berates and punches Ralph for "disrespecting" the Bada Bing. Only privately does he lament the killing of Tracee. A commentary on the heartless and impenitent nature of these individuals is made earlier in the episode by Meadow's university roommate, Caitlin. After having seen the movie *Freaks* (1932), a particularly disturbing film, she asks an emotionally indifferent Meadow, "Why is other people's pain a source of entertainment?" The senseless tragedy of thoroughbred Tracee's death is further intensified if we recall Tom Hagen's sepulchral commentary to the death of a Las Vegas prostitute in *The Godfather Part II*: "It'll be as though," he tells the distraught Senator Pat Geary, "she never existed."[31]

Tony's externalization of his own self-contempt takes the form of suffered indifference towards others, especially women, while idealizing a rapport with non-psychologically threatening agents, in his case, animals. Ducks, bears, dogs, and horses hold special sway over him. Animals see but cannot witness. Their eyes stare back with unblinking indifference, waiting for the onlooker to bestow emotion and animate a response. Pie-O-My's vacuous stare while lying ill in its stall soothes Tony. The horse's presence calms him, motivates him to unearth entombed feelings never spent on others. But it is not until episode V.7, appropriately named "In Camelot," that we truly understand the underpinnings of this unweaned emotion. Appropriately, it is a visual memory of his father and of himself that jogs a startling subconscious emotional epiphany and changes an ideal image from the past, a vision of Camelot, into an incubus of Hades. The glorification of his father (the affirmation of manhood and reason for Tony's mobster life) to the detriment of his mother (the ontological insecurity unleashed by the negation of his feminine side) reaches an implosive climax. Confronted with a photograph of his childhood pet dog Tippy (long assumed dead but in reality given as a present by his father to his mistress Fran Felstein), the unexpected memory detonates the pain of self-abnegation. All the hopelessness of his neurotic self comes into clear, painful relief as his inner eye reveals the memory of one of his father's deceitful betrayals that affected not only his mother's health but also his own diminishing sense of worth. The happy eyes of former pet Tippy with his new owner cannot be explained away with a cursory deflection to his mother's hate for the dog and her wish to have it removed from the household. Once Tony realizes that his father lied to him regarding the fate of his pet and ties this falsehood to his father's sham story regarding his whereabouts (he was with his goomah Fran Feinstein) while his mother suffered a life-threatening miscarriage, his own collusion with his father, seen in retrospect, seriously compromises his ontic selfhood. The memory of his youthful lie to his mother trades one complex set of half-understood feelings for another more piquant set of debilitating emotions. But he realizes that he is powerless, trapped in the visual cross-hairs of his own deceptions to family, wife, colleagues, even himself. He remains forever suspended, caught between images from the past that he cannot change and surrounded by images in the present that remind him of a past that he does not wish to see.

The commissioned self-portrait with the horse Pie-O-My is a rejoinder to these wilfully submerged memories. Tony is portrayed as a successful horse owner, glass of champagne in one hand, proudly holding the reigns of his winning thoroughbred with the other. He is serene, strong, and silent, an allusion to the title of the episode "The Strong, Silent Type" IV.10. The painting of himself as a respectable horse owner places him in haughty company. It portends another turning point in Tony's voyage towards cognizance and in our journey within his inner sanctum. The idea for the portrait began as a sexual flirtation with the Gloria Trillo look-alike Valentina La Paz. The imaginary pastoral world in the painting is meant to signal a new version and vision of Tony as a corporate boss, a self-image he relishes and wishes to broadcast to others. Unfortunately, the return of his first cousin Anthony "Tony B." Blundetto from an extended prison stint coupled with the death of Pie-O-My and his murdering of Ralph Cifaretto remind him of his real world status. The new image of himself in the painting quickly sours as memories of the past torment his relations with Tony B. This engenders an anxious state of uncertainty and insecurity that comes to inhabit both his waking and sleeping hours. Not only is Tony flustered with his cousin's constant comedic barbs but is also fraught with a deeply entrenched guilt for having abandoned his cousin one fateful night when they were teenagers. On that particular evening, Tony suffered a panic attack when he should have been highjacking trucks with his cousin, and he fell and hurt himself. He went to the hospital for stitches to a gash on his forehead, and his cousin was arrested. The gash became a public mark of Cain he would unavoidably face in the mirror forever after. Once arrested, Tony B. was incarcerated and faced years of obscurity. Tony's rise to public prominence (the figure in the painting) was thus the direct result of a debilitating genetic defect that elevated his secret weakness (panic attacks) to a determinant life factor.

The direct outcome of this factor rendered his rival, Tony B., invisible. The title of the episode in which Tony B. returns to visibility, "Two Tonys" V.1, speaks clearly to the central issues of self-being versus self-loathing, of honesty versus panic attacks, all mixed into the brew of family love and jealously. Tony's newly resurrected panic pivots around his sudden lack of ontological autonomy. His sense of public identity is being drained by the comedic posturing of his newly visible cousin, Tony B., by the vexing usurpations of his authority, and by his own petrification of himself as an object (the image of himself in the painting) in scenarios he no longer fully controls. The painting with Pie-O-My extemporizes all these internalized malignancies in an unwanted compulsiveness that come to the fore in fits of anger and anxiety. The painting comes to symbolize a public testimony to his growing sense of a newly constructed identity gone desperately wrong. The emotional connection he establishes with the painting is apophatic. The emotional denial it engenders may be directly linked to his refusal to comprehend the message of the emblematic mural that hangs over his matrimonial bed. In short, the painted image of the eyes that fixate Tony from his self-portrait remind him that the structures of his immediate masculine reality have lost their meaning due to the subliminal message of feminine propriety embedded in his heraldic crest. The return of this wilfully hidden and purposefully invisible guilt reminds him of the nefarious duty he will be obliged to commit several episodes later (i.e., the killing of his cousin Tony B.).

His cousin Tony B. has become a loose cannon, accepting contract killings from "Little" Carmine Lupertazzi's supporters Rusty Millio and Angelo Garepe. Tony B.'s murder of Joe "Peeps" Peparelli drags Tony's family into the power struggle of New York's Lupertazzi family. He is thus a liability to his crew and an untrustworthy blood relative. But Tony must be careful and not penetrate the debilities of his soul or listen to the remorseful murmuring of his heart lest he hesitate. Especially now, after the death of Pie-O-My, the murder of Ralph Cifaretto, coupled with his cousin's untimely return into the fold and regrettable freelance actions, Tony simply cannot bear to view the painting of himself with the now-dead horse. He has he yet come to psychological terms with his heraldic heritage and struggles with the demands it imposes such as that of killing his own cousin. His only recourse is to avoid the mounting confusion between public display and inner necessity. He therefore orders that the painting (thus his divided self) be destroyed (burned, aptly) in a fit of self-serving and all-consuming pathos.

Soon afterward, in "All Due Respect" V.13, his troubled wandering blindly leads him to Paulie "Walnuts" Gualtieri's house where, to his surprise, the painting of Pie-O-My, altered with his image now in a general's uniform, hangs over Paulie's mantel. Tony is furious as a spate of unavoidable memories swell to the fore. He has truly lost control not only of reality but also of its visual representation. He berates Paulie for salvaging his image and complains of being dressed like a lawn jockey, of being portrayed as a visual laughing stock, literally disrespected by his men. Paulie retorts earnestly. The altered Tony, to his mind, is a leader, dressed as Napoleon. It's no joke, "something that captures more of what you're really all about ... that's not a lawn jockey, it's a general ... not a real general from history. It's you!" Paulie is oblivious to Tony's inner eye. He does not believe that he has deformed the boss's image but instead cleverly distended his masculine cache. But Tony cannot bear the analogy, nor does he truly want the responsibility that Paulie's words portend or that the painted image implies. He tears down the painting and, in a fit of anger, unceremoniously tosses it into a garbage dumpster. He has placed his painted image (thus himself) in the trash. But as he gapes at the painting that is so indecorously lodged in the garbage, he is haunted by the self-reflecting mirror image before him: the clenched right fist, the gold-handled sabre, the painted eyes that fixate his own eyes in frozen mortifying judgment. Tony has just confessed to Dr. Melfi that he "is very confused," and that all his choices "were wrong." All his life choices, all the wrong choices as he has just confided, have brought him to this new juncture, to the schizophrenic impasse of denying the vital essence of his self in order to preserve his being. While staring at the painting, Tony is offered a moment of conscious self-awareness. These are moments when the viewer is invited to penetrate his mind, to see with his eyes, to peer into the recesses of his soul and become eyewitness to sensations *inside* his body. This is such a moment. His introspection imbues the scene with profound solitude and despair. He is a vacuum, as empty as the dark eyes he sees on the painted canvas. But he is fully aware that the darkness and the emptiness he espies in those eyes mirror the soulless monster that gazes into their profundity.[32]

In this episode ("All Due Respect" V.13), Chase has effectively juxtaposed Tony's war with the New York families with a program about the Second World War on The History Channel. While he watches the atrocities of war, the newly exacerbated war with New York torments him. As the history program weaves in and out of the episode, Tony learns of German General Erwin Rommel's leadership qualities and of his "sixth sense of sizing-up a situation." Tony sees himself as a painted general. He now imagines himself poised to battle in his own personal war and appropriates tidbits of information about Rommel that help legitimize his reeling from the weight of the dilemma he faces. How does he "size-up his situation?" Does he have the resoluteness of Rommel? Can he be as decisive? Can he rely on a "sixth sense"? Should he or should he not murder his first cousin and childhood soul mate Tony Blundetto? Johnny "Sack" Sacrimoni is demanding his death in order to appease his second-in-command Phil Leotardo. By killing his cousin, Tony would solve his problems with the New York families and thwart a possible gangland war. The close-up of Tony gazing into his own painted eyes unleashes a spate of thoughts that deepen his existential dilemma while heightening the necessity of a swift decision. His entire essence revolves around this decisive and defining visual vortex. Does he follow the neurotic inner self of the disembodied hero doing his duty, or the projected self of loving cousin?

Tony is not an automata; he has choices. Nevertheless, the rule-laden performance of his duties is the only reality he knows. He must remain coherent, stay in uniform; he must project, like the staid Japanese Samurai warrior statue on Dr. Melfi's office shelf and the painted image on the canvas before him, the image of the good and obedient soldier. The painting becomes the mediating object of his fateful decision. The burden of responsibility (we remember the earlier conversation with Silvio Dante at the Bada Bing in this episode concerning responsibility) is ponderous and lonely, just as it was for General Rommel. As the camera probes the inner black of his eye, he resolves to kill his cousin Tony B. He'll do so for the pressing and barbed sake of survival and for sense of duty to family. But the act is as hideous as Michael Corleone's killing of his brother Alfredo in *The Godfather Part II*. Blood may be blood, but business is business. The murder is an act of blind desperation, the desire to remain oneself as objectified Other while remaining squarely within the subjective skein of unchanging relations with those around him. After the deed, he returns to the Bada Bing. His men all give him a reassuring eye and pay him all due, if not perfunctory, public respect.

But Tony is also painfully aware that he is both the vexed seer and stigmatized seen. He realizes all too well, now, that he is morbidly persecuted by the real, surreal, and even painted images that he has chosen to advance and that the cost of their maintenance, beyond all the images public and private, is his self. Ironically, the title of the episode, "All Due Respect," potentializes the forestalling of his inner feelings in lieu of the shallow posturing that is the norm within his mob realm of private, public, real, and imagined painted fiction.

Chapter Two

When I Grow Up I Want to Be an American

> Picture yourself on a boat on Ellis Island, how does that sound?
> Comic at the Greengrove Retirement Residence paraphrasing
> "Lucy in the Sky with Diamonds" by The Beatles
> ("The Legend of Tennessee Moltisanti" I.8)

> The new world is upside down
> And the cafoni can smile
> For the coat of arms had no renown
> And calluses are in style
> La Sciabola by Eduardo Migliaccio (known as "Farfariello")

Ethnic Prologue

As the camera pans upwards from mud-caked boots, we see what appears to be a migrant worker slowly approaching a white clapboard country house ("Calling All Cars" 4.11). We recognize a stumbling and uncharacteristically hesitant Tony Soprano; nervous, sleeveless, wearing a sweat-stained undershirt, unshaven. His demeanour is reserved, his posture contrite. He knocks on the rickety screen door of the clapboard country house and respectfully waits, hands clasped and fidgeting in front of him in a typical sign of peasant submission. As he attempts to peer through the lace curtains, the inner door slowly and ominously creaks open. The camera's long shot frames his figure in the door jamb. As the camera angle shifts from exterior long shot to close-up of Tony's face to the dark interior staircase, we hear him speak. At first a meek, trembling "Allo?" Then Silence. Then again a more forceful "Allo!" Again silence. "I'ma 'ere fo' da masona jobbe." The voice is Tony's but the accent is southern Italian broken English; the tone is humble, even servile. The camera shifts between close-ups of Tony's face and the empty interior space as a black-draped figure appears and slowly descends the darkened staircase. As he peers into the grim interior the figure stops at mid-stair. The viewer notes that the silhouette is eerily reminiscent of Tony's dead mother, Livia Soprano. Further silence. Only the whistling wind and restless crickets cut the dense air. He speaks to the figure: "Me no ... speaka da eenglish. Me deespeeeache." He slowly opens the squeaking door and moves towards the interior of the home.

The scene abruptly shifts to Tony as he awakens brusquely from this troubling dream. He is in a Miami hotel room. Rising from a sweat-soaked bed, he lumbers to the bathroom, mistakenly turning on the heat lamp instead of the bathroom light. The red lamp lends an infernal, bedeviling glow to his features as he peers first into the mirror and then at his sweaty bed linen. His breathing is laboured, tortured. Seeking respite, he moves to the window. As he draws the drapes, we see an earthly paradise of white sand, blue skies, and green palm trees swaying in a soft breeze, which contrasts sharply with the inferno of the red-lit bathroom and menacing blackness of the bedroom. He exhales a sigh of deep-felt relief. As a close-up of his face fills the screen, the viewer peers into his gaze. The sun shines, the waves splash. Tony is generations removed from the clapboard house, yet it is eerily present, its shadows haunt his thoughts. As he basks in the warm morning sun seemingly suspended in mid-air, a disquieted Tony embodies the drama of his ancestors' past as the Beach Boys intone the 1960s classic "Surfin' U.S.A." The scene aptly portrays the angst of living on the hyphen of ethnicity. The dark, surly, and rotund immigrant son will never bask in the full sunlight of the American experience. He will never be the carefree, free lovin', "bushy, bushy" blond-haired and tanned surfer boy, surfin' through life in the good ol' US of A. That these emotions ferment in the breast of Tony Soprano might surprise the viewer. Is Chase adding another human facet to Tony's reprehensible character? How do we interpret the scene? A key towards interpretation was provided earlier in the episode by Tony himself.

Satisfied with the initial results of his three years in therapy, and convinced that he has been cured and is no longer in need of the weekly confessions, he has resolved to end his sessions with Dr. Melfi. Rather than expressing gratitude for the good doctor's patient efforts, his tone is relentlessly negative and reveals the uncharitable malevolence of the character traits inherited from his mother. "All this fuckin' self-knowledge. What the fuck has it got me? ... Pain and truth. C'mon. I'm a fat fuckin'crook from New Jersey."[1] This self-denigrating portrayal is understandable, given Tony's vertical split between acting like a manipulative unappreciative monster (his mother) and the violent broker of illegal business activity (his father). Sensing his feelings of rejection and exclusion, Dr. Melfi delves his vulnerability: "Anthony, now that the panic attacks and the base-line depression have been dealt with, the real work can begin ... When we're not constantly having to put out fires, we can really delve into who you are and what you're really after in your very brief time on this earth."

But Tony remains inflexible. He feels he has travelled far enough on his road to wholeness and is tired of the voyage. But the closing of one door, like the opening of the screen door in his dream, unleashes a flood of submerged anxieties. The vision of his mother's silhouette on the darkened staircase is now doubly poignant. Mother Livia is the castrating voice that lurks in his unconscious ("I could stick this fork in your eye!" "Down Neck" I.7). She is the hounding semblance, his mother's son, the shadow in the wrinkles he sees every time he scrutinizes his face in the mirror. Livia was not a loving mother but a malevolent Medea.[2] Yet Tony cannot tolerate the possibility of hating her to the point of denying his self and his heritage. "Hate your mother," he blusters to Dr. Melfi. "You're supposed to take care of your mother" ("46 Long" I.2). He subsequently rescripts his past, refusing to admit he once contemplated killing her after the botched assassination attempt on his life: Dr. Melfi: "You tried to smother your mother with a pillow." Tony: "The fuck I did. I grabbed a pillow but it was ... just to keep my hands occupied" ("Members Only" VI.1).[3] Even after her death, Tony bridles at the mere mention of her name. He is comically aware of her rash obduracy as profiled in the viewer's very first glimpse of the mother–son rapport in the pilot episode as she sidesteps any move away from her eternally suffering mother stance. But Tony is inexorably yoked to the travesty of her motherhood and, subsequently, to the cumbersome burden of his genetic heritage.

We recall that he dreams of being a babe suckling at an idealized mother's breast in "Isabella" I.12. Interestingly, the future dream that portrays him as an immigrant worker and his awakening into the bright light of Florida sunshine come at the midway point of the series. If the protective, sheltering, brown-haired Isabella had been Tony's mother, he might never have come to America or, if he had, he may have become the swarthy but honest immigrant labourer of his dream and not a rancorous mob boss. Altered identities and identity crises are the leitmotif of the series. The tendency is apparent from Tony's first encounter with Dr. Melfi. When Tony imagines himself a babe in the arms of a different mother, he is imagining a different life path, a different story to narrate to the psychiatrist and to himself. Interestingly, in this same episode his real mother, Livia, begins to feign a loss of her identity by simulating Alzheimer's disease in order to escape incrimination in the botched murder attempt on her son. Tony often speaks of an alternative life path that would have led westward and where he may have become a lawn-chair salesman. In "Join the Club" VI.2, this alter ego materializes in the character of Albert Finnerty, a successful optics salesman living in California. Furthermore, he is constantly reminded by his dispassionate Uncle Junior that he could have been a sports star (echoing Terry Malloy's "I cudda' been a contender" refrain in *On the Waterfront*, 1954), but he was never good enough.

That Tony is restless in his skin is an understatement. He is tired of confronting his many-faceted self in therapy, and worn out from facing the senselessness of life and realizing that its meaningless pit is filled with routine actions. He prefers to avoid existential issues, choosing to remain within a comfortable false-self system that frees him from these moments of personal turbulence. While Tony thinks he can resolve many of his personal and professional concerns through evasion, his mother's voice and her memory are constant reminders of the vulnerable underbelly of his false self. She returns to haunt him in his dreams. Apparently, so does his ethnicity.

Ethnicity: Business or Nostalgia?

One purpose of this chapter is to discuss the latent subtending ethnic momentum of the series. Ethnic identity and all its ramifications with respect to ethnic pride is an issue that cannot be censored when discussing *The Sopranos*. The series follows an interesting political posture with respect to ethnicity because, instead of attempting to ameliorate controversial media portrayals of I-Am mobsters by desensationalizing them in the media, David Chase presents these fabricated prepackaged images for what they truly are: products of a media industry that is ultimately not interested in ethnic defamation but only in financially profitable ethnic characters. It is not an issue of I-Am stereotypes as portrayed in *The Sopranos* but rather of a Pan-American pop media culture that has become vulgar and offensive to all peoples, not just I-Ams. The notion of stereotype suggests that these televised ethnic characters are not fully a part of their own ethnicity, not really Italians, not really Poles, not really Russians, not really, in the final analysis, Americans. They are instead an odd sort of something that has been concocted in between. Whatever that something, they are too much or not enough of the proposed equation. This begs the question of lack. Most often these hyphenated characters are not culturally conversant enough in their own heritage, otherwise they would realize that they are the scions of cultures that help spawn the culture in which they live and thrive. Sometimes these characterizations move beyond official stereotype and into the hype of reverse discrimination. In essence, they become too hyphenated; too self-conscious of their cultural foibles; so embroiled in the shallow proliferation of their proto-heritage that they become dangerously thin-skinned and contentious.

These are issues often raised during American political campaigns. Most recently, in 1988 and 2004, Civil Rights activists Jessie Jackson and Al Sharpton, both presidential hopefuls, were accused of being *too Black*, too radical, too entrenched in ghetto realities to be politically and philosophically objective. Conversely, in 2008 Barack Obama was just not Black enough, with reference obviously being made to his white mother but also, given his upbringing, to his perceived lack of touch with real Black Americans. The same occurred with Mario Cuomo of New York, considered *too Italian* for the presidency while Rudolph Giuliani's loose family mores made him *not Italian enough*. In these and other instances, the media creates a verbal/visual narrative that both sustains and negates the very personages it seeks to create or, by default, destroy and delete. The viewer is compliant in the invention of either a false identity, in the formulation of deleterious impressions, in creating suspicion and fear, or in the manipulation of a television image to foster empathy, familiarity, and trust.

Without a doubt, television and mass media have affected and shaped American lives.[4] As one of the major influential technologies in recent history, the market-oriented television system has created characters that serve as examples and as illustrated moral lessons to the nation's citizens. Television can be a powerful influence in developing value systems and cultural behaviour. Television programming and its characters were designed to exude honesty and moral certitude to a growing population. Television executive Huw Wheldon summed up the sentiment when he stated that television's role was "to make the good popular, and the popular good."[5] In the 1950s and 1960s, TV programs promoted the reassuring sense that life was good and getting better, a feeling that ran throughout much of society and that is bemoaned in Tony Soprano's latent end-of-century despondency of "having come in too late." In this burgeoning consumer utopia, law enforcement and its agents became the protagonists of programs that satisfied the moralistic exigencies mainstream conservative America and of the nascent TV industry. Popular and long-running radio programs such as *Dragnet* (1951–9) and *The Untouchables* (1959–63) became the franchise archetypes for an unending stream of television police dramas with white cops usually chasing visible minorities. Today's popular TV shows *CSI* (2000–), *America's Most Wanted* (1988–2011), and *COPS* (1989–) continue the tradition but place second- and third-generation immigrant descendants at the helm, often parachuting them into situations at odds with their own watered-down cultures. In these programs, lawlessness remains at the periphery of the true American law-and-order experience while criminals are spotlighted as the malevolent exception to the melting pot norm. Crime, in these programs, does not pay.[6]

As a potent cultural disseminator, television programming has long been charged with filtering the message of nation building and the construction of a visual and ideological national identity. Effective programming has contributed to the individual's sense of political unity, social responsibility, and belonging to a larger community. Television's immediacy became an instrument of politics, an institution with weight and import, a vehicle for educating its audience into malleable citizens. The suburbanization of America coincided with the televisualization of its citizens. As the American frontier expanded, so did the technology and content of the small screen. Television could entertain or inform, communicate or propagandize. It could be folksy and culturalistic or technophilic and futuristic. The history of American television is replete with a coterie of interchangeable and inauthentic ethnic characters that belie a latent colonial tokenism and politically incorrect representations. Parcelled glimpses of random I-Am ethnicity in popular programs such as *Welcome Back, Kotter* (1975–9), *Happy Days* (1974–84), and *Everybody Loves Raymond* (1996–2005), among many others, offer stereotyped visions of characters usually spoofed for comedic effect rather than racial slur. These depictions of colourful anecdotal characters typically offer a panoply of wily Bensonhurst street types, wide-eyed apple-pie teens, big-nosed Italian diner owners, stingy Scots, hard-nosed Latin greasers, surly Russians, and street-wise Blacks that help to fend-off criticism by contrasting an unsubtle view of our culture, and casting our ways as effectively innocuous, if not cute.

More recent programs such as *Growing Up Gotti* (2004–5), *Jersey Shore* (2009–12), *Jersey Couture* (2010–12), *Jerseylicious* (2010–), and *Bitchin' Kitchen* (2010–) all follow the same formula: take a successful concept, add I-Ams, sprinkle some ethnic vulgarity and achieve immediate success. These programs, however, are infinitely more pernicious than the self-effacing silliness of earlier programs and possibly reflect a universal lapse into socially accepted moral chaos. They promote a hyperbolic, vitriolic, comedy-driven, and benevolent smear against everyone and everything. As Stephen Marche ponders, "What's so wrong with a little bigotry? Stereotypes have become meaningless, and that means we can finally start enjoying them."[7] Beyond such enlightened perspectives, these programs do little to promote either national unity or diversity; rather, they merely prolong the same tired stereotypes, only on a more vulgar and insidious scale.

Though over-the-top depictions of I-Ams, African-Americans on *30 Rock* (2006–13), or New York Jews on *Entourage* (2004–11), *Seinfeld* (1984–98), and *Curb Your Enthusiasm* (2000–), now make regular appearances in America's TV rooms, ethnic minorities have been relatively absent from America's TV rooms. The contemporary exploitive integration of these bereft realities with no redeeming values into regular programming can be viewed as destructive and culturally retrograde. The weight of centuries of tradition can be erased with a single humorous television image. History becomes a sanitized story related by winners to the comical marginalization of others. These images may then be deployed by society to legitimize social exclusion. Unfortunately, they are often appropriated by the delegitimized victims to engender a false history of their own collective past.[8] It could be argued that an invented media ethnicity allowed I-Ams to find a niche, a place where mainstream images were internalized, accepted, redeployed as a version of a possible and empowered ethnic self with a recognizable identity. The relentless stereotyping of I-Ams as violent and vicious low-lifes was covertly mitigated by an attractive underlying layer of loyalty, love, and compassion for one's own kind. The price to be paid by the immigrant was a type of split identity. On the one hand, I-Ams are portrayed with inferior ethno-racial traits; on the other, they occupy powerful social positions. In the realm of representation, these caricatures and slurs serve to entrench a visual culture that is readily incorporated as real. By sprinkling-in a healthy dose of ethnic markers, the images become self-reflective narratives of characters whose very existence is no longer threatened by outside forces. Some would call this buying into the American Dream. The story thus becomes one of personal, not collectively ethnic, survival. Enter *The Sopranos*.

The series provoked a wave of anti-defamation rhetoric from a number of Italian-American organizations.[9] Here it was, they claimed, another television program that further entrenched the caricatured image of the I-Am gangster in the American psyche, and used comedy to boot. Boycotts were called, marches were held, protests were lodged. But this kind of ethnocentrism concerned solely with smitten personal pride only blurred the real issues of false identity and Otherness that were so often imitated by that same ethnic youth the detractors were trying to save. The fanatics simply did not allow for discussions of dissent and for the realities presented on a daily basis on the streets of the nation. Yet, as a growing coterie of academics and commentators began to extol the socio-political and cultural quality of the series, the novelty of strong characters wrought with debilitating nuances, all set within an I-Am Mafia subculture, generated a narrative momentum that was uncommon for the media but especially novel for television.

One of the most intriguing aspects about *The Sopranos* is the way in which it challenges not only its own medium but also its own ethnic message. Whether questioning the fashionable conventions of prime-time television, endorsing controversial gangster stereotypes, or refuting condescending critics, the series both invites and answers criticism regarding its own artistic culpability. The most compelling issue David Chase stares down, to my mind, is ethnicity, the conditioning arbiter of the legitimized violence in the series, the watershed of purposeful and justified ethnic authenticity. But it is the manner in which ethnicity is highlighted in *The Sopranos* that makes it unique in the history of television. Though the series is rooted in the specifics of the Mafia code, much of the drama occurs when mainstream mores confront traditional ethnic sensibilities.

The series does not hide its ethnicity. Its very title, *The Sopranos*, is a pregnant marker of Italianicity, a strident attractor of possible scorn and acrimony. The pistol, ingeniously holstered in the sinister blood-red Soprano insignia of the series' name, immediately defines place, standing, and territory within ethnic identity and gangster tradition. Tony's ride from the bowels of New York to the heights of New Jersey further defines ethnicity as positionality. It's all about location. It's a long way, physically and emotionally, from the New York harbour and the produce-cart-laden streets of Little Italy. Yet, despite the palatial Soprano home perched on a hill in the upscale professional New Jersey neighbourhood of North Caldwell, and despite all the cultural baggage the Italianate name carries, the family could still be living in the old neighbourhood of Newark's North Ward (also known as First Ward or Seventh Avenue). First impressions don't change; the opening sequence merely reinforces the notion that perhaps the Sopranos, like their ancestors and despite their money, are upstart misfits.

America has always promoted a national image that rallies around the plastic identity of the One as a representative paradigm of the Other. It is a politics of sameness that eschews the multiple models of pluralism and multiculturalism in favour of cookie-cutter malls and bland suburban sprawl. In *The Sopranos*, however, the individual's sense of self-in-nation is configured within a definite model of multicultural empowerment that promotes the individual beyond the restrictive area of collective tradition and difference. There exists, indeed, a plurality of ways of belonging to the American Dream that move beyond limiting identity labels, beyond the restrictive visual panorama of television culture. As Michael Fischer has argued, "ethnicity is something reinvented and reinterpreted with each generation by each individual ... Ethnicity is not something that is simply passed on from generation to generation, taught and learned; it is something dynamic, often unsuccessfully repressed or avoided."[10]

The drama of ethnic assimilation versus rejection of heritage is one component of the success of the series. In essence, Chase is replacing the ideal of a melting-pot national culture with that of a more realistic parochial and pluralistic American landscape. Towards this end, the I-Am centre of the series is surrounded by a Russian, Jewish, Oriental, Middle Eastern, and African-American periphery. This focus leads to two complimentary, if not paradoxical, phenomena. On the one hand, the depreciating confidence of a singular national identity is undermined, replaced by an overarching individuality that craves success at any cost. On the other, the increasing reliance on traditional group ties and assertion of the ethnic self bemoans the rupture of a cohesive social fabric and the emergence of pockets of increasingly diverse insularity. Ethnic assimilation in *The Sopranos* is achieved not by conforming to law and order but instead by blossoming into the shadowy nooks of the family business. The series thus smoothly circumvents the usual repression of the ethnic Other normally seen in police action series by allowing the individual to prosper within a labyrinthine world of intrigue and malevolence that prospers in spite of the law. There is no question that this tendency begins with the birth of frontier America, finds its consolidation in the outlaw figures of both the cowboy and the gangster, and finds its most sublime expression in the ethnic opera *The Godfather* (1972). The sublimely charismatic Don Vito Corleone achieved prominence in America by creating his own economy, exploiting an ethnic subculture, and controlling an economic socio-political state of his own making outside the law. He was the revered prince of the underworld masquerading as the generous chair of the local neighbourhood watch, able to dispense an avalanche of vigilante justice previously unmatched in gangster films. Viewers embraced his benevolence, admired the increasingly evanescent virtues of trust and family loyalty he steadfastly represented, even though these same values were tinged with hues of darkness and were spawned by the same devil that would eventually cause their demise.

The Sopranos surpasses this trust placed in the godfather character first by socially and publicly enabling the ethnic criminal and, second, by enacting the visceral drama of social assimilation repeatedly throughout the series. These elements move the series beyond facile categorizations of defamation and stereotype that were heaped upon it by detractors. The storylines mark a radical thematic departure for the medium. The criminal is now glorified, wrongdoing is rewarded handsomely, and law enforcement is not only peripheral but it is also never a real threat to the stability of either the protagonist or to the continuation of the series itself. In fact, the law rarely presents an effective menace to the villains and often appears more complicit than antagonistic.[11] When interaction unavoidably occurs between the forces of good and evil, it is almost playful, more sport and comedic relief rather than traditional police drama.

Take for example, "Mr. Ruggerio's Neighborhood," the opening episode of Season III where FBI Special Agent-in-Charge Dwight Harris and his men connive to plant a wiretap in Tony's home. The series portrays them as if they were Keystone Kops. They bungle everything. Their speculations regarding Livia Soprano (will she testify against her son?), Richie Aprile (has he been wacked?), Salvatore "Pussy" Bonpensiero (is he in some compost heap?) are laughable miscues. Agents illegally rifle through Soprano mail, move through the house without a proper warrant, even Agent Harris has his cover as an insect exterminator blown when he is "made" by Tony as he drives by the fake exterminator van. The entire episode satirizes earlier cop shows as the FBI antics are accompanied by music from the old *Peter Gunn* series, mixed with Sting's pop hit "Every Breath You Take" ("I'll be watching you" is the lyric constantly played as soundtrack). Even Tony is caught singing the razzing lyrics "I'm a fool to do your dirty work" from the Steely Dan song "Dirty Work" while driving. The agents eventually replace a study lamp found in the Soprano's basement with a meticulously reconstructed (and wired with a bug) replica lamp from FBI headquarters. Unfortunately, the only information they garner from the Soprano household is about nutritional roughage and dental floss. Meadow eventually takes the doctored lamp to college, effectively neutralizing the FBI bugging. As a counterfoil to the agents' burlesque antics, Paulie "Walnuts" Gualtieri comically rages against the dangers of germs (bugs) on shoe laces and pant cuffs. In an episode whose central theme is covert listening devices, or bugs, the manic concern for technical and sanitary cleanliness is a perennial nuisance.

Seemingly separated only by the slimmest line of morality, Chase inverts the traditional cops-and-robbers relationship, making the criminal the object of identification, if not sympathy, and the law enforcement agent the unwilling antenna of scorn and derision. What he is really saying is that, in essence, the New Jersey I-Ams are a tightly knit community held together by emotional attachments, local culture, and material interests while New Jersey cops are a group of disconnected, unsettled, and befuddled ethnic individuals who are not bereft of their roots but simply distanced from them. Indeed, local FBI Chief Frank Cubitoso, agents Deborah Ciccerone Waldrup, Robyn Sanseverino, and Frank Grasso, are I-Ams and may come from the same neighbourhood as Tony. Special Agent Harris especially, a non I-Am but definitely sympathetic, walks the same streets as Tony, frequents the same corners, and eats the same sandwiches at Satriale's Pork Store. We eventually see him in dalliance with a partner FBI agent, his own goomah in other words, in "The Blue Comet" VI.20, thereby drawing even closer affinities with Tony and the gang. The fact that he saves Tony by freely offering information regarding his personal safety when the New York families are out to whack him only serves to endear him to the viewer. He has become one of the gang. It seems that both Harris and Tony were raised to embrace the same masculine etiology and are, in fact, both part of secretive card-carrying, coded, and unforgiving brotherhoods. Only difference is that one is legal, the other isn't. Interestingly, the soon to be departed FBI informant Salvatore "Big Pussy" Bonpensiero views his unfortunate coercion as a move from the realm of illegality to one of respectability in "Knight in White Satin Armor" II.12. He envisions himself in the world of law enforcement, a realm he considers similar to that of the mob save the minor detail of legality. Agent Skip Lipari even suggests it's a case of Stockholm syndrome when referring to the delusional informer.

The boundaries are indeed porous and need constant delimiting in order to remain clear. Tony regularly sends party platters to FBI Chief Frank Cubitoso who willingly accepts the mocking generosity and passionately enjoys the capicollo. He "just can't resist the lard breath," ("Knight in White Satin Armor" II.12). When the chief summons Tony and plays the recording of his mother Livia and Uncle Junior plotting his assassination in "Isabella" I.12, he does not gloat over his victim's distress at hearing his two closest relatives plotting to kill him. Rather, he speaks of sharing the same reality, background and traditions, and openly commiserates with Tony and his all-too real grief at the thought of being targeted by his own mother. Chief Cubitoso: "You and I are not compari Tony. You on the one hand, me and Agent Grasso on the other, even though our ancestors all hail from the same sunny peninsula. But we do share some cultural ideas: religious, culinary, matriarchal." Though diametrically opposed philosophically, they carry the same baggage and understand each other's need to survive as professionally engaged opposites and opponents. They are both aware and genuinely interested in taking care of their own kind amidst the sweeping changes that swirl around them. In essence, the characters that are successful in the series, like Agent Cubitoso and Tony, understand their roots but grow beyond the shadow of their limitations. For them especially, ethnic origins are not a site of nostalgia but a source of personal initiative and possibilities.

In this sense, *The Sopranos* breaks new ground because the traditional law-and-order plotline of controlling ethnic outsiders through their vilification as sociopaths and social misfits is ruptured. Instead, ethnics are part of the establishment, part of an impulsively fluid American mythology of wealth and prosperity that openly privileges greed while discreetly providing the dubious means to achieve those very ends. The notion that law enforcement re-establishes proper social order through the dead bodies of law breakers never occurs. In this series, the years leading up to the end of the millennium are demystified to reveal what it means to live through them. Indeed, it's the bad guy who wins while ethnics, whether law-abiding or law-breaking, are here to stay. Ultimately, then, there will be no ethnic conflagration, no saving America from ethnic criminality save for the justice meted out by the very same perpetrators the system defends. Instead, the series advances a poetic use of violence for thematic ends. In this world, Tony is an anointed patriarch, a mob kingpin able to outrun legal encroachments and generational upstarts. He is the archetypal gangster who will not die; a permanent fixture, a paradigm of power in the American cultural and business landscape.[12]

It must be emphasized here that Tony is not really Italian, as his trip to Naples in "Commendatori" II.4 aptly demonstrates. He is marginally Italian-American. He is not an old-world Mustache Pete mobster laden with the historical burden of social inferiority and forced assimilation but a hip, modern, socially maladjusted New Jersey I-Am. His family problems, his cultural mores are generic and, arguably, geographically specific. He is part of an invisible minority, a subculture that straddles the categories of American and I-Am with all the socio-political and cultural irregularities this represents. His ethnicity is itself stereotypical, a type of shield worn irreverently; it is an expediency that allows him to flexibly conform to situations as required. I would offer that though he extols the petty virtues of his Jersey neighbourhood, his ethnic image is chameleonic, granting him the socio-economic power that he feels he is wrongly denied by a bigoted American establishment in the outside world, while providing protection and continuation of identity in the privacy of his home. Similarly, his business practices are rationalized to reflect, to his mind, common corporate practice: a sort of sanctioned institutionalized violence that finds its origins with the robber barons of early twentieth-century America. Here is Tony's version of the rich and complex, often tragic but also triumphant epic of the I-Am experience:

> When America opened the floodgates and let us Italians in, what do you think they were doin' it for? Because they were tryin' to save us from poverty? No, they did it because they needed us; they needed us to build their cities and dig their subways and make 'em richer. The Carnegies and the Rockefellers, they needed worker bees, and there we were. But some of us didn't want to swarm around their hive and lose who we were. We wanted to stay Italian and preserve the things that meant something to us – honor, and family, and loyalty. And some of us wanted a piece of the action. Now we weren't educated like the Americans, but we had the balls to take what we wanted, and those other fucks, those ... the J.P. Morgans,

they were crooks and killers too, but that was the business, right? The American way ... ("From Where to Eternity" II.9)

Tony is just one of the common folk demanding a piece of the corporate pie. He resides on the margins of an ethnically spawned world that is much less picturesque than it is often romantically painted. His ultimate bargaining point is non-capitulation. The most expedient tactic is normally murder. His justification is rationalized and rote: "We wanted to stay Italian and preserve ... honor, family, and loyalty ... The American way."

Tony's real dilemma is not gangster chic or corporate envy but instead a corroded and confused ethnicity. The codes that sustain his hyphenated lifestyle are corrupted, the very foundations of his essence, as he knows them, have been diluted. Stereotyped by consumerism, milked by advertising, strained by economic opportunism, the Honoured Society has lost its self-serving legitimacy. He bemoans both the old ways of his mobster father ("Lately, I feel I came in at the end of something. The best is over," "The Sopranos" I.1), not really knowledgeable of that past. He laments the disappearance of his boyhood hero Gary Cooper ("Whatever happened to Gary Cooper? Now that was an American"), yet thinks nothing of helping to destroy his little piece of America, his old ethnic neighbourhood, by selling landmark family businesses to developers: "What the fuck is happening to this neighborhood?" a disconsolate Paulie "Patsy" Parisi exclaims as the local chicken store, from which he regularly extorts protection payment, is gentrified into a Jamba Juice franchise in "Johnny Cakes" VI.8. Both archetypes hover in his psyche and images of the father and the hero appear at key moments of the series. They are constant reminders that he is living on the hyphen and, similar to his ethnic culture, is squarely in the maelstrom of an identity crisis having to live between two cultures, one more public than the other.[13] "Who am I? Where am I going?" he asks while in a coma ("Join the Club" VI.2).[14] The words echo in his therapy sessions with Dr. Melfi and resonate throughout the series. To Tony's queries we may add the questions: "How Italian am I? How American should I be?" This sense of displacement is a common disquieting denominator that often perturbs many I-Ams in some way. Carmela feels the same disorientation. Her Parisian sojourn in "Cold Stones" VI.11 causes her to question personal issues of vital quotidian notoriety, "Nobody knows us here, Ro. Can you believe that!" and to explore her inauthentic ethnic myths: "When you actually die life goes on without you like it does in Paris when we're not here ... it all just gets washed away." Whether the result of institutionalized socio-historical conditions or the individual single-minded search for illusionary rootedness, the shared commonality of social marginality too often defines, creates, and helps maintain a false and mythical group identity.

What Melting Pot?

In *The Sopranos* there is a rainbow of ethnic characterizations that re-enact, in varying degrees, the ritual of choice that confronts immigrants and minorities daily. By incorporating Black characters as rappers, poor or affluent drug addicts, and HUD scam artists; Jews as mobsters, hotel owners, or avaricious loan sharks; Middle Easterners as probable terrorists; Slavs and Russians as organized crime members, the series adds to the sounding board of ethnic inclusion/exclusion, similarity/difference, oppression/repression. These ethnic masks are an empowering vehicle for facile discrimination. In Sopranoland everyone gets their chance to get caught-up in the tension of cultural confrontation and indictable collusion. As the series travels through the bowels of the New Jersey Meadowlands, each encounter brushes against the darker side of the American experience. Residents of these communities may be united in their perception of social integration, but they remain divided because their relationships are built upon those societal interstices that breed conflict between contending groups. Sheltered and protected by the group, the meaning of life for the individual is based on interpersonal networks, a hidden ethnocentrism that promotes in-depth personal relations as the precondition for any meaningful activity. The result is an imperative to rule for the group and an inability to act for the social Other.

The Italian immigrant faced the dilemma of assimilation as a vital compromise that sapped any notion of happiness and fortune they may have harboured upon leaving the relative normalcy of their villages. Sustained by the fixed traditions of their village, yet inspired by the notions of a new life, the relatively stable bedrock of family and tradition seemed to be the price of integrative admission to the great American dream. For this reason, it was not uncommon for enterprising individuals to promote the preservation of personal, family, and cultural honour and pride. To create, in other words, a community dynamic that worked within the institutions of the group. The ultimatum of respect often moved them, however, beyond the recognized limits of the law. As E. Anthony Rotundo puts it:

> Whatever else organized crime may be, it is a vehicle for recreating an Italian village in a New World and preserving in the New World the old ways upon which village life had rested. By existing outside the law, an organized crime syndicate throws up invisible walls that create space for the imagined village inside the very heart of an unsuspecting modern America. Within those walls, the remembered values of the village can flourish. To those who built it, this village organization was Cosa Nostra – "our thing."[15]

Restaurant owner and chef Artie Bucco, for example, is not concerned about breaking the mobster stereotype but instead thrives on the limits of its cultural culinary lore. He is portrayed as a typical I-Am who grew up knowing who the gangsters were and has remained sympathetic to his lifelong friend Tony Soprano. He relies on the gangsters' business and regularly interacts with them in his restaurant. Despite his wife Charmaine's adamant disapproval, he admires their untouchable world of crime, even envies their lifestyle. Though likeable, his figure is rather gelatinous, spongy, prone to emotional overplay. He is a borderline promoter of an authentic I-Am voice, not really understanding his roots, content to foster his version of Jersey Italian cuisine to like-minded clients. But it must be added that this image, rather than being offensive, renders his character and locale popular and attractive. Though the visual markers of Italianicity are kitsch, they reflect a familiar view of the I-Am as an affable everyman that is sometimes victimized by circumstances. His one attempt at illegal gain fails miserably, ending with an attempted suicide provoked by shame. After Tony comes to his financial rescue, he realizes that the aid comes at the end of a long and botched process initiated by his own incompetency and Tony's predatory foresight. The implication, of course, is that not that all I-Ams are latent criminals but that the codes of Italianicity often encapsulate the characters in awkward positions of counterpoint. Artie represents the silent majority of I-Ams who may decry the notoriety of the mob but envy the power the mob wields.

Dr. Bruce Cusamano, by way of contrast, boasts no affiliation with his Soprano neighbours but his bravado allows him to brag that he lives in the safest neighbourhood in New Jersey. As an educated professional, he has chosen to distance himself both from his traditions and the I-Am community. Tony, an oafish sort and a gangster to boot, is a source of chagrin for both him and his wife. Dr. Cusamano belongs to an exclusive Anglicized country club and, though he may unknowingly be their token Italian, he survives because he has rejected his own ethnicity in favour of gratuity and deference. Like Amerigo Bonasera in the opening chapter of *The Godfather*, Dr. Cusamano can bluster: "I believe in America. America has made my fortune."[16] He lives with the naive pseudo-conviction that there is a hard line between crime and the American institutions of truth and honour. Yet he also understands that the road to financial success is to pledge allegiance to twisted social affairs and backroom corporate deals. Accordingly, the Cusamanos inhabit a landscaped haven of false conjecture and loathing pretension. Tony disparages the doctor in a telling conversation with Dr. Melfi in "A Hit Is a Hit" I.10:

DR. MELFI: Am I to understand that you don't consider yourself white?
TONY: I don't mean white like Caucasian. I mean a white man, like our friend Cusamano. Now he's Italian but he's American. He's what my old man would've called a wonder bread WOP. He eats his Sunday gravy out of a jar.

The Cusamano character type is reprised in a later episode ("Marco Polo" V.8) by Russ Fegoli, a doctor in international affairs and a retired American ambassador to the Holy See. In this episode, Carmela's mother acts as the conscience of a self-deprecating I-Am community doing everything in her power to shield her supposedly up-street friends from the low-brow, sausage-toting figure of Tony. Her dilemma is not Tony's criminal history; she has lived with his nefarious side since the marriage of her daughter, but rather his ethnic wholeness. He's just *too Italian* (or what passes for Italian in New Jersey) for her tastes, a family embarrassment, an obvious insult to her diplomatic friends. He has not grown away from his roots and displays mannerisms too reminiscent of Mulberry Street vendors and hawkers. As he struts into the garden party clad in loud floral shirt, shorts, sockless leather loafers, and adorned with a string of Satriale's sausages dangling around his neck, she cringes in shame. The Fegolis share her visible consternation.

"A doctor in the house," Tony boisterously exclaims as he is introduced to Dr. Fegoli. "Well that's good 'cause somebody usually goes down at these things." The joke is not well received. When the good doctor condescendingly informs Tony that his degree is not in medicine but in international affairs, Tony's mother-in-law reprovingly chimes-in: "From Princeton." Chase provides both jocularity and a dissonant counterfoil to the diplomat's pretensions by inserting an idle bystander's deflating comment "G.I. Bill." The remark serves to hold Fegoli's feet to the fire by revealing his down-scale pedestrian roots. The university degree was not achieved because of social pedigree but because of a government handout to returning underprivileged veteran soldiers.

Tony's remaining comments also deride his reputation in typical *Soprano* repartee. Father-in-law: "Russ had an audience with four popes." Tony: "Oh. What section did you all sit in?" By this point, the mocking complete, Tony is free to abandon the pretentious show. But there is still more to come. Russ and his ilk do not take the public humiliation lightly. Later on during the party, in a deliberate attempt to belittle Tony's gift of a Beretta Rifle to his father-in-law, Russ recounts a visit to the Beretta factory in Italy stating: "The best pieces they never export." Tony and his guests have been duly mortified and viciously humbled by the vitriolic doctor. At party's end, Carmela's obsequious mother apologies to the Fegolis "for everything." The "everything" is in obvious deference to Tony, his friends, and their tainted culture of contaminated ethnic difference. Interestingly, though on the brink of divorce, Carmela vehemently defends Tony and her lifestyle, harshly chastising her mother for her callous bigotry.

> CARMELA: You're sorry for what? ... I wanna hear.
> MOTHER: Ah, please Carmela. The off-color jokes, the sausage twirling.
> CARMELA: Tony.
> MOTHER: These are cultured Italians. Russ is a successful diplomat. This was a shock to them.
> CARMELA: He's such a diplomat he insults his host! You know what he said to Tony. He's a pompous man, he always was.

Carmela's words display a deepening sense of betrayal by her mother and a burgeoning personal ethnic pride. Their argument adumbrates the possible conflicts played out with her mother in the past. She reminds her mother that the snobbish former ambassador was once part of the gang in their old neighbourhood.

> CARMELA: That's why you didn't want Tony here. It had nothing to do with the marital situation. All along it was so your cultured Italian friends, who were born and raised on Arthur Avenue I might add, wouldn't meet your *gavone* son-in-law.[17]

The cat's out of the bag, Carmela's mother reveals her true colours:

> MOTHER: He made us all look like *gavones*.
> CARMELA: Whatever we are I am proud of it, unlike you obviously.
> MOTHER: I've always been proud of my heritage.
> CARMELA: That's bullshit! I remember you telling Aunt Rose you were happy De Angelis didn't end in a vowel ... And when Meadow came out, "Oh my God she's so dark!"

Carmela's closing comments are biting. They could be a rallying anthem for David Chase as she decries those closet Italians who remain hidden lest they be touched with the brush of popular Italian culture.

> CARMELA: There are Italians all around with their closet self-loathing; I just never wanted to believe my mother was one of 'em ... Your secret is out.

In essence, Russ Fegoli, with all his pretensions, and others like him shelter a deep-seated culpability of cultural inferiority that ultimately results in public self-destruction. Not comfortable within their ethnic skins, they become ambassadors of personal suicide and social patricide. These Russ Fegoli clones do not nurture and grow from their roots; instead, they prefer to stifle and kill them. They are ultimately rootless and have rejected the acceptable rules of comportment for organizing and living one's life. Unable to sustain or happily revisit the outmoded forms and practices of their youth, they can never partake of the evolved sensibilities of the I-Am community. Ultimately, they don't melt in the pot because they find the company meddlesome and loathsome. Instead, they burn off any allegiance with their former neighbourhood, their shameful relatives, and ultimately their ethnic selves. As wonder bread wops they wilfully embrace the outward semblance of Italianicity when politically expeditious, but they are embarrassingly devoid of any sustaining compassion.

Because of their rejection of their own tradition and cosy acceptance of more palatable and profitable American mores, these characters are made to suffer a variety of indignities by the Soprano family. For example, when Carmela requires a letter of recommendation for her daughter Meadow's admission to Georgetown University, she threatens a Cusamano aunt, a lawyer and Georgetown alumna ("Full Leather Jacket" II.8). Earlier in the series, in a scene reminiscent of *The Godfather Part II*,[18] Tony asks an intimidated Dr. Cusamano, sarcastically baptized "Cooz" by Tony, to hide a mysterious box for safe keeping ("A Hit Is a

Hit" I.10). The box contains nothing but sand. The viewer and the Cusamanos, however, are allowed to suspect the worst. An embittered Tony also threatens to violently assault FBI Agent Grasso for betraying his own people by joining law enforcement in "The Legend of Tennessee Moltisanti" I.8. The expression used by Tony, "*Ti faccio un culo cosi'!*" (I'll fix your ass!) is a phrase that historically represents a symbolic, and in many cases physical, act of male domination over a vanquished opponent. Taken literally, the act and the hand gesture implying the act, connote rape and sodomy. In modern Italian usage it can be used to signify a beating. The message is clear: the only real protection for an individual is to be found in the authority provided by tradition, even if that cultural, social, and sexual tradition is tainted with the likes of Tony Soprano.

But this bunker-mentality paradigm, with its illusion of personal control, ethnic loyalty, and economic stability, has unfortunately become tenuous. It resonates with the same exhaustion and uneasiness that infects corporate America. As Tony acknowledges to Carmela when discussing how to discipline their teenage daughter Meadow for having a party at her grandmother's then-empty house, "Let's not overplay our hand, 'cuz if she finds out we're powerless, we're fucked!" ("Toodle-Fucking-oo" II.3). The phrase could easily be applied to the devolving social trajectory taking place.

As the obligations of fealty become unsettled in a world that no longer preserves the traditional lines of generational interaction and cultural transmission, the line between affection and hostility can indeed be indistinct. Such is the case with Richard La Penna, estranged husband of Dr. Melfi. A short-lived character, he is the foil Chase employs to chastise activists in the I-Am community objecting to the series and its portrayal of I-Am gangster stereotypes; a one-trick pony for Chase's on-screen rebuttal. He is perhaps the least sympathetic character in the series and receives little airtime, just enough to spout his reactionary diatribe to his wife. He is definitely on the wrong side of ethnic identification in a series where Paulie "Walnuts" Gualtieri is able to spout vulgar indignation that Starbucks has ripped off Italian culture by selling espresso coffee ("Fuckin' Italian people. How did we miss out on this?" "46 Long" I.2) and Father Phil Intintola affectionately refers to Robert De Niro as Bobby D ("College" I.6). While La Penna's objections are strident and he feels himself enslaved to an ethnic media image viscerally disembowelled by characters such as his ex-wife's patient, he is also visibly pained by the rebuff American culture holds for him. Ultimately, as we shall see, Richard La Penna perceives himself as a victim of an all-encompassing stereotype relentlessly exploited by American media.

Except for two references made by Tony to his children about their great-grandfather the mason, nowhere are there discussions of the waves of immigration that forged the New Jersey sociocultural cityscape. At the same time, while immigration and the lore of yesteryear are obviously not the main concern of *The Sopranos*, issues of ethnic difference bubble close to the surface of the series and often occupy symbolic central positions within narrative plot lines. Ethnicity is an issue that each important character in the series confronts and which is highlighted by Chase in many different settings. Chase's sympathy clearly rests with the rejection of mainstream culture and the embracing of ethnic traditions. The code is simple: follow traditions, respect one's elders, live close to home. In this world, characters are guilty and punishable to the degree that they deviate from acceptable norms of tradition and family.

The code is more complex, however, when the family is also a *famiglia*. In The *Godfather Part II*, Michael Corleone's question to Mamma Corleone about the possibility of a man losing his family plays upon the double entendre of the mob's penchant for viewing their collective affairs as extended blood relations. The notion of both nuclear and extended family in Italy, especially southern Italy, has been studied and widely debated by anthropologists, sociologists, literary critics, and journalists.[19] I cannot agree with many of *The Sopranos'* commentators who, for whatever reason, have seen the Mafia as a way of "recreating an Italian village in the New World."[20] This is an erroneous and romanticized notion of a pre-industrialized Italy often subject to medieval mores and local banditry. Mafia families and blood families are distinct entities. To suggest that peninsular southern Italians are latently criminal and therefore beholden to feudal power structures, and that these patterns of patronage were exported with the emigrants, is not only insulting but part of the sensationalism that the series, to my mind, attempts to address. Most knowledgeable observers recognized that crime, disorganized or organized, was not imported from Sicily or Naples, but learned in the streets of urban America, where the children did indeed catch "the spirit of the new country."[21]

The Sopranos is not about Italians, not about Italian-Americans. Rather, it chronicles the evolving family life of an I-Am family whose wage earner is the boss of a Mafia family. Smudging the line between the legitimate pursuits of the vast majority of hyphenated Italians worldwide and the illegitimate brutalities of the characters portrayed in the series is biased media fodder. Invariably, the loneliness, dislocation, and threatened violence of the New World bred an irreverent tension in the early immigrant enclaves as many suffered the unjust economic imbalances that exploited them. What immigrants mostly felt, however, was a sense of loss, a gnawing nostalgia for old ways that did not, I must insist, invariably extend to criminality. Loss subtends the fear of losing traditions, faith, customs, and one's way in the New World. This sense of impending loss adumbrates the entire narrative of *The Sopranos* and is critical to understanding the drama of ethnic culture as represented in its characters.[22]

From the outset, Tony's dilemma is the loss of continuity and constancy. He is anxiety ridden, insecure, hostile, and unpredictable. He suffers from depression. In order to survive he must undergo a period of individuation and create a reliable existential framework that satisfies his narcissistic needs and heals the wounds of his childhood. Our glimpses into the home of Johnny and Livia Soprano reveal a second generation mob-centric culture dissonant with the legitimate working-class ethnic neighbourhood and dependent upon the continuation of hypocritical public and private relations. The Soprano children straddle categories of stereotypical representations of their culture while they themselves evolve to become controlling Others. Depression, doubt, and inner emptiness are the price they pay for this control. Siblings Janice, Tony, and Barbara Soprano represent typical reactions to the drama of the ethnic child forever in search of their true selves in a home that, because of its double-barrelled difference (ethnic and criminally connected), is dysfunctional and unbalanced. To further complicate matters, their father is a psychopath, the mother a narcissistic personality incapable of love. Both Janice and Barbara resolve their dilemmas by leaving the private torture of home and the public shame of neighbourhood. Barbara marries outside her skin and remains culturally indifferent to her roots. Janice renames herself Parvati (a benevolent Hindu goddess that often assumes wrathful incarnations) and finds liberation in the pursuit of drug-induced soul searching and self-loathing on the Pacific coast. Both remain as far from the Jersey shore as possible. Only middle son Tony musters the obligatory courage to remain. It is a Faustian bargain that respects family tradition and permits swift admission into the lucrative underworld of crime but ultimately deprives him of positive ontological affirmation.

Tony's children relive the same drama. Though peripheral to the real action of the series, they are central to understanding the inevitable personal conflict that pursues them once they perceive the duality of their lives. Meadow MariAngela and Anthony Junior are presented as frivolous, sometimes disrespectful, but always typical teenagers sprouting their wings. Unlike their socially secluded parents, they have no buffer in their dealings with the outside world and are often the targets of unsolicited labelling by their friends. Meadow often confronts her friends' devolution from their *famiglia* by chiding their derogatory remarks. A.J., on the other hand, reluctantly discovers that his father's notoriety can be used as an attractive calling card for his high school chums and is often able to profit from the popularity. Their existential angst is trebled and cursed in three ways: first, because they are healthy teenagers experimenting with the world; second, because their world, like that of all immigrant children, is different from the rest; and third, because they bridle against a reality that contains irrevocably embarrassing illegal activity. Their third-generation parents live a quandary similar to that of first-generation immigrant parents but for different reasons. They live with the fear of losing their children not because of a suffered heritage but because of a changing American identity amidst the normal increasing independence of their children and their slow discovery of the family business. It is a drama of a tormented emotional discovery on both sides that is resolved with the acceptance of a unique and all-conditioning family ideology by all parties by series' end.

The first season of the series sets the tone immediately: Tony and Carmela are concerned about their children's growing awareness of family secrets. In "College" I.5 Tony is made to confront his major contradiction by his daughter who asks, "Are you in the Mafia?" His initial reaction, "There is no Mafia," is tempered by revelations concerning income derived from some illegitimate sources. A more contrite father later expresses his rationalizion, "My father was in it, my uncle was in it. There was a time there when the Italian people didn't have a lot of options." To which a sprightly Meadow sarcastically chirps, "You mean like Mario Cuomo?" Despite the loving entente between the two, Meadow is forever blemished, her evolving self-esteem irrevocably compromised by the blatant deception that scaffolds her world. "Sometimes," she confesses to her father in "Bust Out" II.10, "we're all hypocrites." Like her father, she is able to rationalize her choices by deflecting the derogatory designations of her ponderous cultural baggage with intelligent repartee and chaffing wisecracks. Yet, where Tony wrestles with his *anima*, Meadow probes to understand her *animus*.

Both suffer the pain of events that destabilize their world constructions. After the separation of her parents, for example, a surprisingly resolute Meadow confronts her mother, asking how she could put up with the bullshit for all those years ("Whitecaps" IV.13). Yet Meadow acquiesces, her stridency not meant to hurt her mother but instead to voice her own deep-set frustration. Ultimately, she remains faithful and steadfast to Soprano family values. She saves her family's face on numerous occasions. One such instance occurs after Jackie Aprile Jr.'s funeral ("The Army of One" III.13) when she scolds Jackie's sister, Kelly Aprile, for speaking about their fathers' mob connections in front of their friend Mackenzie, a family outsider.

> KELLY: My brother's whole stupid pathetic dream was to follow in our father's footsteps. What? I gotta' paint a picture? He was killed by some fat fuck in see-through socks. Take your pick, they all look alike.

An incredulously disheartened Meadow responds:

> MEADOW: Actually, Kelly, you have no basis to say that.
> KELLY: We used to joke around about our families. What happened to you?

Pouring herself several jiggers of vodka, a surprisingly calm Meadow lays out the party line:

> MEADOW: Look, I know this is a really painful time for you but your brother's best friend was an Israeli X dealer. I met him.
> KELLY: Wow (mockingly) so it was international.
> MEADOW: Just drop it, OK.
> KELLY: Yeah right. I mean, if my dad still controlled all the crime in North Jersey like your dad does now, I'd probably want to drop it too. But then, it might not have happened.

Adorning her best Soprano family false face, Meadow replies:

> MEADOW: Wait. This is way beyond. Our dads are in the garbage business, and it's always good for a laugh, and yeah they brush-up against organized crime but you think they control every slime ball and illegal gun in like a hundred communities! The fact that you would even say this in front of an outsider is amazing to me. Jesus Christ! Some loyalty!

Shortly afterwards, however, the strain of her protracted loyalty is painfully displayed as she blatantly disrespects her family by pitching bread balls at her great-uncle Junior, the public patriarch of her *famiglia*, and disparages his singing as sickly. "This is such bullshit!" she screams at her father as she dashes across the street against oncoming traffic. It seems the strain of wearing a Janus face[23] is often too unbearable, even for Meadow. Nevertheless, she is truly her father's daughter, in one breath confidently defending her family and in the next repentantly disassociating herself from that same family in a fit of petulance and insufferable frustration.

Even when confronting her fiancé Finn Detrolio ("Unidentified Black Males" V.9) in a moment when she should be at her most comfortable and honest, Meadow peevishly defends the very men she knows to be hoodlums:

> FINN: You should've seen these guys. They were laughing, it was fucking sick. Is this what you grew up with?
> MEADOW: What are you talking about?
> FINN: These people. Your dad's friends.
> MEADOW: I never saw one bit of violence growing up.
> FINN: And what about your dad's road rage? And didn't you tell me you had a boyfriend once that was killed, shot to death or something?

To which Meadow calmly and reservedly replies:

> MEADOW: First of all he was killed by drug dealers. African-Americans if it makes you feel any better.

She then waxes academically, a Soprano apologist for Tony Soprano "end of story" rationalizations:

> MEADOW: You know you talk about these guys like it's an anthropology class. The truth is they bring certain modes of conflict resolution from all the way back in the old country and the poverty of the Mezzogiorno where all higher authority was corrupt.

Significantly, the scene shifts to a cemetery, the ultimate "end-of-story" mode of conflict resolution in Sopranoland.

On another occasion ("Live Free or Die" VI.6) she defends her father and his ilk to live free or die with impassioned indignity, accusing the federal government of heavy-handed intimidation at the wedding of John Sacrimoni's daughter:

> MEADOW: And you look at my father's friend, federal marshall's dragging him out of his own daughter's wedding; he hasn't even been tried yet, you're innocent in this country until proven guilty.

An unmoved Finn replies:

> FINN: Yeah, but Johnny Macaroni was indicted for murder.
> MEADOW: They couldn't let him stay fifteen more minutes ... You know why they did that? To humiliate him in front of everyone. Metal detectors, frisking, my father with his shoes, it was pure harassment.
> FINN: But the guy's lucky they did let him out.
> MEADOW: So white-collar criminals can destroy people's lives and steal their pensions and it's no big deal to you?

As Finn attempts to dislodge himself from the vexing argument, Meadow resumes her pointed attack, accusing Finn of negating his immigrant heritage, returning again to an apology that expresses the essence of her own divided identity.

> MEADOW: Let's talk about it, so we can stop with the macaroni cracks. Weird since you're part Italian yourself.
> FINN: My dad's so deracinated ...
> MEADOW: The way he prefers it. All those hysterical jokes about Italian cheeses and smelly feet.
> FINN: Why are you picking a fight?
> MEADOW: I'm not, but you're slamming my family.
> FINN: You weren't there for the grand inquisition of Vito. I was in the back of a butcher shop with your uncle Paulie ratting out a guy I don't even know. What do you think is going to happen to Vito for being gay? And don't give me any of that poverty of the Mezzogiorno bullshit. We're in fuckin' Caldwell, New Jersey, and you're on your high horse about justice. They are gonna' meet it out themselves.

A disgusted Meadow mumbles the words "Listen to him" under her breath and leaves the scene. Like her father, she needs to carefully avoid regarding the touchstone of reality lest she corrode the underpinnings of her inner self. As with Tony, Meadow's use of the word family is fraught with pregnant ambiguity. Her signalling of personal disapproval moves beyond the offence language used by Finn and draws upon defence mechanisms that both shield and distance the duplicitous reality in which she constantly lives. In this manner, she avoids personal and public social anxiety by never really being in the true company of others, even her fiancé whom she will not marry. She chooses instead, like her father, to play an elaborate game of pretense and equivocation; always not quite herself but instead hiding her being-in-the-world behind extraneous trappings that define her exterior roles: teenager, college student, future lawyer, and daddy's girl.

Similar to the plight of her third-generation father, her restless search for a sense of self beyond the family often leads her away from both the fiercely held legends of the home ("You'd think there never was a Michelangelo," "The Legend of Tennessee Moltisanti" I.8) and the wrenching bigotry faced outside their pseudo-ethnic lifestyle. Undoubtedly, the site of emerging subjective awareness in the maturing immigrant child requires that it be one of transformed identity; a construction of self that either supersedes immediate parental obstacles or forever succumbs to their debilitating narrative. The potential to acquire voice in these offspring is thus relegated to a restricted space that considers it in relation only to their ability to deny a portion of themselves and become, in essence, a tormented invisible minority.[24]

In these instances, parents may either promote their children's freedom from their father's legacy (Salvatore "Big Pussy" Bonpensiero's sons are in medical school; mob boss Jackie Aprile Sr. wished a similar academic road for his son Jackie Jr.; Tony wishes to save [his word] his son A.J.), and therefore die emotionally from a loss of self and family, or encourage them to embrace the old ways (in the manner of Richie Aprile, Ralph Cifaretto, Carmine Lupertazzi). It is a standard generational paradox that *The Sopranos* plays out in the realm of criminality, compounded by the sword of generational ethnic assimilation. Meadow, like her father, eventually chooses to avoid transcendence and remain forever anchored to the predatory and pernicious facet of her inner self. She remains true to her heraldic emblem. She will apply her talents to protect the sinister dealings of secretive criminals and not enter the more sanguine and publicly respected realm of pediatrics as her parents had aspired for her.

MEADOW: The world is a sad, fucked-up place.
TONY: If there's so much suffering in the world, why did you go off the pediatrician bit?

MEADOW: We talked about that.
TONY: Yeah, you said you wanted to be a lawyer for Black people.
MEADOW: Oh, that's all I said. Really? What I said was the state can crush the individual.
TONY: New Jersey?
MEADOW: The government, specifically the federal government.
TONY: What about little babies, in the face of meningitis?
MEADOW: You know what really turned me? Seeing the way Italians are treated. Like Mom says. And if we can have our rights trampled like that, imagine what it's like for recent arrivals.

And then, in a final acerbic, brash, and scorching kick to her father's plans of distancing his daughter from his business, she confesses that she is inspired to defend men like her father because, she confides, "If I hadn't seen you dragged away all those times by the FBI, then I'd probably be a boring suburban doctor." The scene drips with brazen irony as Tony is left contemplating whether he should be a proud mobster or remorseful father ("Made in America" VI.21).

Meadow's stance presupposes her capacity to maintain a firm and vibrant inner reality that remains separate from the problematic outer world that envelops her. This inner self is both regularly destroyed and simultaneously quantified by the external outer persona she emanates. This self depends entirely upon social circumstance. This dialectical relationship with both self and others is the price she pays for her precarious vibrancy. The cost leaves her irreconcilably split, volatilized and, like her father, able to truly believe and convincingly relate the most egregious lies for the sake of maintaining a public face. Though Meadow is a fourth-generation child, because of the overwhelming Mafia heritage in the home, she displays the tendency of many third-generation immigrant children who tend to be more extroverted and engage, as Jerry Mangione states, in

> acting out behavior often of a psychopathic type. There [is] anger in their complaints, directed not only towards their family but also towards American society. While the mental disorders of the third generation are extreme cases representing a tiny percentage of the Italian American population, they suggest the fear, anger, hurt, and inferiority which all generations experienced to some degree, though generally secretly among the first and second generations.[25]

What is revelatory, however, and emblematic for Meadow, is that she is not really compromising her values, she is merely living up to them. Though she berates the criminal nature of her father's business (privately and within the family bosom), she also deplores the legal abuse of past and recent immigrants by the federal government (publicly now and, it can be assumed, in her future career as a lawyer). In *The Sopranos*, stereotyping is only a small part of the characters' alluring social criticism. After all, ethnic identity in the series is a duplicitous game that most often fades into criminality.

To Be or Not to Be a Mobster

Like movies and "that smell in Blockbuster" ("The Legend of Tennessee Moltisanti" I.8), ethincity and the Soprano odour of criminality are central to the identity conundrum that haunts many of the main characters and colours their public and private relations. These characters suffer, in varying degrees, from an attraction/negation to "ethnic-itus." They endeavour to rest on the good part of their heritage while walking the tightrope that sometimes ties them to the coarser constituents of their selves. For this reason, racial slurs and antipathy towards all peoples, all colours, and all creeds are evenly sprinkled throughout the series while questions of ethnic stereotypes are never dismissed but always tackled head-on. At the same time, the series does not play with truisms of the typical ethnic Italian Other but rather with the silent and latent stereotype within I-Am culture and specifically with the conundrum "to be or not to be" a mobster. This is the crux at the heart of Tony's many liminal relationships – people that defer respect to his mob station but who are terrified of proximity and personal implication. These characters are always I-Ams and include Carmela, Dr. Melfi, Dr. Cusamano, Dave Scatino, Artie Bucco, Gloria Trillo, Finn De Trolio, even the spiritually wayward Father Intintola. All savour the excitement of vicarious identification with Tony and his ilk but fear culpability. All are cognizant of his dark side but often bask in the generosity of his light. Whether for social notoriety (Dr. Cusamano) or culinary intimacy (Father Intintola), business opportunity (Artie Bucco) or sexual companionship (Gloria Trillo), they are close to Tony for immediate convenience, and any entreaty to change or alter his life course is weak because they are essentially self-serving.

Truth is, the dilemma in the series is not between Americanization and retention of pseudo-Italian roots from the old country, as many have contended. The pull between the cultures is clearly not between an Italian and an American ethos. For all their so-called Italianate-Americanized trappings, Tony and his brand are New Jersey I-Ams with no clue of their ancestral roots or culture beyond that planted and grown on their Jersey shore. As fourth-generation immigrant children, Davey Scatino, Artie Bucco, Dr. Cusamano, and, we may include for that matter, Dr. Melfi and her estranged husband Richard La Penna, to name a few, find the sources of their misunderstood heritage in the public media, the local streets, and uppity academia. They mispronounce Italian words, call tomato sauce gravy (an East coast usage), *cafone* becomes *gavone*, *capicollo* is *gabigool*, and so on. They often display a serendipitous interest for things Italian. Carmela enjoys the pop tenor Andrea Bocelli; faux Renaissance paintings grace her bedroom walls. Even the learned Dr. Melfi, with a remark that may be interpreted as either ironic or sarcastic, professes a fondness for Venetian Murano glass while dining at the Cusamano's ("A Hit Is a Hit" I.10). In "The Ride" VI.9, she confesses her emotional attachment to the neighbourhood annual Feast of St. Elzear festival, stating to Tony, "The thing for us kids was to throw sugar on each other from the zeppole."

We recall, too, that in "Commendatori" II.4, Tony, Christopher Moltisanti, and Paulie "Walnuts" Gualtieri flounder in Naples. They have little or no knowledge of their mother country and are dumbfounded by Italian food, ancient customs, and superstitions. They simply don't understand the layout of the land nor do they fathom the richness of the culture. Paulie's closest contact with his ancestral roots is an indelicately disinterested prostitute from his grandfather's town of origin. Christopher's Italian sojourn extends through the point of a syringe of non-discriminating and non-generic heroin. Tony, on the other hand, receives receives an Italian-style Mafia lesson when he witnesses Furio Giunta casually smack a young ruffian in front of routinely indifferent Neapolitan carabineers and the boy's sobbing mother. He learns Neapolitan folklore at the able hands (and manicured, hex-free fingers) of his distant female cousin Annalisa Zucca, who just so happens to be the capo of the local mob family. This is obviously a process both of the deconstruction of inauthentic I-Am myths *and* the reconstruction of an individual ethnic mythos responding to the personal, and nefarious, exigencies of Tony Soprano. Just as older generational ways and parental traditions were to be questioned and possibly re-evaluated, these same generational motivations were never to be forgotten. His Italian education helps Tony accept the underworld into which he was born and, for the sake of comfort and facile wealth, remain a gangster. For Tony, and apparently for Chase, it's all a matter of personal choice, not of group dynamic, lineage, or heritage.

What, then, makes some people identify themselves as Italians in North America? What are the social, cultural, psychological, linguistic, even personal motivations that lead one to distinguish oneself and identify with an ethnic group? For Richard Gambino, the I-Am experience in North America is trapped in "inauthentic myths,"[26] the same ones the series repeats and continues to popularize. Social caricatures, street tales, media portrayals all contribute to a "surrealistic limbo" in which it is impossible for I-Ams to reify an authentic and fully developed identity. Like those liminal characters that cling to Tony, many I-Ams unthinkingly hold myths about themselves that are a perverse deformation of the spirit of their true ethnic character (whatever that may be).[27] Early in the series we are presented typical and stereotypical instances of ethno-labelling in manners of dress, comportment, food, and language. These are often comedic moments. Paulie "Walnuts" Gualtieri, we recall, decries trendy coffee shops stealing his heritage in "46 Long" I.2:

> Fuckin' Italian people. How did we miss out on this? ... Fuckin' espresso, cappuccino; we invented this shit and all these other c. suckers are getting rich on this shit ... And it's not just the money, it's a pride thing. All our food: pizza, calzone, buffalo mozzarell', olive oil. These fucks have nuthin'. They ate puzzi before we gave them the gift of our cuisine.

Stereotyped I-Ams adhere and sustain their much ballyhooed stereotypes. It's the only reality they know. In this same episode, for instance, the demise of the Mafia is discussed by a former mob soldier on television as if it were a Golden Age fiction while real-life mobsters watch and count their apparently fictitious monetary gains. The layers of deception are both engaging and entertaining. Yet these tongue-in-cheek tirades set-up the viewer for an onslaught of more subtle innuendos that expose deeper concerns.

A more sober and salient discussion occurs when Chase juxtaposes two socially distinct and ethically appositional families in the series: the Melfis and the Sopranos. We are introduced to their not-so-unique ethnic family dynamics over the most emblematic of I-Am traditions, family dinner in "The Legend of Tennessee Moltisanti" I.8. In the Melfi home, son Jason's use of the term *ginzo* (a derogatory term, we are informed by Richard La Penna, Dr. Melfi's estranged husband, is derived from the word *guinea*) sparks a discussion about Dr. Melfi's unnamed patient.

> RICHARD: People like him are the reason Italian-Americans have such a bad image ... Ask any American to describe an Italian-American in this country and invariably he's gonna' reference *The Godfather*, *Goodfellas*, and the rest are gonna' mention pizza.

To which Jason cracks, "Good movies" and "Good movies to eat pizza by."

The conversations then turns to what will become a familiar Sopranos rejoinder as Richard continues to advance arguments against media stereotyping of I-Ams:

> RICHARD: Why do you think we're never going to see an Italian president?
> DR. MELFI: Oh, and that's my patient's fault ... I realize that you're very involved in the anti-defamation lobby, so go after Hollywood if you absolutely have to; leave my patient alone.

But Richard raises the existential stakes by broadening the argument:

> RICHARD: It's a synergy. News items and the constant portrayal of Italian Americans as gangsters.
> JASON: Wasn't the Italian anti-def deal started by Joe Colombo, a mobster?
> RICHARD: Italians against discrimination did a study and at its height the Mafia in this country had less than five thousand members and yet, that tiny insignificant fraction casts such a dark shadow over twenty million hard-working Americans.
> JASON: Dad, at this point in our cultural history, mob movies are classic American cinema, like westerns.

Grandfather chimes in:

> GRANDFATHER: I have to agree there, Richard. You know you never saw the Scotch Irish pissin' and moanin' about always being portrayed as rustlers and gunslingers.

Then grandfather closes the dwindling argument by toasting: "To we, the twenty million." The use of the personal subject pronoun "we" instead of the object pronoun "us" is significant and turns the entire discussion into an educated-intellectual artifice placing the speaker as first, separate, and distinct. They are portentous words swirling in a glass of wine, Chase's way of transferring the dialogue from a passive group dynamic (us) to an individual subjective and active responsibility (we).

This is the first of several instances where Dr. Melfi will not allow her former husband to pin his personal life modality, success, or failure on the coat tails of I-Ams. The Soprano household, in the same episode, entertains a similar pride-inspired discussion but, as always, at a more pedestrian, if not less genteel and prosaic, level. The family's encounter during an FBI house raid that involves the bumbling I-Am FBI Agent Grasso sparks Tony's ire at the notion that a fellow *paisan* would join the enemy.

> TONY: I know those feds are doin' their job but it pisses me off the way they act ... And the guy that broke the bowl, he did that on purpose.
> CARMELA: Oh, I don't think so. The guy was just a klutz.
> TONY: What was his last name? Rizzo, Razzo, what?
> CARMELA: Grasso.
> TONY: Grasso. You think it's a coincidence they sent him? If he wasn't Italian he'd be back at the office sweepin' up, the stupid jerk. They probably frisk him every night before he goes home.
> A.J.: Why?
> TONY: Why? Because he has a vowel at the end of his name, that's why: Grasso. I mean what's he think he's gonna make it to the top by arresting his own people? ... He'll see. He'll learn.
> A.J.: We have a vowel.
> TONY: Effin' right and you be proud of it.

Then, similar to the Melfi household, the discussion turns the corner to false pretense and public posturing:

> TONY: Jesus Christ, you'd think there never was a Michelangelo, the way they treat people.
> CARMELA: Did you know that an Italian invented the telephone?
> A.J.: Alexander Graham Bell was Italian?
> TONY: You see! You see what I'm talkin'... Antonio Meucci invented the telephone and he got robbed. Everybody knows that.

Meadow derails her father's excursion into ethnocentric history by stating:

MEADOW: Who invented the Mafia? ... The Cosa Nostra, who invented that? ... Wasn't it Salvatore Lucania better known as Charlie Lucky Luciano who organized the five families – Lucchese, Gambino, Bonanno, Profaci.

Visibly perturbed by his daughter's non-relevant and purposefully instigative historical information, he snorts:

TONY: Is there something you wanna say to me?

She replies mockingly:

MEADOW: I just like history like you, Dad.

Carmela ably steers the conversation back towards safer ethnic shores by asking A.J.:

CARMELA: A.J., did you know that John Cabot was Italian?

A watershed of examples extolling the feats of Italians in America, including the Bank of America (founded by Amadeo Giannini), Mother Cabrini, Sacco and Vanzetti, and ending, appropriately, with the name Francis Albert (Sinatra) completes the Soprano family's personalized ethnic walk of fame.

Chase often incorporates the outside criticism launched at the series for perpetuating I-Am media stereotypes into the series itself. Many of these moments are a catalyst for a discussion of issues that normally would have never been considered for the small screen. In "Christopher" IV.3, for instance, the series explores the controversy that surrounds the quincentenary of Christopher Columbus's landing on the shores of America in 1492. In short, whether through scholarship or media sound bite, the legendary voyage of Columbus and its subsequent effects were being judged outside of their historical context. Chase tackles both viewpoints by creating a scenario that sees Native Americans protesting the Columbus Day Parade. What follows is an episode stoked with pseudo-I-Am pride.

The episode features a lecture by an intellectually smug Professor Murphy on the changing perspective of I-Am traditions. Prodding her female audience that the time has come to step out of the shadows of victimhood and into the redeeming fashion light of Gucci and Armani, the speaker's promise of wholeness is achieved by adopting and proclaiming the alternative stereotypical trendy media image currently fostered by international marketing. Unfortunately, Professor Murphy ironically discredits her own *Italianicity* by needing a reminder from Father Intintola that her full name is Lallo-Murphy. Her conspicuous mispronunciation of Italian names and products equally signal her pretentious affectations. The implicit irony of this sort of false ethnic posturing reveals both the arbitrariness of her discourse and the misplaced imagocentric motivation of the speaker. The implication is that I-Ams will survive only by disparaging their own hard-won I-Am legacy in favour of a sexy *neo-Italianicity* that is media driven and image conscious. In order to fully comprehend the sarcastic implications of Professor Murphy's lecture, however, it must be viewed within the context of the episode. It is couched between two instances of cultural self-awareness that unmask the delusory foundations of her chimeric arguments. One such moment occurs at the beginning of this turnstile episode; the other at its end.

"Christopher" IV.3 opens with an overhead vertical shot of the Soprano crew sitting outside Satriale's Pork Store. After throwing catcalls towards a passing car with Massachusetts plates, Bobby "Baccalà" Baccilieri Jr. reads a newspaper article aloud announcing the New Jersey Council of Indian Affairs' intention to disrupt the upcoming annual Columbus Day celebrations in Newark.

> BACCALÀ: The New Jersey Council of Indian Affairs has announced plans to disrupt Monday's Columbus Day Parade in Newark. Council chairman Del Redclay, professor of cultural anthropology ... says council members and supporters will lie down in the path of Columbus Day marchers, quote, "In protest of Columbus's role in the genocide of America's native peoples," unquote.

The words spark an animated and biased defence of the Genovese explorer against the damning modern portrayal of him as a predatory slave trader. Silvio Dante especially is enraged by the affront to his presumed heritage. His superficial tribute to his ancestors embodies the conflict between nation-building immigrants and their indigenous counterparts.

> SILVIO: You know what it is? I'll tell you what it is: anti-Italian discrimination. Columbus Day; a day of Italian pride and they want to take it away.

His discourse exemplifies the difficult process of balancing conflicting cultural values. His diatribe against Indians protesting the Columbus Day Parade helps the viewer grasp the magnitude of the abyss that often exists between rival community groups in contemporary America. It recalls the psychological cost of assimilation, the repercussions of tribal genocide, and the continuing real and involuntary daily challenges of Americanization. Chase diffuses and coincidentally derides and amplifies the issue of group rivalry by introducing Italian newcomer Furio Giunta's culturally relative diatribe against mainland northern Italians.

> FURIO: Fuck them. But I never like Columbus. In Napoli, a lot of people are not so happy for Columbus 'cause he was from Genova ... the north of Italy always had the money and the power ... they punish the south since hundreds of years ... even today they put up their nose at us like we're peasants. I hate the nord.

Once again highlighting the Jersey group's insularity (reinforced by the camera long shot of the men sitting in huddled proximity), the men outside Satriale's Pork Store are unaware that Italy is a land of aggravated historical, linguistic, political, and cultural contrasts. Unbeknownst to them, southern Italians (the New Jersey I-Ams represented in the program are all from the southern region of Campania), are northern Italy's discriminated visible minority. Furio's rant is thus both blunt and necessarily discriminatory. As is often the case in the series, the pedestrian stereotypical views of the mostly inept Jersey I-Ams are blunted by a more pointed, yet equally stereotypical and, in this case, venomous rebuttal by a more informed outsider.

Outsiders abound in Sopranoland. In "A Hit Is a Hit" I.10, for example, Massive Genius is an atypical Black gangster rapper that breaks the inner-city stereotype of Blacks held by the Jersey crew. A former inmate, now successful entrepreneur, he embroils the Soprano clan in a legal battle over the rights to songs by Black artists allegedly pilfered by longtime Soprano adviser Hesh Rabkin. Like Professor Lallo-Murphy, Massive Genius is on a quest to reinvent his group's public dignity and place (not in American history but) in American pop culture. Though he may privately express respect for the Italian mob by praising *The Godfather* ("I seen that movie 200 times"), his public sentiments are coloured by the same suave savvy as Professor

Lallo-Murphy. Christopher's vindictive rant, like Furio Giunta's earlier harangue, is visceral:

> CHRISTOPHER: Our thing once ruled the music business ... We bankrolled acts, Blacks, everybody. Paid the DJs or busted heads to get them played on the air.

Again, the thrust is towards reappropriation and redress of perceived past ills. Assimilation has its costs and lies in the unspoken prohibitive barriers between ethnic hierarchies. Hesh, the primary object of Massive Genius' legal scorn, is himself an odd-sort-of-friend of the Soprano family. Though Jewish, he has Tony's ear and was a trusted confidante of Tony's father Johnny Soprano. He suffers discrimination and will not allow even the slightest off-colour remark to pass without severe reprobation either publicly or privately. In "Christopher" IV.3, Hesh is offended by a remark made by a business partner comparing Columbus to Hitler:

> HESH: You're talkin' out of your ass. Columbus and Hitler. You're trivializing the Holocaust. Frankly, Ruben, if you got that kind of covert anti-Semitism, I'd like you to leave my house.

In these two episodes, but then again throughout the series, ethnic slurs (Uncle Ben, Donny Brasco, homey, black-eyed peas, mulies, titzoon), and facile retorts abound. In *The Sopranos*, denigration is always applied even-handedly while discrimination is a balanced social slur for all ethnic groups. Such complex delineations of hackneyed and harmful ethnic myths do not generally sit well with audiences accustomed to lighter television brew. Yet Chase berates both the audience and the perpetrators for their passive acceptance of such views. He challenges them to rethink their judgments, to rethink their ethnicity, their minority stance, indeed their place in the American landscape. This place is not to be measured by consumer product value, as superficially extemporized by Professor Lallo-Murphy's pseudo-ethnicity, by Massive Genius' commercial collision of cultural pecking orders, or by Hesh Rabkin's biased historical ethnocentrism.

Returning to "Christopher" IV.3, we find Professor Lallo-Murphy's intellectualized arguments further deprecated by the final scene of the episode. Silvio Dante has been brooding about the Columbus Day protest for the entire episode, much to the chagrin of a desperately disinterested Tony. By the end of the episode, Tony's reticent approval of Silvio's faux ethnic posturing spills into an argument. Silvio, like Professor Lallo-Murphy, founds his objections on notions of supposed group solidarity. "They discriminate," he states, "against all Italians as a group when they disallow Columbus Day." Tony's retort is predictable since it echoes a leitmotif expressed on numerous occasions:

> TONY: Group! Group! Whatever the fuck happened to Gary Cooper, that's what I'd like to know ... The strong silent type. He did what he had to do ... And did he complain? Did he say, Oh, I come from this poor Texas Irish illiterate background or whatever the fuck, so leave me the fuck out of it because my people got fucked over?[28]

Within a system that is shielded from other value systems, such as that of any actively orthodox ethnic group, an individual is not autonomous and may not have an individual sense of identity beyond the group. But I-Ams, for Tony at least, live in the real world, have a measure of security in the world, and do not need to become victims of other interests or ideologies regardless of the hardships or discrimination they may have individually faced. For Tony, and ultimately David Chase, separation from the group is not estrangement, self-centredness is not selfishness, self-determination (even choosing to become a mobster) is not sinfulness.[29]

Pained irony bleeds through Silvio's attempts to give voice to the retro-crusade he intends to lead. For a moment the viewer forgets that Silvio is a mobster whose major preoccupation is silencing any form of dissent or non-compliance to the mob's perverse norms. But the discrimination his grandparents endured, Tony reminds him, is not his drama. To hear him vindicate the hidden sap of generations of silenced immigrants is rich with displaced concern and pretentious posturing, a jibe, obviously, at Chase's detractors. Tony will remind Silvio that America is the land of opportunity, of self-made men.

> TONY: Let me ask you a question. All the good things you got in your life, did they come to you 'cause you're Calabrese? I'll tell you the answer. The answer is no ... Did you get all this 'cause you're Italian? No. You got it 'cause you're you, 'cause you're smart, 'cause you're whatever the fuck. Where the fuck is our self-esteem? That shit doesn't come from Columbus or *The Godfather* or Chef fuckin' Boyardee.[30]

By divesting Silvio of any pretense to ethnic patrimony, Tony chooses to reassert a traditional (and in his case malevolent) cultural milieu even as remnants of his ethnicity disintegrate all around him. The great American legacy (and tragedy) is that of the self-willed loner, the socially, and often family, orphaned individual that must "make it" on his own wits and physical prowess. Tony is reiterating again the quintessential figure of the American imagination. It is a symbol that is no more powerfully at work than in the screen image of Gary Cooper. Whatever a person's ethnic markings, the self-made man epitomizes the intrinsic American myth of competitive individualism. Silvio "made it" not because he is Calabrian but because he had the courage to follow opportunity. As the screen fades to black, an allusion to the futility of Silvio's arguments, we hear the Newark, New Jersey, I-Am pop group Frankie Valli and The Four Seasons intone the lyrics of their 1964 hit song "Dawn (Go Away)." Thus reminding the viewer, and by extension the floundering Silvio, that indeed "you can't change the places where you were born."

The fact this discussion occurs on Columbus Day is doubly salient. Beyond opening a culture war of discriminatory historical revisionism, Tony, like Columbus, is proving himself to be a gifted and cunning navigator who, blessed by tenacity does not recoil from adversity, is supremely crafty, and, when need be, ruthless. In many ways he resembles the valorous mariner, Italy's first recorded immigrant. He has heroic fortitude and is dogged in pursuing what he perceives to be the greater goal. We should remember, in this context, that we do not intend to laud him; both Tony's ends and his means are confounded by the series' amorality. Yet, among his band of crooked brothers, only he has both a vision and a dream to guide him.

Tony's extemporization on individual worth and merit resonates with a contemporary rereading of America within its new cultural and historical contexts. The fluidity of American life, its continuous touch with old traditions and new migratory influences, furnish the forces that construct an evolving American character. The composite nationality of Americans, their dominant individualism, whether working for good or for evil, are traits that sailed into the waters of the New World with its first explorer and which, perverted or not, persevere in Tony. The fact is, for all his reticence and longing for the past, Tony is a fast-paced, quintessential American millennium man. He accepts the conditions that his frontier furnishes; he is opportunistic at every turn, lest he perish. If we extend the critical context of Tony's words, we find that the reticence of several characters to adapt to this reality is indicative of the fear of loss that an evolving melting pot context often generates. Tony's visceral rant to Silvio is reminiscent of Dr. Melfi's more intellectualized retorts to her former husband's ethno-phanatic raving. Dr. Melfi's private lecture occurs one season earlier than Tony's words to Silvio, but it explicitly sets the tone for Tony's later ex-ethnic exegesis. In "Employee of the Month" III.4, Dr. Melfi and her former husband prepare dinner. In an obvious allusion to the anti-defamation bluster swirling around the series, Richard La Penna excoriates the media for their continued slurring of I-Ams:

>RICHARD: The very idea that ABC would even think of producing that stereotypical gumba fest.
>DR. MELFI: Richard we're an advertisement for the American experiment. We did great.

Undeterred, Richard deepens his revulsion to the media's ethno-packaging of I-Am imagery:

>RICHARD: I'm so fed-up with people assuming I'm a thug because my name ends in a vowel. Undershirts, yelling. Harvard tries to give these sociopaths the tragic grandeur of Al Pacino.

His distaste for programs that display gross stereotypes of I-Ams is clear. Later in the episode, while assisting his former wife after her rape, he is visibly nonplused when he hears that the perpetrator's name is Rossi.

>RICHARD: Rossi. It's an Italian name.

An incredulous and seemingly more enlightened Black female physician attending Dr. Melfi poignantly asks:

>DOCTOR: Am I missing something here?

Richard attempts to shield his smitten ethnic pride:

>RICHARD: The girl said he was Puerto Rican.

Their son Jason bursts into the room and offers a Pan-American harangue that counters his father's embarrassing show of ethnic shame:

> JASON: Jesus, Mom! What did these lousy fuckers do? I can't believe this shit. I'm gonna kill these motherfuckers. Fuck it, Dad! You know the whole world is a fucking sore, nothing but a fucking sore. It's a bunch of animals out there running wild and they're fuckin' winning.

Seemingly bolstered by her son's generic outrage, Dr. Melfi turns her rage towards Richard's all too apparent ethnocentricity:

> DR. MELFI: You should have seen your face when you heard that that fucking shitbag that raped me had an Italian name.
> RICHARD: What? I registered surprise ...
> DR. MELFI: What difference does it make? Are you so ashamed of your background that any misdeed by an Italian somehow damages your self-esteem? ... All fuckin' words about your self-esteem. Or maybe you don't have enough.

The distance between Tony's diatribe against Silvio's imperious ancestral affirmation and Dr. Melfi's call for personal growth and self-affirmation beyond the non-being of ethnic self-denial is small indeed. Both views are faces of the same American coin of individualism and reinforce the series' focus on the cosmopolitanization of "our ethnic thing."[31] True personal worth lies in self-reliance and autonomy. This success-at-any-cost attitude subtends the motivations of these players. Their actions belie the frightening contradictions of a social ethos that privileges just such autonomy while at the same time fostering tension between a perceived malignant ethnic identity and an approbate and pure majority culture. In other words, success, however it is achieved, remains the marrow of America.

It seems that David Chase's series about a mob family is more coterminous with the economic distress of millennium America than with the self-indulgent and ontologically insecure ethnophobes that he continuously disparages. Chase's more enlightened characters are both liberated and successful equal opportunity bigots; contemporary Archie Bunkers[32] whose discriminatory palette is so colourful that it becomes comic to the point of being inconsequential. To view Tony, then, as a symbol of the historical struggle of hyphenated individuals that defines an ethnic identity within an American context is wrong, if not critically malicious. Instead, if the business of Americans is business, as President Calvin Coolidge once supposedly stated, then Tony is its unflinching poster child. His materialist values prevail so strongly that any discussion of ethnicity in *The Sopranos* is clouded and politically motivated. Though there are moments of I-Am pseudo-culture throughout the series, these remain as pockets of misplaced and misunderstood nostalgia that are shallow and non-critical. If anything, in *The Sopranos*, cultures interpenetrate at their crassest level. Not purity, then, but an image of crossings, what Michael Fischer sees as an "inter-reference between two or more cultural traditions."[33] Perhaps "trans-ethnic" or "polyethnic" interactions are more appropriate terms as the narrative that shapes the cultural awareness of the characters is muddled and dubious.[34] "I thought we were Napoli-dapolis or whatever" states A.J., unaware of his own family's origins. His mother corrects him stating that their family is "Napoleetan" but can offer no details or family anecdotes ("For All Debts Public and Private," IV.1). Not interference between groups, then, but inter-reference; an a-moral cross-listing of human assets that fosters an image of crossing invisible borders between groups and classes that weaves the fabric of America. This loss of boundaries is empowering, a cunning act of liberation for Tony personally (the same holds true for Carmela and Dr. Melfi), but it is the bane of characters such as Christopher, Paulie, and Silvio who desperately require fame (we recall Christopher and his fixation with notoriety), ethnic labelling (Paulie in the coffee shop), and historical affirmation (Silvio and Columbus).

So are there any values that the real, non-fictional, I-Am viewing audience can learn from the depiction of mobster I-Ams in *The Sopranos*? What of the proud, strong, self-dependent, and self-sacrificing individuals who comprise the grand majority of I-Ams? What is their legacy? If I-Ams feel betrayed by the series it is because Chase ably twists and distorts the distinctive and fundamental Italian values of family, loyalty, work, and self-respect towards ends that are frightening for their allure. Chase depersonalizes these values, defuses their inflammatory rhetoric and, in many instances, chastises those who pretentiously hold them while simultaneously using irony to spread the malaise. In this sense I agree with Michael Flamini:

> By truthfully facing *The Sopranos* and their tradition, members of the Italian American community might become comfortable enough to say to

other Americans, "Yes that's part of my world, but not all of it. Get over it." Finally, we might be able to move on with our lives in a way that leaves no part of us behind.[35]

In many respects the series does not open a conflict with its detractors as much as it faithfully depicts and unflinchingly uncovers a media morass of postmodern cultural peculation.

In today's America, real ethnic awareness is waning, dissolved in the flotsam of melting-pot commercialization. I-Ams are no longer either culturally minoritized or politically marginalized, while Italian-American tradition has become a marketing tool within the greater master narrative of cultural indifference and unbridled financial profit. That is the potpourri image of contemporary *American-ness*. Within this context, the Soprano family is just as likely to eat Chinese takeout with wine as it is to feast on baked ziti and cold milk. They are, as the final episode title swaggeringly proclaims, mobsters truly made in America.

Chapter Three

God Help the Beast in Me

Observe what a man has in mind to do when his father is living, and then observe what he does when his father is dead. If for three years he makes no changes to his father's ways, he can be said to be a good son.

Confucius

"You can act like a man!"

Don Corleone to Johnny Fontane in *The Godfather* (1972)

"Big Girls Don't Cry."

Frankie Valli and The Four Seasons (1962)

Act Like a Man

Western culture has a long heritage of promoting the feminine and masculine principles within rigidly established schemata of what it means to be a woman and what it means to be a man. Subsequently, men and women have been locked into culturally defined gender roles that eschew difference and consider alterity and difference an unacceptable, if not potentially dangerous, ideological discourse. In the past, any demand for equality that posited sexual difference as a historical gender construct risked contradicting its own symbolic foundation. But being-man and being-woman are both primary forms. And so is difference. Human beings are not merely biological factors but are the result of historical experience that includes inclusion, estrangement, and separateness. Difference essentially implies duality. Reshaping the world to accommodate gender duality entails modification of symbolic, institutional, and economic structures as well as the restructuring of modes of perception that have fomented limiting, often troubling, points of view. Traditionally, the essence of the feminine principle is passivity, visibility, and space. It focuses attention on backgrounds thereby interpreting inflection and nuance by inviting the perceiver to discover the intangible and subtle essence of human experience. It is holistic, essentially non-verbal, and concerns itself with being in the world. The masculine counterpart displays the opposite but complementary functions of speech, abstraction, and linearity. It is purportedly active, processes information logically, and is able to implement its words into direct actions. Generally, the male is able to shut out the background, those feelings that might otherwise distract. This dispassion is indispensable for killing; the opposite of a female's binding love.

One of the most innovative and provocative aspects of *The Sopranos* is undoubtedly the introduction of the feminine principle into the encrypted and closed masculine world of the mob. The Mafia is by definition a secret society that has historically not only excluded the feminine principle but has, in its efforts to remain undiluted and masculine, violently negated anything remotely reminiscent of weak, passive, and unsightly feminine attributes. When Tony vehemently exclaims, "I'm a man, you're a woman. End of story!" ("Pax Soprana," I.6), he is not simply reiterating a transplanted Mediterranean attitude of genealogically inherited male chauvinism. His reasoning is the result of the evolutionary cleaving of the human brain into two distinct lateralizations – the right hemisphere and the left hemisphere that, while appearing symmetrical, are functionally different. The physiological reconfiguration of the brain produced the sharp division of labour between men and women and superinduced the protoplastic social patterns that we normally attribute to the sexes: men were active hunters, women passive gatherers. The eventual dominance of left-brain linear thinking (logic, analysis, abstraction) initiated the political decline of feminine values (holistic qualities that involve feelings, imagery, intuition) and helped usher in an entrenched patriarchy that sometimes blossomed into unbridled misogyny.[1] But the matter is not so clear cut and gender simple.

One of the many chauvinist dictums promulgated by the mob is that "Words are feminine" (*Le parole sono femmine*). This is a Sicilian proverbial disclaimer that extemporizes the heartfelt notion that the description of actions through the use of words are part of the holistic, synthetic, simultaneous, and ultimately passive properties of the right hemisphere, traits normally attributed to women or effeminate (weak) males.[2] These essentialist traits have long been touted in heroic myth and proverbial lore. When seen in this context, words thwart action. They have the power to still and mute the left-brained linear, rational, sequential, abstract, and action-oriented attributes normally associated with the masculine. Long before the days of socially subjugated notions of self and independent personalities, the dynamic difference between males and females fostered archetypes and myths that precognitively anticipated the war of the sexes. Women stilled men's vitality (petrification as exhibited in the Medusa myth, loss of strength in Samson) and were creatures of the heart responsible for unleashing evil upon humanity as expounded in the pagan myths of Tiamat and Pandora, and the Judeo-Christian narrative of Eve. Even death was deduced as a feminization of the vital masculine impulse.[3] Most societies invent creation stories to explain the presence of evil in their midst, all of which can be traced to the wanted restriction of feminine power and subsequent endorsement of masculine principles. Yet the primal dichotomous nature all humans carry within persists.[4] Although these represent aesthetically opposing perceptual modes, they coexist and overlap in each individual. Both men and women carry within their psychic typography generous portions of what Carl Jung calls *anima* and *animus*, the primary anthropomorphic archetypes of the human unconscious.[5] As an enduring part of human evolutionary development, this psychic hermaphroditism became a beneficial and entrenched balancing feature between the sexes that promoted child rearing, fostered culture, and ensured the survival of the species. This dichotomous nature, however, enabled its own hidden agenda. The dominance of an excess of assertive *anima* in males or dominant *animus* in a female was considered a mental disease that manifested itself in abnormal character traits and deviant sexual behaviour. Fear and mistrust subsequently bred a specter of evil officially imprecated by an opportunistic class of chauvinist, and often misogynist, leaders. Fundamentalists especially viewed any deviation from the established socio-political gender norm as a curse visited upon the tribe by disconnected individuals, be they male or female. While the fundamental differentiation between the two sexual principles are complementary forces forever attracted to one another, as polar opposites they are used to establish contextual and categorical impedimenta that must not be broached. The beast in men, in other words, was their feminine Other.

The active engagement with relations of Otherness or alterity is not determined a priori but in specific contexts of tribal, social, and cultural application. Contemporary culture has, for some time, played with the notion of socially acceptable and visually exhibited hermaphroditism. Needless to say, certain types of gendered subjectivism, including same sex, bisexual curiosity, transgender fashion, gay, rave, or simply cutting-edge radical fashion chic, impose an experimentation with new forms of social narrative more adequate to the cognitive aims of these shifting significations. Difficult to ground, the process is a struggle that bears no restrictions. The misogynist days of St. Augustine reverently opining on the evils of womankind or, flash forward, pop philosophers declaring that "men are from Mars, women from Venus" have the redolent odour of ancient history.[6] A social shift has occurred, some would consider it a paradigmatic convulsion that incites our fundamental androgyny, propels the acceptance of any and all sociocultural difference, and installs a too-often ill-tempered political correctness. This shift frequently feeds deeper undercurrents of pent-up misogyny, economic denial, and intolerance of the disenfranchised. The reasons for this change in Western thinking are myriad; the long-term future consequences of the shift are speculative and relatively unclear, but almost always alarmist. Whatever the eventual aftergrowth, it is abundantly apparent that both the medium and the message have changed and that contemporary culture has become either defensive, therefore revisiting and asserting orthodox values, or offensive, thereby aggressively promoting explorations of individual diversity.

This is nothing new. The historical reinforcement of the masculine *animus* at the expense of the feminine *anima* and the corresponding strengthening of left-brain rationalization over right-brain imagination has fostered the suppression of women's role in society and a general past abhorrence of image formation. Misogyny, patriarchy, and iconoclasm are the social manifestations that have fed upon this deep subtending sociological current. But there is a counterculture that runs against cherished masculine energy. The contentious usurping of word-based authorities by the sheer volume and ubiquity of contemporary images invites right-brain pattern skills to participate more fully in our cultural gestalt. Film has replaced the novel, the personal computer spurs an iconic revolution, and television pictures surge further changes in consciousness that promote a feminine world view. Though it is a commonplace in today's culture that the feminine principle has a power undreamed of by even the most sympathetic of past idolaters, image producing media (television, cinema, computers, iPods, iPads, smartphones, etc.) may be spawning a reconfiguration of the brain that only time will coalesce into an organic and discernible future event.[7] We are already engaged in a perceptive process that balances both hemispheres of the brain into greater equilibrium thereby producing more gender harmony and potential transcultural interdependency. For the moment, however, the changing role of men and the increasing entrenchment of heretofore anathematic subcultures in contemporary Western society have led to an appreciable emasculation of masculine paradigms. The gangster figure offers a viable site for investigating the changing social and sexual role of the contemporary American male. The media representation of the gangster "becomes a telling figure in the tale of American race, gender and ethnicity ..." It is a popular trope of the newly problematic mode of being, and remaining, a man's man in America. As such, it posits a symbolic mutilation that may psychologically handicap the transition between a self-identity entrenched in latent chauvinism and one reanimated by a liberally renovated manhood.[8]

Personality is constituted and differentiated through a myriad of life experiences that define character and help to form individual identity. Normally, a child identifies with someone else, usually a parent, and subsequently embodies the traits of his immediate genealogy. In the best scenario, this external example helps to structure the child's inner self by providing physical comfort and psychological security. In a disruptive and emotionally bereft situation, the resulting turmoil may cause grief and personal trauma. Traditions and rituals help assuage the passage of the child into the foreboding world of adulthood helping him to become a functioning member of the social group. Rituals of various kinds are common to all human cultures and though they vary from place to place, historical cultures celebrated a girl's menarche and a boy's pubescence with elaborate rites and ceremonies. A post-pubescent individual enjoyed all the once-prohibited privileges and secrets of the tribe, and gradually came to appreciate all the subtleties of local tradition. The fundamental difference between the male and female transition into puberty is that traditionally a man had to prove himself worthy of his developing manhood. Whether flirting with danger or taking an oath, the male adolescent's initiation ritual inculcates values that are important to his eventual incorporation into the group of dominant males.

Perhaps the best known media-spawned tradition that symbolically marks an insurmountable boundary for outsiders is the Mafia initiation rite of becoming a Made Man. The well-known mise en scène is a blood-sealed pact bathed in the aura of hierarchy and steeped in notions of virility. The bloodletting marks a vital passage, while the rite cements bonds, marks territory, erects barriers exclusive to men indentured to secrecy and committed to violence. The bond can only be broken by death.[9] The entire ritual is laced with homoerotic undertones that outwardly consolidate the masculine absoluteness of the sanguine enclave while internally forging the individual's self-worth within the group. The very sense of being a Mafioso is beholden to this formal staging of a Mafioso masculine identity. A Made Man's ultimate duty is indeed to learn to *act like a man*. This notion has several repercussions within the series, beginning with the nature of sonhood.

Made Men

The Sopranos is a realistic, tongue-in-cheek, and often hysterical exposé of a contemporary I-Am mob family boss grounded on the double entendre of the word *famiglia*. It is predicated on the primal, and in this case dysfunctional, relationship of a son with his mother, hence the need for the main character's need for therapy. Mothering implies the imparting to the child knowledge about the culture and the imprinting of notions of love, respect, honesty, curiosity, and especially self-esteem. For all the emphasis on patriarchy and manly pursuits in the series, it is the lack of a nurturing mother and the image of the evil *magma mater* that seems to condition many of the male characters and foments their misguided notions regarding women. Fathers, however, are also absent. Tony Soprano is the only character who normally interacts with his children, dutifully and intuitively performing his paternal role since he, too, is essentially orphaned.[10] This emotional dysfunctionality marks the manliness of the Soprano crew and conditions their survival in the criminal underworld. It determines their place in the tribal hierarchy. Rather than encountering steeled men whose sense of violent purpose reflects that traditionally encountered in mobster films, these characters display a fragility that undermines their masculinity and consolidates an aberrant sense of sexual identity. The self, in other words, is more conditioned towards feeling than towards reasoning, towards empty rituals rather than empowering gestures; hence, the bumbling and comedic episodes that accompany their interactions with the more seasoned mobsters from New York. Actions are often reactions to self-preservative desires that spring from within but often buckle under the set priorities of the code they have adopted as their life creed and which lead therefore, to internal strife, self-questioning, and subsequent comedic conflict. There are generous portions of both *anima* and *animus* in all the male Sopranos characters. They all live on the razor's edge of public displays of masculinity and private psychological fears of a latent, therefore misunderstood, femininity.

The figure of Tony Soprano, of course, is of primary concern. Beyond the publicized nature of his double life (nurturing father of one family, dreaded boss of another), the root causes of his schizophrenia are a destructive bipolar mother and an absent hoodlum father. The domineering mother deprived him of a viable and stable masculine identity. The absent father compounded the trauma and heightened the mother's debilitating influence. Tony is basically a momma's boy who has sheathed his marshmallow interior with a boisterous external armour. Though confused, he refuses to allow his *anima* to effloresce, much to his psychological detriment. Not only would it not be manly, but in his line of work, it would be deadly (as the ads for the first season proclaimed: "If one family doesn't kill him ... the other family will"). Dr. Melfi's attempts to cure Tony by holding up a mirror to his existential angst result in some of the more tense moments between them and pushes the program to explore issues otherwise alien to this world of guns and vendetta.

As the eldest of three children and the only son of Livia and Giovanni Francis "Johnny Boy" Soprano, Tony is expected to follow in his father's footsteps. Johnny Soprano died when Tony was still a teenager, before the child could be initiated by the father into the world of adults. His father is introduced to us through a series of flashbacks that depict an impulsive hooligan with little regard for the public displays of his violence, even less for their psychological implications on his children. Tony recalls witnessing occasions when his father beat a man senseless on a neighbourhood street corner ("Down Neck" I.7), chopped off Mr. Satriale's pinkie ("Fortunate Son" III.3), and was arrested by police for racketeering ("Down Neck" I.7). Tony observes the merciless and repulsive behaviour of his father first as a casual bystander as a youth and, second, in his mind's eye, as a patient in Dr. Melfi's office. This is a defensive strategy that both distances and compartmentalizes the potential conflict these experienced events should normally procure both in the child *then* and the man *now*. But they don't. This vertical split in his psyche has allowed him to rationalize violence as a means of settling accounts and of doing what's right according to the relived memories of his father. Everything becomes a matter of distorted principle, of misconceived honour and misplaced patriarchal loyalty that is tinged with the same irony and tragic consequences that drive the inward-looking narrative of Michael Corleone.[11] His ritualistic initiation into the world of Made Men, and the idealized memory world of his father, performed the public function of asserting his father's residual definition of manhood. The same ritual, however, did not consolidate a private inner sense of a solid foundation of masculine identity.

Exactly the opposite. Tony uses the mob as an ideal father substitute. The mythic trappings of loyalty, respect, and honour become a substitute for the paternal affection that is lacking in the disincarnated son. The ingrained respect for established hierarchy in the clan is not a positive influence because it is not counterbalanced by affection. Tony is caught in limbo. He is an eternal son, unable to establish a coherent internal structure and therefore develops aggressive attitudes and rampant sexuality that follow lines of childish abstraction and unsatisfied adolescent objectification. His relationship with women is repressive, needy, and shallow. Tony is often chided for his childish behaviour by Carmela. His goomahs question his affection and often feel his self-serving wrath. He attempts to compensate by structuring himself from the outside. The more fragile he feels internally, the harder the outer shell, the more prone to identify with prevailing stereotypes and superficial notions of stolid manhood. Even fellow mobsters question his suitability as a boss given his penchant for changing the rules to suit his temperamental, and often prurient, personal gain. His foray into psychiatry merely exacerbates personal notions of weakness and fragility. A visual sign that he has not grown out of adolescence is the telling remark made to him by Carmine Lupertazzi, a respected old-world Mustache Pete of the New York Lupertazzi crime family: "John said he went to a cookout at your house. A Don doesn't wear shorts" ("For All Debts Public and Private" IV.1).

Tony's lack of attention from his father results in his inability to truly identify with him, regardless of how atrocious his behaviour, to literally grow up and subsequently establish his own courageous identity. Though he remembers his father fondly, he deflects paternal memories and personal trauma with mocking humour. We recall that when Dr. Melfi reacts with sympathetic horror to Tony's account of his witnessing his father's brutal lopping off of Mr. Satriale's pinkie finger with a meat cleaver, he plays down the melodrama and is satirically flippant: "What?" he wisecracks. "Your father never cut off anybody's pinkie?" ("Fortunate Son" III.3). Indeed, returning to the memory of Mr. Satriale's missing pinkie, Tony recalls that while waiting for dinner, his father did not scold him for not obeying his demand that he wait in the car. Instead, his father complimented him. "A lot of boys your age would have run like a little girl, but you stayed" ("Fortunate Son" III.3). The lesson schools him in his father's code of masculinity. A limited and incomplete code since his father's premature death robbed him of a reliable father figure. His father is essentially absent from his physical and psychological teenage formation. Deprived, therefore, of any sort of security and masculine confirmation, he is unable to advance to a psychologically whole adulthood and remains in a state of spiritual and emotional void. In the absence of a legitimate role model, Tony is vexed instead by a substitute surrogate uncle-cum-father whose Alzheimer-induced verbal barbs trigger an affection-starved adult Tony to ask imploringly, "Don't you love me?" ("Where's Johnny?" III.3).[12] Given the emotional void that envelops him, his only recourse is to *act like a man* in the only way he assumes would have met his father's approval. He thus dissipates his public persona (fails at high school football, drops out of college) and creates an ulterior identity by disappearing into the underworld of his father.

As a mobster he is unrecognized by society save for the publicity of his crimes played on the nightly news, disrespected by his family save for his role as economic provider. He is an outsider, a loner condemned to a world of silence where those who speak are a threat to male security and solidarity. His pseudo-independence is really a form of self-absorption, emotional denial, and self-imprisonment. Though he is a father figure to his underlings (although even this fated love is questioned in the series), their incompetence merely belies the structural frailty of his family and of his paternal qualities as leader. His constructed masculine identity needs constant reinforcement and validation by similarly disposed masculine presences that crave the same attention and personal favour. In this sense, his ballooning and hulking exterior is a shield of power and strength that in the end is really just fat.[13] While Tony's corpulence and frame emphatically display his ability to effectively muscle his way within his sacred brotherhood, his actions reveal a seething and frustrated inner child given to limitless self-gratification and gratuitous violence. There are, in essence, two Tonys ("Two Tonys" is the title of episode V.1) – the gentle one that he wishes to display to Dr. Melfi, and the monstrous one that, as the viewer ascertains, moves beyond the double nature of being a family man and into the realm of pathology.

Guy Corneau uses the medieval story of Percival, one of King Arthur's legendary knights, to illustrate the separation between body and mind in the divided male self. For Corneau, in this story, "we see the tragic consequences of constructing masculinity entirely in the outside world and the resulting loss of man's inner identity."[14] He finds the knight's armour a significant symbol of constructed external masculinity. It provides a robust, relatively indestructible structure capable of standing erect even on its own, a symbol of its own volition, withstanding external assaults and protecting his interior vulnerability.[15] Tony's steely frame and studied facade is an apt metaphor for Percival's armour. His story, too, is similar to that of the young medieval knight. Percival lives with his mother, has never known his father, and his brothers have all died at war. Raised by his mother in a world of feminine principles (Tony lives with his mother and sisters), the young man is ill equipped to face the world. At the age of puberty, and against the wishes of his mother, he leaves home to pursue the ideals of chivalry. Before leaving, his mother makes him swear an oath to silence (*omertà*), a pledge that he would hold his tongue in society. On his first adventure he saves a young maiden from the Scarlet Knight whose vermillion armour he steals and dons over the humble peasant clothes sewed for him by his mother. Literally steeled with his newly found, stolen, and grossly misunderstood masculinity, he seduces then abandons the maiden and continues on his journey. After a series of adventures, all of which see women suffer the brunt of his irascible and puerile masculine impulses, Percival is offered redemption. His initiation into Arthur's Knights of the Round Table offered a civilizing subtext premised upon metaphors redolent of feminine connotations: compassion, reflection, nurturing, and kindness. After a troubled period of apprenticeship and learning, a befuddled and desperately fundamentalist knight sets out to conquer the world. Unfortunately, his adventures are continuously self-serving and ill-thought. Though he is revered as a conquering hero, his obsession with male heroism and his staged outward virility exacerbate his meagre regard for women. Instead, he vigorously disassociates himself from what he perceives to be his feminine and plaguing weak inner nature, and projects this troubled self-repulsion onto the outside world.

Tony and Percival exhibit similar characteristics. Both symbolically carry the desultory legacy of the mother beneath their adamantine exteriors. Both were never properly weaned from the mother figure due to the absence of a caring father. Their nascent masculine identities, therefore, relied solely upon the accepted models of comportment provided by male relatives, friends, or male sects vowed to the preservation of masculine principles. The tragic consequence of constructing masculinity in this fashion is the loss of a stable inner core and reliance upon facile and mechanistic rules of comportment. Percival's violence is sanctioned by a misunderstood knightly code; Tony's ruffian antics are shielded by a criminal code of *omertà*. Both crave the reassuring accouterments of traditional symbols and gender-mediated formalities. In both stories, the newly formed man internalizes his latent feminine attributes, ashamed when they surface, concurrently secreting an aggressive external framework to hide the self-perceived inner frailty. In short, not knowing how to act like men, both mimic what is considered acceptable male activity.[16] We recall that at the end of "Boca" I.9, Tony must drink himself senseless in order to overlook his inexcusable blunder at not having whacked Meadow's soccer coach for having molested one of the team members. A disconsolate and "out-of-self" Tony woefully laments his momentary frailty to Carmela: "Carmela. Carmela. I didn't hurt nobody. Call the shrink. Tell her the town's been given a fuckin' bonus." This is outward rage turned inward against himself because he has breached his own manly protocols.[17]

This atypical behaviour causes Tony much confusion, consternation, and conflict both psychologically and physically. The aptitude for abstraction and objectification is subsequently forever lost since the primary life focus is the reinforcement of the ritualistic norms that the individual has grudgingly accepted. Percival's and Tony's search for strong male figures as a substitute for their own diminished self-worth often leads them to develop negatively against the mother and, subsequently, the female. These men structure themselves from the outside, surrounding themselves with the trappings of masculinity since they lack a viable internal gyroscope. The more they feel fragile, the harder the shell that insulates them. From bulging muscles to silent moods, swastika tattoos to suits of armour, stereotypical expressions of male power and strength become a secure refuge and source of fixed masculine inspiration.[18]

Masculinity is thus defined in negative terms. Real men don't cry, are not sensitive; they repress emotion and act macho. Manhood for these individuals is proved through confrontation. To be a man is to amputate one's heart and body and substitute them for an avatar of prolific virility and gender domination. Women are thus appendages ("cunts" Tony calls them, referring to Adriana La Cerva after her murder, but it is clear that he indicts all women; they are conquered handkerchiefs to be tied to Percival's lance), actors in a script of well-worn words, platitudes, and amorous scenarios. Since both are unable to truly understand the ways of the world, radical male bonding becomes the sole medium for their differentiation from the female (mother). Of course this process never properly occurs for either figure due to the lack of a blood father figure. Both succumb to the lure of a male-only society of warriors sworn to fealty and devoted to hierarchy, whose parameters are often clandestine, whose ends may be illegal, but whose ethos is undifferentiated and homophobic. They are trapped in their own listlessness, finding comfort only in the gamut of fantasies of the disincarnated father image that pursues them. Their reality is role playing, of being the tough guy, of climbing to the top of the heap. This constant self-denial, along with the continued abrogation of emotion, subtends an unconscious desire for physical pain that must be satiated through membership into the clan and acceptance through initiation; something both find in their respective brotherhoods.[19] A disconsolate Tony joins the fellowship of the mob; an unredeemable Percival joins the Knights of the Round Table.

The role of the father, here represented as either the Patron Saint of the mob family or as stalwart King Arthur, gives meaning to the disorientation the initiate feels. In order to gain entry into this world of men, youth must learn to suffer, withstand pain, to tame and master the debilities they carry within. The pricking of the finger to draw blood, a wound ritualistically inflicted by the father (Don) of the family, acquires mythic significance, just as significant as the dubbing of a youth into knighthood by the king. Both ceremonies are founts of honour that christen the initiate with an indelible responsibility. But instead of liberating the individual, the ritual imprisons him in a permanent state of dependent immaturity. Absence of the father in a child's life thus trips a process of idealization and allegiance to the image of a substitute father, a Don, a liege. This ideal father poses no limits save those of the caste to which they are beholden. This absence of external social limits again engenders feelings of inadequacy in the individual who is neither willing nor able to respect authority beyond that to which he has expressed fealty. These sons are more apt to become delinquents, abuse drugs and alcohol, revolt against social norms. In spite of all of society's machinery throughout the ages, the tension between the desires of one's own private nature and the moral imperatives of public culture remain. They are manifest in many of our myths; they are dissentiently bequeathed by Tony to his son Anthony Junior.

Mad Sons

The figure of the son is one of those ethno-packaged stereotypical frames of Italian Americana. Sometimes buffoonish (Vinnie Barbarino of *Welcome Back, Kotter*, 1975–9), sometimes sexy (Tony Manero of *Saturday Night Fever*, 1977), sometimes oafish (Marty Piletti of *Marty*, 1955), often virulent and emotionally disturbed (Charlie of *Mean Streets*, 1973), the media portrait of I-Am sons paints them as lost private souls in search of a different, and liberating, public identity. Invariably, all push forward towards a melting pot resolution rather than reaching into their own cultural past in search of the stability of their nebulous origins. In short, though their ontogeny is ethnic, their actions and motivations move beyond the neighbourhood and towards New World sovereignty, individuality, and power. In all these cases, it is the mother who represents culture and is the de facto guiding principle in the youth's life. When the mother is absent, the character is normally portrayed as an intemperate loner with no family ties, and cast as the mythic lone heroe of past and present lore.When the father is absent, the character is cast as being deprived of the emotional confirmation and unreserved security of a father's true, active, guiding, and sustained presence, and he is unable to successfully advance to adulthood. Such is the case with Tony Soprano; but he vows it will not be so for his son.

It was to be different for A.J. While the overbearing mother–son relationship he suffers is encrypted into the media psyche of I-Am portrayals of sons, in *The Sopranos*, Tony is not an absent father. Quite the contrary. Having tacitly understood the dilemma of his own inherent inadequacies, he wants to "save this kid" (Tony's words) not only from the psychological trauma of growing up Soprano but also from the strong-arm tactics, murders, attacks, and threats useful to the quotidian world that he inhabits. The fact that A.J. suffers from panic attacks, a genetic tic Tony discovers runs in the family (his father, Hesh Rabkin reveals, also suffered from fainting spells, "In Camelot" V.7), only exacerbates his feelings of inadequacy as a role model for his son. "I want him to like me ... not be like me," Tony confesses to Dr. Melfi. But it seems inevitable that A.J. will eventually follow in the footsteps of his father. Offspring maintain an unwilled yet slavish adherence to genetically preprogrammed behaviour, reinforcing the adage that one may free things from alien or accidental laws, but not from the laws of their own nature. Throughout the series, A.J. enacts a process of disidentification from his father that seems perfectly normal for any growing teen. Irresponsible capriciousness, impulsive school pranks, psychologically confirmed fidgeting, attest to his attention-grabbing moments that serve to foment the tension that sporadically erupts between father and son. His juvenile pranks, association with unsavoury friends, disrespect for authority, even his stress-induced panic attacks are all symptomatic of A.J.'s unconscious cultivation/rejection of the father figure. These moments erect barriers to that same figure he craves and secretly nurtures. His mythological idealization of the father results from a negative father complex that prevents him from acknowledging Tony's good side. Yet this same idealization induces him to rebel against his own commitments towards a separate wholeness apart from the father.

A.J. eventually succumbs to the lure of the father's legacy not because he has no occupational alternatives or life choices, but because he was born into the heredity of silence that marks the world of his family. "Walk Like a Man" VI.17, an episode that sees his existential crisis come to a head, begins with a rare view of the mural in the master bedroom, which was identifed above as being the female heart of the family's inner sanctum. The viewer first encounters this mural upon the death of Livia Soprano; it is the heraldic master text of the Soprano family inheritance. It is interesting that it should appear again at this juncture of A.J.'s evolving story. This heraldic crest is indeed an emblem of his undeniable birthright. Though he is yet to become privy to the mural's message and seems driven by the helter-skelter winds of his troubled teenage years, the existential vessel of his life is never really threatened, his life path never really questioned. Though he may suffer the anxiety of non-being and outwardly manifest behaviour aberrant to his father's will, this non-being is part of his own finitude. The path he eventually accepts at his father's side, random as it may seem, is forged in the same crucible as that of his father. It belongs to that same being-self that transcends any possible threat of non-being because he too, like his sister, will live towards, and not away from, Soprano family values.[20]

For this reason, when Tony is in a coma, A.J. refuses to publicly acknowledge the possibility of his death, preferring to act like the man his father would have wanted. When he refers to his mortally wounded father as Anthony Soprano mob boss, not father, he is replicating Michael Corleone's bedside pact with Vito Corleone in *The Godfather* ("I'm with you, Pop") as mob boss. Like Michael, a different A.J. resurrects the morning after his overnight stay at the hospital with his father. Out of the public eye, A.J. is able to regress and regenerate a private bond with his albeit unconscious genetic imprinter. The overnight vigil reinforces an indelible connection to what he knows is the repulsive side of his own Soprano nature. He comes away with the courage, but not the smarts, to take his first steps towards ritual acts of spiritual self-affirmation. The spectacle of his father's open wound implies that the masculine principle has been severed in the household and that it is incumbent upon A.J. to publicly redress the treachery perpetrated by a blood relative, his great-uncle Corrado "Junior" Soprano. The location of the wound is also important. It is in the middle of the body, the region that divides the upper and lower body, separating the organs that contain the noble attributes (brain, heart) from the more inferior ones (intestines, genitals). The wound is life threatening, but not fatal. It does, however, present a veiled reference to castration. Tony has symbolically lost the power to engender and regenerate. Along with avenging his father, A.J. is precociously summoned to assume the vital role of family genitor. But the wound has also disincarnated Tony spiritually. Unbeknownst to A.J., his father is navigating the dark seas of transcendental awareness while in his coma. It is as if he has been cleaved from the repulsive side of his nature, hence the prolonged coma dream of another, more solar life as Albert Finnerty. In much the same manner that shamans helped initiates navigate that crack in the universe that leads to an entirely different order of reality, so too Tony's silent presence permits A.J. to contemplate his own inner logic and dreams, to face his non-being in the most radical way in order to set himself on the path that eventually leads to his essential Soprano being.

The moment portends an inevitable undermining of the viewer's rational expectations. Instead of appearing weak, A.J. summons up a concentrated rush of strength typical of youth undergoing rites of initiation and, after his requisite night of waiting, swears to his father that he will begin his journey towards manhood by avenging family honour. Faced with the dilemma of "what to do" after being continuously chastised by parents for his indifference, the oath represents an intensification of masculinity and those values traditionally linked to the masculine principle. The fact that he sports long hair in these scenes only reinforces the approaching metaphysical death and rebirth of the individual. Long hair is a cultural marker connoting different significations, depending upon social status, religious restrictions, or stages of life. In some primitive cultures, long hair is a phallic image of virility, a symbolic reliving of the primal rite of passage from the position of weak prey to mature predator. A.J.'s newly found resolve places him on a course of deliberate predatory action that is marked, in his case, by mob mores but that follow the path of the classic hero.[21] These mores include the rejection of others' feelings, a denial of social responsibility, and the imposition of physical, non-intellectual, control. Through A.J., the viewer is allowed to intimate the turbulent teen years of Tony when he, too, we are informed by his uncle in the pilot episode, had long hair and smoked pot ("The Sopranos" I.1). His sluggishness and incompetence (he is reminded by his mother), ineptitude at sports (annoyingly prodded by his Uncle Junior), and "slacker attitude" (for which Coach Molinaro admonishes him in "The Test Dream" V.11), connect father and son in a trans-generational dance of missed vital cues. The coach's words are particularly hurtful. He accuses Tony of wasting his life, of not living up to his leadership potential. These words haunt Tony throughout his life as attested to by the admitted frequency of "the Molinaro Dream" (as he calls it) to Carmela. This misguided youthful ambition is revisited upon his son's increasingly deviant antics. Tony's father, we recall, died before Tony embarked upon his own career of ravenous gangsterism. Did Tony, too, make a silent pact with his absent father to follow in his footsteps? Were his wayward antics as a teen a similar revolt against a pained decision to join the underworld?

The hospital vow that A.J. swears before his father is a sacred covenant, an awesome bloodletting that must be confronted and fulfilled if he is to transition successfully from paradigms of weakness (absence, partiality, foolishness, silence, continence, etc.) to positions of strength (presence, totality, sagacity, speech, sexuality, etc.). Like his father before him, he asseverates his fealty to a father figure who, for all practical purposes, has been reduced to a corpse in a darkened hospital room. Like his father, A.J. is sublimating conscious growth in favour of reckless instinct. Unfortunately, A.J.'s misplaced filial loyalties foment a rage that leads him to an ill-thought-out and dreadfully fumbled attempt at murdering his great-uncle Junior. He does so to garner favour with his father, to psychologically fulfil the passage to manhood, to become a (Made) man. But the botched attack infuriates Tony and he confronts his son fuelled by generational angst and the exploded personal expectations for his son:

> TONY: Stupid fuckin' moron. Do you realize what could have happened to you if we didn't have connections? Some cop goes by the book and they charge you with attempted murder. You hear me! Attempted murder! Then what! Then what!
> A.J.: So what? He shot you! You just gonna let him get away with it!
> TONY: I told you that's my fuckin' business not yours! And what did you do? Nothin'! Zero! A big fuckin' jerkoff!

> A.J.: Fuck you!
> TONY: I otta' break your fuckin' neck!

A.J.'s tears break Tony's barrage of insults. A sympathetic father consoles his son.

> TONY: Stop cryin'! Stop cryin'! I guess your heart was in the right place, A.J. But it's wrong ... It's not in your nature.

The belittlement embitters A.J. Tony has questioned his genealogy, marked him with the sign of Cain, and flagrantly branded him an outsider to his father's realm. Because of his public failure he remains an exclusively private figure whose past portends no future. Essentially reduced to a non-entity, he remains betwixt and between, stuck in the throes of the rite of passage. While the filial tie remains because of descent and emotional bonds, the son has failed the rite of incorporation and remains symbolically detached from the community of men that Tony Soprano so zealously represents. The father's condescending tone reinforces the indeterminate attributes that define the son's liminal condition:

> TONY: You're a nice guy and that's a good thing for Christ sakes! ... I mean it. You're a good guy and I'm very grateful.

The son now confronts his father, in essence exploring the limits of his own present and future identity by emptying the content of his most precious memory of his father at his progenitor's feet:

> A.J.: Well you're a fuckin' hypocrite, 'cause every time we watch *Godfather*, when Michael Corleone shoots those guys at the restaurant, those assholes that tried to kill his dad, you sit there with your fuckin' bowl of ice cream and you say it's your favourite scene of all time!

A.J.'s motivations are rooted not only in the Mafia-inspired signs and gestures of pop culture but also in the emotional aspirations and empathy of his father. Both the fumbled action of killing his great-uncle and his heartfelt confession to his father assume multiple resonances. A.J. is making his voice heard by confronting his own disincarnated masculinity and the problems it has engendered. His androgynous appearance, unkempt hair, and deliberate neglect of personal care are typical of initiatory patterns. Like any initiate, he follows the footsteps of those male elders he must respect but fears to emulate. The price is high. In his father's world, murder is an acceptable gesture. The act would have marked him as being on the path towards manhood. It would have also suppressed his feelings of ineptitude and those realms of human weakness which do not fit the mould of the Mafioso. After all, had not his father become a legend by becoming a Made Man after usurping the normal rules of comportment and jumping the queue to "make his bones"?

In "Amour Fou" III.12, we are informed that a precocious teenage Tony earned his Mafia stripes by highjacking a weekly poker game run by the bosses of the family. There were no injuries and the stolen money was equitably returned. The incident, however, confirmed the young thug's courage and capabilities. He quickly moved up the ranks to eventually become boss. Teenage Tony's misguided but successful act of bravado is revisited in his son's singular act of ill-conceived courage. One would think Tony would be proud of a teenage boy who attempts to emulate his father's gestures in order to become a true son of the father. A successful murder could have been an official passage from adolescence to manhood, an attempt for A.J. to recover possession of his body and emotions. Tony may chastise him for regressing to the use of movie models, for acting, in other words, like a child, but cannot repress the fatherly warmth. Tony fully understands that A.J. is not a budding Made Man but merely a Mad Boy who is beginning to understand his nefarious pedigree and who wrestles with his own probable destiny. A suppliant father gently admonishes his child: "Jesus Christ, A.J. You make me wanna cry. It's a movie. You gotta grow up. You're not a kid anymore. You hear me? You gotta grow up." Chase allows the moment to move beyond the actual business of (a) a father reprimanding a son and, (b) A.J.'s failure to successfully transition the rites which accompany every change of place, state, social position, and age by installing (c) a metacritique of the fictions of Mafia culture. Viewers of *The Sopranos*, after all, are not uninitiated, nor are they innocent. They, too, however, like A.J., are bogged down in the loss of meaning that the multi-voicing of movie mob stereotypes entrenches. By castigating A.J., Tony is demystifying the socially assigned gangster resonances and the critically assigned aesthetic assumptions in these films. It is as if the viewer is being chastised for understanding the intertextual references between *The Sopranos* and Mafia movies that include *The Godfather*. Just as Tony's bad parenting has forever scarred A.J., these movies have marked the viewer with an indelible societal stain.

While the father in Tony acknowledges that indeed *The Godfather* is "only a movie," he envelops his son in a language he himself knows is not worth learning. In essence, Tony refuses to imprint A.J. because he senses his own emotional fragments in the trembling child. He can see the wrenching and painful ritual of becoming a man that is etched in the features of A.J.'s face. Appropriately, in "Walk Like a Man" VI.17, the viewer once again sees Tony with the same look of aggrieved vexation as he sits in Dr. Melfi's anteroom. Importantly, he is no longer framed between the green statue's legs. We are almost at series' end and Tony has travelled far from his initial rudderless musings about his own manhood. No longer confused, he glares at the statue, fully cognizant of its debilitating meaning. He is concerned for the well-being of his son vis-à-vis the green virago's generational influence. Unlike the opening scene of the pilot episode, no words are spoken by Dr. Melfi. It is Tony who speaks. He is calling it quits. "It's over." Or so he thinks. But he grudgingly admits that his son is in need of counselling. He is contemplating suicide and is questioning, as is Tony, Soprano family values. Those private values ensconced in his bedroom mural and the feminine beast Soprano men carry within have assailed A.J. The equilibrium of male identity is a fragile one. A.J. repudiates his mother, which is normal for a boy attempting to wrest his body away from the mother, and prefers to live with his father, but he swings constantly between the nostalgia for a regression back to the security of the wholesome feminine and the inevitable individuality of the masculine. The muddled dropping of the knife when attempting to kill his great-uncle not only demonstrates his ineptitude to fulfil the traditional male role of hunter but also alludes to the castrated stance that plumets him into a regressive angst. This process of disidentification threatens his self-worth both privately as a son and publicly as a functioning member of his social circle. The inability to successfully complete the task of avenging his father precipitates his crossing the fault line on his way towards a premature psychological and physical death.

Ritualistic rites of passage are loaded with the metaphoric power of narrative and the theatrical complexity of tradition. Every action, every symbolic item opens a space where dramas may be enacted to alter social roles or status. Within this transitional space or limen, the actant is separated from the every day and enacts socially subversive and ritually inversive structures that are related to some empirical item of experience. To be sure, the cultural and social dimensions of this predictably confrontational adventure shapes the fortunes of the inductee as he is eventually incorporated into the customary routines of the group or, upon failure, rejected into the limbo of ostracism. Unfortunately, A.J.'s basic building blocks of life are resting on nefarious ground. His cosmogonic narrative is limited to his experience as a member of a New Jersey I-Am mob family, while his role models have been gleaned from mobster films. He learns at a young age the power of his surname when a rival he confronts on the school grounds over owed money retreats from the predictable schoolyard brawl because he fears the Soprano reputation ("Meadowlands" I.4). This unfortunate secret weapon affects his social demeanour as a teen. As he strives to distance himself from his family, his shyness bespeaks a deprecating swagger that strives to mask the powerful lure of his birthright. But he cannot escape the legacy he uncomfortably bears. He bridles when his New York friends brag to others that his father is *"capo di tutti i capi"* ("Johnny Cakes" VI.8). In order to escape this existential merry-go-round, he must perform a revelatory act. Using Victor Turner's words, he must "go into the hole of life and pass through the tunnel to the hole of death."[22] A.J.'s bungled attempted murder of his "mummy uncle"[23] is just such a hole. It is a liminal experience shrouded in the exegesis of ritual. One that he hopes will allow him entry into the world of men, the unfortunate but only world he truly craves, the world of his father. But the botched murder attempt is indeed revelatory. It reveals A.J.'s continuing liminality and exposes his implicit ineptitude. Unable to gain entry into the world of men, he withdraws to the comfort of adolescence, spends his time watching cartoons, and submits to a limbo of statuslessness.[24] As he slowly regains a shadowy semblance of his unfortunate former self, his path sets him on a precarious course that leads back to the polarizing routines he had so wished to conquer. Dead-end jobs, alcohol, and drugs do little to assuage a gnawing inner void. Once again his peers esteem his company for his name, not his virtue.

A.J.'s relation with Blanca Selgada is an effort to exorcise his odious heritage, to begin a new white page (the name Blanca means white in Spanish), to initiate a sobering chapter replete with personified images of a new imaginative fiction. Like Kay Adams in *The Godfather* films, Blanca is a life line, the access way to a new gene pool and newfound responsibilities as a companion.[25] The semantic valence of the gesture is heroic. The fact that he wilfully accepts the fictional role of father to her child crystallizes his detachment from his own father by placing him on the same paternal footing, something that normally happens when a son marries and fathers a child. Tony the father is no longer a threat because he is no longer a rival. The nature of their relationship thus changes. The newly hatched positioning, however, is ultimately solipsistic. A.J.'s fictions are deep and have their own body and their own will. As such, they remain closed to any outside rationalization.

At this point, Chase introduces an interesting parallel storyline to augment A.J.'s transformative narrative. Having learned of his father's homosexuality, Vito Spatafore's young son abruptly changes his placid identity and becomes a despondent, psychologically ravaged teen with identity confusion ("Chasing It" VI.15).The similarities in their woes are strident. Both teens risk being labelled losers by their more socially adept peers. Both seek socially meaningful contexts outside of their heredity in order to live the symbolic structures of their befuddled psyches. Both react from the midst of depression. Father Tony is the mediating force, the shaman who understands the incumbencies that coexist between the two youths. He is called upon by Vito's mother to heal her son. His initial reaction to young Vito Spatafore is patent: "Your dad's gone. You're the man now. Start acting like it." Unable and unwilling to dedicate his time to the wayward young Vito, Tony deflects personal responsibility and opts to send the boy to a tough-love youth camp. At the same time, A.J. attempts to "man-up" for Blanca in "Kaisha" VI.12 by getting rid of noisy neighbourhood lugs hanging out beneath Blanca's window. He too deflects manly responsibility and opts for negotiation instead of violence. He barters his new bike in lieu of his self-admittedly inadequate fists. The gesture renders him a Shakespearean fool masked in ridicule, absurdly lashing out at the world as he quotes Rodney King calling for an end to all wars, flippantly railing against the vicissitudes of global strife. The context of these symbolic behaviours suggests that both are chimeric individuals that do not accept the DNA bequeathed them. They are unhappy wanderers in search of another father. The dispatching of Vito Jr. places him outside the viewer's, and Tony's, purview. A.J., however, remains embroiled in separation, stewing in his own juices[26] as he is unable to transition to a healing haven.

His continuing rites of separation come to an abrupt end with the loss of Blanca. After she returns his engagement ring ("Chasing It" VI.16), A.J.'s drive for self-affirmation devolves into a quest for self-destruction. He again falls into depression. At this juncture the malady is more mature, riveted in existential angst rather that adolescent disquiet. His therapy confirms a deep-set antipathy towards his embodied heritage. His grandmother's prophetic panegyric rave haunts him: "It's all a big nothing. In the end, your friends and family let you down. In the end you die in your own arms" ("D-Girl" II.7 and "The Second Coming" VI. 19), while the morbidly toxic and chiliastic poetry of Yeats' "The Second Coming" sanctions his apocalyptic resolve. In the end, A.J.'s imploding images are his keepers. He becomes instead the oblique paradigm of his own introspective fiction. Having exhausted what he considers his options, he surrenders to the lure of non-being. The anxiety attendant on his fears of being crushed, engulfed, and overwhelmed by the realness of his false aliveness slowly lead him towards his ultimate act of defiance. A.J. attempts suicide by trying to drown himself in the family pool in "The Second Coming" VI.19. For all its disturbing aspects, the blundered stunt (the cinder block he ties to his foot is on too long a rope) bursts asunder his unified world of protracted childhood. It is a voluntary act that seals a violent contact with the reality of the universe and destroys the blind dependency he has constructed around himself. Ever louder than the words he belches at his father following the botched attempt on his great-uncle's life, the inelegant ineptitude of the act only heightens the incalculable importance of shattering the constraints of the father. He must develop a new existential narrative. But in order to undercut his condition of grotesque impotence, to halt his spiritual demise, he has to die physically It is a causal schema whose unfolding unveils the earnest intentionality of personal salvation and the embracing of a new untold story. A.J. is essentially born again; extracted from the symbolic baptismal water by his father. The episode is appropriately titled "The Second Coming" VI.19.

Tony is indeed incensed; unable to comprehend his son's gesture but cognizant of its hidden connotations. Like a desperate mother, he coddles the water-soaked body of his son in an exquisitely posed pietà posture; this son who has just attempted to take the life he begat and that he no longer admonishes to "grow up." Lovingly stroking his head in much the same manner that his imaginary mother gently stroked his own infant head in "Isabella" I.12, both return to childhood, to a preternatural space of comfort and affection, before the trauma of growing-up Soprano had become the fodder for suicide.[27]

While recovering from his mental breakdown in a psychiatric hospital, A.J. spots Rhiannon Flammer,[28] a patient recovering from anorexia and a member of the social group he used to frequent while clubbing in Manhattan. They renew their friendship and after leaving hospital decide to become a couple. Their reciprocal passion eventually leads them on a drive in A.J.'s new SUV (which Tony bought for him) into the woods. A.J. parks on a pile of leaves and, as he and Rhiannon become overheated in the car, the SUV's catalytic converter overheats to the point of igniting the dry leaves ("Made in America" VI.21). The two transitioning souls emerge from potential death unscathed. One could stretch the metaphor to state that they have survived their baptism by fire. But A.J. is still running from himself. He still needs to prove that he can indeed "act like a man" and so decides to join the Army. As if to adumbrate his son's newfound resolve, when Tony encounters A.J. jogging roadside, he lowers the window of his SUV and sings bars of the *Rocky* (1976) theme song.[29] Though A.J. had once boasted to his friends that "There's no fuckin' way I'm goin' in the Army" ("Everybody Hurts" IV.6) he is a signature away from joining the ranks. Tony has no choice but to co-opt his son into the family business. This is a misguided, but expected, move to prevent his son from leaving the fold. Carmela favours the decision. She had expressed reservations about sending A.J. to a military academy in order to straighten out the boy and considers a military career equally inappropriate. She is not contrary to removing A.J. from one cadre of gendered rules, regulations, and regimentation (the Army) and placing him squarely into a similarly ritualized, illegal, and secret organization called the family business. The trade-off is that their son remains a fortiori under their control. A.J. willingly capitulates and receives a renewed lease on a future life of corrupted prosperity. With Carmela's blessing, Tony arranges an entry-level job producing pornographic films. Suddenly the clouds over sad sack A.J. dissipate. No longer subjugated to existential angst or obsessed with the plight of the world, he has learned that concern for humanity is admirable but illegality and wealth is an easier road to travel. As we see him settle into his black BMW M3 and drive to Montclair High School to pick up Rhiannon, his blond girlfriend, the viewer intimates a similar scenario lived by a teenage Tony and his blond heart-throb Carmela. A.J. is indeed his father's son. But the viewer knows that while Tony is not the monolithic and unthinking man his father was, A.J. will never reach the nefarious heights of his father. Tony is nevertheless hopefully optimistic that A.J. will carry on in the business, competently or not, however the case may be. After all, Tony often opines, blood is blood. But, of course. Tony Soprano, we are reminded by Fred Gadarphé, "is the last of the wiseguys."[30] In this sense, A.J. represents the coming apart or "unravelling" of the wiseguy paradigm because any prediction of his viability as a successful underworld character is wrought with uncertainty and proven ineptitude. Just as Tony comes to accept his fate, so too will A.J. In the last episode of the series, "Made in America," he will reiterate his father's words from the last episode of season two, "Funhouse." "Concentrate on the good things," he elatedly pronounces, much to the approbation of both his doting mother and his incredulous, though superbly appreciative and grateful father.

The Brotherhood of Prodigal Sons

For all of the men initiated into the brotherhood, weaker members are problematic. These indeterminate characters are anything but anomalous but carry an undeniable visual weight. Their presence within the group preserves the male's innate allure of the feminine while reaffirming an entrapping male discourse. As has been stated, feminine space for these men is an anathema compounded by the absence of a father figure and the remnants of a maternal presence that has been dismissed, marginalized, or recontextualized into an easily digestible masculine context. First rule of the club: women are to be seen, not heard; exploited, not encouraged. Mob men do not honour women who are not their mothers but instead sequester their rights, use them as sexual fodder, post their scantily clad images on their club walls to satisfy their lustful yearnings. They are easily replaceable, as exemplified by the sanctioned proclivity to have not only a wife but also a goomah, and any other extracurricular sexual dalliances on demand. They are interchangeable, as illustrated in the many dream sequences in which Tony's female partners and acquaintances often morph into one another during sex. Tony's and his cohorts' dominance over this changing array is guaranteed by a network of long-established patriarchal tropes that reinforce the phallocentric organization of power and left-brain linear communication. All of Tony's business relationships, victims, and underlings are grounded in this visible masculine energy. Silvio Dante and the crew, Tony's Jewish lawyer Neil Mink, Dr. Melfi with her continuing therapy, Carmela with her acquiescence – all are relative cooperators of this well-defined authoritarian narrative. Rule number two: the image of the mother, and no other woman, is the default mode for the hereditary silence that accompanies the latent sexual desire of these men for the mother figure throughout life. The powerful seduction of the mother figure, if not naturally cleaved by the presence of a loving father, can cause a pseudo-dependence on the symbolic mother that inhibits men from fully inhabiting their own bodies. Tony's dysfunctional love–hate relationship with his mother is documented throughout the series. He vehemently rebuffs any inference of an Oedipus complex during his sessions with Dr. Melfi. Though he marginalizes his mother's phlegmatic presence in his life he cannot eradicate his idealized image of her, however toxic that image may truly be. A.J.'s relationship with his mother seems typical and normal, given the extenuating circumstances surrounding his youth. Christopher Moltisanti's mother Jo Anne Moltisanti is a drunk, useless to her son, an unavoidable family appendage that serves only to remind him of his tendencies towards self-destruction. As if to punctuate the importance of the overpowering mother archetype, Chase introduces a brief storyline that bolsters the heredity silence and angst that plagues these children of Percival.

Paulie "Walnuts" Gualtieri discovers in "The Fleshy Part of the Thigh" VI.4 that Marianucci "Nucci" Gualtieri, the woman he cherishes as his mother, is really his aunt. Though Marianucci has nurtured and raised him as her son since he was a babe, he finds out that his birth mother is her sister Donatucci Gualtieri, the women he knows as his aunt "Dottie." It seems his biological mother, "Dottie," became pregnant after an interlude with an American soldier during the Second World War. Ashamed by her act and shunned by the family, "Nucci" adopted the newborn to hide the scandal, and "Dottie" entered a nunnery. The women simply changed places; the mother became the aunt, the aunt the mother. The revelation is unnerving, so much so that an emotionally befuddled and psychologically reeling Paulie envisions the Virgin Mary Queen of the Heavens, the mother of all mothers, floating above the Bada Bing stripper concourse ("The Ride" VI.9). This virtual incarnation of the Madonna (mother as sacred, woman as profane) archetype persecutes Paulie as he settles into an identity stupor. All humans have predetermined patterns of behaviour that are activated at congruous junctures of existence. These structures include the ability to meet and accept a father and a mother. In order to actualize these potential archetypes, one must meet someone sufficiently resembling the internalized fantasy in order to turn on the program. Paulie's predicament is that his idealized model of traditional motherhood has been erased, violently expunged by the biting words of a humble and truly contrite mother-nun. The model of masculinity he has forged and nurtured his entire life has suddenly become a sham. Visibly shaken by the emotional tailspin that has corroded his world view, he turns to the sole rock of security and wisdom that remains, his boss and surrogate father-figure Tony. He attempts to give classical expression in rational terms to his tale of woe, but is fraught with the angst of inauthenticity and nullification. "Worse thing," he confesses to Tony, "I'm not who I am. It's like my whole life is a joke. A big fuckin' joke on me" ("The Fleshy Part of the Thigh" VI.4).

In the same episode Paulie meets hospital patient John Schwinn, played by Hal Holbrook. A group of patients is watching a boxing match on TV. The usual sporting remarks are made by the animated bunch when a visibly rattled Paulie empathizes with the boxers and exclaims:

> PAULIE: I tell ya', we're each and every one of us alone in the ring fighting for our lives.

A cerebral Schwinn corrects Paulie using Austrian physicist Erwin Schroedinger's quantum mechanical explanation as an educated response for the unseen order in the universe.[31]

> SCHWINN: It's an illusion those boxers are separate entities. We're all part of the same quantum field. Nothing is separate, everything is connected. The universe is just a big soup of molecules bumping up against one another. The shapes we see exist only in our own consciousness.

Fellow patient Reginal G. the rapper adroitly summarizes the scientist's philosophical response with a streetwise quip: "Everythang is everythang."[32] This being the case, Paulie's self-serving lamentations for a cause-effect world are an outdated fantasy. Objective reality is a dream, a search for an unseen order that lies beyond the ontological reality to which he has grown accustomed. In short, the facade of his life has been predicated upon his own puerile passions and anxieties. If everything is everything, according to Schrodinger, it really doesn't matter if his dying aunt "Dottie" Gualtieri is his biological mother and his adoptive mother "Nucci" is his aunt or vice versa since we are all part of the same maelstrom. But Paulie's reasoning betrays a limited cognitive function that is existentially detached from his emotional centre. He is stuck on the frozen image of himself as "Nucci's" legitimate son and will never have the courage to affirm his own illegitimate nature over what is accidental or incidental to him.

A sanguine Tony also reprimands him, reminding him in typical capo fashion that none of the self-pity matters because we're all "part of something bigger." After a period of childish petulance and unpardonable acts towards his now deposed mother-figure, he meekly settles upon a suffered and pitiful vision of motherhood and succumbs anew not to "Nucci's" loving care but to satisfy his own preternatural need for a normal and undifferentiated mother–son relationship. Within this masculine mob narrative, the mother–son bond is a reified, sanctified, archetypal herald to be celebrated and supported at all costs. This narrative replaces epistemological zeal with miserly narcissism thereby outlining a falsely reified world model that only permits conformity. It is precisely this conformity that arouses the disruptive forces of secrecy and psychological fragmentation that forcefully subtends the visual and accepted public identity of manhood so vital to the continuation of mob patriarchy.

Issues of motherhood are not so simple for perennial misfit Christopher Moltisanti, Tony's proclaimed surrogate son. The viewer's first long look at Christopher is in "The Legend of Tennessee Moltisanti" I.8, an episode laden with ethnic identity issues and aptly named for Christopher's sidelong aspirations to become the next Tennessee Williams. It would be difficult, however, to accuse him of cultural elitism. Rather, Christopher views the lure of creative writing, pedestrian as his skills may be, as an extension and intensification of his own fictitious reality. Writing is Christopher's attempt to bring an aesthetic order to his personal chaos, something Tony cannot condone since it (a) places Christopher beyond Tony's (and Chase's) verbal control by granting him authorial independence; (b) disrupts the debilitating feodality of Mafia masculine hegemony by introducing the feminine principle of creativity; and (c) creates an unreliable narrative that will jeopardize his own existence and that of his mob family. Ultimately, writing offers Christopher the possibility of salvation, a slipping from the bonds he has vouchsafed. It will become his fatal flaw. It is worth recalling that Christopher's death is ultimately precipitated by the screenplay he penned titled *Cleaver*, a poorly written B movie (un)consciously based on the sexual exploits of his boss Tony with his own fiancé Adriana La Cerva.

Ever-conscious of his image, this would-be public enemy's primary source of inspiration is the fantasy world of gangster celluloid. An unfledged moviephile who gets high on the smell of Blockbuster, he believes what he sees and views his life through the filter of re-enacted scenes and disremembered movie dialogue. Unfortunately, the scenes are always misinterpreted, the dialogue always skewed. The miscues in his life are many. In the pilot episode, he insists on calling Emil Kolar, the Czech-American thug he is about to kill, email. His incoherent rodomontade on not knowing the difference between Polacks and Czechs or the existence of sausages beyond Jimmy Dean or Satriale Italian sausages does much to bolster the dumb innocence his face proclaims and his actions confirm. While disposing of Emil's corpse with Salvatore "Big Pussy" Bonpensiero, he compares the scene to the killing of Luca Brasi in *The Godfather* but mispronounces the name, calling him Louis Brasi. "Big Pussy" corrects him: "Luca Brasi, Luca ... There's differences, Christopher, OK, from the Luca Brasi situation and this." But it makes no difference to Christopher since he is incapable of transcending the immediate realm of superficial passions and deep-set anxieties. These instances mark him for a path of social abnegation and uneasy, inescapable, ontic self-negation. He is portrayed as an incompetent loser, a tainted putative punk whose romanticized movie vision of mob life is destined to sour.

Chase stokes the fires of Christopher's distorted cinematic imagination by inserting intertextual information that permits the ideal viewer to penetrate the psyche of this deeply flawed, often negative, even unlikeable character by referencing former roles of Michael Imperioli, the actor who plays Christopher. As already mentioned, Michael parodies his role as "Spider" in Martin Scorsese's film *Goodfellas* (1990) when his character Christopher reprises the poker scene in which an irrationally volatile Tommy De Meo, played by Joe Pesci, shoots him in the foot, and then kills him at the next card game in a fit of cowboy bravado ("Big Girls Don't Cry" II.5). In *The Sopranos*, an impatient Christopher bullies a young bakery clerk, shooting him in the foot when the latter fails to recognize the imminent threat and render the requisite respect the gun-toting thug demands. In "Live Free or Die" VI.6, Chase again references a former Michael Imperioli role. As the Soprano crew discusses Vito Spatafore's homosexuality, Christopher states: "I wanna kill the fat faggot, myself. It'd be a fuckin' honour. Cut off his *braciole* and feed it to him." The line recalls Michael's role as private D'Ambrosio in the film *Dead Presidents* (1995) in which the unfortunate D'Ambrosio is captured by the North Vietnamese, disemboweled, and castrated. The reference to *braciole*, a thinly sliced piece of meat rolled into a roulade, is colourfully demonstrative. Art imitating art imitating art. The metatextual implications are fraught with Christopher's inability to live his life without disappearing into the fiction of his own film fantasies. Appropriately, Christopher maintains that his personal woes are the result of a missing narrative arc or transformative vital experience, the type that consolidates a protagonist's legitimacy in a plot line. He feels his narrative is chock-full of frayed strands and incomplete story threads that are dull, tedious, and go nowhere. Yet he frays the only lifelines he truly possesses when he abuses his fiancée Adriana La Cerva and disrespects his mentor Tony Soprano. Since he is unable to distinguish between natural desires and those which spring from perversely distorted urgencies, he eventually kills both relationships: Adriana is fed to the mob; Tony is killed symbolically in the film *Cleaver*. His malevolence knows no bounds.

Life for Christopher is a series of abstracted fictions of ambivalence – and these guiding antithetical fictions create an inconclusiveness that thwarts any real existential progress. His many extraneous escapades are an attempt to create a life trajectory outside the clandestine realm of the hypermasculinity he both loathes and craves. It is interesting that he spends much of the series unconscious. Psychic hermaphroditism projects just such oppositions between conscious and unconscious, masculine and feminine, public and private, likes and dislikes.[33] For Christopher, what is natural is the unnatural, all of which is impossible to satiate because his ambitions are fuelled by subjective inarticulate needs.

Writing is an attempt to articulate and exorcise the existential conundrums that assail him, escape into the light of literary imagination, a right-brain excursion into a parallel space that permits creativity and freedom. These alternate worlds lead him to understand that his own world is nothing more than a mob construct. He has tried to understand it from the inside but is uncomfortable with its unidirectional flow, feels restricted by its monocular views. While he obeys the rules, he repudiates the existential consequences; he longs for the regimentation expecting rewards, but bridles against the sophomoric pettiness. He indulges in drugs and alcohol with the same bipolar and contradictory energy. Hence the attempts at sobriety and the resolution to create his own undifferentiated space away from the meddling Soprano crew all go for naught since all is predicated upon behavioural false-self systems.

What truly sets Christopher apart, however, is his inability to reason and to make valid inferences. He repeatedly lacks the courage to affirm a self-centred, individualized, self-determining self. He is a cynic possessing no criterion of truth, no set of values, rejecting whatever he doesn't understand, a carcass empty of meaning and vital essence. Not courage but weakness induces him to declare himself as a part of the Soprano crew. It is interesting that he attempts to transcend his insecure nature by using the written word. Yet, though he wishes to be a writer, he is dreadfully inarticulate. His movie manuscript ("The Legend of Tennessee Moltisanti" I.8) is replete with misspelled words and faultily reasoned segues. He dreams of Hollywood cinema and lucrative contracts, but his only real contact with the brutal reality of Hollywood is in "D-Girl" II.7, where again his only cache is that he is an inarticulate mobster able to add crass realism to staged mob fiction. Christopher is indeed an anomaly. He buckles against authority, yet joins a male-only club rooted in conformity and hierarchy. As such, he craves company yet uses his friends to promote his own apartness and perceived state of lone wolf. Ultimately, it is precisely his chronic neurotic anxiety that sets him apart from the other characters in the series. He misappropriates language, is unable to express his needs, is hot tempered and quick to exacerbate situations with violence. An apt description, one must admit, of Tony Soprano. Both are caught in similar nets of contending existential contingencies, hence the mutual affinity between the two. The attraction is tempered, however, with cautious contempt. As the series progresses, Tony learns to affirm his individual selfhood in spite of these conditioning deficiencies, while Christopher is simply snared in their debilitating finitude. This pouting gangster, a role he reprises in a scene from the 1955 film *Rebel Without a Cause* in "Big Girls Don't Cry" II.5, is a retro-gender model of the eternal child: men who cry but women act surprised when they actually do. Christopher's tormented immaturity is thus his greatest source of attraction and vulnerability. Tony prosaically calls the syndrome "cowboy-itus" or, the urge to be caught. The trouble is that Christopher does not realize the self-destructive motivations of his actions. Though he is a Made Man, he never truly learns to act like one.

If A.J.'s adolescent concerns are that "it's all a big nothing," Christopher's enduring anguish implies that there is indeed a world beyond the self-imposed norms he has accepted. The meaninglessness he feels springs from the inability to summon the courage to be himself beyond the conformist courage to be a part. This is the reason why his relationships, both aesthetic and personal, share the maniacal mantra of distraction and failure since he has no real functioning relationship with any female. Adriana La Cerva is merely a foil for his falsifications. She is a cover-up, a means of detachment. His ego drives the necessity of being caught up in this love story, in the possibility of a soulful history. But their tragicomic relationship is a hallucinatory search for control rather than reflection. Since his psyche mangles his subjectivity, he will forever remain a reticent son to his drunken Medean mother, never a loving partner to his mate. He remains a reluctant rationalist, able to sacrifice the one female who truly loves him, Adriana, in order to remain firmly embedded in his image-driven masculine discourse. Wilfully assenting to the tabloid images his confused psyche engenders, he eventually marries not Adriana but an epistemologically abstract surrogate partner and dutifully begets an offspring. But the rendition of this concocted marital reality into a ground for self-knowledge is ultimately futile.

Against this metaphysical artifice stands Tony Soprano, the stalwart boss who redoubles his trenchant and conniving influence over his chosen successor because he also acts as a surrogate father to Christopher. Christopher's paradoxical hunger for visual confirmation (publicity) and gangster notoriety (privacy) are a continuing source of consternation for Tony, a stalwart fan of the silent Gary Cooper archetype. He cannot condone his protégé's overt displays of bravado nor his proclivity for the pen over the sword. Alpha males simply don't expose the chinks in their armour, let alone write about them. Tony's murder of this wayward putative son in "Kennedy and Heidi" VI.18 by suffocation is a brutal "end-of-story" solution, a terminal response to Christopher's compulsive voyeurism and misplaced storytelling. The gruesome death is an announced eventuality, prophesied at the end of the pilot episode, and reiterated often throughout the series. Christopher's demise is Tony's self-promise of a new beginning unencumbered by images and "those distractions" that he admonishes Christopher to avoid. Tony's holistic structure is a system of inevitable interrelations that will not tolerate digression. The unexpected and horrific killing freezes temporality into an ever-repeated motion that guarantees its endless repetition as well as Tony's continued dominance and control over the masculine sphere.

The quest for manhood and the all-encompassing need to *act like a man* causes consternation and pain for many male characters who must follow the Mafia code regardless of their innermost feelings. The unending search for personal validity that cascades into the need for a legitimate sense of sonship and of belonging to a confirming and gratifying social norm is tainted by the inability of these men to both relate emotionally and cleave effectively from their fantasies of a mother archetype. This triggers an absence of coherent vital limits and a distorted conception of the archetype of the father figure. Any clan that premises its legitimacy on the hypermasculine desire to maintain this sort of false selfhood is doomed to a symbolically mutilated membership.

We have seen how Christopher's periphery exploits into his own feminine recesses inevitably sanction his demise, how Tony's polyphonic dogmatism, A.J.'s adjacent similarities, and Paulie's emotional capitulation condition and taint their acts with self-serving deceit. No one is saved from this merry-go-round of masculine malignancy. In "Boca" I.9, for example, a fitfully enamoured and surprisingly virile Corrado "Junior" Soprano abruptly ends his relationship with his longtime partner Roberta because of her verbal indiscretion about his prowess at oral sex. As a respected and elder mob boss, Corrado cannot publicly display a perceived weakness because it destabilizes his public mask and threatens his need for an unchanging mob lexicon. He chides Roberta when he demands her silence: "They think if you'll suck pussy, you'll suck anything." The act, in other words, challenges established mob notions of masculinity and therefore eviscerates his public identity.[34]

Proper male behaviour for Mediterranean cultures is traditionally rooted in the notion of *ombredad* or, more commonly, *omertà* and entails the controlling of one's public behaviour. This notion of manhood is firmly embedded in the restraining of one's emotions, silent governance of one's authority, coolness and measured detachment in one's actions. For example, John Sacrimoni's tears at his daughter's wedding in "Mr. and Mrs. John Sacrimoni Request" VI.5 earns Phil Leotardo's scorn: "If they can make him cry and if he's that weak, what the fuck else can they make him do?" On the other hand, a public display of virile bravado demonstrates the length these men travel in order to hide their latent insecurities. In "University" III.6, Ralph Cifaretto has just chided girlfriend Tracee for attempting to kiss him after performing oral sex on a coterie of clients. He publicly rebukes her, offended at the notion of kissing her tainted lips. He immediately turns, however, and kisses Gigi Cestone, a fellow mobster. Because of the proximity of word and deed, Ralph's kissing of Gigi raises the same question of tainted lips and public acts. Ralph forestalls the expected mockery from Gigi by stating that he "has a cousin who's a fag." The insertion of a fat cigar into his mouth, however, and the viewer's privileged knowledge of his proclivity for anal penetration by his female sexual partners grossly differs his overstepping of legitimately accepted norms. For these men, the anxiety of emptiness and meaninglessness beyond the confines of the mob is never overtaken by the anxiety of guilt and condemnation.

Returning to Corrado, Roberta's inevitable surreptitious revelation to female friends of his proclivity and bravura at oral sex similarly moves beyond the circumscription of all accepted mob boundaries. Interestingly again, his subjectivity is impregnated with language. For Corrado, the most vital being is the being which has the word and is bonded to silence. Roberta's verbal transgression effectively destroys their relationship and, though a self-liberating gesture, it usurps the vitality of his private and public action. The once loquacious and generously suave Corrado has suddenly been struck dumb, petrified by the words of a female. Within the parameters of acceptable masculine strength, the opening of the heart to another occurs only in the most extreme of circumstances; the loss of a loved one, the death of a father. Mob propriety and business priorities do not permit the sharing of what is considered the weak and imperfect emotions of humanity. To act otherwise would reveal these rigidly adhered to principles as sham. Yet Corrado is vexed by his own deterministic view. He perseveres with the power of a self-affirmation that acts in spite of personal cost. As he exits the fateful scene of his break-up with Roberta, his mind is so pervaded with cascading images about the cost of what it means to act like a man that any attempt at verbalization is nullified by inaudible, but painfully visual, grief.

Public misreckoning of a mobster' reputation cannot interfere with the studied staging of a man's Mafioso identity. Such is the case when Christopher Moltisanti would rather die by Tony's bullet than live with the consequences of rumours that his fiancée Adriana and his boss Tony have had an affair ("Irregular Around the Margins," V.5). Tony attempts to privately convince Christopher to accept his explanations of innocence, but Christopher prefers to suffer the inevitable public consequences of his indignation. And so, on a lonely highway surrounded by his peers, Tony, holding his nephew by his now familiar scruff, tells him to "tell me right now that you can take it into your heart that I did not do this shit, or this is as far as we go." A cocked pistol lodged into Christopher's face does nothing to change his mind. A compromise is reached when Tony Blundetto intervenes with a possible second narrative: If Adriana had been pleasuring Tony while driving there would be no seatbelt bruises on her shoulders. Later, even after hearing evidence by the physician attending Adriana that both passengers were indeed wearing seatbelts and therefore not engaged in oral sex at the time of their accident, Christopher remains obdurate and disheartened:

> CHRISTOPHER: What do you want from me? I guess I believe you ... But at this point now it don't make no difference. Even if it wasn't true, it's what people think.
> TONY: What do you care what people think? You know the truth.
> CHRISTOPHER: I gotta live in the world. And now I look like Joe Jerkoff.

Though Tony argues that what others believe is of no consequence, it matters little to a publicly emasculated mobster.

Christopher's cynicism stems from his disbelief in reason. He has no answers to questions of meaning, no criterion for truth. The bane of all these men is iconoclasm, or fear of images and spoken words. Their neuroses are a reaction to the anticipated muteness or public death that must occur when the imperative of bonded secrecy is broken. The material sign of the word must not infiltrate the unilogical structure of their male-gendered world. Any intrusion, be it real or intimated, would still male discourse with its debilitating stare, much like the figure of Medusa in mythology. Artie Bucco, for example, is verbally castrated by his wife Charmaine when she chastises him for associating with the hoodlums at the Bada Bing in "Boca" I.9. This humiliation of being "ball-less" is similar to the chiding and mirthful smiles that accompany Corrado "Junior" Soprano after Roberta's revelations. Those same smiles hound Coach Don Hauser for not accepting a sexual tour of the backroom with one of the Bada Bing strippers. The refusal to publicly display one's manhood or the mere perception that one's manhood is compromised are equally reproached by real men with "balls" as subversive, something to be mocked. When Tony eventually learns that the coach is a "ball-less" pervert that seduces his teenage soccer players the only retribution to this detestable debauchery (the coach's wrong use of his balls) is vigilante justice. Artie Bucco, of course, is not part of Tony's crew but his daughter plays on the same soccer team. Artie's dilemma of ball-less-ness leads him to sit amid the hanging green balls of his tomato plants where he confesses to his wife, "If I had any balls I would do it myself." He is reassured by wife Charmaine, "You do have balls. That's why you're not like him [Tony Soprano]." Tony himself is fraught with subconscious fears of losing his family and of castration, of literally losing his "balls," as exemplified in his dream about losing his penis to a duck related to Dr. Melfi in the pilot episode.

In this instance, but there are many throughout the series, any pleasure that the male character might achieve through the contemplation of beauty, of the female, of the image, or of the imaginary, is subverted by the unending involutions of the fearful male subject upon its masculine self. The hypocrisy of all concerned, Carmela notes, is rampant. It is interesting that when Carmela reveals their Uncle Junior's bedroom talents she and Tony are sitting underneath their bedroom mural. The need for men to hide their feminine, ball-less natures is nowhere more apparent than in the physical seclusion of this painting in the Soprano bedroom. These men are caught in a network of false appearances in which a real identity is purposefully difficult to locate because it is so painstakingly hidden.

The equilibrium of masculine identity, we have posited, is fragile in this series. It is tenuously balanced between the interdiction of one's own feminine attributes and the subliminal nostalgia for the gentility buried within every man. If it is true that men must prove their masculinity over and over again as a defence against any perceived intrusion of their latent femininity, then any lapse in one's guard may spell doom. But the courage to be, to truly *act like a man*, is an ontological posture that affirms one's essence in spite of those elements in one's existence in conflict. For Plato, courage occupies a central position in the creation of the soul. The courageous element in man helps bridge the cleavage between reason and desire.[35] The erection of artificial masculine boundaries to proscribe natural feminine contingencies cruelly disintegrates the bonds that lead to salvation and instead install a narrative of guilt and renunciation. Such is the fate of Soprano capo Vito Spatafore.

A minor character known for his girth and his earning prowess, his short-lived Season VI odyssey in search of sensual redemption begins with his new svelte image proudly displayed in the opening sequence of the final season. Vito has slimmed down to an uneasy low-carb veggie-laden diet of public blandness. Gone, supposedly, is the conspicuous gluttony. Gone, it seems, is the insatiable appetite. But a new spectre of a defanged and domesticated mobster figure emerges. His latent femininity has come to life, inspired by all the gender-liberating dreams he may have always harboured but forever feared. His newfound courage to display the bridge between his publicly straight and privately gay natures is determinately pathological because it flaunts mobster proscriptions.

Any suspicions the astute viewer may have entertained regarding Vito's sexual leanings are validated in "Unidentified Black Males" V.9

when a sleep-deprived Finn Detrolio arrives at the construction site where he works to find Vito sexually pleasuring a male security guard. Admitting culpability, Vito makes contrition by proffering baseball tickets to an emotionally beset and homophobic Finn. The perfect limp foil for the sexually aggressive predator Vito, Finn once again demonstrates his ferociously disconcerting unwillingness to battle against conflict and diversity, preferring instead to withdraw into his own perspective of intolerance. Finn's discourse of ratiocinative ineptitude extends, we have seen, to all facets of his class, ethnicity, and gender. He is the indefectible idiot, agonizing over the encroaching sociocultural narratives that just won't leave him alone. Taking pride in the deracinated nature of his father's existence, he is desensitized, devitalized, de-eroticized, disempowered, and eventually destroyed (obliterated from the story by Meadow without so much as a whimper) by his own vital inadequacy.

Returning to Vito, beyond the minor implications of this prefatory transgression, his irreconcilable moment of ontic self-affirmation arrives in a gay bar in New York's club district. Dressed in leather tights and chains, his fabricated armour is forever chinked when two Jersey thugs spot him cavorting with a similarly clad male companion. Vito's dancing around the prescribed boundaries erected by his mob clan (as opposed to Tony's singing), may give vent to his cross-gender wanderlust, but his discovery on the dance floor dressed in dominatrix leather and chains sanctions the eventual pummelling of his Janus identity. The surprising revelation of Vito's abominable indiscretion sets in motion a chain of events that ultimately negates both his public and private image within the masculine context. Indeed, the direct conflict between the muffled subversion that the feminine represents is nowhere more primordially expressed than in this flagrant usurping of the masculine logic that characterizes the stability of the Soprano world. A Mafioso is compelled to stifle those motivations that do not fit the ends of the organization he has joined. Self-control, denial of one's emotions and the rejection of others' emotions are the unwavering bedrock of the creed. It is thus interesting that Vito chooses a super-macho appearance to display his alter ego because the sadomasochistic garb, replete with implications of inflicting physical or mental pain on willing partners, aptly mirrors the gratification he receives by imparting pain and suffering on unwilling clients, both sexual and otherwise. In both instances, Vito is displaying his true self in a vain attempt to retain an outward masculine armour of virility and macho control. The term macho carries multiple meanings, with both positive and negative connotations.

The positive characteristics of the Spanish word have been lost in mainstream English usage, where the term is used almost exclusively to refer to hypermasculine aggressive attitudes. Traditionally, however, the word carried positive associations. To be macho was to be well-respected in the community, a man embodying traits such as courage, valour, honour, and gentility.[36]

Vito's revelation is indeed a surprising twist in the Soprano narrative. A peripheral figure throughout the series, our perception of the comically rotund and waddling Vito is dramatically altered. But so, too, is Tony's and, with him, that of his entire crew. Vito's shedding of fatness for fitness runs counter to the series' idealized presentation of girth as a signifier of success. From Tony to Salvatore "Big Pussy" Bonpensiero to Bobby "Baccalà" Baccilieri Jr., the standardized body image for the Jersey mobster is overindulgence, voracious greed, and cumbersome portliness. As Avi Santo argues, "On *The Sopranos*, fitness seems intricately connected to dandyism and male bodily display."[37] What are we to assume, then, of Vito's new corporate body image? What repercussions can the introduction of this variable serve to the notion of acting like a man?

Vito's domination of appetite and the reinvention of his public body image through self-sacrifice visually separate him from his self-indulgent and wilfully beefy cohorts. He has, by losing weight, broken the social contract of ubiquitous largesse requisite of a successful mobster. By displaying his body in tights, he has called attention to his desire to be publicly noticed. His new image thus acts as a sort of moral counterweight to a culture of reclusiveness. If fatness, for the gangster, embodies the destructiveness of power rooted in both outwardly displayed force and inward amoral certainty, then Vito's newfound nutritional sobriety initiates an unsolicited interior group struggle that threatens to emasculate the crew. Vito no longer eats or drinks like a mobster, nor does he indulge in the pleasures of his goomah, much to the consternation of his incredulous peers. While still possessing many bad habits, hubris and ambition are his primary faults. He is not shunned by Tony since he remains the crew's top earner. He has, however, rocked the boat. He has finally grown up and has become the man no mobster father ever wanted. In Vito's case, to grow up and act like a man entails a rejection of the publicly displayed notion of manhood and the acceptance of his true inner essence.

Having shed his former identity, his open homosexuality expresses an unconscious search for the father and for a new and different masculine identity. His escape to New Hampshire is an initiation ritual that forces him to consider his genetic inheritance, to rediscover resources within himself, and, ultimately, to surrender to his own physicality. Vito imagines himself in heroic playfulness. His jaunt in the tamed wilds of rural New England pushes him beyond the zero-sum game of the New Jersey identity police. The newly satiated Vito has all the makings of a virgin-cum-whore. He is fat, curvaceous in body shape, ravenous in his sexual yearnings. His tryst with Jim "Johnny Cakes" reinforces his resolve to no longer live a life of solitude and silence but courageously embrace the self-affirmation of being in spite of the threat of non-being. In essence, Vito finds partial liberation of his identity and momentarily enjoys open sexuality before imploding in his own recurring hetero-homo incubus. In the end, his short-lived adventure could be ascribed a modicum of real courage. Yet, while he has crossed the limen of his latent desire, his return to New Jersey to literally face the music is pure ego immolation.

Vito's adventure demonstrates how mobster modes are all an expected act, ways of comportment that ordain and separate Made Men from all other men, but especially gay ones. He may be torn between the power of the mob and the pleasures of the bed but he is fully cognizant of the antithetical credo he must enact to remain a viable member of the clan. His unfortunate end at the hands of his brother-in-law Phil Leotardo in "Cold Stones" VI.11 bespeaks of reprobate intolerance and kills any cross-casting of transcending values. The mutually exclusive enclaves simply won't allow capitulation. While Vito may dream of a cross-class, polyethnic, transgendered place, his fruitless pursuit to reconcile the two life strategies he lives by inventing a liberating paradigm of a separate but equal space is his ultimate character failure. Such a recalibration of his character would have rivaled even Tony's rise from bumbling urban teen to urbane, psychologically handicapped mob boss struggling to contain his self-absorbed macho frontierism in a veneer of emasculated docility. Vito is not as obsessed as Tony to reinvent or even re-examine himself. There is no self-scrutiny by Vito in random mirrors, no self-driven forays into the recesses of the soul in response to life's vicissitudes. Vito cries where Tony rants; implores where Tony raves. Interestingly, Vito is hobbled; a limping and, by symbolic extension, impotent male. He is no match for Tony's physical prowess. He cannot joust Tony's salacious animal masculinity. Few men in the series can. Where Tony is an alpha male predator, Vito is the unfortunate perennial prey. It could be said that Vito's character is a thwarted attempt to go beyond the gangster figure, updating a pseudo-romantic mantra of worn stereotypes. Tony, on the other hand, is a literalization of the contemporary gangster-cum-businessman-cum-entrepreneurs' psycho-social profile and, as such, a template for masculinity in an American postfeminist world. Vito may have chosen to ideally remain under the sexual radar by transferring his dominatrix act to a more open and accepting Florida seascape, but Tony has groomed himself to be nothing less than dominator of the New Jersey shore. Again, both may be compared and identified by their performance in their evolving roles. But where Tony consolidates an immanent presence, Vito is doomed to tainted absence.

A truly heroic act of being is Tony's sufferance of Vito the bad boy despite the latter's flagrant dismissal of mob norms. Courage always harbours risk. But Tony, too, has experienced the anxiety of emptiness and meaninglessness that torments Vito, and he senses that Vito's transformation is rooted in the same anxiety of guilt and in the risk of losing oneself in the self-reflexivity of the mob world. He, too, has attempted to broach the rigid veneer of male stoicism. His foray into psychiatry has exposed embedded issues his peers disregard. He suffers the eviscerating absence of true masculine love.[38] And, indeed, Tony's perspicacious intent to transcend the norm moves him towards the limen of non-being and emotional ruin. But, just as Vito's return to his New Jersey clan is a misguided, but necessary, step in his plan of public rebirth, Tony's voyage towards miscreant manhood is an agonizing acknowledgment of his own disruptive liminality. What Tony ultimately learns from Vito is that a man who is out of touch with his impulses never feels himself to be a man and can actually begin to fear the loss of his masculinity. The resultant feelings of vulnerability that hound Tony as displayed in his many dreams and that persecute the group during these sexually stoked episodes unfortunately endorse Vito's brutal killing and settling of mob accounts. Yet, for all of their public postures of manhood, of disinspired emotional containment and of ultimate sexual repression, only Tony lives the crucible of psychological self-inquiry and personal growth. All his deeds, nefarious as they may be, ultimately lead to his assertion "I get it" in "Kennedy and Heidi" VI.18. What he "gets" is the answer to the questions first heard in "Funhouse" II.13: "Where you goin'? What're you lookin' for?" to which he had replied "I dunno" and "Somebody's lookin' for me." The same questions he himself asks when he awakens from his coma in "Mayham" VI.3: "Where am I? Where am I goin'?" What he finally "gets" as he relishes the epiphany, arms outstretched towards the rising desert sun, is the monstrous and liberating assurance that he has become the image of the mob boss he has long cherished. He knows who he is. He knows where he is going.[39] In "Sons" V.13, Tony lectures John Sacrimoni on mobster facts of life: "What we are here for in the end is to put food on the table for our families, our sons ... the future, that's what's important." Coupled with the psychic adroitness of what it takes to act like a man within the brutal and unforgiving world he has chosen to inhabit, he can unflinchingly and without remorse confess to his son, like his father before him, "This is my livelihood. It's how I put food on the table" ("Fortunate Son" III.3).[40]

Chapter Four

Two Tonys: Drawing Conclusions from Mediated Mob Images

Tony Soprano: "We wanted to stay Italian. Preserve ... honor, family, loyalty, the American Way."

"From Where to Eternity" II.9

Respect. It is a love and a rage. The love you already know about, lurking in all the clichés of ethnicity: pungent, generic. Like garlic, it stays with you.

Alane Salierno Mason, "Respect," *Beyond The Godfather*

"L'il boy, in this business there's only one law you gotta follow to keep out of trouble ... Do it first, do it yourself, and keep on doing it."

Tony Camonte to Guino Rinaldo in *Scarface* (1932)

"I'm Not Like Everybody Else."

The Kinks (1966)[1]

World Construction

The TV screen frames a close-up of Christopher Moltisanti and Tony Soprano butting heads, locked together like virulent rams, eye to eye, chin to chin, hot breath to bellowing hot breath. Tony holds Christopher by the lapels, hovering over the younger thug in menacing pose, spouting vitriol, demanding respect ("Amour Fou" III.12). But we've seen this scene before. Years before, at the end of the pilot episode, a despondent Christopher pouts over Tony's lack of recognition for his role in resolving the impending garbage dispute with the upstart Czechs. "A simple 'Way to go Chris' over the Triborough contract would have been nice," he churlishly spouts. At this early juncture of the series, a surprisingly empathetic boss acknowledges his nephew's lament and blames his own inherent shortcomings. "You're right," he admits. "You're right. I have no defense. It's how I was parented, never supported; never complimented." But, as we recall, the conciliatory small talk of that summer day turns virulent, poisoned by the wrath of Tony's explosive fury. As Christopher blithely reveals his temperamental intentions to write Hollywood scripts about the mob, Tony's temper flares as he menacingly collars his nephew and spits: "I'll fuckin' kill you. What are you gonna do, go Henry Hill on me now! You know how many mobsters are sellin' screenplays and screwin' everything up!" Then, like a passing spring storm, the mood again becomes conciliatory as Tony lovingly disables Christopher's visible angst by appealing to his nephew's instinctive need for fatherly direction. "Forget Hollywood screenplays," Tony soothes while stroking the young man's face. "Forget those distractions. You got work to do; new avenues. Everything's gonna be alright from here on end. Look, it's a beautiful day ..."

But though the construct of the two scenes may be familiar, the self-reflecting echoes collide and clash to elicit a starkly different afterimage. The characters are more mature in their roles, the vital stakes of their conversation much higher. Not a bright summer sun but a pale glow highlights their profiles; they are surrounded not by warm skies but by foreboding tempestuous darkness. The chiaroscuro effect is gripping, dense with poignant implications. The low light and subdued hues soften the contours of the central characters, framing them with a painterly setting that reduplicates the painting directly behind them. The temporal memory of the earlier scene ensconced in our memory is the same. A wilfully defiant underling has boldly questioned Tony's authority, imputed his ulterior motives. That fixed point in time is where we start. But Christopher now bolts forward and oversteps his measure of correctness by recklessly dismissing his affection for the boss. He disrespectfully declares "I loved you" with the verb in the past tense. The verb wilfully extends any and all emotion that is framed by the current scene to a before and an after. The song of change does not sit well with Tony. A recognizable rage overwhelms him. His temples throb as revelation and knowledge become chaos and bewilderment. Christopher has summed up the past of an entire life, profaned the very sources of expression. The soothing light becomes infernal as an infuriated Tony lunges at the young man, the full weight of his agency expressed both in his physical girth and in his pointed power and focused verbal precision. Paraphrasing Niccolò Machiavelli he boils: "Well you don't love me anymore that breaks my heart ... but you don't gotta' love me, but you will respect me!"[2] ("Amour Fou" III.12).

Tony's deep-set love for his nephew has always triumphed in these situations and has permitted an uneasy resolution without continued confrontation. This time, however, the tension does not dissipate. Christopher pulls away, pumped with wanton bravado, and fumingly exits the scene, leaving Tony, and the viewer, to expect future explosive ramifications. A glowering Tony remains alone in the scene frame. A painting hangs on the wall directly behind him. It looms large and acquires immediate poignancy as it occupies the entire screen. The confrontation between Christopher and Tony finds pathetic fallacy in the swirling mass of dark, brownish storm clouds that surround the behemoth that is Tony. A brewing storm is an apt and facile analogy of the painting. Closer examination of the cloud formations, however, reveals the painted faces of two sneering tigers. They appear, nose to nose, eye to eye, chin to chin, and revolve around a turbulent celestial vortex. One of the tigers is larger; his arched back poised in a threatening stance, claws and teeth at the ready. He looms over the smaller tiger. The painting is a visual analogy to the scene we have just witnessed between the two men. Like the frothing behemoth that has just collared his younger nephew, within the painting, as well as in the series, further lethal action is anticipated.

The real pathos of the scene, however, is reserved for "the beast in me," the (un)willing but essential catalyst of the series examined in chapter 3. Here the beast is on public display hovering behind Tony's massive shoulders. But it is also a private subjective perception of his tormented psyche. Tony glances but remains oblivious to the two swirling beasts behind him. Instead, he maintains furtively passive to its implied message, intent instead on pursuing this personal plot line to its predestined and malevolent end. The painted reality screeches danger, it portends discord and family strife. Yet, if he would only turn to see the approaching storm as it is displayed by the glaring tigers, he would comprehend the full import of his plight and understand that the unsavory situation with Christopher must not be allowed to brew. But he doesn't; and so the future remains predictable, at least for the ideal viewer. The eventual death of his nephew by his own hands is still a paradoxical obscurity. Like the tiger statue that commands attention on the fireplace mantle of the Soprano home; like the snarling tiger tattoo that Tony sports on his right shoulder; like the painted mural in the

Soprano master bedroom, the hidden, yet simultaneously visible emblems of Tony's true self and probable future remain sheltered to him.

The paintings and emblems that swirl around Tony represent perceptive ambiguities that imply the existence of a horizon that is shielded from him because their disambiguation varies with the modifications of his states of being. Each viewing of these emblems during the course of the series suggests to the viewer the unperceived sides of a continuous ambiguity for Tony. Moreover, each perception itself extends horizons that encompass other interpretative possibilities that may occur when one deliberately changes the direction of perception. Turning one's eyes one way instead of another, for instance. The moment of seeing this particular painting of swirling tigers signals impending doom for the observant and informed viewer, but not for Tony. Characteristically, he turns his eyes, he moves away. But the fleeting cognitive experience manifests itself in a series of polyvalent experiences. Tony's survival instinct now compels him to rethink his strategies regarding the wayward Christopher and muster the will to overcome, and eventually resolve, their ongoing drama. The near equation of two painted tigers and the two raging beasts that are Tony and Christopher – and we will extend the metaphor to Tony and his wife Carmela, Tony and his mother Livia, Tony and Gloria Trillo, Tony and whomever he crosses or is crossed by in the series – is a parallel perceptive process of equal importance to the actualization of the storyline and of Tony's character development. If Tony's drama is that of a patient attempting to fully discern and secure his own dematerialized image as an I-Am mobster stereotype, the insertion of the painted tigers into the series at this strategic moment helps to define his place in an evolving depiction that must be measured against an all-too familiar panoply of media stereotypes.

Tony Soprano is the latest of a long and popular line of I-Am characters that are on one side of the law or the other. To name a few: on this side of the law are Marty in *Marty* (1955), Tony Manero in *Saturday Night Fever* (1977), and Rocky Balboa in *Rocky* (1976); on that side of the law are Rico Bandello in *Little Caesar* (1931), Tony Camonte in *Scarface* (1983), and the Corleone family in *The Godfather Trilogy* (1972, 1974, 1990); those who sit on the ambiguous fence of comedy include Vinnie Barbarino in *Welcome Back, Kotter* (1975–9); and those who promote cultural self-effacement and ethnic parody include Ray Romano in *Everybody Loves Raymond* (1996–2005). The common trait of these characters is that they want to "be somebody." All wish to establish a presence that moves beyond their own respective neighbourhoods. They unwittingly extol the prime immigrant motif of mobility, are wiseguys, comedic or otherwise, with a lot to prove and everything to gain.[3] Tony Soprano is the most burly and surly; the roughest hard guy with the smoothest edges. He is an exquisitely sad menace; a man haunted and hunted; a walking controversy incarnate. There is no middle ground with Tony. In fact, it is precisely the lack of stable middle ground, his desperate need to find (discover) a dependable central core that is at the root of his existential dilemma and motivates the story arcs or "touchstones," as David Chase terms them, of the series. Not until he is at peace with his violent self, until he fully understands his pedigree (heraldic crest) and is able to consolidate both his public (boss) and private (father) roles will he truly find himself. Only then will the series end. But who is Tony Soprano? What does he represent? Is he just a sidetracked misunderstood social misfit, one who "despite everything," according to Dr. Melfi, is "a very conventional man" ("Amour Fou" III.12)? Or is he the end of a long parade of I-Am stereotypes bent on sullying the character of the silent majority of hard-working and law-abiding I-Ams? Is he that powerful an image?

Unlike the myriad of literary characters that populate I-Am novels, or the relatively popular Hollywood films featuring I-Am characters, Tony's greatest dilemma is that he is a loveable beast. A veritable mixture of fatherly Don Corleone sweetness (*The Godfather*, 1972) and Tommy DeVito ruthlessness (*Goodfellas*, 1990), he represents "the historical culmination of a long process of assimilation of Hollywood Italian images into the mainstream of American popular culture."[4] He is a compelling high-water mark of wiseguy entertainment wrapped in contemporary ethno-social I-Am and American issues. Tony is a target both for fictional rival families and real angered I-Ams enraged by his mobster image and the media hype he resuscitates. What is unique about Tony is that he is able to dispatch both with on-screen bravado. His retorts are classic. To his daughter when she scolds his old-fashioned reasoning: "You see, out there it's the nineties, but in this house it's 1954" ("Nobody Knows Anything" I.11). To Dr. Melfi as he rationalizes his vindictive nature: "Revenge is like servin' cold cuts" ("Two Tonys" V.1). To Dr. Melfi again as he bemoans life's boredom: "Every day is a gift ... does it have to be a pair of socks?" ("The Ride" VI.9). Tony's philosophy is botched, often hokey, but clear-cut. The daily struggle is heroic, even mythic if we consider the series an I-Am tragedy with an inevitable American destiny. Neither ashamed nor hampered by his I-Am origins, he instead flaunts his *guido* youth with imperviously ripened swagger.[5] Tony, by his own painful admission, is just "a fat fuckin' crook from New Jersey" ("Calling All Cars" IV.11). Weaned on the darker strains of New Jersey I-Am neighbourhood street smarts, Tony's ubertext on what it means to be a mobster is Tommy Powers in *The Public Enemy* (1931), his music template is mainstream 1960s and 1970s Top 40 Pop Charts, his intellectual horizons are bounded by the New Jersey shore ... and one semester of college. The only time he displays a perceivable discomfort with his fiefdom occurs after his return from Italy in "Commendatori" II.4. On the ride home from the Newark airport he is palpably disturbed as the sunny bright landscape of Italy he still holds in his eyes is substituted by the grey monotone of the Jersey industrial lowlands. Yet, whatever his place, Tony owns his public identity and flaunts it regardless of geography. Violently ruthless, wilfully delusional, suffering from bipolar depression, his meteoric rise in the underworld could well mirror an eventual precipitous demonic fall.

David Chase places the source of his adult psychosis at the feet of his dysfunctional parents. His mother is an overbearing borderline narcissist lacking empathy and remorse; his father was capo of the original Soprano crew that controlled the Down Neck neighbourhood of Newark, then a capo in the DiMeo crew that ran North Jersey. He was a criminal sociopath, a narcissist whose few moments in flashback footage reveal a parasitic lifestyle predicated on unscrupulous antisocial violence. Careful not to influence his children the same way, Tony often speaks of his dream for their success in the legitimate world. His efforts at shielding them from knowing the truth about his occupation, however, are thwarted by midnight FBI home raids, gold Krugerrands found by his children during Easter Egg hunts, mob pages on the internet that highlight the DiMeo crime syndicate, and the extended family of *family* uncles that resemble *The Godfather* movie characters. A man of immense appetite, his irrepressible cravings lead to passionate consumption and the ultimate destruction of the object possessed. Tony is the archetypal hero of his own prescribed realm, set against his own will, a divided self whose publicly advertised predicament ("If one family doesn't kill him ... the other family will") sets him apart from the secondary characters of the series, and moves him towards an atypical and idiosyncratic destiny.

What ultimately distinguishes Tony from his peers is his desire to discover his vital iter, or way in the world. He wishes to understand his foibles, to develop strategies to better control his fate. It is an ancient quest for identity, even if that destiny leads to the affirmation of self as a ruthless monster. This singular focus is an attribute his peers envy and his competitors conveniently lack. By social necessity and psychological identity, he is a chameleonic character, able to alternate between personalities and identities fluidly, seamlessly, with credibility and conviction. Though not a deep thinker, he is able to consider alternative opinions, rapidly appropriate opposing points of view and perspectives, swiftly assess courses of action and execute a plan. Tony's unbridled drive to set things straight for himself is both his most appealing and least preferred attribute for it leads him, throughout the series, to unwillingly confront his false self in order to wilfully preserve his dispassionate and deadly lethal Other.

In the work *Thinking Geometrically*,[6] J.T. Waisanen postulates the notion of geometric thinking that, I would advance, may be assumed as an interpretative strategy to comprehend the multimodal space of Tony Soprano. Thinking geometrically is the ability to deal imaginatively with the multiple, that is, the numerous and simultaneous dimensions of complex and variable objects and relations in a structured, yet dynamic and interactive fashion. In a sense, this means being able to construct mental models, to compare these models to real events, and to modify both the model's and one's own behaviour to arrive at a better fit between imaginative constructions and events in real space. It is a way of negotiating the chaos of contemporary aesthetics, the intricate challenges of new conceptions of time and space, gender, and social identity. It forebodes methods for salvaging the inevitable fragmentation of the self via the demystification and commercialization of nearly everything and anything. It is the realization that falseness and charade are the overriding parables of our turbulent times and that, indeed, multiplicity and uncertainty may be the cause of all the turbulence. This miasmic state of affairs is sometimes referred to as postmodernism, a contemporary cultural movement that promotes the fragment, the endless permutations of subject, the blurring of boundaries, the absence of certainty, all played-out in the arena of indifferent irony.

The Sopranos, and Tony's snippet-based and impulsive perceptions of reality, is part of this present-day culture of disintegration. While the series seduces its viewers to suspend reason in exchange for prototypical interpretations of stereotyped mobsters, these characterizations often privilege contradiction, self-parody, and an introverted, though dynamic, formalism. When taken to their extreme, these trendy categorizations move interpretation into sectors of attenuation that portend audience stress and thwarted expectations. All this manipulative hypothesizing by the writers most often leads to ethically complicated situations and an amoral and all-things-possible universe. There is no question that *The Sopranos* is a product of a congested and generally superficial mannerist modern culture. However, as Linda Hutcheon so cogently notes when speaking of the debilitating effects of postmodernism's construction of arguments on constantly shifting ground, while "the center may not hold ... it is still an attractive fiction of order and unity that postmodern art and theory continue to exploit and subvert."[7]

Tony is just such an attractive polivalent centre. Exploited, subverted, manipulator and manipulated, his predicament is closer to that of the geometrically thinking Jason Bourne character of Robert Ludlum's *The Bourne Identity*[8] than it is to any former literary or cinematic mob boss. The Bourne character is a chameleonic protagonist lost between alternate personalities. In search of memory, in essence his self, the character is able to visualize himself in multiple dimensions and possible planes of action. His discarding of a recovered monstrous and despicable self in favour of an honest law-abiding recluse is in stark contrast with the Tony Soprano character. Though he may flounder in an American culture that is bereft of cultural unity, political authority, a veritable "ersatz mass culture" of "commodified artifice"[9] that permits illegality, he is nevertheless provided opportunities for change that intimate new continuities and alternative life structures. This subtending assurance provides him the ability to visualize events and manipulate various plans of actions that lead to diverse ends, one legal, the other illegal. Since he is able to swiftly negotiate through the disintegration of traditional order all around him and the unresolved contradictions of his own personal history, in many ways he unmasks the continuities that are taken for granted by others or have been supplanted by ironic indifference in everyday social discourse. His narrative may thus appear discontinuous, but it is always governed by rules, be they momentarily transcendental or, more normally, because the series is about mobsters, easily criminal. His actions may appear random, but they impact upon the story in ways that insinuate a linear discourse that may be indifferent to the vast majority of viewers but that nevertheless is economically, socially, politically, and culturally relevant. Rather than seeding chaos, Tony reflects a contemporary malady, an aesthetics of willed indifference towards others or, as Charles Newman has stated regarding the dynamics of the rethinking of modernity, "Post-Modernism" – and here I would insert Tony Soprano – "reflects not a radical uncertainty so much as an unconsidered suspension of judgment."[10]

Thinking geometrically is clearly the watermark of Tony Soprano's character and the distinguishing factor that separates him from his cohorts. It is the difference between the real Tony, truly revealed and fully corporeal(-ized) only at series' end, and the confused, assuming Tony who muddles through the series in search of his despicable self. It is also the reason that the monstrous Tony eventually prevails. Tony works within a complex realm of possibilities and various planes of action. Juggling his skills between domesticity, normalcy, culpability, and criminality, his ability to competently manipulate the transformations among these different points of view ensures his survival. His effortless shifts between his extreme personae reflect his control of the situational exigencies each mode of self requires. Tony's volatility, however, is prime schizophrenia. Calm reasoning and unattached concern often morphs into violent action and conflict with the slightest provocation. The instances are many but are all memorable. They happen repeatedly: between Tony and his drug-addicted nephew Christopher, ultimately culminating with murder ("Kennedy and Heidi" VI.18); with Dr. Melfi as he routinely stomps out of her office, once overturning her table, at another violently accosting her after Gloria Trillo's suicide ("Everybody Hurts" IV.6). Loving vexation for A.J.'s lackadaisical antics results in a smashed SUV windshield and a soft-spoken caveat to his son: "Don't put me to the test" ("Cold Stones" VI.11). The unfortunate brunt of Tony's most repeated and misguided beatings is Georgie, the Bada Bing bartender. Upset with his mother's inanity, Tony mercilessly hammers him with a telephone receiver in "46 Long" I.2. In "Cold Cuts" V.10, he damages Georgie's hearing. The perennially provoked Tony dispenses pain equally.[11] In all these instances, the prevaricated angst inflamed in immediately preceding situations stokes his volatile docility into expected chain-reaction repercussions. For Tony, it is the immediate situational plane that determines the course of action to be assumed, not his personal desires. Constantly crossing the thin line between one self and another, Tony's weakest and most revelatory moments occur when he uses his personal will to thwart the logical action the immediate situational plane demands. We recall his reaction to not having punished the pedophile soccer coach in "Boca" I.9. He has been reprimanded by Dr. Melfi, threatened by wimpy friend Artie Bucco. His decision to allow the police to arrest the coach runs against his code of meting out vigilante justice. His inebriated state at the end of the episode displays a character in turmoil, a model citizen wrestling with his inner mobster nature.

In these moments, Tony reveals a wholly impersonal and even inhuman ethos that thinks globally but constructs a chilling salutary distance from this weaker self through alcohol, sex and drugs. Does he distinguish between fundamental categories of good and evil, truth and lies? Do we simply consider him a volatile schizophrenic? The character is too complex to reduce him to a reductive binary paradigm. Obviously these are ambiguities and distinctions that are not to be overlooked in the face of his characterization. Indeed, Tony is not a suitable model for everyday practice, although he often justifies himself, as does Michael Corleone, by comparing his activities to those of corporate America: "It's not personal, it's business."[12] What sustains our interest in his character is precisely this primary attribute of multiple world construction that allows him to navigate the treacherous, violent, and often illusory environments that constitute his everyday existence ... and survive. We are engrossed by his ability to view the larger picture in his mind's eye while only partial views are available to the senses of others. We sustain his temperament because we come to understand his awe-shucks attitude as a foil for his own (and through cathartic empathy, our own) misgivings and shortcomings. At these moments he may appear insincere (kissing Uncle Junior while knowing he is the architect of the attempt on his life), but he is a survivor and, because he acts intuitively and masterfully, exercises a parallel thought process that expresses multiplex contingencies at any given moment.

Duplicity or Deceit?

Tony and the viewer are repeatedly reminded of the subterfuge of duplicity throughout the series. One feature of this subterfuge is a sense of freedom from the loss of self that would occur if one were to abandon oneself to any sense of the real consequences of one's actions. Tony feels he is not really responsible for his actions because his point of view is unequivocal and committed. He may go through the motions but he is really not doing anything wrong because the structural succession of his actions is a tonal, not a moral, centre that affects the principles of causality. From an existential purview, his real actions are the result of his imagination while the physical consequences of these actions are perpetrated by a disembodied self that rationalizes its own existence beyond personal consequences.[13] In "College" I.5, Nathaniel Hawthorne's words, which are inscribed on the impressive marble lintel of Bowdoin College, could be used to confirm the viewer's initial impressions of Tony at the beginning of the series. But the inscription is not inserted to vindicate Tony's duplicitous nature; at least not yet. Even the casual viewer has become aware, notwithstanding the short span of the series at this juncture, of his Janus volatility. A conventional conclusion is that the words are an apt commentary upon Tony's actions in this particular episode. Yet, while Tony may read the words ("No man can wear one face to himself and another to the multitude without finally getting bewildered as to which may be true"), his dumfounded stare, similar to the one that opens the series with Tony staring quizzically at the statue of the green virago in Dr. Melfi's anteroom, transmits to the viewer that he does not fully comprehend their meaning; again, at least not yet.

The words are instead a testimony, at this early stage, of Tony's *mal*-adaptation and present lack of self-insight. The viewer has just witnessed him acting as both a devoted father to his daughter and as savage avenger of the mobster turned informer Fabian "Febby" Petrullio. The cold-hearted transference is not explicitly enacted as a dialectical relationship between a good self and an evil one but instead as a parallel process that runs its course in the same individual subject as normal routine. Although Tony may lack the formal systems for managing the multidimensionality of events in the real world, he still successfully copes with the unpredictability and contingencies of the world through decisive action. This is mirrored in the many moments of duplicity and choice that occur during this particular episode. Tony must decide whether to admit or deny to his daughter that he has criminal ties; he must decide whether to turn left or right on a highway (either way, interestingly, leads to Colby College), and whether to kill Petrullio himself or call for help. He must wade through various possibilities of names and aliases; he must invent parallel tales to persuade a doubting Meadow of his whereabouts. The binary nature of the episode is highlighted at episode's end when Tony is placed at the beginning of a forking path as ducks ominously fly overhead.

Fabian "Febby" Petrullio must also decide whether to shoot Tony at the motel while he accompanies a drunken Meadow into her room or wait for a better occasion; he must decide whether to take flight or settle accounts, to remain anonymous or reassume a former personality. Meadow must either believe her father or continue denying her intuition. She must decide a future career path: one leads to law, the other medicine. She must choose an appropriate college: one near, Columbia, or one far, Stanford. She must ultimately also come to terms with the fragility of her own duplicitous nature. In all these cases, the characters seem to act outside of time and space and move seamlessly through, around, and above normal contingencies. Tony especially, but Meadow, too, moves thought beyond what he perceives and projects routes of action free of impediment. He controls unexpected events by connecting them into plausible narrative sequences that move beyond the immediate. The simultaneity experienced in this early episode is a revelation of what will become a series-long compulsion. Part of Tony's lore is the uncanny knack he has of relocating himself into a realm of more complex dimensionality where the end always justifies the means.

But isn't the viewer also manipulated by the didactic inferences of the Hawthorne citation? Does the ideal viewer vicariously suffer the same moral conundrum as Tony? After all, while we may be repulsed by Tony's actions we are simultaneously gratified by the meted out vengeance. Doesn't the viewer sometimes dream of being as unrestrained and successful as our favourite mob boss? As Noel Carroll maintains, "We have a pro-attitude toward Tony because he actualizes, albeit fictionally, the sort of abandon we want for ourselves–the capacity to pursue our desires unshackled and, in a large measure, unpunished."[14] The inscription thus acquires a double didactic tone. Like the veil in Hawthorne's short story "The Minister's Black Veil,"[15] it both reveals sin and slyly conceals any underlying culpability. If Tony seems uncomfortable as he reads the words, so do the viewers as we become aware of our own surreptitious self-veiling. We, too, are tinged with guilt as we begin, at this early stage of the series, to explore not only the themes of sin, repentance, and morality but also our growing fondness for this public display of our mutually inherent dark nature.[16]

Tony's duplicity is not an aberration, a protracted mania that torments him daily and often hampers relevant action in his search for wholeness and ontological security. Quite the contrary. The inscription is merely a reminder of his (and the viewer's) Janus face. This is why he is so addicted to scrutinizing his face in mirrors. Does he hate the face he sees in the mirror? Does he recognize the face in the mirror? Does the face remind him of his mother? It is made obvious in the final episodes of the series and made explicit by his sister Janice's comments that Tony displays his mother's "vindictive" attributes ("Soprano Home Movies" VI.13):

> JANICE: I'm more like my dad than ... Tony for example.
> CARMELA: So what are you saying, he's more like your mother?

The shade of Livia Soprano does indeed haunt Tony throughout the series, taunting him to forever remain the good son while compelling him to do exactly the opposite. This inner self-loathing manifests itself in mirrors and is experienced as a threat to public identity. Tony the son cannot tolerate the possibility of being a mobster that hates his mother, yet is petrified by the face that stares back from the mirror. "Wishing your mother dead?" he admonishes Dr. Melfi in "Proshai, Livushka" III.2. "Is that being a good son? ... Bad sons, they should fuckin' die! That's a fuckin' miserable thing to be, a bad son." He eventually turns his lifelong public compliance to his mother's well-being into an attack upon those very foundations, thereby risking the experience of helplessness and bewilderment that, however, is the logical start to being a whole self.

It is precisely this false-self system that Dr. Melfi, in good faith, attempts to cure. She realizes that while Tony attempts to maintain a smooth relationship with the outer world, the maternal shrapnel he carries in the body directs the destructive impulses of his soul. But Tony is not interested in removing the embedded projectiles.Instead, he often sounds a lot like his mother, echoing her fatalism, displaying a similar egotistical temperament. In "All Due Respect" V.13, for example, Silvio Dante speaks frankly of Tony's leadership qualities but also concedes his greatest defect.

> DANTE: You got a problem with authority. This attitude of yours is a lot of what makes you an effective leader. But we all got flaws. Even you. Seven Deadly Sins and yours is Pride.

Tony responds in kind:

> TONY: You got no fuckin' idea what it's like to be number one ... It's too much to deal with almost.

Then, taking a page from his mother's book of angst-filled quips, he adds: "You're completely alone with it all."[17] Tony may protest his lot but as the well-meaning doctor herself will come to realize, his sessions cultivate a formula that permits him to fully actualize himself, to become the evil face he scrutinizes in the mirror, to live the heredity he carries within. Rather than succumbing to catatonic withdrawal and passivity, he forestalls engulfment by his alter ego Albert Finnerty (the submerged self that Dr. Melfi wishes to exhume) and becomes the hardened pathological monster that eventually fully actualizes his true nature at the end of the series. Tony's initial longing for the "good ol' days" is thus not a temporary psychological impediment but the effective recompense for that vital promise that is, for Tony, the Mafia. He will not find peace, then, until he is able to effectively achieve a semblance of that same old style and reassuring Gary Cooper code of silence he craves.

Towards this end, Tony decides to be the active agent of change and not its victim. With varying levels of success, he contends with the unpredictability and contingencies of the world by adjusting the rules to suit himself and moves through his public and private space with deliberate action. When a targeted mark, a Hassidic Jew, is not cooperative, he threatens to castrate him. When the victim ennobles his intransigence by retelling the story of Masada[18] and intimates a similar moral victory asking: "And the Romans, where are they now?" Tony rewrites history and menacingly responds: "You're lookin' at 'em asshole" ("Denial, Anger, Acceptance" I.3). If a childhood chum, Davey Scatino, is a compulsive gambler, he exploits him by enabling his habit. "You told me not to get in the game. Why'd you let me do it?" a supplicant Scatino beseeches Tony. "Well I knew you had this business here, Davey. It's my nature; the frog and the scorpion, ya' know ... you're not the first guy to get busted out. This is how a guy like me makes a livin'" ("Bust Out" II.10). All the while, Tony justifies his motives with arguments of Natural Order and Selection with himself on the peak of the pecking order.

Another childhood friend, Artie Bucco, will intuit the same natural predatory instinct in Tony after his ill-advised investment in French vodka in "Everybody Hurts" IV.6. Fearing the inevitable consequences of having squandered the money loaned to him by Tony, he candidly lauds his friend's ability to have anticipated the impending financial debacle, yet still guarantee a profitable outcome for himself.

> ARTIE: The cobwebs have been removed ... You saw this whole thing, didn't you? You knew exactly what was gonna happen. You can see twenty moves down the road. Please, I don't blame you, I envy you. It's like an instinct, like a hawk sees a little mouse moving around a cornfield from a mile up.

TONY: You think it's my fault you're fuckin' lyin' in here?
ARTIE: It's just that somebody mentions fifty grand to bank roll a French *digestif* and your mind goes through all the permutations at internet speed and realizes oh, worst case scenario, I eat for free.

Tony is infuriated at Artie's all too accurate assessment of the same predatory instincts he confesses to Davey Scatino not because it is offensive but because it is so apparent and revelatory. He repudiates not the message but the messenger:

TONY: You fuckin' suicide. You're disgraceful ... You don't care what people think. Well I do. Enough people hate me.

Later, however, while in session with Dr. Melfi, he deliberates Artie's assessment.

TONY: So he says I planned it all along, that I could see twenty steps down the road how it was gonna go and how he was gonna get screwed.
DR. MELFI: Did you?
TONY: I don't know. According to him it's subconscious, second nature.
DR. MELFI: But the accusation bothers you.
TONY: Is that the kind of person I am? A hawk? It's an animal!
DR. MELFI: Well, as I understand it, you make a lot of your living through usury.

Dr. Melfi reminds Tony that it is indeed in his nature to be rapacious, and that the picture his inner eye has of himself is indeed the person perceived by others. Oddly enough, this recognition of his predatory identity safeguards his mobster image. Though he may sometimes question his self as a virtually disembodied separateness, and therefore not responsible for his actions, there are no discrepancies, no real cracks, in his multilayered and parallelepiped world view. He remains, willingly and with all the accouterments the position demands, the painted general he had callously thrown into the trash dumpster.

Again, the ability to think geometrically, to view his duplicity as a positive force, is the difference between Tony and Davey Scatino, Tony and Artie Bucco, Tony and his peers. His actions are never happenstance, not casual, never coerced, as is the case with many of his cohorts. Instead, every move in his repertoire is fatefully studied and innately insightful, even when spontaneous. Seemingly unlimited in experience in whatever domain he occupies, Tony's greater awareness of the complex machinations of the worlds he inhabits make him acutely aware of how unstable these worlds have become. His running preoccupation with his children, his unyielding relationship with his wife Carmela, and his brutal dealings with business associates attest, again, to his ability to assess situations and cultivate appropriate contingencies about them simultaneously. He is thus not a victimized reader of the Hawthorne epithet but rather, at this point in the series, a more cognizant practitioner of its inextricably unambiguous import. He's merely surprised that anyone would notice and that others, notably the great men he religiously watches on The History Channel, would share the same qualities. Tony legitimizes his own raison d'être vicariously through their examples. Because of all this, it is easy to overlook the fact that this skill of flexible ratiocination requires the exercise of a new kind of imagination. Moving beyond the on-screen documentary evidence of dialogue, characters, action, setting, theme, and style, Tony is able to envision narrative outcomes that are as relevant and as piercing as a fired projectile. His multiple perspectives and synthetic thinking serve as a contemporary model for rational thought for they place him both within the particular event being experienced and concurrently beyond the local time and space of any situation. Traditionally, one would say he understands the proverbial limits of those around him and plays to their non-apparent weaknesses.

Take, for example, his ability to visualize events and characters in multidimensional planes of action beyond the real. This normally happens during his dreams ("alternate universes," as Chase prefers to call them).[19] This sort of out-of-body experience is normally typical of tribal shamans and mythical oracles. His dreams are more than tableaus of traditional Freudian archetypes for they not only reveal his subconscious to the viewer but also furnish solutions to him regarding pressing life-altering queries. Tony's dreams are modulated reflections that assess the worldly contingencies that assail him. They privilege possibility and as such his dreamscapes posit solutions that empower his multimodal creative thinking. A meta-intelligence is at work, one that conceives interpenetrating dimensions of visual coordinates that looks at things from points of view of a more complex dimensionality. This roving inner eye imagines alternative worlds and allows him to prove Salvatore "Big Pussy" Bonpensiero's betrayal (Tony dreams he is a fish in "Funhouse" II.13), to intuit Dr. Melfi's smoldering sexual tension (Tony dreams about hot interludes with Dr. Melfi in "Pax Soprana" I.6), to reify the ramifications of killing his cousin Tony Blundetto (Tony imagines himself as a general who must carry out a difficult task in

"The Strong Silent Type" IV.10). Whether chemically induced by Prozac, alcohol, peyote, or emotionally triggered by guilt, repression, or anger, these oneiric revelations add to the mystique of Tony (and are a convenient literary expedient for David Chase and his writers as they are able to project future action). By intentionalizing these moments and rendering them hypertextually relevant to the narrative, Tony is able to foreshadow future schemes that are dependent upon the meaning of these imbedded thoughts and memories, which move beyond the normal narrative equation offered to other characters.

Tony's divided self and these multiple possible worlds are correlated. He is the portal of their reification. It is thus necessary for him to maintain distinction and apartness while determining which natural course is most germane to his life struggles. This unique and prototypical mindset allows him to drive the entire series for he is able to control, connect, and compare imaginary musings with the physical and imagined evidence he observes. This is why he is such a fan of The History Channel. For Tony, there are no contexts without primary texts in the first place. In this sense, Tony's models all come from an imagined canonical past not relegated solely to The History Channel but taken from his own family history, from mob-related anecdotes, from Hollywood movies, and from life experience. Yet, though he cultivates the messages of these paths to self-knowledge, he never cites past family exploits, never imitates actors (a favourite pastime of both Silvio Dante and Ralph Cifaretto). He may momentarily enjoy reminiscences of mob hits, but he suffers the loose lips of his peers, despises the haughty monologues of Michele "Feech" La Manna, and is especially critical of Paulie "Walnuts" Gualtieri's tendency to drone endlessly about the good ol' days. "Remember when," he tells Paulie in an episode appropriately entitled "Remember When" VI.15, "is the lowest form of conversation." Nor does he regale his immediate family with ancestral family stories or berate his sisters for abandoning the roost. Instead, he bemoans the contemporary movie-centred and publicity manic malaise that grips the new age mob, bridles at Uncle "Junior" Corrado's constant reliving if the past (until he is told of his uncle's Alzheimer's) and privileges acting within clearly established present realities based upon traditional codes. This is paramount to his everyday existence. Tony prefers to distill the myriad influence of movies, stories of the past, the brief historical sequences viewed on The History Channel to a linear, logical, and fundamentally simple formula of current intent and future action. By practising what he sees, he allows the past to define current events and change the parameters of potential action to a manageable single point of view.

Indeed, though Tony may not fully understand the theoretical framework of historical discourse, the lack of explanatory power has no effect on his adopting the examples of great men in history or examples from his mob heritage as effective imaginative constructs; another vital tool for his gun belt. Particularly informative to Tony, for example, are the words used to describe Field Marshall Erwin Rommel in "All Due Respect" V.13: "His plans were often startling, instinctive, spontaneous, and not infrequently obscure. His men idolized him and had boundless faith in him." As Tony slurps ice cream, Carmela slips to his side on the sofa just as Rommel's wife is described as a teenage sweetheart and lifelong love. The parallel between Rommel and Tony's perception of self is reinforced in his next session with Dr. Melfi. He speaks of his recurring dream of high school Coach Molinaro. He reveals how the coach once told him that he was special, "a leader of men." Tony's need for affirmation through the due respect of his men spurs him to mediate the television messages into practical and homicidal application. The lessons of history, of family, of non-ending personal stories, and mob movies allow him a plurivalent perspective that his peers lack. They establish a consistent frame of reference that shape, even in a limited manner, the logical expression of the best course of action to pursue. The linguistic and visual experiences become a path to knowledge that redefine and renegotiate the scope of his life's dialectic. Ultimately, these lessons in literacy reinforce Tony's continuing self-affirmation as a viable mob boss able to hold his own with the New York mob.

Tony is often publicly disparaged by the larger mob families of New York. Phil Leotardo especially takes a contemptuous view of Tony's apparent lack of tradition when he bemoans the lack of family honour and formal ritual in the Soprano crew. "The pygmy thing over in Jersey ... they make anybody and everybody over there. And the way that they do it is all fucked-up. Guys don't get their finger pricked, there's no sword and gun on the table. Either it has meaning or no meaning," he bleats in "Blue Comet" VI.20. But Tony understands the haughty vilification of his crew; he understands the psychologically complex combination of fear and bravado that established New York families harbour for rival New Jersey upstarts. So he chides his crew to move beyond these personal quibbles and to "Get beyond the petty bull shit. You're part of something bigger," he reminds them in "The Fleshy

Part of the Thigh" VI.4. Not group weakness but personal strength, not public hesitancy but private certainty. The threat of elimination by their New York counterparts is thereby assuaged by what Plato terms the *methexis*, or mode of participation of the individual in the universal. Tony is thus able not only to justify his actions by learning from those who came before him, but also to find satisfaction as a participant in a much larger cause by applying what he distills from the lessons that history, his family, his therapist, and his own actions teach him. These actions move beyond the domestic business spheres of neighbouring Mafia families. Tony instead relocates his immediate predicaments into a realm of complex dimensionality thereby legitimizing his decisions and actions to produce satisfactory and mutually accepted results for himself and his men. He may confuse the political philosopher with perfume and call him "Matchabelli," but Tony is indeed Machiavellian. He may only peruse *The Art of War* by Sun Tzu, but fully intuits the oriental strategies that lead to clear-cut victories. At the very least, the multifarious systems of communication, the remembered and imagined texts handed down through history by family, friends, and the media give him a sense of purpose and place. At the most, they are motivational instructions that allow him to intervene aggressively in the world and flourish as a calculating and tenacious mob boss.

Word and Image

The role of visual imagery, we have seen, be it historical, actual, fictive, or imagined, is crucial to Tony's picturing of himself and in the projection of future scenarios to his cohorts of their business and family relationships. Projection, from the Latin *projectio*, or throwing forward, involves a conjecture of events and conditions extrapolated from knowledge of the present and the past in order to envision a plausible future. This schema functions like an imaginative utopic discourse. This new visual narrative is necessarily oral-aural and is connected to the form of its content by strict semantic functions. The contingencies that are envisioned are thus not only related to the accidental events or unfortunate occurrence. Rather, the evolution of events is tempered by logical coherence, rational necessity, and, because we are in the realm of narrative, also constructed through words. As *The Sopranos* evolve as a series, a whole network of signals and references anchor the story in a self-referential and reverberating history. The more densely these nodes intersect, the more the viewer feels compelled to comprehend the potential narrative. The very centre of this world is Tony Soprano, since he provides the textual conditions of possibility for interpretation. For example, in "The Test Dream" V.11, Tony and Carmela see their immediate future selves preparing to leave the house on a television screen. When an old western comes on screen, Tony is enthralled and stops to watch. "It's so much more interesting than life," he confesses to Carmela. She responds: "Are you kidding? It is your life." That may be, and indeed Tony's life may metaphysically resemble a Hollywood movie script. Yet, unlike his underlings, Tony, we have seen, does not mimic film characters; he enjoys, but does not encourage, banter about the mob. Fully ingrained in the present yet future calculating business and personal trajectories, his image schema is entirely different. He understands that while it is impossible to find decent plumbers to apply grout (a conversation held with daughter Meadow in the pilot episode), the value of their past work should not be forgotten nor diminished by today's shoddy standards. The past in other words should not substitute reality through its parody. This hegemonic strategy has neat aetiological chains grounded in reality and edited by Tony into a suitable language for everyday mise-en-scène legitimizing. Both the act of visual projection and mnemonic reflection upon one's own embodiment, or image (even on a television screen) are tools for exercising his spatial imagination. Both are never neutral activities; each is dependent upon the entrenched power of language.

Tony is an able teller of stories, and his chronicles involve relations between memories, historical events, world affairs, and imagined necessities that he relates publicly to both his families and furtively to Dr. Melfi while in session. He lives through what he appropriates from these experiences and lives the realm that he creates through their telling. This self-conceived reality corroborates an ouroborous effect that permits him to deceive others while remaining undeceived. It's an interesting alchemy that concocts a never-ending entwining of disparate selves and social roles. It enables an ability to interface the rituals of being a mob boss while satisfying the rites of a family man. Tony relentlessly dices language to self-serving bits and details. It's all perspective, rather than truth, a way of seeing and depicting the world even when the fidelity of the image remains wilfully obscure. As the series progresses, his language evolves and demonstrates what Noam Chomsky calls "the environmental challenge" of his station in life. Tony is never allowed to truly express himself because the "prevailing orthodoxy," in this case the proscriptive norms and deterministic rituals of mobster life, is governed by the "general tacit agreement" to keep hidden the uncomfortable facts and facets of his venomous trade.[20] Tony's heartfelt concern for his mob family extends as far as power, money, and action are a form of speech with wide-ranging effects that aggrandize his own personal profit. It is important to note, then, that Tony is at a loss for language only when he confronts Dr. Melfi, when the doctor's expected returns are coloured by his significant personal loss. Let us return, here, to the beginning of the series and our first encounter with the two main characters in order to explore the most dynamic of the series' narrative interactions from the vantage point of language.

From a Platonic vantage, Tony Soprano begins the series in a state of metaphoric darkness. He is trapped, much like the prisoners of Plato's Cave,[21] inside the tautological web that conditions his apperception of the world. He is about to exit from the cave and enter into the overwhelming light by revealing stories that cannot be told. These mental constructs act as his guiding fictions; governing fantasies that fuel his feelings of insecurity. The viewer's initial impression of him completely ensconced within the thighs of the brazen green nude female statue in Dr. Melfi's anteroom in the opening scene of the series, suggests that at the very least he is trapped within the vice of feminine influence. The statue governs the scene, reducing Tony to a petite figure gawking open-mouthed at the statuesque monster. Indeed, the statue displays an autonomous strength of character not usually associated with what, at least in Tony's world, is presumed to be the weaker sex. Though the statue strikes a pose similar to the dancers he ogles daily at the Bada Bing strip club, he appears uncomfortable with the unblushing virago. The best he can do, it seems, is to cower. Our initial visual image of Tony is of an emasculated, flinching, befuddled, and classically petrified male: a prisoner frozen in time, stilled by the Medusa figure before him.[22]

This posture of the statue with its arms sassily held above its head is visually mimicked by Dr. Melfi after Tony storms out of his first session with her. Carmela is also placed before the statue as she waits to speak with Dr. Melfi in "Second Opinion" III.7. This opening shot is thus an important marker-scene. It posits a leitmotif of the main character of our story. Tony, for all his macho bravado, is threatened by female energy. This image of his latent weakness is imprinted in audience memory and becomes the indelible thumb print that conditions any future responses the viewer may engender about Tony. The proto-image sets the stage for future intercodal relationships that will inform the nature and workings of his multifaceted personalities. Is he a hulking mobster or a wimpy marshmallow?

But there is more to the commonplace conventionality of this incipient marker-scene that sets up another traditional literary paradigm: the writer, David Chase, has presented a spatial image (a silent icon) of the main protagonist of his story. In the same way that the opening descriptive passages of a romantic novel set the silent stage for the eventual story of the novel's characters, here too the viewer is enveloped in a prolonged descriptive silence. The scene is static, an odd opening sequence for a mob series. The viewer is permitted slowly to examine every point of the visual field in successive saccades. The cameraman opted for a depth of field that focuses upon the central figure dressed in black while the legs of the statue appear as two out-of-focus green pillars. This selective vantage enhances the arrested, non-moving image of Tony. It is especially easy to know where Chase wanted the audience's eye to come to rest. There are many ways of seeing the world, but obviously, the viewer is being conditioned to this snapshot vision of the single stationary eye. As the viewer surveys the scene from this limited perspective, any silent musings (and perhaps Tony's) are abruptly interrupted by sound, by a verbal utterance. In a traditional novel, this is the point where the imperfect verb tense of the predicate gives sway to perfect verb tenses. In other words, the descriptive passages are about to end, the reader is adeptly dropped into the action. Similarly, on the television screen, the palpable visual silence of the stilled image of Tony is directly overtaken by motion and temporality. The camera shifts to Dr. Melfi as she enters the anteroom. It is important to note that not until Dr. Melfi opens the series with a verbal utterance (considered masculine) does the visual description end and action (considered feminine) commence. When Dr. Melfi peers into the scene and says "Mr. Soprano?" she introduces action, in the form of language, and opens the series to its framing tale of verbal psychoanalysis. She initiates a dialogue with Tony, and with the audience, whose primary enterprise is the spoken word. Language in the series is a distended projection of fragmentary world views. It is sometimes properly used, most often misused; it is often abused, rarely sanitized, and usually ethnicized. Language is recurrently inappropriate, it can be misappropriated; or it may denote power; an utterance that makes one cower. Dr. Melfi's short and cogent vocalization wraps the spatial import of the befuddled image of a silent and wordless Tony sitting on a couch within her psychoanalytic cage of syntax, her future snare of semantics, her manoeuvred conditioning of revelatory words. Language is the starting point. It will occasion the disruption of Tony's sense of being that is inextricably bound up with his body image and the words he uses to feel embodied.

From the outset, then, the passive visual image of Tony is set in epistemological spatial contrast with the active, assertive, and aural words of Dr. Melfi. She has turned the tables on Tony, has subverted his normally assertive masculine energy, turning him into a passive image to be studied, not feared. Indeed, the crux of the series is her attempt to focus his attention on his inner anima, to make him acknowledge both the feminine virago of the green statue he seems to fear as well as the import of the heraldic feminine imagery depicted in his bedroom mural. As if to reinscribe the subversive authority and intimate connection between the green statue in the vestibule and Dr. Melfi, after Tony storms out of the office in a pique of anger, she places her arms over her head and crosses her hands behind her head. We see her from the rear, her pose echoing the virago in her lobby. The statue, an ideal embodiment of Dr. Melfi, will now begin to look back. Where the image (Tony) appears weak and confused, words (Dr. Melfi) impart strength, power, and certainty. Effective communication is the vehicle of her therapy. She is, after all, empowered to heal by using the logic of left brain techniques to cure the meanderings of the right hemisphere – a practice once reserved to the male shaman of primitive tribes. Her well-rehearsed locutions offer metaphors of sight and of potential insight. Instead of theorizing healing, she evinces modes of representation in order to achieve wisdom and revelation. Her words effectively heal when they reactualize deeply embedded memories, thereby releasing the patient into an epiphany of sensations and subliminal images. On the other hand, non-communication is Tony's realm of practical expertise. In his domain, candour and clarity of speech are marks of betrayal. Distortion, subterfuge, euphemism, and outright lie are the signposts of normal business. Absence of language, in favour of gesture and silent code, is the hallmark of Mafia allegiance and dependency. The Mafia code of *omertà* sanctions a violent assault on liberal language expression and begets a secrecy that demands taciturn contact (spatial continuity) and collusion. In Tony's world, silence is power; its marshalling and persuasive potential a controlling social mechanism.

Dr. Melfi and Tony are thus at opposing ends of the language-power spectrum. Both employ language and its absence in their own way to control and mould their environments. Both are able to utilize their considerable persuasive skills to achieve precise objectives within their mutually exclusive realms. Both recognize their mutual strengths. They therefore afford the other respect (usually) and differential decorum. The ability of these two diametrically diverse characters to master their respective linguistic domains thus determines their status within their professionally, socially, and morally circumscribed realms.

This sober stand-off conditions their responses to each other while they are normally engaged in Dr. Melfi's office. The linguistic determinism of their roles is apparent in the very first exchange between the doctor and her patient ("The Sopranos" I.1). The audience becomes aware that Tony's world is a fabricated linguistic fallacy. It is grounded in appropriated images and gestures from a limited cultural system that maps his world in circularity. His signifiers float in a distorted realm of euphemism (where a mob boss can become a "waste management consultant") and comical inversions (a viscous beating becomes friendly banter: "we had coffee"),[23] where psychological processes are conditioned by a system of miscreant values. On the other hand, Dr. Melfi's strives to empty her patient's circular utopia by exposing its mimetic fallacies. By investigating the unconscious infra-structural patterns of the stories he recounts, she deciphers their figurative content and eventually exposes their true meaning (the symbolic order of the mother, the blood imagery of capicollo, for example) to her patient, Tony. Dr. Melfi is in the business of redeeming troubled souls; Tony in taking them. She is empowered by the word. He is besot by them. The success of Dr. Melfi's therapy rests upon her ability to translate embedded emotions and memories into spoken language. Tony, on the other hand, is debilitated by honest dialogue. His leadership relies upon the ability to translate stereotypical mob images and prototypical immigrant cultural memories into effective linguistic deception. Yet both willingly attempt a rapprochement of these distinct and patently divorced realities within the confines of psychiatry. This, ultimately, is the true draw of the series. Just as Tony and Dr. Melfi are equally seduced by the confessional interplay of psychiatrist and analysand, so too the viewer is drawn into the narrative and feels compelled to remain enmeshed in both the institutional and the thematically repetitive drama. This is a radical passage; a pure act of creation that moves from nature to culture. The essential purpose of this narrative is to produce a coherent explanation of Tony's fin-de-siècle malaise despite being constricted, interestingly in both cases, by the professional (Dr. Melfi's code of ethics) and cultural (Tony's Mafia code of ritual) imprimatur of *omertà*.

If Tony's singing in a psychiatrist's office forebodes career-ending consequences, that is, loss of life, Dr. Melfi's professional restrictions of secrecy are no less impelling and would also be career-ending, that is, loss of licence. Her reasons for studying psychiatry are never delved into, yet it is intimated that she required control of personal, possibly ethnic, angst and chose her profession to better understand her being. As the reader of Tony's verbal narrative text, she must focus on a therapeutic interpretation of an ethnic story she probably knows too well. As she listens to her patient, however, she becomes aware of his unreliability as a narrator as well as of the malevolence of his character. She also becomes consumed by the seductiveness of his subversive narrative and her own vulnerability to its doubly prohibitive (male-charged and ethnic) allure. She is enthralled enough by his Mafia aura to peer out of Dr. Bruce Cusamano's bathroom window one evening to view Tony's neighbouring home. When I-Am guests at his dinner party disparage I-Am propensity towards kitsch, she defends the image of her shared Italian heritage with pride ("I like Murano glass," "A Hit Is a Hit" I.10). But she, too, displays socially imposed limits. She rejects Tony's cheapening of their common Italian lineage. When he condescendingly asks her, "What part of the Boot you from, Hon?" she coldly corrects him by asserting her public linguistic marker: "Dr. Melfi," she reminds him ("The Sopranos" I.1). Her rejection of his amorous entreaties is curt and laced with confident bravado. Her pained though unambiguous "No!" at the albeit alluring prospective of siccing Tony's vigilante justice on her rapist is chilling in its unequivocal moral resoluteness ("Employee of the Month" III.4). By interpreting Tony's lies, Dr. Melfi is painfully cognizant that she empowers her own enduring ethnic enigma, hence her own dependency upon therapy and private sessions with her own therapist regarding self-worth and identity.

Tony's foray into therapy stems from loss of consciousness; panic attacks that open an incidental space of uncontrollable discourse. These attacks are micro-discourses that interrupt the normal paradigmatic strata of mob syntagma. While under the effects of an attack (we must include the long coma sequence in Season VI), Tony is similar to an iconic object because his whole function as a text is suspended. He is observed, not heard. Since speech is stifled, he no longer produces meaning but is displaced, fixed in spatialized temporality, unable to impose narrative signification. The series arises from his attempts to verbalize the root causes of this trauma, a predicament that he attributes to a sense of dread and existential malaise. It could be said that he must learn to heal a weakened public image as a physically vulnerable mob boss. He must be taught to construct a stable self that does not faint in public. But he can no longer, apparently, solely depend upon words to redress his apology.

Tony intuitively understands that oral language is fleeting; it occupies no physical space and, most importantly from a legal standpoint, leaves no incriminating trace. He knows that the absence of speech subtends the shadowy semblances of his world and guarantees his survival. Once language is written, or it appears in recorded format, or is corroborated by written testimony, it escapes the jungle of hearsay and becomes legal tender. He is preoccupied of becoming a case study for Dr. Melfi. In "Moe and Joe" VI.10, for example, Tony recounts an incident in childhood when sister Janice had tape recorded an argument between himself and his younger sister Barbara:

> TONY: She stood in the hallway and she tape recorded me and Barb having a fight. And she held that cassette tape over my head for a month. Fuckin' extortionist. Made me make her bed, get her shit.
> DR. MELFI: Did she do that to Barbara, too?

Tony, angered and incredulous, responds:

> TONY: That's not the fuckin' point. I've been comin' here what five years now and you still don't understand what it means to tape someone in my family! You still don't fuckin' get this!

The good doctor obviously doesn't, shielded and empowered as she is by the written word and its sanctioning thrust. Tony, however, has been bred to mistrust written, but especially recorded, text. He thus spends the better part of his life withdrawing from written language. He prefers furtive encounters steeped in mystery, whispered instructions, business transactions executed in blood, coded gestures deficient of traceable intention. Images are safer; what is seen by the eye is fleeting, passing, easily misinterpreted.

Tony's multifaceted though sinisterly grounded world is marked by fabricated representations and poorly remembered words and images. He usually misinterprets these images and misappropriates the accompanying words with a conspicuous Archie Bunker–like innocence (Hannibal Lecture, for instance, instead of Hannibal Lector). He is condemned to display a studied image of outward male bravado but is often tapered to reveal a sometimes comical and faint-prone gangster figure: "I find I have to be the sad clown, laughing on the outside crying on the inside" ("The Sopranos" I.1). Tony's machismo, from this vantage, is just another word, an empty paradigmatic construct precariously erected and simultaneously emasculated by the very images that erect its facade. This character weakness augers his submission to the temptation of using what his world of codefied masculine ego abhors – words. When he breaks the code of linguistic silence, when he lies about his panic attacks, when he uses spoken language to fabricate a viable reality construct in Dr. Melfi's office, he no longer acts in the way he has been taught a man should. *Real* men, in Tony's undifferentiated apperception of the world, act in silence. They proffer no excuses. They conjure approbative *absence* in taciturn alliances that ultimately refer to the power construct of embodied illicit *presence*. Tony's existential quandary can be summed up accordingly: he has come to understand the unvoiced actions of his trade as well as the images that cripple his psyche. Tony's strength follows consequently: he does not succumb to the logic of reality, preferring instead to use the antitheses of his reality as an opportunity to exert more power in forceful actions. He, therefore, does not deconstruct his own stereotype by dismantling mob constructs as one would normally expect from psychoanalytic therapy, but uses therapy to foster a magic of power that consolidates his personal world view.

The ideal viewer is aware from the series' opening scene that any attempt by Tony to act towards an understanding of self through words has been stilled by the petrifying stare of the Medusa female. This has been his vital dilemma. As he struggled with the narrative life story he was compelled to relate to Dr. Melfi, he felt himself slipping through the crevices of confessional language. The process was just too revelatory. Tony is hard pressed to identify with the intimate structures of his duplicitous nature because the malevolent image of his neurotic disorder strikes notes to strident to bear.

Dr. Melfi's reality, on the other hand, depends solely upon the psychoanalytic certainty of abstract linguistic signs. The written and spoken word is her chosen realm. An academy of texts, professional literature, and a canon of corroborated medical facts establish credentials that have created the self that sustains her being. Her reasoning is linear, rational, orthodox, all tacit masculine qualities. Her personal weakness is involuntarily submitting to the lure of the irrational gloss, to the bait of Tony and his attractive villainy, to the temptation of his bad-boy image. She is seduced by his bacchanal sloth and enticed by his subversive cultural message. In many respects, Tony is the modern echo of a primitive warrior, an alpha male; the prohibited fruit dangled before young impressionable women. Dr. Melfi knows she fits Tony's preternatural image of femininity. She is dark, from "the Boot," seductively intelligent, and dangerously independent. But he married a fair-skinned New Jersey Italian blond. Interestingly, Jennifer Melfi chose to marry a relatively innocuous I-Am male.

Both characters seem steeped in contradictions. These motivations bind them to often unbearable, or at least discomfiting compromises. These moments carry the viewer into the heart of theoretical discourse itself. What, indeed, is the difference between the latent image of what they perceive, of what they crave, and the destructive content of one others' secrets? What would happen if one or the other chose to disengage from their distinctive opening stances and enact a supplementary narrative by moving towards the other's realm? In other words, is it possible for Tony and Dr. Melfi to pursue their tantalizing imagocentric mania for each other? Can they overcome the strictures of their self-imposed logocentrism and create a *different* story?

The forging of a new equilibrium portends a realignment of priorities. Obviously, they are both inextricably bound to a sense of continuity that cannot deny empirical reality. And, of course, it simply cannot happen because the mutual exclusivity of their respective domains ultimately determines the outcome of their respective fates. At series' end, it is precisely their acceptance or rejection of their hyper relation with words that will sanction the finality of *The Sopranos*. Neither relinquishes masculine dominance to become subordinate. Neither betrays the honour of their professions to engage in a politically correct deterritorialization. Power, in this case, is the ability to stop the proliferation of possibilities to suit particular ends. Before the drama is allowed to climax, however, both interlocuters must come to terms with their separate worlds, accept their shrunken parameters, and evermore remain asunder. For Tony, Dr. Melfi will remain a morality-laden afterthought. For Dr. Melfi, Tony prevails as the loathsome underbelly of the seductive face of American enterprise.

A Blacker Shade of Pale

When Tony exclaims, "I get it!" in "Kennedy and Heidi" VI.18, he has just awakened from a peyote-induced delirium. It is a sort of transcendental awareness, induced by drugs and consummated in the barren desert heat of Nevada, that springboards him to a new level of cognition, of anagnorisis. He exclaims to the universe, and to himself, that he has exited Plato's Cave. The shadows and the simulacra of reality have dissipated as he stands on the threshold between orality and literacy. What remains is clarity. He can see plainly. He can speak unequivocally. The word-riddled anomalies and image-laden memories that have heretofore battled for his soul have found respite in a newly conquered personal serenity. He now wholly accepts both the visual projection and the verbal construct of himself as a mobster. The repeated query: "Who am I? Where am I going?" that reverberated throughout the series, but which found material expression during his prolonged coma (Season VI.1, 2, 3) has now been answered. He will not be hampered by the green statue's subtending psychological subversion, no longer encumbered by Coach Molinaro dreams or the alter ego of an optics salesman. Shortly, even Dr. Melfi's reprobate monologues will be fodder for the past. On the practical front, Carmela's hollow and familiar lamentations, his crew's ingenuous inadequacies, his children's unfolding histories will no longer entangle him, no longer embroil him in protracted anxiety. He no longer need abide debilitating notions of Vito Spatafore's latent homosexuality, his crew's homophobia, his uncle's mental irrationality. Such issues no longer affect his life. They have been laid to rest. It is indeed interesting that A.J.'s transference of identification from mother to the father, Meadow's switch from the nurturing profession of doctor to the male-dominated realm of law, and Carmela's newfound motherly resolve all come to the fore precisely at this moment in the series. Life is good, it seems, as reflective hesitancy dissolves in the thinning desert mist.

This vital life change signals a metaphorical bridging between the left and right hemispheres of the brain and the harmonization of their concomitant attributes. Tony's once-divided psychic sensibilities[24] have been healed. From the viewpoint of narrative, self-understanding is the healing fiction that permits him to leave behind acts of linear time and construct new acts of the imagination. As he becomes ever more whole and comfortable in his dastardly skin, so does his salutary perspective on the happenings around him. The pain of finding a comfortable and sustainable mimesis (in either word or image) of his divided self, the dilemma of facing his morally bereft choices, have come to a head and have been resolved. The "fat fuckin crook" can now iterate unmistakable locutions of self-knowledge. He can say, "I'm a miserable prick," and mean it. The difference between then ("Calling All Cars" IV.11) and now (series end) is that he is no longer caught in an interminable uroboric paradox. He has broken the habit of equating the past with the present. His life has ceased to cipher a coded message but has become instead an irrefutable, albeit disreputably notorious, display of unmasked authenticity. He may now actually nurture his chosen realm. He has survived multiple attempts on his life, murdered his closest friends, suffocated his nephew. But he has also revealed a well-spoken and intelligent alter ego while in coma. Only now is he able to transit to a new differentiated space and wilfully acknowledge the tattooed beast that graces his arm. The tiger is the apex predator that has replaced the symbolic image of his Medean mother; it resides within, a psychic vessel of fervent urgency, prophesy, and mission.[25]

Throughout the series the viewer has been invited to read words on the television screen along with Tony. We recall especially the image of the Nathaniel Hawthorne quotation sculpted into stone. There will no longer be "Two Tonys," an apt title of the opening episode of Season V. That season began the structural removal of the series' conflicting points of view. The viewer is asked to rethink *The Sopranos'* social map as a metaphor for an imagined world built on the represented order imposed by Tony. As he slowly sloughs off his existential tiredness, he may move towards his moment of lucidity. To paraphrase Phil Leotardo in "The Blue Comet" VI.20, Tony "decapitates, and does business with whatever is left." The character that emerges at series' end is a fully assembled mobster firmly embedded at the crux of his own personal empire.[26]

In the final episode, the viewer is again invited to read along with Tony while he's sitting at Holsten's Diner. As he searches through song titles on the tableside jukebox, the words build a storyline that resonate in his life and read as thematic signposts of his six-season journey: "Those Were the Days"; "This Magic Moment"; "Who Will You Run To?"; "Don't Stop Believin'"; "I've Gotta Be Me."[27] His entire life has been spread out before him and he, along with the viewer, reads the emblematic abstract all at once. Scrolling through the titles one notes their melancholic conclusiveness but more importantly the resoluteness of the final song title that is never uttered by Tony but read by both character and viewer: "I've Gotta Be Me." The title defines the man and empowers his self-validating visual-verbal myth. Moreover, all his inarticulate desires and unfathomable fears have been summed up in this concluding text of musical monologue.

A similarly complex change also occurs with Dr. Melfi, Tony's psychic foil and series travelling companion. Equally pained by subjectivity, feelings, and torments, her deepening discoveries of her motivations for tolerating Tony revise the incoherence of her story. As she moves from a position of interpretive commentator of Tony's fictions to author of her own literal truth, she must reject any hysterical or paranoid corroboration in his case history. Though she has not heeded the repeated warnings of her own psychiatrist regarding the endorsement of Tony's criminality through therapy (in essence she mistrusts the intentionality of what is uttered by her own therapist, remarkable and revealing), Dr. Melfi's emotionally compromised stance regarding Tony changes once her visual fixation with dangerously tantalizing image is subordinated to the renewed empowerment of the bedrock of her professional life, the written word.

The preponderance of written words presented on the television screen in the final episodes of *The Sopranos* is indicative of an unfolding, if not unravelling, of the elements and relations that have created the images in which the audience has so pleasurably engaged. When the story begins to "tell itself" as it arises by displaying the words read by the characters, this can be understood as a textual mark of simultaneity and co-presence. The viewer, the character, and even the writer, are literally on the same page. The whole is offered for micro-inspection. No hidden surfaces or secrets remain. The action of the series that began in the opening scene of the pilot episode with active verbs is about to once again become descriptive, leaving only the echo of actions that are about to end. But isn't this what the viewer expected from the very start? The first move in the narrative, we have contended, is affected by the arrival of Dr. Melfi as she takes her place within the profane world of Tony Soprano. The final move is marked by her return into the hallowed space of her profession sans Tony Soprano. Both Dr. Melfi and Tony are woven into the carpet of this figurative picture. Each is valorized in a contrary way. Each painstakingly constructs a model of reality where it is the contradictions of the language they employ that cancel each other out and eventually become mutually exclusive. The result is a homogeneous unity where underlying personal tension and pathologically morbid structures may be momentarily masked only to be fully revealed in the remaining word traces – song titles for Tony, academic text for Dr. Melfi – that sanction the death knell of the series.

In "The Blue Comet" VI.20, the audience enters Dr. Melfi's bedroom and finds her reading in bed. Ominous words scroll slowly onto the television screen. The stalwart images of ink, pillars of canonic strength firmly embedded in paper stock, acquire symbolic relevance and counteract any specious spatial imagery that might remain of Tony Soprano. Dr. Melfi and viewer read the article's title: "The Criminal Personality" by Samuel Yockelson and Stanton E. Samenov. (Page is turned) "The criminal's sentimentality reveals itself in compassion for babies and pets." (Cut to Dr. Melfi turning page) "The criminal uses insight to justify heinous acts." (Cut to a visibly worried Dr. Melfi) "Therapy has potential for non-criminals; for criminals, it becomes one more criminal operation."

Reading these words changes her (and the viewer's) perception of Tony. Rather than threatening her identity, the article reconstitutes her authority by reconstructing not only what has happened throughout the series but also how it felt, how it appeared, and how it was experienced. In a flash, Dr. Melfi explodes the experiential density of the visual details and literally joins the viewer as she now bears witness to what the audience has always known. The written word (*ecriture*), with all its intellectual and sociocultural baggage, now eclipses the spoken word (*phone*)[28] and undermines her former tainted interpretation of Tony. The written text reclaims special status, refutes any venturesome psycho-rhetoric. As Dr. Melfi replaces her trust in the canonical authority of the text, we, too, as readers, diminish the distance between our own possible repulsion towards Tony and any potential remnant of emotional attraction the viewer may still harbour. Reading thus becomes an assertive enactment of selfhood even for the viewer. This sort of conversion is adumbrated when Artie Bucco rediscovers his selfhood in the handwritten recipes of his father ("Luxury Lounge" VI.7), when A.J. reads Yeats ("The Second Coming" VI.19), and earlier when Christopher loses his false self in the spelling errors of his poorly written manuscript and tosses it into the incinerator ("Mr. Ruggerio's Neighborhood" III.1).The written texts in these instances bear witness to acts of recollection. They are memory sites, accounts of the temporal processes that produced convenient images for the time but are now superseded.

For Dr. Melfi, the written word is a liberating gesture. Not until she reads the written text and is set straight by its linear logic and staid solemn syntax is she able to rationally and intellectually undo her imagocentric attraction to the likeable bad-boy mobster. The left, analytical side of Dr. Melfi's brain now assumes control. She will listen to reason (a functional trait of the left brain) and not be swayed by the nurturing side (and traditionally feminine trait) of her right brain. Though she had been reproved on several occasions to reject Tony, the oral reprimand was not convincing. Scrolling through the text from left to right, however, imparts the same unilateral force and purposeful direction as throwing a lance or firing a gun. The same verbal aggression Tony imparts upon his foes subtends the potent cutting prose of the Yockelson and Samenov article. Both assertive gestures, one corporeal, one mental, are disruptive acts. Tony's spoken words kill victims; the article kills Dr. Melfi's relationship with Tony.

In essence, Tony is defeated not by the feminine, intuitive, right-brained side of his nature – as we have been led to expect by the series since he follows therapy to resolve this chronic issue – but by Dr. Melfi's decision to abruptly declare a terminus to the words of therapy. Her action reinforces, ironically, the left-brained masculine principle. If the right brain deals with gestalts and with being, the left elucidates the world through language, its unique form of symbolization. Writing (and the reading of written words) makes ideas visible by presenting the obscure and the incomprehensible through graphic language. The wilful absence of language is a paralysing, if not frightful, monstrosity. The outright destruction of words, from this point of view, precipitates sinister and dangerous alterity. It is interesting, then, that during their very last session ("The Blue Comet" VI.20), Dr. Melfi berates Tony (the language is tellingly precise) for "defacing my reading materials" by tearing pages from her anteroom magazines. She literally accuses him of stealing her words for his own malevolent use. The significance of the utterance is lost on Tony, but not on the ideal viewer/reader who is privy to the doctor's newfound resolve. She scolds him for his disregard for "the body of work that's gone into building-up this science." Dr. Melfi now venomously relinquishes her linguistic primacy, and thereby her synthesizing control, over Tony (and thus her own latent yearning for completion in the subaltern image he projects) when she allows the written word, and morality, to regain primacy in her intellectual life. No longer disabled by a subversive imagocentric interpretation of issues, the revelatory prerogative of logocentric values legitimizes a newfound intellectual resolve to act like a man and kill her relationship with Tony. Her slamming the door shut on her ex-patient is an "end-of-story" gesture that declares her freedom. It also mirrors her act of opening that same door to commence the series. It's a story of in and out, of limens; of the great demarcation between the inner man and the outer world. As in Greek tragedy, their sessions have been cathartic and have revealed their inner foibles, their strengths, their anomalies. Both now accept their fates. Dr. Melfi has become as hardened as her male antagonist and, by aborting their temporal flow, has halted the storyline. There is no more story, no more Tony Soprano, no more psychological drama to narrativize. Tony has also readily accepted his destiny and, like the best of tragic heroes, secures his place in the flow of time. The difference, however, is while she has ineluctably reaffirmed the canonical *logos* of America the good, Tony has become ever more ensconced within the American *imagos* of a successful at any cost, morally corrupted, yet socially accepted, and dispassionate outlaw. In essence, the final episode of the series can be viewed as an epilogue, an impious projection of mob boss Tony Soprano's recreant life beyond therapy. When viewed with the pilot episode, the two become part of a frame tale, brilliant first and last acts of David Chase's world view.

The series, then, is not about killing Tony Soprano, as many expected and wished for and chastised David Chase for not fulfilling the bloody expectations of mob-story convention. The series finds its foundation and also its conciliation in the provocative antagonism between the actions of a mobster and the progressive accumulation of insight into the salacious, and forever silent, underpinnings of the cost of success in America. It is a hidden underbelly that both frightens and allures. It is "an America at every level at war with itself."[29] The sessions between Tony and Dr. Melfi are thus a confessional ritual, the unction of contradictory poles where the repetition of deeds are unfolded and ordered, where morality is callously cancelled and surreptitiously affirmed. All along, the series has been inward looking; about making Tony whole. It has always been about a guy that walks into a psychiatrist's office, confused about his evolving state in the world, uncomfortable with, but resigned to, the nature of his unconventional life beyond the normal bounds of convention; buoyed by the seductive materiality of attainment. An American Everyman of heroic magnitude. It was about addressing psychological issues that had rendered him a halved individual unable to feel like a legitimate mobster because he craved a spatial fix (for images, i.e., a longing for his symbolic mother, legitimacy in the world of the father, normalcy and acceptance) while yearning for the freedom of temporal flow and syntax (for words, i.e., the death of the mother, the lack of a father, uniqueness and solitude). Despite the existential strictures, Tony performs the passage into his new reality admirably. He masterfully toes the line between perception and reality while all (a)moral denotations regarding the political, social, and economic constitution of the structures of his world remain shrouded in the cultural duplicity of pain and anxiety, joy and tranquillity.

Hence the controversial ending of the series that leaves closure dangling and promotes open readings and thematic ambiguity. As the rock band Journey intones, life indeed goes on and on and on ... for Tony, for his family, for the mob, for Dr. Melfi, for America. We simply don't really know how. Chase has fittingly acknowledged and exploited a disturbing millennium consciousness that questions the validity of American mores while promoting the American paradigm of progress, as dim as that light may seem:

> People have said that the Soprano family's whole life goes in the toilet in the last episode, that the parents' whole twisted lifestyle is visited on the children. And that's true – to a certain extent. But look at it: A.J.'s not going to become a citizen-soldier or join the Peace Corps to try to help the world; he'll probably be a low-level movie producer. But he's not going to be a killer like his father, is he? Meadow may not become a pediatrician or even a lawyer, but she's not going to be a housewife-whore like her mother. She'll learn to operate in the world in a way that Carmela never did. It's not ideal. It's not what the parents dreamed of. But it's better than it was. Tiny, little bits of progress – that's how it works.[30]

In essence, Chase has reintroduced the notion of individual growth and progress as a limited *process* to be measured not in the soul-deadening juggernaut of alienation, but in the interface of eternal paradox. The ending reaffirms this delicate, vital, and dangerous minuet between self-fulfilment and self-destruction. This tone is reflected in the overall style of the series but nowhere more than in the final sequence where any mundane referential remnant of the conventions of mob movies and mob speak is subverted by a playfully elegant and ultimately disruptive writing style that questions those very mob codes and conventions that subtend the mobster mystique and thereby perpetuate the ethnic stereotype. As the family (Tony, Carmela, and son A.J.) await the completion of their private circle (daughter Meadow) in the public space of Holsten's Diner, the intimacy and warmth of the locale is paradoxically fraught with menace and impending dread. Will this be the final family gathering? Will Tony be shot? And what of those intimidating individuals? Are they here to eat or harm? Finally, why is Meadow having so much trouble parking? Is she, in the event of the unthinkable, to be the sole family survivor? As the visual images clash in a crescendo of impelling uncertainties, Chase permits the viewer to speculate sequences, to ponder upshots, to highlight the possibilities and become part of the creative communion. The unresolved paradigms mimic the subtending, though momentarily subdued, antagonisms of the characters. By placing the tools of his craft directly in the lap of his viewers, by encouraging them to speculate out loud, Chase exposes the eternal struggle between contesting modes of perception and leaves all issues deliciously unresolved. The only certainty, the centrality of Tony as malevolent Mafioso may have been vouchsafed; but the phantasmagoric construct is engulfed, at series' end, by the final image of total ineluctable darkness.[31]

Chapter Five

An Appendix of Verbal Bits and Visual Bytes

All attention must take place against a background of inattention.

E.H. Gombrich

David expects you to commit to details as much as he does. Nothing's left to chance ... It's never "Carmela goes to the door and the delivery boy gives her the birthday cake." It's "Carmela goes to the door and the delivery boy is a nineteen-year-old Brazilian guy wearing an Artuso's Pastry Shop Baseball cap – and he has a lisp." Or, they'll go to the hospital and the emergency room doctor is "a Sikh with a turban but no accent." And then when they cast it, they really go find that nineteen-year-old Brazilian or that Sikh.

Michael Imperioli cited in Brett Martin, *The Sopranos: The Complete Book*

Another distinctive feature of *The Sopranos* language is Chase's love for old-fashioned Italian-American slang. When Fat Dom was stabbed at Satriale's Pork Store, Chase wrote a line for Silvio: "We've got to clean this up. Go get some biangalin ..." The great thing is that David doesn't care if most of the audience has no idea what Silvio said. He's happy if three percent will be delighted by hearing that word.

Terence Winter cited in Bertt Martin, *The Sopranos: The Complete Book*

Introduction

My first-year-university-level course *The Sopranos*: Cultural Contexts for Critical Thinking was conceived to examine the conceptual models about ethnic assimilation that have traditionally competed in North America and that have welded to form contemporary American society. Drawing upon HBO's popular and perennially controversial series,

I wanted students to probe notions of artistic representation and reconsider ways of interpreting, in this case, a television program. I hoped that by the end of the semester each student would develop a unique perspective on a particular aspect of the series and relate it to the world around them. I purposefully chose *The Sopranos* because it provided a real and immediate means to ponder visual representation in the pop intellectual territory in which the students live. Indeed, some entered the course under the mistaken impression that we'd spend the semester watching the series and discussing their half-baked notions about individual episodes and favourite characters. The ideas of these individuals contained such contradictions that they found it difficult to defend often outlandish positions since they were unhinged from the story and unfettered critically. Not trained in knowing what to look for, they needed guidance. For the most part, however, as the class grew within David Chase's cultural construction of end-of-millennium America, most understood, sooner or later, that no fiction, however popular, however relevant, however disliked, however irreverent, is ever intellectually innocent. A finely wrought and exquisitely written series can be a clear window on an opaque world. However, the formulas of representation of that world are conditioned by the viewer's own individual visions and cultural codes as well as the artist's motivations and idiosyncrasies. Most importantly, however, the students learned from my analyses of the series and from their debating with one another that effective interpretation always begins and must relentlessly depend upon the text.

To make the eighty-six episodes manageable, students were expected to view the entire series outside the classroom setting; classroom time was spent examining particular episodes and scenes and grappling with storyline events chosen by me. I used a variety of critical approaches when presenting an episode being sure to highlight the tight and coherent shape of each as if it were a freestanding work of fiction. I then focused on the ongoing and expansive characterization that marked the creative link to the Bildungsroman and serial novels of the nineteenth century. In this manner, I privileged a coherent step-by-step analysis that highlighted lateral connections over a narrative arc. My choice of topic and viewpoint was guided by a comparative methodology that translated interdisciplinary and parallel interrelationships into leitmotifs that engaged students to challenge and redesign their appreciation of aesthetic and historical experience embodied in the arts. My pedagogical view thus mirrored the world view of the series since it rejected simple characterization and plot in favour of real life complications and inconsistencies. I therefore chose scenes that best exemplified specific perspectives that lent themselves to a developing critique of open-endedness. Though I always provided my own interpretation, I allowed the material to pose the problem and adjusted my reading of the scenes accordingly. In this manner, words that once meant nothing to the students beyond their function of dialogue, actions that seemed relevant only to the immediate issue at hand, became concepts that, when retooled from a theoretical context, engaged the students in multiform literary, filmic, philosophical, political, and social critique. As I described the possible theoretical and critical underpinnings as well as the intertextual allusions that helped form my tentative conclusions, students became empowered with the interpretative skills by which to propose and support their own variegated, but always informed, analyses.

I am convinced that students learn more from the practical application of knowledge than from any theoretical master-knower proclamations. To prepare students to freely speak in class in a reasoned manner should be the aim of any instructor. Towards this end, I provided relevant critical material that helped them perceive the issues that subtend the series. These readings ranged from articles covering gender studies, feminism criticism, ethnicity, characterization, mobster stereotypes, and I-Am language and culture, to a potpourri of related sociopolitical arguments that both enhanced and problematized their apperception of the series. The most successful students actively deconstructed individual scenes or characters by dethroning their own preconceived notions of predetermined value. Others found the necessity to make lateral connections between the many visual cues in the series daunting, but accepted the challenge and eventually moved from their comfortable perch of traditional viewing entertainment. All ultimately came away from the course with a newly found sense of cultural empowerment and expanding critical acumen.

If watching films and television programs were as simple as observing what is seen on the screen and understanding only what is scripted by the characters, all films and programs would enunciate exclusively that which has already been determined by the media's own conventions. Fortunately, however, these media systems, let's call them codes, allow viewers to enunciate suppositions and events that the code did not fully anticipate, to see beyond the composite images the creator has divined, to render meta-semiotic judgments that reveal unexpected epiphanies that lead the viewer behind the scenes and further into the minds of both the characters and of their creator. For example,

Hollywood settings are chock-full of objects. These objects, call them props, can be used to frame and focus a field of vision in the photographic sense of the term. Sometimes props enhance the difference between the characters and what surrounds them. Sometimes they help characterize the subject in the scene by providing obvious visual support. Props can give the subject depth, provide a nuance, intimate an added meaning. Elsewhere they may reveal a character's shortsightedness. This occurs when the character in the scene sees less than what the viewer sees or has difficulty understanding the aggregate of features and objects in his surroundings. In these cases, it is the informed viewer that supplements the message and constructs a potential virtual dimension that is wilfully more cogent than that of the unreliable character. By measuring the amount of information the character perceives, one may deduce whether a character is round, flat, focal, supportive, generic, and so forth. Perhaps the character is particularly astute and is able to ferret out, as is the case with story protagonist Tony Soprano, ambiance nuances that confirm his suspicions and validate the viewer's impressions. Sometimes the character is merely two-dimensional or flawed, like Christopher Moltisanti. Confined to the limits of his story, he is unable to extend his influence beyond his arc because of his own deleterious confines. Unlike Tony, he simply doesn't learn to see the props and is incapable of playing the interpretative game of clue finding. Settings and props form the gestalt for the program's virtual dimension and are ultimately measured both by the characters and the ideal viewer.

The visual cues of a television program are part of a metaphoric network of cultural discourse that articulate a complex poetics of visual detailing. More often than not, viewers are hardly aware of them. Entire backdrops can fade away in a flash as attention is focused on the central action and dialogue of the scene and not the peripheral contingencies. But very often the background posters, the books held in a character's hand, the seemingly innocuous objects seen behind a character jump to the forefront. In these instances, the props may have a particular relation to that character and are a possible tool for either defining character traits or may, at the least, add depth and interest to the overall story. While the viewer may not immediately appreciate their wordless flavour, visual impressions of their passing through the scene remain wrapped in the shadows of subliminal awareness. They foster latent structuring metaphors that provide the articulations necessary in the always problematic development and description of fictional characters.

Ultimately, these visual subtexts harbour invaluable clues that advance the eventual resolution of *The Sopranos* story. This self-consciously marginal dimension varies each time one watches. It is commonplace to say that on a second viewing an attentive viewer may notice things that were missed the first time. This implicit inexhaustibility of the interpretation of texts allows, even induces, innovative viewings that provoke fortuitous links between the many seemingly disparate visual sightings. "It's almost like he's [Chase] asking us all to make up our own minds, which is extraordinary. Usually in TV they lead you by the nose, but David really wants you to think."[1]

The Sopranos is a lush and richly adorned series. The appointments of its settings are trendy New Jersey and, save for relatively few sojourns into areas outside Sopranoland, reflect precisely the sort of space these characters would normally inhabit, the types of posters, art, and statuary that would inhabit their living space. Upscale homes for the bosses, seedy strip joints, greasy spoons, and tawdry backrooms of putrid meat shops are everyday consumption and add realism to the mobster brand. Within this realm, the observant eye is bombarded with background objects, the attentive ear overhears periphery dialogues that add authenticity and map out a recognizable Soprano terrain. But often the props and visual paraphernalia that clutter the scene, the dialogue heard from television sets, are strategically positioned between the synapses of character dialogue, and between the sight lines of conversing actors. At times, these precisely parcelled moments seem to take over. Contemporary pop posters or recognizable artworks surge to the fore and proffer unexpected commentary behind the characters, a television dialogue playing on a distant TV set may fill in the blank spaces of silence in character dialogue. Whatever the instance, this often conspicuous visual and aural information becomes the fortuitous happenstance that drives the series' contextual momentum.

We are, essentially, creatures of images (moving and not) of words (spoken, written, or heard). They construct our everyday world with laden symbols, proliferative signage; they create our world through shared messages. Reality is an empty canvas waiting to be filled and, in our media-saturated world, humanity seems poised to fill it. In the realm of film, images and words are "the basic story stuff"[2] that animate and give life to a work. In *The Sopranos*, the ideal viewer is invited to augment the series content, in essence to write more script, by fleshing-out the characters and scenes vis-à-vis the words and images that surround them. This mix between written and spoken text engages the ideal viewer in ever-new-ways, keeping him/her constantly surprised, senses heightened, inferences abounding. As the ideal viewer takes inferential walks[3] beyond the visual text on the television screen, layers of potential meaning are superimposed upon the storyline. David Chase privileges just this type of intertextual competence in his ideal viewer for he has carefully included all sorts of extra-story references to intertextually subtend and extend his intratextual storylines. The visual/verbal moments of added experience, the props, are part of a value chain that moves from the writer's inception to the ideal viewer's experience. This shared experience creates a pleasurable secondary world that augments the normal viewer's understanding and response to the series and incites him/her to probe even more, in essence becoming Chase's ideal viewer. To his credit, Chase makes the experience a labyrinthine sojourn as complex and serpentine as his imagination and television media would allow. The multi-tracked and laterally connected arguments are pieces of an evolving puzzle; complex symmetries and subversive complementarities part of a decipherable grid that adds to *The Sopranos'* aesthetic message. It's all about organizational learning and operational cuing. The cues may often be missed. But once the viewer catches-on to the game and is willing to actively participate in the construction of a more complete story, he/she discovers that depth is always more telling than the surface, that background noise usually conditions foreground clarity, and that more often than not that which seems filler is actually thematic sustenance. The ideal viewer is essentially invited into the show, coaxed and teased to make intra- and extratextual connections and complete the message by making intelligent inferences.

In *The Principles of Painting*, Roger de Piles states, "Painting should call out to the viewer ... and the surprised viewer should go to it, as if entering a conversation."[4] If viewing *The Sopranos* provides a multilevelled occasion for a lively interactive dialogical interpretation, then the viewer's conversation with the series is measurably enhanced when considering the words and images that depict Sopranoland. Whether espying a rock-band poster, recognizing a classic painting, reading a newspaper headline, contemplating a family photograph, or eavesdropping on a television program, the ideal viewer is invited to transform these everyday banal objects of a domestic setting into an enhanced commentary. During these moments, it is as if the viewer is blowing-up details, reassembling what he/she sees, and making lateral connections as if unravelling an ever-evolving rebus. The space of the series is thus not necessarily contained only by the stage of its theatre. Its actions, emotions, themes, and style can be mirrored in the accoutrements that transform television drama into a shared fictional reality.

In this realm of open-ended interpretation, each ideal viewer's conversation with the series is affected by what he/she knows or believes – according to his/her cultural baggage. It is not solely a question of mechanically reacting to media stimuli. While looking may be an act of choice, observing, surveying, deciphering, decoding, and analysing the relation between the seemingly trivial words and random images detailed in these scenes and the larger story is a continually active, intellectually fluid, and critically guided methodology governed by the interpretative strategies brought to the conversation. If we accept this reciprocal bond between an ideal viewer and an ideal text, then the enjoyment of discovering the stories that are explicitly or secretly woven into the design of the series through examining the use of seemingly innocuous props greatly enhances the viewer's pleasure and rewards critical curiosity with interpretative empowerment.

* * *

The following appendix is a casebook of the wide range of practical textual examples that I have used to discuss and analyse *The Sopranos*. My purpose is to briefly note entertaining, and always fascinating, visual mise-en-abîme moments in the series that, when taken together, generate a supplementary subtext that thematically subtends and ideologically extends the series. The samples are limited to those moments where an apparently inconsequential background noise or a fleeting glance at words or images in ambient surroundings provide a source that weaves itself into the main text. I use them to address the teaching of theory from an implicit pedagogical strategy that privileges the hands-on and practical approach of confronting what is seen on the television screen with critical discourse. I have found that this experience of close analysis challenges students to interpret and engage different meanings just as they might when reading a novel and, most importantly, never to assume reductive meanings when our challenge is to problematize simplicity by uncovering its deceivingly intricate subtexture. My commentary is limited to a descriptive detail, sometimes elaborated, most often understated, sometimes merely noted. I wish to provide a lead and to allow further signification and intertextual inferences by whomever wishes to elaborate these *in nuce* notions.

An Appendix of Verbal Bits and Visual Bytes   203

What follows, then, is a potpourri of selected visual bytes and verbal bits that animate many scenes of *The Sopranos* and which in turn create a looping Mobius dialogue within the series. The list is meant to be a loose snapshot of my viewings and is infinitely inconclusive; every viewing of an episode, every reviewing of these scenes for classroom discussion, reveals evermore possibilities that should be added to this open-ended list. Here, then, I suggest possibilities instead of coverage. I also do not include many moments already mentioned or discussed earlier. I hope that the appending of these samples at the end of this study provides an extension of the ideal viewer's interpretative pleasure and that these visual subtexts translate into a narrative echo that resonates in a continuing and more engaged aesthetic appreciation of *The Sopranos*. These samples function to empower and engage the user to carefully observe, read, speak, and negotiate interpretations situated within each sample's position in the overall network of thematic correspondences. They are not a bankable set of mastered facts but rather bits and bytes of a larger discourse yet to be engaged. They are arranged by thematic categories in order to facilitate use. When taken together, they forward an active exercising of the issues we have argued in this text.

* * *

Paintings

The many paintings that adorn *The Soprano* sets provide supplemental receptive experiences for the viewer. Obviously, paintings are not the casual forte of *The Sopranos* mob families. This shark-skin-suited culture is more comfortable with sexually provocative posters than conventional works of great art. Indeed, apart from the original paintings hanging in Dr. Melfi's office and home and the Pablo Picasso originals in A.J. girlfriend Devon's upscale home, the walls of these mobsters are normally cluttered with kitschy murals of pseudo-Italian landscapes and cheap imitations of known originals. The samples range from Artie Bucco's paintings of the Bay of Naples and the Roman Forum in his restaurants, the mural of a Venetian gondola in the Canal Grande in Carmine Lupertazzi's newly opened restaurant, to the *trompel'oeil* mural in "Little" Carmine Lupertazzi Jr.'s Florida home. These nostalgia-ridden canvases colour the series' action within definite low-brow I-Am parameters. The "working crew," as they are disparagingly referred to by the New York families, may suffer all the indignation heaped upon them by their culturally hip big city brothers for being uncouth, but their own public locales and private homes are equally lacking in New Yorker panache. On both sides of the Hudson River, the paintings exhibited in background typically speak towards the stereotypical association of mobsters with scaloppini, romanticized Italian panoramas, and checkered tablecloths; all part of their exaggerated sensual appetites and minimal intellectual enlightenment.

But the art on display, nevertheless, tells a pertinent story. Beyond the Soprano bedroom mural and those paintings in Dr. Melfi's office anteroom already discussed at length, the choice of paintings that are seen in the series unintentionally or intentionally holds a sympathetic or castigating mirror to this world and opens these colourful vistas to playful considerations.

Samples

- When the Sopranos visit Green Grove in "Meadowlands" I.4, Tony and his mother Livia settle in front of a large painting of women seated in a hierarchical pose. The women in the painting stare out onto the reality before them. Tony is completely surrounded by their painted figures; his black shirt places him squarely within the frame of the chiaroscuro painting. The Green Grove painting adumbrates, both imagistically and metaphorically, the Soprano bedroom mural of posed women the viewer will behold on the day Livia dies in "Proshai, Livushka" III.2.
- Tony and his crew bosses chat in front of a pastoral painting depicting an English fox hunt in "Boca" I.9. The classically bedecked horsemen striding their horses eerily foreshadows Tony's retouched painting of himself in similar dress with Pie-O-My in "All Due Respect" V.13.
- Authentic Pablo Picasso paintings adorn the walls of A.J.'s girlfriend Devon's home in "Everybody Hurts" IV.6. Devon's natural authenticity and unpretentious attitude offsets A.J.'s studied airs as he attempts to impress his girlfriend with what he comes to realize is mere Soprano kitsch.
- In "Rat Pack" V.2, Tony is given a reproduction of the famous 1960s Rat Pack featuring Frank Sinatra, Sammy Davis, and Dean Martin by "Black Jack" Mazzarone. Tony immediately identifies with the tenor and characters of the painting and appreciates the gesture. More important than religion and family, he turns a distracting

family photo and a picture of the Virgin Mary on his mantel face down to make room for the canvas. The painting unfortunately also reminds Tony once again that "he came in late" and that the camaraderie and trust of the legendary Pack is now only a faded memory. In the same episode, he tosses the work into the river after realizing that the painting is also a metaphor for Mazzarone, a "rat" on the FBI informer's list.

- Perhaps the most self-conscious moment of ethnic kitsch appears in "Marco Polo" V.8. The episode opens upon a gold-gilded Venetian chandelier. A huge imitation Renaissance-style painting is slowly panned. A bare-bosomed maiden looks on with vicarious interest onto the unfolding scene, one hand partially covering her breast, the other timidly resting upon her chin. Two naked putti attend to her needs. The camera follows the maiden's line of vision into the room, falling upon another painting of a faux window with balcony and accompanying view of the Bay of Naples. "Little" Carmine Lupertazzi Jr. enters the room with his guests and illuminates them with his critical commentary. He pretentiously speaks of "trump pay le oil," a grossly mispronounced malapropism for the painterly technique of creating images on canvas so real that they seem to *trompe l'oile* or fool the eye. He then proudly and naively adds that it was done by a local artist from West Hampstead. The modesty of the painted maiden also contrasts sharply with the topless Bada Bing dancers that closed the preceding episode.

Posters

Whether used as props or to fill background settings, these seemingly casual visual texts are instead remarkable micro-narratives riddled with puns. Posters present both graphic and textual elements and are a non-discrete metalanguage of distinctive sociocultural features. The tools of advertisers, propagandists, anyone wishing to propose a public message, posters efficiently bestow any set designer a font of interminable information. Posters are an esoteric culture. When they are displayed in private rooms, they offer insights into the inhabitant's current interests or future dreams. Appropriately, specific locales in the series display semantically relevant posters. Satriale's Pork Store surrounds its customers with informative posters of meat cuts, its storefront advertising posters blare commercialized neighbourhood ethnicity. The Bada Bing, a purveyor of a different sort of meat, is adorned with sexy pin-up calendars, boxing posters, and the odd, faded travel poster of Italy. Hospital posters offer patient care information. Rock-band posters denote the musical interests and growing age of the Soprano teens. All these posters may or may not be familiar to the viewer. Nevertheless, they add authenticity and depth to the settings. The placards, posted bills, and commercial and artistic posters suggest supplemental messages to the specific episode's themes and actions. In these instances, the posters extend the viewer experience, take the viewer closer to the bone of the characters' reality, and place the viewer within the same communication field. They are a prime example of movement from the series towards the viewer because in all cases they are real posters, many of which the viewer may be familiar with or may actually own.

Samples

- In Episodes 1 through 4 of Season I, the viewer enters the bedrooms of Meadow and A.J. on numerous occasions. As young teens, their walls display posters that situate them within their relative age groups. Meadow's walls are adorned with posters of Natanuf (a Cincinnati-based female pop-rap duo), *House of GVSB* (this is the title of the fourth album by the female hard-core band Girls Against Boys), and Lisa Loeb (a popular singer-songwriter know for lyrics exalting compassion and self-reliance). These musical tastes are symbolic systems, concrete means for identifying with peers. They also constitute a semiotic portrait of Meadow as an independently minded youth on a path towards intelligent self-reliance. A poster of a butterfly near her computer indicates she has shed her cocoon and, like a butterfly, will be difficult to pin down.
- A.J.'s room is messier and displays posters coded towards a cliquish behavioural style pertinent to his age. His musical choices are more impulsive, loud, and raucous. Stuck Mojo (a heavy metal band preaching rage), *Irreligious* (the name of the second album by the Portuguese irreverently gothic metal band Moonspell), and Nevermore (an American heavy metal band featuring trash and grunge music). These bands promote a sort of tribal communication among those who are in the groove and outside the mainstream. Though A.J. may simply relate to these groups as a normal youth in transference, their messages of emotional upheaval, anger, macabre angst, and madness forebode the budding youth's protracted and difficult socialization and attempted suicide.

- Subsequent visits to their rooms in Season VI reveal appropriately matured teenagerhood. In "Join the Club" VI.2, we discover that Meadow's tastes include an increasing intellectual sophistication and reverence for artists. Her walls are now adorned with posters of Henri Matisse, Ernst Fruhling, and Pablo Picasso. A.J.'s room is less festooned with posters as his interests have turned to esoteric internet sites. Two occasions, however, clearly display posters that supply an alternative message to his immediate existential dilemma. In "Mayham" VI.3, a furious Carmela storms into her son's room and berates him for breaking the family code of *omertà*. A.J. has spoken to television news reporters about his father. His unexpected performance has appeared on the local news, playing into the hands of information-hungry media and effectively calling unwanted attention to the Soprano home. As Carmela exits his room, an Under Amour Boyz poster located near the door imploringly asks A.J. to heed its message and Protect This House. On another parental visit to his room, an earnest and consoling father attempts to rejuvenate a sullen A.J.'s morale after losing his fiancé Blanca Selgado in "Walk Like a Man" VI.17. A poster with the words Sugarcult: Start Static can be seen on A.J.'s door. Beginning anew from a stable, static position is Tony's hope for his son. But the title of the hit single from the Sugarcult's hit album *Pretty Girl* only serves to reinforce A.J.'s rocky and unstable self-deprecating demeanour. Because of the song "Pretty Girl," he remains forever pining and ever forlorn for his lost pretty girl.
- Tony ridicules his Uncle Junior as he is fitted with an oxygen mask by his doctor in "House Arrest" II.11. Uncle Junior looks clownish indeed, but he serves Tony well as a fake boss, and the mask fits his role as court jester. It is Tony who really wears the crown in the family as attested by the crown that is visible above his head in the Barone Sanitation poster several scenes later while he sits in his Barone office.
- The auspicious hospital poster in "Pine Barrens" III.11, that reads Don't Get Left in the Rain, aptly captions Paulie's and Christopher's romp in the snowy wilds of the Pine Barrens of New Jersey. The same poster will reappear in "The Fleshy Part of the Thigh" V.4 as Tony is discharged from hospital. As Paulie and Christopher are about to be left out in the rain (snow actually), Tony hopes to leave the rain behind.

- Ralph Cifaretto's ex-wife beats him with anguished anger after their son has been impaled with an arrow and lies in a coma in "Whoever Did This" IV.9. As the two ex-spouses battle, a Safe Families: Everybody Needs One poster looms behind them lending sarcastic commentary to a couple that has done nothing to ensure a safe family home for their son. Meadow and A.J. appear seated before the same poster after the attempted murder on their father in "Isabella" XII.1.
- A William Wegman poster of dogs in "In Camelot" V.7 momentarily stalls Tony's pelvic thrusts while he mounts Valentina La Paz doggy-style. The dogs remind him of Tippy, a childhood pet, and of his father. When Livia had insisted the dog be put down, Tony's father instead gave the dog to his goomah Fran Feinstein's son. The action may have saved Tippy but it now gives Tony pause.
- Christopher Moltisanti pays a punitive visit to his recovery support partner J.T. in "Camelot" V.7. J.T., it seems, is delinquent in payments to Christopher. The *Dr. Strangelove* movie poster he smashes over J.T.'s head physically manifests the new sort of topsy-turvy strange love that will now overtake their spiritual healing. J.T. is eventually killed by Christopher.
- In "Kaisha" VI.12, Tony closes the deal to sell his old-neighbourhood property to Jamba Juice. While Tony sits in her realty office, a poster of the architectural project behind the real estate agent Juliana Skiff reads Horizons: A Better Way to Build. The slogan "Vertical Living" is promoted as a hook for the new high-rise condominiums. The ads "Better Way to Build" echoes Tony's newfound resolve to find a "Better Way to Live" by not mixing business with pleasure. Later, while signing contract papers in Juliana's apartment, Tony feels compelled, at least on this one occasion, to abstain from the pleasures of horizontal play. "Vertical Living" (abstaining from sex), and not horizontal play, is Tony's new motto.
- Silvio Dante hangs a poster for the porn film *The Perfect Secretary* in "Moe n' Joe" VI.10, unknowingly intimating the newfound intimacy that has surfaced between wayward Vito Spatafore and short-order cook Jim "Johnny Cakes." The female figure in the poster is pictured from the rear with caption that reads "Carmen's first anal scene." The abundant derrière is an unsubtle allusion to the portly Vito and his romp in the sack with "Johnny Cakes" in the preceding scene.

Photographs

Because of their ability to mechanically capture moments of reality, photographs traditionally have been considered a faithful reproduction of the world and are therefore unique to the moment they are displayed. We are so accustomed to being addressed by photographs that we hardly notice their impact. Invariably, when the camera focuses on a photograph and the viewer is permitted to linger and consider it, along with the character who is gazing at the same photograph and its content, the viewer is invited to assume unspoken and unseen realities that concern the people represented in the photo as well as the possible/impossible relations the beholder of the photograph in the series may entertain. It is as if a window has been opened by the photograph, one that initiates, or ends, an endless chain of domestic symbols, framed for the viewer's inspection and providing a secret key to the characters' soul and memory, thus photographs reduce a universally shared sentiment to the singularly felt emotion.

Memories of things past, usually uncomfortable in this landscape of murder and violence, are also perceived from the standpoint of the viewer who then moves beyond the frame of the photo. In one instant, the viewer may conjure, through the illusion of self-reflection with the character in the photograph (or the character viewing the photograph), an imaginary temporal quality. The photographs create empathy between character and viewer because they seem to metaphorically reflect shared emotion. The viewer is suddenly transported into the characters' fictional time, shares his/her imagined past, travels to the very source of vital expression. The Sopranos photo album enhances the words and actions of the series and helps create the empathy the audience holds for many of its characters.

Samples

- The parade of photographs begins in "46 Long" I.2 as a visibly morose and emotionally troubled Tony removes family photos from his mother's mantle. The experience triggers a panic attack, the second attack the viewer has witnessed. At this early juncture of the series the viewer is yet unaware of the real underlying motivations of these attacks and, for the moment, is free to assume that memories of mother and father overwhelm him in this private experience of heightened self-awareness. In the very next scene, Dr. Melfi suggests to Tony that a possible reason for his feelings of helplessness and anxiety is an underlying anger, even hatred, towards his mother. On the suggestion that he "own" his anger rather than "displace it," he storms out of the session despondently berating the doctor for even suggesting the possibility of hating one's mother. In the very next scene, however, Tony's memories of mom violently erupt as he displaces all his surging rage onto Georgie the Bada Bing bartender's skull, a convenient substitute for his mother but an unfortunate victim of time and place.

- In "Meadowlands" I.4, a pubescent A.J. views the M.O.B. Megabytes of Bad Guys website. As photographs of mobsters and ancestry graphs fill the screen, he turns to view a photograph of himself and his father with new eyes. He has only just begun to comprehend the true extensions of his extended family.
- The photograph of mother Livia proudly displaying an infant Tony sharply contrasts with the television newscaster's words concerning the attempted gangland slaying of Tony Soprano in "Isabella" I.12.
- FBI photographs of mobsters make cameo appearances throughout the series as the viewer is made privy to the FBI's wall of nefarious fame in "Mr. Ruggerio's Neighborhood" III.1. As FBI Agent Frank Cubitoso tosses Salvatore "Big Pussy" Bonpensiero's photograph into the trash, he unknowingly confirms that which the viewer already knows. "Big Pussy" sleeps with the fishes like Luca Brasi, *The Godfather* character he had cited in the pilot episode.
- A collage of Jackie Aprile Jr.'s high school photographs near his coffin attest to a young life spent too soon in "The Army of One" III.12. These images are a necessary and equally unfortunate reality in Sopranoland. They may either remind a relative of a painful personal loss or a mobster of a successful hit. The connection between football, life, and death, Tony's unfulfilled football career, and A.J.'s panic attacks will be extended throughout the remainder of the series.
- Livia Soprano's professionally posed photograph, eyes raised upwards, stares menacingly at mourners at her wake in "Proshai, Livushka" III.2. The image contrasts sharply with the woman portrayed in the series. Not until "In Camelot" V.7 will viewers see a gentle version of Livia as she lies in hospital after a miscarriage.
- Christopher smokes near a photograph of his father after having killed his supposed murderer the night before in "For All Debts Public and Private" IV.1. He is in his mother's kitchen and

photographs of himself as a child and assorted family members are taped to the refrigerator. Christopher's addition to the collage will be a picture of Andrew Jackson on a $20 greenback.
- A family photograph is the sole witness to the suicide hanging of Gene Pontecorvo in "Members Only" VI.1. The photograph serves as both memory and motivator as Tony has just rejected Gene's request to leave the Mafia and retire to Florida. The protracted scene of his body swinging by a rope is accompanied by swing music from Uncle Junior's house as the scene shifts to Tony preparing pasta and swaying to the beat. At a moment when all FBI informers have been neutralized, a jovial Tony is unaware of the rainstorm and the fire (from the accompanying music lyric "Comes a rainstorm, put your rubbers on your feet/Comes the fire ...") that is about to inundate and overpower him.
- After Phil Leotardo places the urn containing his brother Billy Leotardo's ashes on the mantle over the Leotardo family bar, he holds an impromptu history lesson for the grandchildren of the family in "Stage 5" VI.14. Using the bait of Leonardo Da Vinci, he reveals that the original family was Leonardo, not Leotardo. The change in spelling occurred on Ellis Island. When asked how this could happen he responds: "Because they're stupid, that's why, and jealous. They disrespected a proud Italian heritage and named us after a ballet costume." An exasperated grandfather is then informed by his granddaughter that tutus are for ballet, leotards for modern dance. His only consolation, as the scene shifts, is a grandson's affirmation that "there's no difference." The scene closes with a slow pan of photographs of defunct family members displayed over the bar. This is *la famiglia*'s wall of the dead. The viewer recognizes Carmine Lupertazzi, Billy Leotardo, and John Sacrimoni. The viewer also senses an ominous sense of future retribution and a deep-set willingness on the part of Phil to help increase the Soprano photo obituary.
- Uncle Junior autographs photos of a handcuffed self that he puts up for sale on eBay in "Remember When" VI.15. For Junior it's "a sick fuckin' world" as he literally sells himself for sodas. In the next scene, the viewer is given a stroll down memory lane with old family photographs as Peter "Beansie" Gaeta entertains Tony and Paulie "Walnuts" Gualtieri in Florida. The photos of Paulie as a young hood and of Johnny and Uncle Junior in front of Satriale's Pork Store strike a deeply embedded memory valence filled with

nostalgic family stories. Tony revels in the memories, but they contrast sharply with the crass selling of Uncle Junior's self-image for immediate satisfaction of candy bars while institutionalized.
- Rosalie Aprile flips through photographs of her trip to Paris with Carmela Soprano in "The Blue Comet" VI.20. In one photo, the two pose as characters in a French painting. The faux Parisian picture/painting holds special significance at this late juncture of the Soprano story. We recall that during her Parisian sojourn, Carmela explores her own mortality by exploding the inauthentic myths of her faux Italian Jerseyian Mafia heritage. She marvels at the possibility of anonymity, of new beginnings, of history's encompassing temporal eraser. The assumed identity in the faux photo, even in jest, recalls her unsuccessful attempts to abandon her past and assume a different identity on several occasions during the series. Tony's disconcerting news that Bobby "Baccalà" Baccilieri Jr. is dead, that Silvio is mortally wounded in hospital, and that he, too, is in danger, is revealed while the viewer sees this particular photo. Carmela's past, incorporated here in Tony's voice, reminds both the viewer and Carmela that frivolity has also become a thing of the past. Her hens are coming home to roost.
- Christopher Moltisanti's photograph in "Made in America" VI.21 holds special sway over Paulie "Walnuts" Gualtieri. He believes Christopher's soul has migrated to a pesky orange cat that sits before and endlessly stares at the photo of Christopher regardless of where it is placed. The two series-long companions, Paulie and Christopher, are spiritually reunited, albeit as man and cat. At series' end, Paulie tans in the sun, while Bacia Galup, the mysterious cat, accompanies him in front of Satriale's Pork Store.

Verbal Subtexts

David Chase intersperses the series with resonant and evocative verbal texts that are pictured within the narrative as imagery. These inserted strings of words open a dialectical field of forces that depend upon the viewer's understanding of their signification. In essence, Chase installs a double voice, a double relation of language as signifying system and as visual experience. This occurs when the viewer reads billboards, newspaper headlines, or briefly glimpses typed or written words on notes. These subtexts appear in different scenarios and are meant to achieve different purposes in the story. Since they are read by both character and viewer, they are passing but important written notes, lines from a letter, and so on that introduce a fixed temporality, a frozen moment in the character's time. These words provide a subtending commentary to the viewer. The message of these texts may offer a critical purview or an optional perspective otherwise absent from character dialogue but important to the story and character development. Billboards and public signage on store fronts, for example, are public messages that are ubiquitous. One would normally expect to view them as the characters travel the streets of New Jersey.

The starting point for the interpretation of billboard space is the semantic space of the field itself. This field is situated within recognizable institutions and discourses that are already immanent in the words and in the fabric of a description. The landmark life-size pig atop Satriale's Pork Store, to cite an obvious sample, is an advertising marker, a neighbourhood icon signalling product, culture, ethnicity. It also metaphorically alludes to its clientele's restless propensity for excess in sensual depravity – wine, women, and bullets. The fact that the butcher shop serves as an expeditious on-site disposal for human carnage enhances the pig's image-text as a complex medium. In another example, the Suckling Pigs Any Size sign that is often fore-grounded throughout the series, supplements the Satriale pig with blaring efficacy. In "House Arrest" II.11, for example, Agent Dwight Harris, Agent Joe Marquez, and Tony Soprano discuss the New York Nets and the New York Knicks as Paulie "Walnuts" Gualtieri, Salvatore "Big Pussy" Bonpensiero, and the rest of the crew look on; they are just a bunch of ol' pals chitchatting about sports. As the camera slowly pans outward and upward, the Suckling Pigs sign comes into view and hovers above their heads. The message seems clear, the viewer is invited to choose a pig, any size, as they stand, sit, converse, relax: makes no difference.

Samples: Brief Notes

- A view of Christopher Moltisanti's manuscript in "The Legend of Tennessee Moltisanti" I.8 confirms the viewer's suspicion that Christopher is not the sharpest pencil in the Soprano pencil case: "I thought I was daed but I manuged to get the drip on him." His glaring "spellin'" errors corroborate his befuddled notions of mob honour, respect, and loyalty as they comingle with equally muddled perceptions of literary fame.

- A verbal metaphor uttered by Livia Soprano comparing her daughter Janice to a snake in "A Guy Walks into a Psychiatrist's Office" II.1 becomes a visual reality. As soon as Janice the snake slithers back into brother Tony's life, she immediately schemes to grab all she can from her exasperated sibling. After their first meeting beside the Soprano pool, Tony and the viewer look into the pool and see the water vacuum hose slithering along the pool bottom. Its motions resemble those of a water snake.
- The standard FBI Warning that prefaces all DVD movies is doubly resonant when Tony and crew watch *The Godfather* in "Commendatori" II.4. But interestingly, the DVD player goes on the blink and they can't watch the film in the end. Instead, Christopher bashes the machine to pieces. Their favourite film is not to be copied or distributed without permission. The warning says nothing, however, about duplicating the actions in the film.
- While attending an acting workshop in "Big Girls Don't Cry" II.5, Christopher Moltisanti is asked to read from *Rebel Without a Cause*. His passionate and tearful performance as Jim belies the title of the episode. His enraged beating of the actor playing his father underscores Christopher's enduring resentment of his own fatherless past. He is indeed a rebel in search of a cause.
- In "The Happy Wanderer" II.6, Dr. Melfi cites author and anthropologist Carlo Castaneda: "Live every moment as if it were your last dance on earth." The author becomes relevant in "Kennedy and Heidi" VI.18. While in Las Vegas, Tony discovers a new, peyote-induced meaning to life that is strikingly similar to the Yaqui way of knowledge inspired by Castaneda.
- Livia Soprano enlightens her nephew A.J. about the hazards of wearing safety belts and the impossibility of escaping an incinerated car in "The Happy Wanderer" II.6. In "Made in America" VI.21, her words become reality as A.J.'s SUV bursts into flames while he and his girlfriend Rhiannon are inside – unbeknownst to A.J., the SUV is parked on top of a bed of dry leaves and the engine has overheated.
- In an effort to thwart Meadow's aspirations to leave home for California, Carmela prefers to trash the letter from The University of California, Berkeley informing Meadow that her application is incomplete in "The Happy Wanderer" II.6. Carmela feels that by destroying the message she will better influence Meadow's choice of college. She remorsefully retrieves the envelope and dutifully gives

it to her daughter. Meadow's queries about the trash-soiled letter reveal her perception of the Soprano's standard dirty practices.
- Immediately following grandmother Livia's death, A.J. reads the 1922 Robert Frost poem "Stopping by Woods on a Snowy Evening" in "Proshai, Livushka" III.2. Unable to understand the symbolic resonances of the work – life, obligations, sadness, death – the boy simply cannot connect the poem's meaning and place in his life at this moment of personal loss. The ominous creaking of floorboards in the hallway, however, causes him to sense the spirit of his grandmother's presence in the words he has just read. As he peers into the darkness of the hallway he calls out, "Grandma?"
- Written condolences addressed to Tony for the loss of his mother from the FBI Organized Crime Division are both salutary and sarcastic in "Proshai, Livushka" III.2. The written text may be linked to the aural text of Livia and Uncle Junior plotting Tony's death.
- Just as Tony and Carmela confess to Dr. Melfi that "we're learnin' how to communicate" in "Pine Barrens" III.11, Meadow and Jackie Aprile Jr. are "learnin'" about the vast linguistic abyss that separates their intellectual lives by playing Scrabble. The word "oblique" earns Meadow thirty-six points – and Jackie's churlish objection "No Spanish." A suffering Meadow provides synonyms for the word and finishes her lesson with the retort, "C'mon. You're in college." Jackie's contributions to the game with the monosyllabic three-point words "ass," "the," and "poo" place him in the same English league as Christopher Moltisanti; a perception not lost on a feverish and saddened Meadow who fully comprehends her intellectual incompatibility with the burgeoning Christopher-clone wanna-be thug.
- In "The Army of One" III.13, a fugitive Jackie Jr. hides out at the home of a Black drug dealer after the botched poker-game hit. He is asked by the dealer's bright little daughter if he plays chess. Crying, Jackie answers, "No." The little girl informs him that she does because "my daddy taught me." Her unintentionally insightful words fill Jackie with deep remorse and filial sadness. Like Christopher, the absence of a fatherly presence in his life portends the loss of emotional and spiritual stability. Both die young. The template for the fatherless youth becoming a wayward young thug is Tony Soprano. The viewer has already seen him mindlessly doodling while his empire crumbles around him in "House Arrest" II.11.

- Meadow's increasing existential plight is mirrored in the only available college course still accepting students in "No-Show" IV.2. The course title, Morality, Self, and Society, needs little commentary. The course requires no prerequisites. But of course, Meadow arrives with the overladen baggage of Soprano amoral societal ethics.
- A sly knowing nod is offered to the viewer as coerced, compromised, and unwilling FBI informant Adriana La Cerva peruses greeting cards in "Watching Too Much Television" IV.7. Like an inauspicious fortune-cookie message, the card instructs Adriana on how to perform her new Janus role as mobster girlfriend and mob rat: "Now, if I can only remember to fake it."
- An unscrupulous Janice Soprano attempts an end-around play in order to win the heart, or at least the attention, of grief-stricken Bobby "Baccalà" Baccilieri Jr. in "Calling All Cars" IV.11. She uses email to trick Bobby's children into using the words of the Ouija board to contact their dead mother. Their fright causes Bobby to solicit Janice's sympathetic care to console his children.
- Carmela's mob wives' movie club is stunned into crucified silence by the huge FBI warning prohibiting criminal copyright infringement before viewing the film *Citizen Kane* (1941) in "Rat Pack" V.2. The FBI warning is a chilling reminder of their station in life.
- Dr. Melfi reads Tony's note excusing himself for his behaviour in "All Happy Families" V.4. Her own analyst surmises that the toiletries that accompanied Tony's note suggest ablution, a cleansing gesture on Tony's part. Tony's words, however, spark Dr. Melfi's ire and remind the viewer that they have yet to meet again to exchange words as doctor and patient. They have yet to cleanse the bad feelings and no amount of Tide detergent will help.
- A tongue-in-cheek retro-comment occurs in "Moe n' Joe" VI.10 as Tony carries a box with the tag *Sands of Iwo Jima* Box DVD Set. The box is a visual reminder of the box of sand maliciously handed to neighbour Dr. Cusamano by Tony to hold for safekeeping in "A Hit Is a Hit" I.10.
- The label Fresh All Natural Turkey slapped on the wrapping of a dead frozen bird in "Kaisha" VI.12 sparks a discussion between Tony and Carmela about a hospitalized Liz La Cerva whose wings (arms) have been clipped (tied to the hospital bed) because of an attempted suicide. Liz is convinced that her daughter Adriana has been murdered, while Tony insists, using an aviary metaphor, that Adriana has simply flown the coop. The viewer knows the truth,

turkeys don't fly, and Adriana, despite her recurring appearance in Carmela's dreams, remains frozen in the cold New Jersey ground.
- William Wordsworth appears in the series on a classroom blackboard in "Kennedy and Heidi" VI.18. The words "Getting and spending we lay waste our powers" fuel A.J.'s increasing despondency towards contemporary material values.

Samples: Signs, Billboards

- We can't seem to get away from pigs in *The Sopranos*. They grace Satriale's Pork Store's interior walls. Their reach becomes international when, in "Cold Stones" VI.11, Carmela photographs the neon sign of the Parisian restaurant Pied de Cochon. The sign appropriately features a pig. The neon porker, replete with bottle and glass in hand, portends the excesses of the Soprano crew who appear in the very next scene eating and drinking in Satriale's backroom office. The off-colour joke regarding ducks and pigs told by Pasquale "Patsy" Parise reinforces the metaphorical connection.
- Christopher Moltisanti and Adriana La Cerva wait impatiently in line for burger baskets at a Black burger joint amid Black customers in an apparently Black neighbourhood in "A Hit Is a Hit" I.10. The small poster with Arabic script hanging on the wall directly behind them contradicts all viewer assumptions. Though situated in a Black neighbourhood, Kansas Fried chicken is another white franchise for Black America.
- As if the viewer needs any further visual cuing, the speedboat on which Tony dispatches Chucky Signori by pulling a gun out of the mouth of a red snapper in "I Dream of Jennie Cusamano" I.14 is called *Villain III*. Though not the third villain to meet his end in the series to this point, he is indeed the third hit sanctioned by the Soprano boss.
- In "Guy Walks into a Psychiatrist's Office" II.1, Tony suffers a panic attack while driving and crashes into a billboard announcing Summit People Find Answers, Not Excuses. Tony's life is filled with excuses these days as Salvatore "Big Pussy" Bonpensiero reappears on his doorstep, Janice returns to the Soprano fold from Seattle, and Christopher slacks off on his office duties. When Tony seeks out Dr. Melfi, who must run her practice from a motel room, and finds her having a meal at a nearby diner, she protests his presence. In

response, he supplies his own excuses that only infuriate the good doctor. Some people just can't follow advertised billboard advice.
- The iconic Any Size Suckling Pigs sign behind Bobby "Baccalà" Baccilieri Jr. in a "Guy Walks into a Psychiatrist's Office" II.1 needs no explanation. Both images are symbols of excess and unbridled appetite.
- In "Commendatori" II.4, FBI informant Salvatore "Big Pussy" Bonpensiero meets Agent Skip Lipari at the Party Box party store. The irony is that "Big Pussy's" life as an informant is anything but joyous and carefree. As the two converse beneath the party store sign, neither really have anything to celebrate.
- The Uncle Ben's Converted Rice logo in "Proshai, Livushka" III.2 reminds Tony of Meadow's new "butterhead" friend Noah Tannenbaum. The Black-American icon exacerbates his capicollo-induced panic attack.
- In "Another Toothpick" III.5, Bobby "Baccalà" Sr. suffers a heart attack while leaving the scene of his last hit. His car comes to rest at the base of a billboard that proclaims Your Ad Here. The message of the billboard indicates that this is an empty space waiting to be filled with advertising. This episode, however, is replete with death, dead mobsters, and old folks leaving empty spaces that now await new additions to the mob family.
- In "The Telltale Moozadell" III.9, Paulie "Walnuts" Gualtieri and Tony watch a nature program about snakes on TV. Paulie irksomely rambles on about their spontaneous reproduction, and Tony mulls over allusions to the biblical snake in the earthly paradise of Adam and Eve. In a subsequent scene, the two independent conversations are brought together as subtending drama that accompanies Tony and Gloria in their own offbeat paradise, the serpent's exhibit at the zoo.
- An impatient Jackie Aprile Jr. and his sidekicks attempt to make their marks in the mob world by shooting-up Eugene Pontecorvo's card game in "Amor Fou" III.12. He wishes to replicate the same gesture that years earlier had catapulted Tony Soprano and his own father into the ranks of Made Men. After Jackie and his cohorts enter the room with guns at the ready, a small sign behind them suggests that their dopey antic could have been avoided if only they had heeded its message: No Hope in Dope. Jackie and sidekicks are killed for their misguided antics.
- A Century 21 real estate sign in "Eloise" IV.12 signals the definitive end of Carmela's infatuation with Furio Giunta. His house for sale,

she no longer has any excuses for visiting Furio, who just happens to have left the country. Real estate listings are another of Carmela's go-between texts. These are props or excuses she uses to facilitate her entreaties towards men.

- Among the get well cards pinned to the bulletin board in Tony's hospital room, a hand-printed Ojibwa saying holds centre stage in "Mayham" VI.3: "Sometimes I go about in pity for myself, and all the while, a great wind carries me across the sky." After reading the saying aloud, Christopher Moltisanti asks Tony, "Who put this up?" A medicine-laden and semi-conscious Tony does not answer. In the next episode, Tony informs the nurse that his sister Janice "put it up," something she will later deny. He then annoyingly adds that it is still pinned to the board because "My daughter likes it." The esoteric and now mysteriously placed saying acquires added meaning. Meadow has never deferred to the saying. However, viewers are aware of the rustling winds in the trees that accompany Tony throughout the series and may intuit a connection. The wind becomes relevant when his ducks take flight in the pilot episode, and when the wind blows through the empty boughs around his empty pool at series' end. This same wind acquires a voice during Tony's coma. It is Meadow's distant voice that acts as a sustaining force as she calls him back from the clutches of death, her voice seemingly emanating out of the wind that rustles the trees as he re-emerges into consciousness.
- While visiting prisoner John Sacrimoni in "Mr. and Mrs. John Sacrimoni Request" VI.5, the younger, and anorexic, of the Sacrimoni sisters exclaims, "Jesus, can we ever talk about anything in this family besides food!" The next scene opens with a close-up of the Satriale's Pork Store's sign: Satriale's Any Size Suckling Pigs. To extend the anorexic versus porker metaphor, in the next scene we enter Satriale's backroom only to view the Soprano crew heavyweight porkers Vito Spatafore and company.
- After Carlo Gervasi retrieves the severed frozen head of Dominic "Fat Dom" Gamiello and unceremoniously disposes of it down a sewer drain, the very next scene opens with a shot of the neon sign for Sheephead's Hair Design in "Kaisha" VI.12.
- In "Kaisha" VI.12, the restaurant sign Restaurant Diner: Baking Done on Premises gets double duty. As Christopher Moltisanti and latest goomah Julianna Skiff bellyache their respective disquiet (Christopher bemoans his life in the mob, Julianna is restive about their dissolving relationship), the restaurant sign behind them is

strategically cropped to read "aking Done on Premises" – a fitting description of the lamentations taking place. Once outside the restaurant, the two continue to follow the sign's tutelage. Indeed, while Christopher and Julianna's *"aking"* is done on the premises, their *"baking"* is performed in the car while parked in the restaurant lot.
- At series' end, A.J. has become a lone wolf, a small independent porn producer in his father's business. The sign on his company door, Lone Wolves Productions, clearly signals his newly found freedom from worry and woe in "Made in America" VI.21.

Newspapers

Newspaper headlines are a regular feature of Sopranoland. They blare at the viewer from Tony's very first walk down his driveway in the pilot episode. They accompany the viewer through the series with the regularity of a subscription. The headlines adumbrate future events or confirm past-plot turns on a regular basis. They also serve to situate the series in a particular real time and place since names and dates are always visible. As set-pieces they offer no ambiguity and provide transparent access, a sense of eyewitness authenticity. Pivotal moments in the series are usually corniced by headlines set in newspaper type that the viewer reads on the television screen along with the character, usually Tony. These newspaper titles inform both the character and the viewer and, in this sense, place the two, again, on a similar temporal plane. The newspapers lend an air of reality. If it's in the paper, it must be true. The fact that the newspaper is usually New Jersey's largest local newspaper, *The Star-Ledger*, merely adds to the interdimensional posturing between the world out there and world of *The Sopranos*. But the fabricated headlines also remind us that indeed it's all only fiction. Nevertheless, reading along with Tony moves the viewer closer to the action and into the silent reading space of the scene.

Samples

- In "The Legend of Tennessee Moltisanti" I.8, a frazzled and notoriety-seeking Christopher Moltisanti suffers his non-existence and public invisibility with wanton angst. His dream is to become a potential FBI target and see his name in print. When he finally receives mention in *The Star-Ledger* as a "reputed gangster," his

newly printed image births a mobster construct that is infused with delusions of unbridled grandeur. Poesis as therapy.
- Tony reads of Coach Don Hauser's imminent move to the University of Rhode Island in "Boca" I.9. The newspaper announcement precipitates a series of non-actions by Tony and his crew that culminate in the coach's eventual arrest by the police rather than death at the hands of Tony.
- Salvatore "Big Pussy" Bonpensiero reads *Waste News* in "D-Girl" II.7. Tony reads the same trade magazine in "House Arrest" II.11 as the garbage wars heat up and garbage woes assail Barone Sanitation customers.
- Season Three begins with *The Star-Ledger* headlines blaring "Mob Competition for Garbage Contract Heats Up." As the camera moves down to the words "Violence Feared," we hear Agent Skip Lipari in a voiceover inform the FBI agents in the room that "it's time to consider Salvatore Bonpensiero compost." "Big Pussy" in other words, is just another piece of "garbage" since it is assumed he has been disposed of by Tony for betraying his oath of *omertà*. The competition between the mob and the FBI for "Big Pussy's" soul has ended. The feared violence that the paper announces ensues in "Proshai, Livushka" III.2 as the episode opens with an exploding garbage truck. The event merits another headline story and subsequent byline: "Second Firebomb in Sanitation War – Retaliation Expected."
- In a flashback scene in "Fortunate Son" III.2, Johnny Soprano reads the sports pages. The Detroit Pistons and now defunct Baltimore Bullets (1963–73), as well as the name Lew Alcindor (Kareem Abdul-Jabbar's Christian name before he became a Muslim in 1971) next to Wilt "The Stilt" Chamberlain's name, situate the action in the mid-1960s, the Golden Age of the National Basketball Association.
- Uncle Junior's amorous fantasies about actress Angie Dickinson appear in newsprint. While sedated for his operation, he dreams that *The Star-Ledger* appears with the headline "Soprano Wins Freedom: Star Witness Weds Angie Dickinson" in "Second Opinion" III.7.
- Season IV opens with Carmela reading about the Italian custom of "raccomandazioni," or political favouritism, in *The New York Times* to A.J. in "For all Debts Public and Private" IV.1. While Carmela may decry the graft, extortion, and favouritism rampant in Italian politics, these same vices are matters of normal public and private practice in the Soprano household. Tony trudges down his

driveway to retrieve *The Star-Ledger*. He reads the headline "Next Year Starts Now." So do all of the above vices.
- While Tony stews in his guilt after he suspects Carmela has discovered Valentina La Paz's silver-tipped fingernail while folding his pants in "Mergers and Acquisitions" IV.8, Carmela loses herself in the morning paper with knowing smile and cunning silence.
- Episode 1 of Season V, "Two Tonys," begins with somber visual notes of desolation and loss: a rusting BBQ, a tarpaulin-covered pool, a leaf-strewn patio, a darkened empty house whose windows signal the absence of normal Soprano family bliss. As the camera slowly pans down the front drive, the viewer no longer sees Tony trudging in slippers and trademark white terrycloth bathrobe to retrieve the morning paper. Instead, Meadow runs over *The Star-Ledger* with her beat-up convertible; further testimony that Tony no longer lives here. As for the newspaper, it's all old news, nothing worth reading today.
- While under house arrest in "In Camelot" V.7, Uncle Junior scours the newspaper Obituary Section in order to gain permission to attend the funerals of his friends. The spate of funerals eventually overwhelms him and reminds him of his own waning mortality.
- Uncle Junior may have dreamed of winning his freedom but the consequences of his trial are less winsome. *The Star-Ledger* announces: "Cushy Psyche Lock-up for Don Squirrel-Leone," an obvious public slight to his character and mob reputation in "Mr. and Mrs. John Sacrimoni Request" VI.5.
- In "Cold Stones" VI.11, *The Star-Ledger* held by Tony informs the viewer that "The Corzine Era Begins." The headline refers to the real Jon Corzine's election as the fifty-fourth governor of New Jersey in 2006. Corzine, a lawyer and politician with a checkered career, is one of those real people in the real world that Chase uses to actualize the Soprano narrative. As for the headline, the real new era for New Jersey bodes well for the fictional era of *The Sopranos*.
- Vito Spatafore's children read "Alleged Capo Slain" in *The Star-Ledger* in "Cold Stones" VI.11 and painfully learn that their father was not a spy, and that he had lied to cover his homosexuality.
- Always the publicity hound, Christopher Moltisanti reads about his Hollywood antics in "Luxury Lounge" VI.14. His wrangling with actress Lauren Bacall expressed in the headline "Swag Grab Nabs Industry Blab" amuses the ever-belligerent, publicity-hungry assailant.

- The sight of the newspaper ad offering "Two-fers Night" at his beloved Vesuvio restaurant in "Luxury Lounge" VI.14 is the final nail in Artie Bucco's descending professional and personal trajectory. As busloads of senior citizens line-up for free food, Artie knows he has hit rock bottom in his career.
- Silvio Dante and Paulie "Walnuts" Gualtieri read a tabloid headline in "The Blue Comet" VI.20. Unfortunately, the message "DBL UKE SLY IN QUEENS" (Double Ukrainian Slaying in Queens) and accompanying photograph of a Phil Leotardo look-alike attest to another botched hit by the Soprano crew. Their surrogate Italian hitmen have hit the wrong man.
- Even Dr. David Chase makes a cameo photo appearance on the front page of *The Star-Ledger* in "A Hit Is a Hit" I.10.

Books

The ultimate and most dense site for verbal subtexts is books and their message-laden covers, which offer potent sites for secondary interpretation. As works of literature they are full, replete, and imbued with cultural presence; they offer a verbal discourse that is at once self-reflective and self-subverting because they are products of the real world outside *The Sopranos* fictional world. They are liberally dispersed throughout the series and key characters are seen reading books. Holding a book on-screen may exemplify nothing other than that which the viewer sees. But once the visual sign is constituted in this fashion on the television screen and the viewer reads the book title, the ideal viewer refunctionalizes the intellectual prompt and virtually enters the series as a potential reader of the visualized book. If the viewer is already familiar with the book on display, he/she is immediately engaged with the character in ever-new-ways. These may include a sympathetic bonding with the character, a better understanding of the character's words, or a different interpretation of the character's gestures. These books thus represent furtive enigmas, beckoning portals to a supplementary fictional world that is shared with both the character and the viewer if both have the key (i.e., have read the book). For the ideal viewer who has not read the book, the presence of these mise-en-abîme narratives are an anticipated will to knowledge, the longing to understand why this particular narrative has been inserted within the story at this particular juncture. Thus, a potential visual contract is installed, along with a promise to read the book in question in order to penetrate and become a part of the series, to cosy up, in other words, with its on-screen readers.

Book titles can lend insight to both the character and plot of an episode. From Nathaniel Hawthorne to Edgar Rice Burroughs, Niccolò Machiavelli to Carlos Castaneda, from Sun Tzu's *Art of War* to Arthur Miller's *Death of a Salesman*, book titles, references, peripheral citations, and direct quotations pepper the series and give it a logocentric corporeality. *The Sopranos* thus becomes a site where a fertile combination of words as dialogue and words as book titles on the television screen take the viewer to the limen of writer David Chase's artistic inspiration. The creative staging of such word and image relations is an orchestrated effort to further explicate, elucidate, and broaden the narrative scope of *The Sopranos*. One might say that these sample books "illustrate" the series in much the same way a suite of images always illuminated the classic *livre d'artiste* of the late 1890s.

Samples

- The parade of covers begins in the pilot episode as Tony waxes over ducks while perusing *The Audubon Society Encyclopedia of North American Birds*. Used as a convenient symbol for lost glory days and the potential loss of family in this episode, the latent affection for birds and animals come to represent a nefarious character trait of Tony's psychophysic personality.
- In "46 Long" I.2, Salvatore "Big Pussy" Bonpensiero reads the self-help book *Healthy Living* as he contemplates how to mend his own deteriorating life. Unbeknownst to his peers and the viewer at this juncture, he has been co-opted as an informant by the FBI, something the viewer learns along with Tony in a later episode. The inclusion of this book at this point in the story is a retro-signal that he is already an informer.
- As the line between her professional and personal relationship with her patient Tony becomes increasingly blurred in "Pax Soprana" I.6, Dr. Melfi sits at home and reads T.C. Boyles *Riven Rock*. The novel explores the nature of psychiatric care but especially the dynamics of male–female relationships, something that is definitely troubling Dr. Melfi as she begins to question her attraction to her patient. One of the main characters of the story, Katherine, is a sexually deprived member of upper crust, early 1900s Santa Barbara society who must deal with tumultuous romances, desperate psychotic events,

and the evermore disturbing intermingling of social classes and encroaching ethnicities that constitute America. These are the same issues that haunt Dr. Melfi and with which she will need to deal before series' end.
- In "Nobody Knows Anything" I.11, a book lies on the kitchen counter next to the Soprano kitchen television set. The book's title is *Fit for Life*, a self-help lifestyle bestseller about weight loss. The authors classify foods into two groups: "living foods" that cleanse the body, "dead foods" that clog it. Tony has just discovered Salvatore "Big Pussy" Bonpensiero's FBI wire. He now must decide whether his longtime friend is still "fit for life" or ready to sleep with the fishes. He opts to cleanse his crew by clogging the New York–New Jersey Estuary with another dead body.
- In "Bust Out" II.10, a book cover holds sway and eminent peril over Tony: *Anarchy, State, and Utopia* by Robert Nozick. It is read by the sole witness to the hit on Matthew Bevilaqua by Tony and Salvatore "Big Pussy" Bonpensiero. The witness is an unsuspecting do-gooder, a utopian idealist that tells the police that it is his duty to report what he saw. The book's title reflects his romantic intentions to organize society according to utopian tonal values. When confronted, however, by Paulie "Walnuts" Gualtieri and subtly informed of the possible personal ramifications of his public witnessing of an alleged private event, he quickly withdraws into the anarchy of Soprano silence.
- Frank McCourt's bestselling memoir *'Tis* is seductively placed next to trays of Italian cookies in "House Arrest" II.11. Carmela and her afternoon reading circle are critiquing the work. Their literary commentary could easily be applied to *The Sopranos* cast of characters as issues of motherhood, fatherhood, alcoholism, and wealth are covered with humoured banter. As Tony shuffles into the kitchen, unshaven, hair dishevelled, bathrobe unceremoniously revealing pajama bottoms and T-shirt, we hear Carmela make reference to author McCourt, but her comment could easily be construed as a sly intertextual compliment to writer David Chase and his depiction of Tony: "It's all in the writing," she says. "It's like he makes certain choices about how he is going to portray people."
- *Chicken Soup for the Soul* is read in bed by Irina Peltsin, Tony's needy Russian mistress, in "House Arrest" II.11. Tony's loving retort to her verbal inanity is to quip a more appropriate title. He tells her to try reading *"Tomato Sauce for Your Ass."*

- Silvio's tenuous literary acumen is confirmed in "The Knight in White Satin Armor" II.12 when he counsels a suicidal Irina Peltsin to read *Passages*. "It's a book," he tells her, not really knowing the book's subject matter. The full title is *Passages: Predictable Crises of Adult Life* by Gail Sheehy.
- The epigraph that opens *Le Rouge et le Noir* by Stendhal, "*La vérité, l'âpre vérité*" (The truth, the harsh truth), aptly counterposes the hypocrisy, deceit, pretension, and materialism that permeates episode II.12, "Knight in White Satin Armor." The closing scene of Carmela and Tony sitting on the sofa dressed in red (Carmela) and black (Tony) readily extemporizes the same bereft morality as the novel. Carmela's closing quip to her philandering husband, "I'll commit suicide" (in reference to Irina Peltsin's attempted suicide) only reinforces the duplicitous game played in the Soprano household.
- *The Grandma Memory Book* that grandmother Livia Soprano does not complete with personal memories of her grandchildren is a further indication that writing gentle memories (a right-brain activity) is impossible for the surly, left brained, calculating, and sinister non-grandmother Livia ("Proshai, Livushka" III.2).
- While the book never appears on screen, *Crime and Punishment* by Fyodor Dostoyevsky is a recommended penitent read for recalcitrant Tony. It is suggested to Carmela by a Jewish psychiatrist in "Second Opinion" III.7.
- Tony discusses *The Art of War* by Sun Tzu in "He is Risen" III.8. His interpretation is priceless: "Most of the guys I know read Prince Matchabelli ... he's OK. But this book is much better about strategy."
- Meadow claims to have spent her summer reading "half the literary canon" by the pool, or so she says, in "No-Show" IV.2. A perturbed and perspicacious Carmela sarcastically inquires whether Mary Higgins Clark, a contemporary American writer of suspense novels (and the book Meadow has in hand), is part of that illustrious group of canonic writers.
- A.J. is seen reading *A People's History of the United States* for his history course in "Christopher" IV.3. His parents object to the author's comparing the historical Christopher Columbus to modern criminals accused with crimes against humanity. A.J. counters their discontent by blurting, "It's the truth. It's in my history book." To which Tony irreverently retorts, "So you finally read a book and its

bullshit ... in this house Christopher Columbus is a hero. End of story!"
- Tony's deprecating wit is displayed when discussing *Billy Budd*, a short novel by Herman Melville, with Meadow's college roommates in "Eloise" IV.12. To Carmela's petulant insistence that the novel is not about homoeroticism in a military context, Tony jests, "Must be a gay book, Billy Budd's the ship's florist, right?"
- *Death in Venice* by Thomas Mann is compulsory reading for A.J. in "Eloise" IV.12. Death and Venice are also on the minds of both the New Jersey and New York families as tensions rise after Tony's crew vandalizes Carmine Lupertazzi's restaurant mural of a Venetian gondola.
- In "Two Tonys" V.1, the two personalities so blatantly endorsed in the episode title is cleverly extended and thematically enhanced as recalcitrant alcoholic Christopher Moltisanti reads the book *My Search for Bill W*. The work is a biography of Bill Wilson, founder of Alcoholics Anonymous, and a man who apparently displayed seven personalities. Good reading for both Tony and Christopher who gingerly walk the line between their disquietingly multiple personalities.
- In the dream sequence of "The Test Dream" V.11, Tony retires to the men's room ostensibly to retrieve a hidden pistol in a spoof of the famous *The Godfather* scene with Michael Corleone. Instead, we see him at the urinal discussing his preparedness for the task at hand with detective Vin Makazian. He pulls *The Valachi Papers* by Peter Maas out of his pocket to prove his readiness. Tony says he's "done his homework." The phrase holds a double valence. It can refer to Tony's ambitions not to follow in the footsteps of mobster-turned-informant Joe Valacci. The choice of this particular text, however, also reflects upon David Chase having done his homework. The publication of this novel was hotly contested by the American Italian Defamation Council, which promoted a national campaign against the book claiming that it violated the civil rights of everyday I-Ams. In 1968, U.S. Attorney General Nicholas Katzenbach asked a district court to stop Maas from publishing the book. The book was later published with revisions and as a third-person account. By citing *The Valachi Papers*, Chase is once again openly responding to critics that continued to declaim *The Sopranos* as defamatory by citing past examples of similar cases that were blown out of proportion.

- While recovering from his gunshot wound in hospital in "The Fleshy Part of the Thigh" VI.4, Carmela gives Tony a book on dinosaurs. As Tony flips the pages, the pictured prehistoric birds morph into real seagulls that hover above the Barone Sanitation garbage depot. This is an obvious allusion to the infamous ducks of his backyard pool. At the end of this episode, Tony, no longer in hospital, relishes the moment as the wind whistles through the trees in his backyard. The scene again morphs into trees along a New Jersey canal. What appears to be a prehistoric bird beak (from the dinosaur book) enters the scene only to reveal itself as a kayak carried by Mr. Barone's son.
- Before leaving hospital in "The Fleshy Part of the Thigh" VI.4, a spiritually rejuvenated and physically reborn Tony is given a book by Pastor Bob: *Born Again* by Charles Colson. Message clear. Tony seems to have accepted his respite from death and rebirth into a new life by lauding a more philosophical world view when he exclaims to an incredulous sister Janice, "Every day is a gift."
- In a rehabilitating vein of personal salvation, Artie Bucco recovers his culinary ethics and salvages the sanctity of his soul as he lovingly caresses the pages of his father's handwritten recipe cookbook in "Luxury Lounge" VI.7. The simple and straightforward words of the food-stained recipe for *Coniglio della Famiglia* set him back on his path of personal and professional integrity. The fact that he must work with only one hand, his left (the right-brained hand of memory, deep inner peace, and ancestral consciousness) and not the right hand (the left-brained hand of here and now, stress, and connivance) both intensifies and consolidates Arties's newfound heroic contentment.
- Vito Spatafore's proclivity for the male body is made ever clear with his predilection for fitness magazines. In "Johnny Cakes" VI.8, we see him perusing *AB Attack*, a men's health magazine that includes the must-read articles "101 Abs Sculpting Exercises" and "10 Keys to Weight Control."
- While John Sacrimoni suffers in hospital with lung cancer in "Stage 5" VI.14, an impertinent orderly (a former oncologist, Warren Feldman, who killed his wife, her aunt, and the mailman and is serving time in prison) provides a different prognosis to John's affliction. John is seen reading *Reader's Digest*. As if to corroborate the differing medical opinions surrounding his prognosis, the *Digest*'s main article is titled "How Doctors Gamble with Your Life."

- Television personality Geraldo Rivera speaks tongue-in-cheek to mock book *Wise Guide to Wise Guys* author Manny Safier in "Stage 5" VI.14. Safier is played by *The Sopranos* writer Matthew Weiner.
- Phil Leotardo asks his nieces and nephews if they know of Leonardo da Vinci in "Stage 5" VI.14. Their response, "He wrote *The Da Vinci Code*" (by Dan Brown), only exacerbates the ethnocentric ire of the forlorn grandfather.
- The film *Cleaver* in "Stage 5" VI.14 is a case of life imitating art imitating life. As Tony and the entire Soprano cast watch the premier of mobster-horror-slasher flick, they vicariously relive those moments that fellow family member Christopher has minced from mob films and from the events that surround their everyday (filmic) lives. The viewer is left with the notion that everything is indeed a pseudo fiction; a mise-en-abîme game of self-referentiality and intratextuality that is played to its deliciously deleterious end.
- In "Stage 5" VI.14, after watching *Born Yesterday* (1950), starring Broderick Crawford, Tony is not convinced that its plot had inspired *Cleaver*. Tony was not "born yesterday." His intuition that Christopher's film is a blatant and unflattering parody of himself is the straw that eventually stirs his underling's premature demise.
- Silvio Dante is regularly seen reading local hardware flyers and in one instance, in "The Second Coming" VI.19, he's seen holding the self-help book *How to Clean Practically Anything*. As consigliere cum concierge, he is often tasked to clean up the mayhem and the physical remains of Soprano crew activities. He is the crazy glue (we recall that in "No-Show" IV.2 he complains of a dried out tube of crazy glue), the fixer of the family. He is routinely called upon to mend relations between wayward crew members and Tony. The fact that he also repairs broken vases, trophies, and other sundry objects placed upon his cluttered desk only adds to his adhesive functionality and his ability to clean up practically anything.

Carmela and Books

Carmela Soprano is the most ambitious on-screen reader and merits a section dedicated to her readings. She is attached to plenty of books. Some help her understand her son's erratic behaviour: *Help Me Help My Child* by Jill Bloom and *The Wonder of Boys* by Michael Gurian. More casual reading includes Arthur Golden's *Memoirs of a Geisha* (II.9, II.10, II.12), Marion Zimmer Bradley's *The Mists of Avalon* (IV.8), Gustave

Flaubert's *Madame Bovary* and the medieval template of ultimate love, *Abelard and Heloise* (V.6), Sue Grafton's *C Is for Corpse* (VI.2), and Fred Barnes, *Rebel-in-Chief* (VI.17). Whatever the subject matter, however, all of Carmela's books appear at specific moments in her life. Their themes and plots subtend the drama, peril, or personal issues she faces.

Samples

- *The Remains of the Day* by Kazuo Ishiguro and the homonymous film about unrequited love and sensual desperation, becomes Father Phil Intintola and Carmela's go-between text, the agent that mediates their dangerously sensual relationship, in "College" I.5. In the medieval love story reprised by Dante Alighieri in his epic poem *The Divine Comedy*, a lustful couple, Paolo da Verrucchio and Francesca da Rimini, succumb to the sexual tension engendered while reading the ribald passages in the Arthurian tale of *Lancelot du Lac*. A similar sexual tension between Carmela and the sexually aroused priest mounts as they intently watch a thoroughly emasculated butler named Stevens (played by Anthony Hopkins) clutch a book that Miss Kenton (the Emma Watson character) desperately wishes to open. Unlike the recalcitrant Stevens, however, Carmela metaphorically opens her book and confesses her difficult memories, as well as her sexual readiness, to an eagerly expectant Father Phil. Unfortunately, though her words and gestures are provocative, the wine incapacitates the improbable lover-priest and renders him a physically ineffective and anticlimactic partner. The inebriated couple will not suffer the same hellish fate as the legendary Paolo and Francesca.
- The same episode cites an American literary great, Nathaniel Hawthorne, on a school lintel at Bowdoin College. The citation ("No man can wear one face to himself and another to the multitude without finally getting bewildered as to which may be true") visually extemporizes the latent internal disseverance and the improbable sexual inclinations of the wayward priest.
- In "From Where to Eternity" II.9, Carmela chooses the Bible as her bedtime reading. The episode is fraught with images of death, out-of-body experiences, repentant prayer, and redemptive psychiatry. With Bible in hand and brimstone in her fiery tone, Carmela demands that Tony undergo a vasectomy in order to save their family from future, therefore eternal damnation ... if not the shame, of a bastard child.

- Carmela, we have seen, often uses books as go-between facilitators or practical excuses to open a conversation with prospective suitors. Vic the painter's book of paint chips proves to be an unsuccessful go-between text as he realizes that Carmela is the wife of mobster Tony Soprano. The level-headed Vic Musto prefers to leave her decorating to more intrepid, if not foolhardy, suitors in "Knight in White Satin Armor" II.12.
- While visiting Meadow at Columbia University in "Second Opinion" III.7, Carmela picks up one of her daughter's course books, *The Theory of the Leisure Class* by Thorstein Veblen, an early critique of consumerism. Meadow sarcastically intimates to her mother that the Sopranos "are way passed that." To Meadow's haughty riposte Carmela snootily retorts with her own latest reading describing the social woes of contemporary society as they unfold in the idealist commercial novels of writer-activist Barbara Kingsolver.
- *The Mists of Avalon* by Marion Zimmer Bradley ("Mergers and Acquisitions" IV.8) is a story of matriarchal rebellion and subterfuge. Bradley retells the Arthurian legend through the eyes of the marginalized women of King Arthur's court. In essence, *The Mists of Avalon* deconstructs the male-centred myths of Camelot and recasts women's experience as a shift in gender power. The same shift is occurring at this juncture of *The Sopranos*. Carmela is no longer a silent partner. She demands information and a say in family finances. Her newfound resolve extends to her open disapproval of Tony's continuing womanizing. By placing the silver-tipped fingernail that she discovers in his pants pocket on his bed stand, she is surreptitiously informing him that she knows of his affair with Valentina La Paz. In the same episode, she further undermines his patriarchal authority and bolsters her own evolving personal agenda by stealing from the cache of money he has hidden in the bird seed. She has acquired both a voice and a deliberate active stance with respect to her own future security within the family by recasting her character role from her own perspective.
- A home-decorating book for cottages serves as go-between text between a surprisingly willing and anxiously yearning Carmela and love-stricken enforcer Furio Giunta in "Eloise" IV.12. Their conversation is blissfully nuanced. As Carmela speaks of "romantic" spaces, Furio tells her she "is a very special woman." The innocent exchange becomes metaphorically impassioned as Carmela ask if he "has thought about flooring yet," a sexual innuendo that does not

escape a willing Furio. A passing workman's cry of "speak English for Crissakes" to a co-worker sarcastically implores the love-struck wooers to stop speaking in metaphors and address each other with clear language. As they plan a first date to a Color Tile store, a place that Carmela states "has everything" and a place where Furio "would love to go with [Carmela]," they seem to heed the workman's plea as they transparently repeat to each other that "a date is a date."

- Ever concerned about her son's education, Carmela reads the CliffsNotes version of William Golding's *Lord of the Flies* to a dozing A.J. in "Sentimental Education" V.6. The homework assignment is another of her go-between excuses for romance. Is she impatient with A.J. because of his lack of interest in his studies or because her relationship with academic adviser Robert Wegler hinges specifically on A.J.'s academic progress? In either case, the Golding story of disaster when individuals cannot govern their own impulses should be compulsory reading for Carmela as she heads down the path of eventual heartache.
- The novel *Madame Bovary* by Gustav Flaubert ("Sentimental Education" V.6) should signal the beginning of a new bourgeois life for Carmela. The special edition volume is a gift from Robert Wegler delivered to her after their first kiss. It is a go-between text, a prelude to a new hopefully vital life. Its pages, however, should remind Carmela and signal the viewer of the banality of the adulterous affair. The ultimate impossibility of any movement away from the bourgeois norm casts Carmela in the same mundane predicament as Madame Bovary.
- *Abelard and Heloise* ("Sentimental Education" V.6), on the other hand, is a volume Carmela discovers in Robert Wegler's bathroom after their first love session. Its sorrowful tale of impossible love portends the frenzied tragedy of their continuing tryst and parodies the ineffable angst of Carmela's continuing emotional distress. In the same episode, we see Wegler reading *Cold Mountain* by Charles Frazier, itself a tale of personal redemption, lost love, and existential exasperation. He eventually becomes cold as a mountain when he snubs Carmela's affection out of churlish self-pity.
- *Rebel-in-Chief* by Fred Barnes ("Walk Like a Man" VI.17) is a case study of the presidency of George W. Bush. The controversial and eye-opening account of Bush's tenure in office can be read as a primer for Carmela's newly found rebellious, and yes controversial,

spirit of non-conformity. She has sold her spec-house and boldly refuses to share her profit with Tony. It seems her marital interregnum away from Tony has provided resolve, drive, and personal ambition, all qualities attributed to George W. Bush by Fred Barnes.
- *C Is for Corpse* by Sue Grafton ("Kaisha" VI.12) is the novel read by Carmela at Tony's bedside while he is comatose in hospital. Beyond the crime plot, the title of the novel is an obvious allusion to Tony's physical and spiritual absence as mob boss and husband. He has been reduced to a corpse.
- The central book for a characterization of Carmela is *Memoirs of a Geisha* by Arthur Golden. In "Bust Out" II.10, a camera close-up lingers on the figure of the geisha on the book cover as Carmela reads the novel in bed. This is significant. The previous episode, "From Where to Eternity II.9, ends with Carmela reading this same novel in bed. She completes that night's pleasure, and the episode, by giving Tony the series' first passionate kiss. "Bust Out" II.10 finds her still in bed after servicing her master. Her geisha-like submission is new and startling. Like the character in the novel, it is possibly premised on the secretive pact between symbolic master and love slave. In Carmela's case, the pact is an accommodating union between real mob-husband and mistress-wife. The symbolic implications of the geisha image are evocative and far reaching. Does Carmela survive as Tony's wife because she remains a faithful, silent, and obedient geisha? Or is she a tough, resourceful character that will eventually write her own life narrative beyond her subservient role as mob wife? Her emotional "busting out" seems imminent as she flirts with Vic Musto the painter in this same episode. Other flirtations and an affair with Robert Wegler will follow. Importantly, and again for the first time in the series, Carmela physically attacks Tony near this episode's end. She is upset at his neglect of son A.J. While she rails against a startled Tony, a statue of a roaring lioness looks on from the fireplace mantel. Is she really "busting out" now or merely laying the ground for her future inevitable feistiness? Sister-in-law Janice's antics may provide a clue.
- The submissive geisha analogy is pertinent to Janice Soprano's tumultuous relationship with Richie Aprile. In the same episode, "Bust Out" II.10, the viewer learns that Richie forces her to submit to his sexual proclivities by holding a gun to her temple while copulating. Janice eventually kills Richie in "Knight in White Satin Armor" II.12. Tony will inform Carmela of the murder while she is holding

the book *Memoirs of a Geisha*. Carmela will remain wilfuly trapped in her submissive role and tied to reading her book to its conclusion. Janice, on the other hand, has indeed violently "busted out."

Television on TV

Watching television programs alongside Tony Soprano spurs an illuminating and especially fascinating rebuilding of the mechanisms of "watching television" that eclipses all other modes of vision in the series. Purposefully inserted television or movie scenes in a television series are particularly interesting as they offer a metalanguage of playful verbal self-reflexivity and intentional visual self-commentary. We recall briefly that David Chase is an accomplished, though self-admittedly frustrated, television writer eager to change standard television genre by extending its potential artistic capacity. To lend the series an art house subtext, he regularly inserts scenes from classic films, television commercials, and television programs into the normal flow of action thereby creating a new syntax. Once in place, the newly formed semantic cannot be severed without diminishing the message on either television screen. The juxtaposition is a potent creative interaction that permits Chase to change the media norm by truly contributing to the restructuring of the viewer's television experience. Chase is clearly making a case for shifting the traditional thinking of television culture. He is establishing a new metaphor for that imagined world by building a representational order based on a multidimensional visual index. He makes the series richer by pointing elsewhere, by adding connections and referring viewers to a related media vocabulary beyond *The Sopranos*. By employing intertextuality to bind the words and images from the smaller television screens in the series to the words and images surrounding them on the larger television screen, he inserts the series into an infinite network of relations with the symbolic potential of unlimited possibilities.

When the ideal viewer is asked to watch television along with characters who have themselves become viewers, the expression and content of both the series and the intercalated television scenes in question become a mutually inclusive semiosis. These visual/verbal cues achieve a correlational function in the expanding semantic meaning of the series. Chase is not overlapping different codes but using media to comment and augment similar media. He has installed a visual conversation between present and past viewable media. The typology of these inserted visual texts may vary (The History Channel footage of the Second World War, an old film, or a television commercial, for example) and often remain paradigmatically contrary to the action. Their operative intentionality as perlocutionary acts, however, produce a newly inspired signifying effect within *The Sopranos* that is unmistakable and novel. The ideal viewer remains on constant alert, ever surprised, senses heightened because the relationship between the words heard and images viewed on the small meta-television screen within the larger television scene is not disruptive. The merging images and words instead create a quiet and simultaneous complementarity. Both Tony and the viewer are touched by the overpowering gaze of the monocular eye of the small television screen. But Tony especially is affected by the modality of his believing eye. His television programs and the films he chooses to view are a supporting platform for the process of psychological transformation he undergoes during the series. Television is Tony's secondary mode of self-reflection, the first being the psychoanalysis sessions with Dr. Melfi. In both situations he learns modes of interpreting himself and his world and appropriates modes of action that benefit his place within his world. The viewer is allowed to tag along, to watch and listen from an ocular vantage that removes, distances, and simultaneously inserts the viewer into the same labyrinthine quandaries as Tony in order to better comprehend the thought processes of the character.

For example, the actions that transpire on the many television screens that are watched by the characters in the series often faithfully mirror the actions that transpire in that particular episode. Or, they may contradict information previously revealed in the episode and may portend an uncomfortable, unresolved end. At times, the mere recognition of a movie title that is watched on television lends the viewer invaluable corollary information and nuanced extensions of the episode's plotline. In these instances, knowledge of the movie's content or character profiles in the movies invite the viewer to make comparisons with *The Sopranos'* characters or plot in that particular episode. In short, a cause-and-effect process of homogeneous or heterogeneous on-screen acts or words emanating from small television screens equip the informed ideal viewer with a deeper significance of the acts or words that are seen or heard in the series.

Most interesting, however, is Chase's use of intercalated films and their background dialogue that actually enters the world of *The Sopranos* as part of the real dialogue in the scene. In these instances, movie dialogue seamlessly intercalates itself and offers possible responses and/or segues to the characters in the scene. In other words, as the characters talk to one another and ask each other questions, the answers to those questions are not supplied by the on-screen characters but by the movie characters on the television screen they are watching. This is truly an interesting intertextual metadialogical assemblage. As words from a filmic past fill the interstices of Soprano silence, the viewer is witness to a fascinating rupturing of television space and the generation of a new virtual space of mutually inclusive, multilayered, and revisioned multimodal worlds.

Samples

- Tony watches television in bed in "Boca" I.9. The History Channel features a documentary on the German Luftwaffe and the viewer hears the commentary "The Stukas and Messerschmitts have command of the sky" as bombs drop on naval vessels. The Stuka was a German ground-attack aircraft while the Messerschmitt was the new lightweight and highly successful Luftwaffe aircraft designed by the company of that name. Later in bed, Carmela drops a bomb on Tony by updating him with gossip concerning Uncle Junior's "taste for women." Tony will comment that the two bombs of "cunnilingus and psychiatry," as he will call them, have led to the bad blood between his mother, Uncle Junior, and himself. The bombs continue to fall and will eventually lead to a contract on his life by a Stuka (Livia) and a Messerschmitt (Junior).
- Livia Soprano and Uncle Junior are informed of their botched assassination attempt on Tony while watching the nightly news in "Isabella" I.12. The site of Tony being taken to hospital on a gurney with minor wounds worries the duo so much that they march directly to Tony's home in order to save face, their reputations, and their lives.
- As Meadow and her boyfriend neck on the couch in "I Dream of Jeannie Cusamano" I.13, the television screen shows a woman whose head turns into a hideous hydra-like alien about to devour an unsuspecting male suitor in her spreading tendrils. In the scene before we see Meadow and boyfried, the same unexpected though lethal dangers of feminine allure are felt by Jimmy Altieri as he anticipates the pleasures of a hooker. Unfortunately, his brain is about to be split into spreading bloody tendrils after he is shot in the head by Silvio Dante for carrying a wire.

- Familiar family patterns have been torn asunder as the Soprano children are testing the limits of their teenagehood, Carmela becomes a restless housewife, and Tony is facing the prospect of prison for the murder of Matthew Bevilaqua in the episode aptly titled "Bust Out" II.10. Everyone, it seems, is hoping to "bust out" of their immediate predicaments. In the midst of these whirlwinds, Tony watches The History Channel. The commentary on General George Patton captions his own dilemma: "He knows that the controversies that have swirled about him have tarnished his reputation. He desperately wants to vindicate himself in the only way he knows how. In battle." The phone rings and he is informed by Paulie "Walnuts" Gualtieri that there is no more need to fret imprisonment for the murder because "the battle" has been won. The television commentary continues: "Patton's hatred for the enemy is matched only by his fierce concern for his men." As the viewer will come to realize, Tony always follows well-placed advice, especially when it comes from The History Channel. In order to demonstrate his own fierce concern for his men, thereby aligning him with the image of General Patton, Tony visits the paraplegic Peter "Beansie" Gaeta and, in a mock show of concern for his men, forces "Beansie" to accept $50,000 as a donation to the spinal cord foundation. Tony is jubilant, his conscience has been assuaged, his reputation as a caring capo assured.
- Carmela's ongoing unhappiness with her marriage and with philandering husband Tony is mirrored on the television screen in "Knight in White Satin Armor" II.12. Carmela is watching *Champagne for Caesar*, a 1950 comedy starring Ronald Coleman and Celeste Holm. As Tony, the Caesar of his domain and her own supposed knight in black leather jacket, descends the stairs, the viewer hears Ronald Coleman say: "You also pretending when I kiss you?" After Tony exits the house and the camera frames a lonely and melancholy Carmela, the viewer again hears dialogue from the female lead that easily reproduce Carmela's thoughts at this revelatory moment: "I'm ashamed of myself." The male lead replies, "Yes, you ought to be, definitely."
- Richie Aprile watches a boxing match on television in "Knight in White Satin Armor" II.12. Perhaps he is taking pointers for the right jab he serves Janice Soprano later in the same episode.
- After murdering Salvatore "Big Pussy" Bonpensiero, a visibly shaken Tony watches the Motown recording group The Temptations perform on television in "Funhouse" II.13. The lyrics of the

song "Ain't Too Proud to Beg" resonate in Tony's ears as he remembers his friend's pleas for mercy before being shot.
- The film *The Public Enemy* (1931) serves as a parallel running commentary to the events of "Proshai, Livushka" III.2 in which Livia Soprano dies. Tony is seen watching the film intermittently throughout as the events of the episode unfold. From the 1930s-style disclaimer and moralistic opening film credits that proclaim "Tom Powers in 'Public Enemy' and Rico in 'Little Caesar' are not two men, nor are they merely characters – they are a problem that sooner or later we, the public, must solve," to the touching scene of the loving and doting mother preparing the bed for her son's return, Tony's emotional state on the day his own mother dies is played and displayed within the themes and frames of this classic film. As various clips are viewed intermittently by Tony, the viewer is allowed to penetrate his emotional state as it is displayed in his teary eyes.
- An *Entertainment Tonight* segment on Hollywood bombshell Jane Mansfield is Janice Soprano's viewing pleasure in "Fortunate Son" III.3. The full-bodied buxom beauty draws interest from Janice perhaps for their shared physical attributes, perhaps for the beauty's determination to "box into the business" at any cost. Cantankerous insubordination is a definite Janice trait.
- Uncle Junior callously announces his upcoming bout with cancer to Bobby "Baccalà" Baccilieri Jr. while watching *The Devil at 4 O'Clock* (1961) starring Spencer Tracy and Frank Sinatra in "Another Toothpick" III.5. A crestfallen Bobby, whose father has just died of a heart attack, bemoans the somber state of affairs that has befallen the family. Uncle Junior's insistence that he is not attending the elder Baccilieri funeral is echoed in Sinatra's firm words, "I'm not going with you." Bobby's expressive wailing, "My father, now you. What the fuck is happening?" is also flippantly answered for a silent and indifferent Uncle Junior by Sinatra's movie dialogue, "What can you do?"
- Ralph Cifaretto complains about Kirk Douglas's anachronistic crew cut while watching the 1960s film *Spartacus* in "University" III.6. Later in the episode, his own callous recreation of a chain-swinging gladiator at the Bada Bing party (he is imitating Russell Crowe's performance in the 2000 film *Gladiator*) results in Georgie the Bada Bing bartender losing his eye. The scene also reeks with sexual innuendo as the cigar-sucking Ralph calls Georgie a pussy boy. The

viewer later learns that Ralph is the pussy boy since he enjoys anal sex. Is all the macho bravado a studied distraction by Ralph or an unsubtle statement on latent homoeroticism?
- Meadow Soprano and boyfriend Noah Tannenbaum attend a screening of *Dementia 13*, a 1963 film written and directed by Francis Ford Coppola. The film is about a scheming young woman who causes havoc for those around her; an uncomfortable reminder to Meadow of her meddling roommate. Both the movie character and the dishevelled roommate are irreparably irksome and exasperating as their foibles undermine all the female friends around them. The episode is aptly named "University" III.6 as all its characters must learn to contend with adversity lest they risk the same sort of derangement and dementia.
- As Tony and Carmela watch television in bed in "He Is Risen" III.8, a Mercedes-Benz commercial becomes a visual metaphor for Gloria Trillo, the Mercedes saleswoman Tony has just met and with whom he is infatuated. The commercial's rejoinder "here's how you'll get your thrills" spurs Tony to brashly inform an unsuspecting Carmela that he is "thinking of getting one of those." Not knowing that Tony has conflated the Mercedes logo with Gloria's legs, Carmela innocently consents by stating "it's a good idea." As promised in the commercial, thrills and spills with Gloria follow.
- Ralph Cifaretto's apology for his impertinence and disrespect towards Tony as capo reverberates in the soap opera that Uncle Junior is watching in "He Is Risen" III.8. The female lead similarly implores, "I'm so sorry," but to no real avail. Both the male lead and Tony remain aloof and indifferent to the supplications of their underlings.
- Much to his chagrin, New York boss John Sacrimoni learns about the esplanade development while watching television in "He Is Risen" III.8. The project was to have been a joint venture with Tony. The unexpected news precipitates a brooding acrimony towards him.
- In "The Telltale Moozadell" III.9, Tony watches the 1934 W.C. Fields movie *It's a Gift* while eating a slice of Carmela's birthday cake in bed. The viewer is allowed to both see and hear a scene in which a bowling ball slowly bounces down several flights of wooden stairs disturbing a sleeping Fields. The bouncing ball presages the bouncing bowling ball Tony will hear after he has murdered Ralph Cifaretto in "Whoever Did This" IV.9. We recall

that Tony hears the ball bouncing down the basement stairs. We recall, too, that Christopher Moltisanti will place Ralph's severed head in a bowling ball bag. In the same W.C. Fields movie clip, a salesman arrives on the scene asking information about Carl La Fong. He proceeds to spell the name: "Carl La Fong. Capital 'L' small 'a.' Capital 'F' small 'o' small 'n' small 'g.'" This spelling bee publicly forecasts the atrocious spelling skills and puerile vocabulary of Jackie Aprile Jr., Meadow's boyfriend and opponent in a Scrabble game in the very next episode, "To Save Us All from Satan's Power" III.10. Unwittingly, in the same episode, Carmela states that she prefers a better lot for her Columbia University daughter and states that she "is not thrilled about this thing with Jackie and Meadow."

- As Paulie "Walnuts" Gualtieri and Tony watch a nature program about snakes in "The Telltale Moozadell" III.9, Paulie espouses his superficial knowledge about the reptile's reproductive system. Tony rebuts Paulie's humorously solipsist reasoning by citing the Bible, Adam and Eve and the Earthly Paradise. In an upcoming scene, Tony and Gloria Trillo find their own earthly paradise in the reptile house of the local zoo as, like a modern Adam and Eve, they make love before an inquisitive snake.
- The Christmas spirit of consumerism is not the only thing taxing Tony in "To Save Us All from Satan's Power" III.10. As he watches *It's a Wonderful Life* (1946) he exclaims: "Awe Jesus! Enough already!" But the viewer is unsure whether he is tired of completing his Christmas shopping list, annoyed with watching the same old Christmas movie, or dolorously mired in his memories of Salvatore "Big Pussy" Bonpensiero who used to play Santa Clause for the neighbourhood children. Yuletide salvation from Satan's power (i.e., betrayal) is never close at hand but is instead an ever-recurring and disturbing memory.
- Dr. Ira Fried, "the prick doctor," as he calls himself, films a television commercial for erectile dysfunction. In the same episode, the doctor is called upon to remove a bullet lodged near a furious Furio Giunta's private parts in "Amour Fou" III.12.
- Tony settles down, ice cream sundae in hand, to watch the film *Rio Bravo* (1959) in "For All Debts Public and Private" IV.1. While Dean Martin intones the virtues of paucity with his three uncomplaining companions, "just my rifle, pony, and me," an uncharacteristically strident Carmela harangues Tony about her own latest three preoccupations: just my money, the future, and security.

An Appendix of Verbal Bits and Visual Bytes   241

- Carmela's financial worries grow as she ponders Tony's possible/probable work-related death in "For All Debts Public and Private" IV.1 while watching a news report about killings in New York that are mob related.
- A *Magnum P.I.* (1980–8) episode plays on television while Christopher Moltisanti confronts retired policeman Haydu, the supposed killer of his father in "For All Debts Public and Private" IV.1. Christopher turns up the volume to cover his gunshots. As he struts around the room acting the part of hip avenging angel, Christopher relishes the television subtext that sarcastically accompanies his murder of the impoverished policeman: "Police? In a Ferrari? What could be farther from the truth," he scoffs incredulously.
- Carmela complains to Tony that she simply cannot communicate with daughter Meadow, who has threatened to travel to Europe and study in Barcelona, in "No-Show" IV.2. In the very next scene, Adriana La Cerva watches an *Everybody Loves Raymond* (1996–2005) episode as Ray Romano provides an unwanted, but fitting, retort to Carmela's motherly lamentations about Meadow as he states, "Maybe they don't have to talk. Maybe they're the kind of couple that doesn't talk constantly."
- Dr. Melfi's ex-husband Richard LaPenna watches television news coverage as violence erupts between Native American demonstrators and Italian American Pride organizers in "Christopher" IV.3. His comment "This is tragic" serves to counterbalance the elaborately expressed positions of both Tony and Dr. Melfi in the same episode regarding private self-esteem and public ethnic pride.
- Tony is caught by old New York boss Carmine Lupertazzi for hiding profits he feels should rightfully be shared between the New Jersey and New York mob families in "Christopher" IV.3. In the very next scene, a television commercial for Schwab Investment Services presents an elderly family doctor scolding his bedridden patient: "I've been your doctor for thirty years, you still need the thermometer." If Tony wishes to remain successful and keep his "portfolio" intact, he must respect the wishes of the elder Carmine before everyone's temperatures rise.
- A lengthy intrusion of television into the series occurs in "Christopher" IV.3 as panelists on the Montel Williams Show discuss Italian-American issues that include Christopher Columbus, Native American rights, and ethnic discrimination. Although topical and relevant to the episode, the Soprano crew's response is to turn-off the television set. Some things are better left in the dark.

- As Uncle Junior and nephew Tony discuss the impending hit on John Sacrimoni in "The Weight" IV.4, an episode of *Who Wants to Be a Millionaire* can be seen in the background. Junior's comment about the television contestant, "the poor prick" has "used all his life lines," could well apply to the marked figure of Johnny Sack.
- Loud music from A.J.'s room and Carmela's hair blower prohibit Tony from hearing any information about Winston Churchill on The History Channel in "Pie-O-My" IV.5. The viewer hears, however, that at the beginning of the Second World War Churchill answered his country's call. Tony is about to answer a mercy call. The thoroughbred Pie-O-My is ailing and Ralph Cifaretto is nowhere to be found. As he babysits the suffering horse in the track stable, he too will light up a fat cigar, à la Churchill, while contemplating his next move.
- Civilization and Egyptian stonecutters are the farthest things from the drug-stoned minds of Adriana La Cerva and Christopher Moltisanti in "Everybody Hurts" IV.6. The television commentary extols the organizational skills and craftsmanship of the Egyptians, which contrast sharply to the disordered and degenerate scene of drugs and depravity in both their apartment venue and their drug-infested lives.
- Adriana La Cerva learns that mob wives cannot be forced to testify against their mobster husbands while watching television in, appropriately, "Watching Too Much Television" IV.7. She is later informed by a friend, and subsequently from a 1-800 Law-4-You public lawyer, that this is untrue, proving once again that watching too much television can be harmful to one's well-being.
- Carmela remembers Furio Giunta as she watches *The Food Network* personality Mario Batali on the television program *Mario Eats Italy* in "Mergers and Acquisitions" IV.8. As Mario's blond ponytail merges with her amorous memories of Furio Giunta's long dark tresses, she imagines herself transported away in a rapturous Neapolitan love dance.
- Late-night programming on CNN inspires Carmela to "take responsibility" and "have a contingency plan in case your husband does not come home" in "Mergers and Acquisitions" IV.8. After hearing heartbreaking situations in which the husband was the sole financial planner and the wife "did not have much involvement in the finances at the home," she stealthily retrieves $40,000 from Tony's secret stash of cash he has squirreled away in the backyard bird feeder.

- Tony and Christopher watch *The Last Time I Saw Paris* (1954) after having prepared the body of Ralph Cifaretto for subsequent disposal in "Whoever Did This" IV.9. Very little dialogue is actually heard. However, the viewer is allowed to watch a memorable scene in which the main character, Charles Wills, lies in a drunken stupor on a staircase. His liquor bottle falls from his hands and rolls down the stairs, previewing the sound of a bowling ball falling down the basement stairs that will spook both Christopher and Tony in the very next scene. The cold winter landscape in the film clip, the bluish hues offset by the female character's blood red robe reflect the sombre mood that has gripped the two sullen killers who have spent most of the night sopping-up Ralph's red blood.
- In "The Strong Silent Type" IV.10, Christopher watches *The Little Rascals*, a television series of short subjects from the 1930s, 1940s, and 1950s and featuring the antics of a young group of perspicacious and mischievous children. The episode on TV features a gorilla jumping on the backs of unsuspecting children, an illusion to the drug-monkey Christopher carries on his own back. The audible quip "Somebody's going to get something that he ain't expecting," just as Christopher is seen shooting up, reflects both the unexpected mind trips one takes while high on drugs as well as the abrupt phone interruption by Tony, the most unpredictable of rascals.
- The classic film *How to Marry a Millionaire* (1953) provides a not-so-subtle clue to Carmela's thoughts in "Eloise" IV.12. Still pining over the unexpected loss of love interest Furio Giunta, the movie dialogue "I never want to see you again," repeated twice, aptly summarizes her feelings towards her suddenly attentive partner Tony. The words may also euphemistically reiterate John Sacrimoni's feelings towards his boss, Carmine Lupertazzi. John has just asked Tony to wack his boorish boss so he never has to see him again.
- While watching the marines battling on a Pacific beachhead, Tony comments to A.J. that "the Marines had no air cover. It was a slaughter," in "Whitecaps" IV.13. The words aptly describe his inability to take cover from the barrage of accusations fired at him by a combative Carmela in a previous scene.
- Television news coverage informs Tony that his cousin, Tony Blundetto, is about to be released from prison in "Two Tonys" V.1. The news ushers a spate of memories that play themselves out in Season V. An uncharacteristically preoccupied Tony also learns about the other imminent releases from Mafia Class of '04. His

furrowed brow alerts the viewer of future travail as these former crew members return to the fold.
- Emotionally inspired after watching the film *Prince of Tides* (1991) in "Two Tonys" V.1, Tony sends Dr. Melfi a basket of cleaning products, including a box of Tide laundry detergent. He signs the card, "Thinking of you, Your Prince of Tide." The gesture is not enough to wash away the memory of Tony's inappropriate antics for Dr. Melfi.
- Tony is visibly moved while watching the recollections of a war veteran in "Rat Pack" V.2. The veteran speaks of a fellow soldier sacrificing himself for a friend: "All your life you gotta' remember what one guy did because he thought it was his job to do and he took a shot for you." In an episode where everyone is conspicuously self-centred and argumentative about girlfriends and pecking orders, and where informants seem to crawl out of the woodwork like rats, Tony's ideal world of Rat Pack camaraderie has been reduced to a painted dream.
- An increasingly delusional Corrado "Junior" Soprano imagines he sees himself as Larry David of *Curb Your Enthusiasm* (2000–) fame in "Where's Johnny" V.3. In the same episode, an infomercial for Anthony Robins exhorts viewers with an onscreen quote by writer Henry James: "It's time to start living the life you've imagined." A sobering comment for in the very next scene, Uncle Junior, no longer sure of his identity, wanders the streets of his old neighbourhood in search of a past that will help him to "start living the life" he can now only fantazise.
- A *Bob Villa Home Improvement* segment about external home facades in "Where's Johnny" V.3 resonates with the false pretense, or facade, that Tony uses to convince Artie Bucco to move out of his motel room and into Tony's mother's house. He calls Artie a brother, but is only really interested in helping his cousin Tony B. who could use Artie's restaurant linen on his laundry route.
- While impatient preachers in a neighbourhood church are cleansing souls and chastising a befuddled Corrado "Junior" Soprano in "Where's Johnny" V.3, Janice Soprano reads a book titled *Bed Wetting* and watches an infomercial for Joe Mangano's Miracle Clean. A good product to use after one has wet the bed since an increasingly debilitated Uncle Junior is probably on his way to wearing Depends incontinence diapers after aimlessly wandering away from home.

An Appendix of Verbal Bits and Visual Bytes 245

- A wildlife program on prairie dogs and information about their hibernation patterns fits nicely into Uncle Junior's advancing memory loss and cerebral hibernation in "Where's Johnny" V.3. He is about to become as innocuous and harmless as the ubiquitous prairie dog.
- While relaxing in her bubble bath, Carmela watches a movie clip from the film *Frida* (2002) in "All Happy Families" V.4. The children in the film ask Frida: "Why do you and Biba live in two different houses?" Frida replies: "Because we are two different people but our love makes us into one." There is biting irony in the juxtaposition of this particular scene with the spousal reality of Carmela and Tony. While they live in the same house, their mutual hatred keeps them separate. The scene is sandwiched between two scenes of Meadow and boyfriend Finn cavorting on the couch. Surprisingly, they are watching the same film as Carmela. In our first visit with Meadow and Finn, the viewer is allowed to watch the television screen as the male lead, artist Diego Rivera, violently destroys one of his paintings. "Do you want to go back to that!" he shouts to Frida Kahlo, implying the tumultuous nature of their relationship. "Yes. I want to go back to that!" she screams back. As the scene segues to Carmela in her tub, the auditory portion of the film (Diego and Frida screaming) is heard before we see her effectively tying the two scenes together. Carmela's solitude in her home, soaking alone in her tub, contrasts sharply with the heated romance of her daughter and Finn. On our second visit to Meadow's apartment the two lovers fall into each other's embrace, once again enhancing the loneliness of Carmela. The sight of Meadow and Finn fondling each other now morphs into the next scene where their fondling is mimicked on a hotel television monitor. As the camera pulls back, we realize that A.J. and friends are spending the night in New York City and have rented a porno film. It seems love is in the air everywhere in Sopranoland. But Carmela is not part of the reverie. She wants desperately, as Diego and Frida bluster, "to go back to that." But whether that "that" is Tony, her now estranged husband, or rekindled feelings of romance with someone else is still to be determined.
- As a close-up of a bewildered Tony segues into a close-up of a sweating and equally dumbfounded Jackie Gleason from *The Honeymooners* (1955–6), Gleason's stammering "uma-uma-uma-uma" fills the silence and provides Tony's answer to Carmela's demand that he take A.J. to live with him in "All Happy Families"

V.4. Beyond the hilarity, the scene also reminds the viewer of Tony Blundetto's impersonations of Gleason and his unappreciated comparison of the comedian's girth to Tony's satiated and bulging belly.
- Television monitors are the undoing of Feech La Manna's short sojourn from incarceration in "All Happy Families" V.4. Tony conives a plan that has Feech agree to store stolen television monitors in his garage; then Tony arranges for a parole officer to visit Feech's home landing him back in prison. The TV action makes Tony's troubled TV family happy again.
- Christopher Moltisanti's jealousy knows no bounds in "Irregular Around the Margins" V.5. His one-sided boxing match with fiancée Adriana is replicated on the small screen in the very next scene as A.J. watches kick-boxing on television.
- The constant bickering between Tony and Carmela since their separation segues to Uncle Junior's television screen and Federico Fellini's *La Dolce Vita* (1960) in "Marco Polo" V.8. The film's plot about unrequited love and impossible happiness seems to mirror the Soprano family norm at this juncture of the series. Uncle Junior's comment that "even with the captions I can't tell what's what," slyly footnotes the rampant emotional upheaval and monophonic bickering of Tony and Carmela.
- As Tony Blundetto ponders whether to freelance himself to "Little" Carmine Lupertazzi Jr.'s crew to perform a hit for money in "Marco Polo" V.8, his mother watches a Julia Child cooking episode on television. The question "Which instrument will we use to torture this meat?" is followed by the chef's flattening of a beefsteak with a butcher's mallet. The scene foreshadows the pounding Tony B. will eventually receive as a result of his extra-curricular activities. More immediately, the meat of his foot will be flattened and tenderized by a car tire after he shoots Joe "Peeps" Pepparelli and a young prostitute.
- In "Marco Polo" V.8, Uncle Junior once again proves the heritage gap between American Italians and Italians. As *La Dolce Vita* (1960) plays on his television set, he sleeps, then admits to Bobby "Baccalà" Baccilieri Jr. that it makes no difference whether he's awake or sleeping, he doesn't understand the movie in any case.
- Soprano rage goes prime time as Tony watches television news coverage of his sister Janice's attack on a soccer mom in "Cold Cuts" V.10. As psychologist Bela Kakuk describes for the news-watching

audience the ever-increasing incidents of rage-inflicted violence in contemporary society, Tony flies into a rage and charges over to Janice's house.
- Tony learns about contaminated transport containers in "Cold Cuts" V.10. The *60 Minutes* news clip links with the earlier news release featuring his raging sister's attack on a soccer mom. The message is clear: just as containers can carry clandestine toxic waste, so too can Soprano family members conceal toxic rage that can easily infiltrate even the calmest of family scenarios. This is exemplified by Tony's noxious comments at the evening dinner with a surprisingly placid Janice and her family. His instigation regarding Janice's long-lost son Harpo sparks the usual cataclysmic clash with his sister. As the lyrics of the Kinks' song "I'm Not Like Everybody Else" (1966) open the closing credits, we are given the message that indeed Tony is not like everybody else.
- In "The Test Dream" V.11, Tony is allowed to view himself on television as if he were an actor in an ongoing reality series. Television adds a third self-referential dimension to this dream sequence as the real sleeping Tony dreams of an avatar Tony who watches a character Tony on television sets. As turnstile moments of his life are played before him, Tony realizes that he is in a dream but wonders, "Where're we goin'?" The answer is California. As he continues his travels, well-known Hollywood films play before his eyes – *Chinatown* (1974), *High Noon* (1952), *A Christmas Carol* (1938) – and while Tony wants to continue watching the movies because he finds them interesting, Carmela exhorts him that it's not the movies he's watching, "it's your life." This multilayered phantasmagorical realm eventually portrays him in the scene from *The Godfather* (1972) when Michael Corleone is about to exit the restaurant bathroom and kill Virgil "The Turk" Sollozzo and Sargeant Mark McCluskey. In the dream, Tony emerges from the men's room not with a gun but with a copy of *The Valachi Papers* by Peter Maas. As the dream moves through fast-paced editing, crowds pursue him and turn into peasants wearing lederhosen and bearing torches from the film *Frankenstein* (1931). The next sequence shows a teen slasher film whose suspense is contrived as Tony moves through the high school shower stalls replete with ominously dripping water. The darkened and slow-moving corridor scene in the next sequence leads to his momentous rendezvous with Coach Molinaro. Fake chocolate guns and bullets, fingers that shoot, actors that play dead, all lend to the surreal

mixture of dream-film-television reality that comingle to subordinate all points of view to Tony's imaginative constructions.
- Television surveillance of The Crazy Horse nightclub by the FBI in "Long Term Parking" V.12 will initiate the final chapter in Adriana La Cerva's short-term, media-driven life.
- Just as Tony promises Carmela that he will cease his extra-curricular dalliances if she allows him to return home and reconcile their marriage, a football referee's whistle from the television monitor he is attempting to adjust signals a stoppage of play in "Long Term Parking" V.12. The referee's whistle also signals an end to Tony's "playing the field." His cheating has momentarily been blown dead. He has been allowed to return home after promising to be faithful to his marriage vows and after bartering an agreement with Carmela that guarantees her a modicum of financial independence. The Hermes scarf he presents her as a conciliatory gift, however, is strikingly similar to the silk scarf worn by burn victim Valentina La Paz one scene earlier. This subtle visual cue signals to the astute viewer that indeed not much will change with respect to Tony and his goomahs. The insatiable scammer will continue to insolently continue his double life. While a naively empowered Carmela clears the kitchen, Tony watches *It's a Gift*, a 1934 W.C. Fields comedy. Ironically, a demandingly shrewish wife and incompetent business assistant create havoc for the main character of the film. The predicament mirrors Tony's immediate plight as both a nagging and evermore shrewish Carmela and the off-the-wagon and evermore wayward nephew Christopher Moltisanti augur imminent calamity à la W.C. Fields.
- Informed by Adriana La Cerva about her lethal FBI connections, a desperate Christopher screams, "What are we gonna do!" in "Long Term Parking" V.12. The answer is immediately forthcoming as the scene cuts to Tony's television set on which he is watching *The Great Caruso* (1951). "Careful of the ear my son," the elder barber instructs a young apprentice. The barber's warning is a plausible suggestion for Adriana and Christopher to heed as they contemplate either slitting their own throats ear to ear or joining the FBI's witness protection program in order to avoid Tony's expected wrath. This scene from *The Great Caruso* is sandwiched between two key scenes in the episode. In the first scene, Adriana has just confessed her predicament with the FBI to Christopher. Meanwhile, in the second scene, Tony has confessed to his cousin Tony B. the real reason (a

panic attack) he missed their scheduled truck-jacking seventeen years earlier. On that occasion, Tony is taken to hospital by his mother; Tony B. is carted off to prison after being apprehended by the police. As Tony finishes his phone conversation with Tony B., the movie dialogue continues to fill in the silences of this difficult phone conversation. He, too, it seems, is given advice by the barber in *The Great Caruso*: "You broke your *carretto* ... because of singing." The *carretto*, a cart used by street vendors, is a euphemism for an enterprise, for business, and, by extension, for business conducted as usual. This cart, or business as usual, is no longer possible. Everything has been torn asunder and is broken. In the movie, the cart (business) has been broken because the Caruso character has preferred singing instead of attending to family business. In *The Sopranos*, the implied connotation for both Adriana's and Tony's life situations is similarly ravaged and their new paths dreadfully clear. Adriana has just revealed her debilitating burden to Christopher. She has overturned their apple cart; the wheels have come off their future. No more business as usual. Tony, on the other hand, has just sung his deeply hidden secret to his cousin Tony B. He has unburdened a load of guilt from his cart but has severely altered his relationship with his cousin. No more business as usual between them. There are calamitous consequences to both confessions. Just as the singers Enrico Caruso and Mario Lanza meet untimely natural deaths that end their lives and careers, Adriana La Cerva and Tony Blundetto will meet early, but expected, deaths. Their ends, however, will be anything but operatic.

- At the end of this same episode, the barber's words again resonate. After the barber has instructed his young apprentice to watch the ears, he continues by saying, "The things I do for friendship." Friends always lend their ears to a confidante for advice. Tony's situation with nephew Christopher is no different. After learning from him about Adriana's unpardonable transgression, he advises Christopher to allow the chips to fall where they may. He also advises himself to contemplate the unthinkable but necessary act of killing his cousin Tony B. As a grief-stricken Christopher laments the death of Adriana, the movie *The Three Amigos* (1986) plays on a large-screen TV. Christopher's pain at the loss of Adriana is exacerbated by his alcohol and drug-induced stupor. An infuriated Tony, already reeling from his deliberations about killing his cousin, lunges at him and kicks him repeatedly while screaming, "You think you're alone in this!" As the three amigos from the movie look on, Tony contemplates how the three of them, Tony S., Tony B., and Christopher will no longer be three amigos. He is also burdened, like the barber, by the things he must do for friendship, that is, membership in the mob.

- Ears are also important in another of the episodes. In "Isabella" I.12, Uncle Junior and Livia visit Tony after their fumbled attempt on Tony's life. As Livia approaches Tony, she exclaims, "Your ear. It's disfigured." Interestingly, earlier in the episode while in hospital after being injured in the ear by the fumbled attack on his life, Tony is approached by FBI Agent Dwight Harris who admonishes Tony to save himself by joining the FBI Witness Protection Program. Tony lends a deaf ear. In the next episode, "I Dream of Jeannie Cusamano" I.14, ears are again relevant as Tony confesses to his crew that "my ear hurts." He has just returned from receiving an earful of information from an FBI surveillance tape of his mother and uncle plotting his death. Ears, indeed, are a relevant leitmotif as they wind their way through the series and become a metaphor for subterfuge and deception.
- In "Members Only" VI.1, Uncle Junior is seen watching the movie *Paths of Glory* (1957). As the viewer is allowed to watch and listen along with him, all of Uncle Junior's frustrations of a life of missed occasions stream before him on the television screen. His foundering mobster career, his subservience to his younger brother, his unexpected vassalage to his nephew Tony are all condensed in the violent scene between the elder general and upstart commander. The general berates the young commander: "You're a disappointment to me. You're spoiling the keenness of your mind by wallowing in sentimentality." (The reference to keenness of mind refers to Tony as he once admitted to John Sacrimoni in "All Due Respect" V.13 of having an IQ of 136. "It's been tested.") The general continues: "You really did want to save those men, and you were not angling for Miro's command. You're an idealist, and I pity you as I would the village idiot ..." The young commander responds: "I apologize, sir, for not being entirely honest. I apologize for not revealing my true feelings. I apologize, sir, for not telling you that you're a sadistic old man. You can go to hell before I apologize to you now or ever again." At this point Tony enters the room and says, "What're you doin'?" Uncle Junior irritatingly replies, "I lost my uppers ... God fuck it all!" He is

conflating movie characters, Tony's subterfuge, phone pranksters that give him no peace, and the memory of Gennaro "Little Pussy" Malanga (a mobster Uncle Junior wanted to eliminate in the pilot episode but was thwarted by Tony, a slight he has never forgotten) into a knot of explosive angst. He imagines himself as the reprimanding general and Tony as the upstart youngster. He is displacing his pent-up lifelong angst upon his unsuspecting nephew. The movie dialogue fuels his anger and triggers the pernicious chain of events about to unfold. Though Tony attempts to comfort and reassure his befuddled uncle, Uncle Junior shoots his impertinent nephew in a fit of chronic paranoia at episode's end.

- The coma episodes in Season VI.2–3 can be considered a television subtext to the primary television text of *The Sopranos*. The events in the coma dream are a privately construed reality engendered by Tony's subconscious. Interestingly, they are watched by Tony just as he would watch a television program in his real life. The viewer is privy to theses oneiric events because we are allowed to watch along with him. The episodes are chock-full of correlational television innuendo. From Christian crosses to California brush fires, to outright religious messages displayed on a television screen: Are Sin, Disease and Death Real? The coma's entire dream sequence is played as a parallel dimension to the real dimension of Tony's mobster life.
- While recovering in hospital in "The Fleshy Part of the Thigh" VI.4, Tony watches a rerun of *Kung Fu,* a 1970s television series that starred David Carradine. In the series, Kwai Chang Caine, the orphaned son of an American man and Chinese woman, roams the Far West armed only with his martial arts expertise and spiritual training as a Shaolin monk. Tony listens intently as Caine's blind mentor, Master Po, teaches him that "between father and son there is a bridge that neither time nor death can shatter." Tony remarks to Paulie "Walnuts" Gualtieri that he used to watch the program "all the time" as a youngster. To view the scene now, then, implicates deep-set personal resonances. First, Tony has just emerged from a coma in which oriental monks played a large role. The oriental teaching that neither time nor death can shatter the bridge between father and son is about to be tested. His son A.J. has vowed to shorten the gap of the bridge between them by vowing revenge upon "mummy" Uncle Junior. The botched manslaughter attempt will eventually strengthen the bond between father and son and

sanction a future collaboration that time will not shatter. Second, Tony's revelation to Paulie that he "used to watch it all the time when I was a little kid" is important because he is speaking to Paulie. The rough-and-ready thug is the closest elder, other than the now-deposed Uncle Junior, that could possibly act as a surrogate father to him. Indeed, throughout the series Tony respects the often cantankerous mobster simply because he remembers looking to him for guidance. When Paulie remains pensive and silent to Tony's enthusiasm about the program, it is clear that Tony was expecting an affectionate response and not Paulie's absent-minded "What about it?" The moment signals a profound longing of the boy in Tony for a real relationship with his long-departed father. The lasting hurt the viewer senses in Tony after Paulie's emotional indifference bears witness to the bridge of longing for his father that still haunts him and that only time, according to the Buddhist proverb, can shatter.

- Still in hospital, Tony, Paulie "Walnuts" Gualtieri, Reginal G. the rapper, and John Schwinn (played by Hal Holbrook) watch a boxing match on television ("The Fleshy Part of the Thigh" VI.4). Schwinn, a Bell Lab scientist, informs his fellow sport enthusiasts of Erwin Schroedinger's equation. "We're all part of the same quantum field. Nothing is separate, everything is connected. The universe is just a big soup of molecules bumping-up against one another ... " The educated response is followed by a typical Soprano-style pedestrian quip as Reginal G. the rapper adroitly summarizes the scientist's philosophical response by blurting: "Everythang is everything." The words resound in Paulie's mind as he must come to grips with the fact that it really doesn't matter if his dying aunt Dottie Gualtieri is his biological mother and his surrogate mother Marianucci Gualtieri is his aunt or vice versa. Unfortunately for Tony, however, the repercussions do not end with the forlorn Paulie but extend into his trade. The episode deals with the selling of his sanitation business. If, indeed, everything is connected, Barone Sanitation garbage routes can easily morph into Cinelli Sanitation routes without severe repercussions. After intense negotiations with John Sacrimoni, the garbage settles in equitable heaps. Tony eventually acquiesces to the laws of physics as he philosophically confesses to a bedridden Phil Leotardo, "There's enough garbage for everybody."

- Cracks in Vito Spatafore's macho facade continue to widen in "Mr. and Mrs. Sacrimoni Request" VI.5. Immediately following the Sacrimoni wedding, an uncomfortable and emotionally wrenched Vito and his wife watch a romantic scene from *Imitation of Life*, a 1959 film starring Lana Turner and John Gavin on television. "I wanna give you a home. Take care of you. Love you," the Gavin character confides to his enamoured. A testy Vito exits the room, rebuking his wife's implorations to remain at home and, as in the movie, take care of her. Vito is restless and testy. He's off to his night-time escapades.
- In "Johnny Cakes" VI.8, A.J. hones his knife skills by mimicking actors on television while working at Blockbuster. His eventual fumbled attempted murder of his great-uncle Junior can be traced to his belief that real life situations can be remedied via an imitation of media images. As his father will admonish him after his botched attack, he needs to grow up. After all, his father reminds him, they're only movies.
- As Phil Leotardo and his wife console the now widowed wife of Vito Spatafore, beautifully oiled bodies of male body builders strut on the television screen in "Cold Stones" VI.11. The moment is filled with heinous irony and homoerotic angst.
- Tony makes his own connection between *The Sopranos* and The History Channel in "Cold Stones" VI.11. After discussing Carmela's upcoming trip to Paris, he notes the timely coincidence of German soldiers seen walking through the Arc de Triomphe on television.
- In "Kaisha" VI.12, Tony learns of President Abraham Lincoln's bouts with depression while watching The History Channel: "For some people, depression is a form of forced introversion." These are the same words he has repeatedly heard from Dr. Melfi, and they provide one more arrow for his quiver of self-abnegation.
- The closing scene of "Kaisha" VI.12 features a Soprano family Christmas. As a bored Bobby "Baccalà" Baccilieri Jr. zaps through holiday movies on television, the dialogue of *A Christmas Carol* (1951) and *Casablanca* (1942) captions the actions of family members and accentuates increasingly tenuous relations. The movie dialogue is adroitly juxtaposed with relevant moments of silence that occur in *The Soprano*'s story text. For example, as A.J.'s girlfriend Blanca's child Hector runs to the mountain of presents beneath the Christmas tree, we hear a character from *A Christmas Carol* shout: "Pass out the presents!" There are three citations from the film *Casablanca*.

(1) As an increasingly petulant Tony suffers as he watches Christopher unload the entire ice bucket into his drink. The movie dialogue conveniently substitutes Tony's thoughts: "It's none of your business." "I'll make it my business." "This is my place. Either lay off politics [ice] or get out!"

(2) The television blasts "Here's to America!" just as A.J. reacts to his father's suggestion that he should have been consulted about Blanca's necklace. Tony is implying that he could have acquired a stolen one for less. A.J. defiantly states that he is free to do as he chooses, just like any other American.

(3) "My dear mademoiselle perhaps you have already observed that in Casablanca human life is cheap." A famous line uttered by Major Heinrik Strasser becomes an admonition to Ilsa Lund to consider the house she has entered and the business of its inhabitants. The fact that the Soprano home is bedecked in white decorations (it has become, visually, a casa blanca, or a white house) punctuates the intertextual connections between this scene and the movie classic.

- Home movies of himself as a child viewed on television in "Soprano Home Movies" VI.13 remind Tony of an irretrievable innocence forever lost in the graft of his family business. When linked with the flashback scenes of his youth, the home movies offer a striking glimpse into the tormented heart of the toughened mobster.
- "Walk Like a Man" VI.17 begins with a view of the Soprano heraldic crest that hangs in the inner sanctum of the master bedroom. As Tony leaves the sanctity of the master bedroom and descends the stairs to the kitchen he sings: "When I was a child I had a fever, my hands felt just like two blue mooooos ..." his voice trailing. He stops as he espies son A.J. watching *Tom and Jerry* cartoons on television, just like a child. The frivolous cartoon images, coupled with the subsequent juvenile image of A.J., are in stark contrast with the gravity of the family crest's private message of maturity, tenacious strength, and solemn severity. The view of the mural at this juncture is a sign that his identity crisis is in full swing. A.J.'s attempt to begin life on a new white canvas by adopting a Latino profile replete with ready-made family with Blanca and son has gone bust. He must now cope with the ensuing depression of having lost in love and, more importantly, of having failed to create an identity away from his heraldic legacy. A.J.'s answer is to watch cartoons. Later in the same episode, Tony again descends the staircase, this time in pensive silence and

sees a reclining A.J. watching a sparring scene from the movie *Annapolis* (2006). The story is about a young man struggling to survive the rigours of the naval academy. The movie dialogue vicariously supplies Tony's all-too obvious thoughts since it could very well represent a virtual dialogue between himself and A.J.: "I'm just a guy looking to punch you in the mouth," he imagines himself saying to his son. "Oh, you can take a punch. I guess we knew that already, didn't we? You can actually land a punch, too. You're pretty good ... against a thirty-six-year old out-of-shape lieutenant." The scene drips with irony, sarcasm, cynicism, and desperate love.
- After killing Christopher Moltisanti by ruthlessly clamping shut his nostrils in "Kennedy and Heidi" VI.18, Tony is awakened in bed by Carmela who complains of his snoring, a problem associated, interestingly, with blocked nasal passages. Together they watch television in bed and view an old *Dick Cavett Show* episode in which Cavett interviews Katharine Hepburn. "They got-on to me after a while," Hepburn confesses, "... I couldn't act." Tony hopes that no one will ever catch-on to his murdering Christopher and hopes he can keep performing his act of playing dumb and innocent about his role in both Christopher's and Adriana La Cerva's demise.
- While in a mental health hospital, A.J. watches a popular television commercial for sleeping medication in "The Second Coming" VI.19. The ad features an insomniac man, a talking beaver, and Abraham Lincoln. In "Kaisha" VI.12, we recall Tony watching a program on The History Channel that revealed Abraham Lincoln's bouts with depression and included the commentary "For some people depression is a form of forced introversion." The medication commercial applies equally to both Tony and A.J. Evermore his father's son, A.J. lives the full Soprano gamut of internal rage, misplaced ambition, and unresolved angst.
- A.J.'s continuing penchant for self-destruction is reflected in his choice of television programs in "The Blue Comet" VI.20. While in hospital he watches cartoon depictions of total annihilation. At home, he watches PBS footage of suicide bombings in Iran. These programs condition his delusional decision to save the world by joining the American Armed Forces.
- The FBI watches Bobby "Baccalà" Baccilieri Jr.'s funeral on television screens in "Made in America" VI.21. The series is in its final episode. The fact that the FBI watches the funeral on television

suggests that the series is just that: something to be watched on television. May as well watch *The Godfather* funerals; it's all just celluloid.
- While watching footage of al-Qaeda in "Made in America" VI.21, FBI Agent Harris is informed of the Phil Leotardo killing. His unequivocal "Yes! We're gonna win this thing!" reveals his long-standing latent admiration for Tony and his pleasure, at series' end, at the Soprano family victory.

Statues

From statues in Dr. Melfi's office, to modern statuary in the Museum of Modern Art, from high art to neighbourhood monuments, three-dimensional sculpted figures occupy important spaces and play important roles along the Soprano itinerary.

Samples

- A bust of former President Ronald Reagan with blossoming full lips in "College" I.5 is enough to confirm Tony's suspicions that Fabian "Febby" Petrullio, former Soprano family member now in the FBI Witness Protection Program, is hiding in New England. The association between loose lips, singing to the police, and breaking the code of *omertà* are conflated in Fabian's penchant for sculpting large-lipped statues. This is the first of a long list of visual metaphors and verbal innuendos related to the mouth collated with inferences of male debility.
- The bat-wielding statue of comedian Lou Costello in Paterson, New Jersey, lends subtle comic relief to the conversations that are held in its shadow. In "Big Girls Don't Cry" II.5, Paulie "Walnuts" Gualtieri plays comical second banana to Tony's straight-man routine as he informs Paulie of his "bump up" or promotion over the more severe and troubled Salvatore "Big Pussy" Bonpensiero. Later in the same episode, Tony refuses to play second banana to his sister Janice Soprano. Called by the bank to guarantee his sister's mortgage application, an irate Tony could very well be wondering "Who's on first base?" in his family! Wielding the telephone as a baseball bat he smashes the receiver against the wall, eventually throwing it towards Carmela who demands that he "Grow the fuck up!" But Tony won't grow up; it's too early in the series. Appropriately, he

later enters the juvenile space of A.J.'s room and attempts to co-opt his son into his comic routine by quipping that he smashed the phone because he "got a job at Radio Shack as a product tester" and was "giving that phone an F for durability." But A.J. doesn't bite. As Tony turns to leave A.J.'s room, he draws the viewer's line of sight to figurines of baseball players atop A.J.'s dresser. The centre statuette looms over the other figurines much as the Lou Costello monument hovers over whoever meets beneath his statue. The Empire State Building is in the background. A glance at the baseball players and their bats by Tony plants the seed for the eventual lead pipe beating of a delinquent brothel owner by Soprano enforcer Furio Giunta. Earlier in the episode a less virile Christopher Moltisanti could only stick the same owner in the nose with a small wooden paint brush. Interestingly, though Furio wields a bat, super virile Tony doesn't need one to defeat his foe. He uses his hand to squeeze the balls of an irksome Russian loudmouth at the Newark marina. Bats and balls abound in this "swinging" episode.
- In "Big Girls Don't Cry" II.5, a statue of a legless torso appears behind Dr. Melfi. The statue alludes to the paraplegic state of Peter "Beansie" Gaeta who has been mercilessly run over by Richie Aprile.
- A stern-faced statue of Jesus Christ looks down upon a disconsolate Paulie "Walnuts" Gualtieri in "From Where to Eternity" II.9. Paulie has decided to angrily cut-off all donations to his church since his money has not bought him the spiritual protection he expected. To his mind, he has kicked-up the required money to his spiritual boss, but to no avail. Paulie has another bitter disappointment with the church in "The Ride" VI.9. He is charged with running the annual feast of St. Elzear, but is more preoccupied with his recent prognosis of prostate cancer. Disgruntled on both counts, he balks at Father José's attempts to extort even more money for the festival. He therefore spitefully allows the statue of St. Elzear to parade the streets without his traditional gold hat, he skimps on festival costs, and he refuses to pay the required insurance premium for carnival rides. Guilt ridden but unrepentant, the apparition of a statue of the Virgin Mary as the Queen of Redemption on the Bada Bing stripper stage only adds to his troubled melancholy and increasing spiritual consternation.
- After Gloria Trillo launches a grilled steak at Tony in "Pine Barrens" III.11, Dr. Melfi's green statue, surrounded by the musical strands of *Sposa son disprezzata* (I am wife and I am scorned) by Geminiano

Giacomelli, makes a cameo appearance. Tony has come to complain of Gloria's erratic, self-centred, and essentially wacky behaviour. The furrowed brow and jeering stare of the statue should have alerted him to the consequences of dealing with scorned women, but he is too attracted by their seductive lure. As the music segues into the beginning of the next episode, Dr. Melfi's final query to Tony, "Does that remind you of any other woman?" hangs suspended on the musical notes. As the next episode begins, "Amour Fou" III.12, the viewer finds Carmela surrounded by statues of contorted figures at the Museum of Modern Art in New York City. The green virago statue of the preceding episode and the black statues of this episode are studies in postural contrast. The liberated strength of the anteroom statue is counter posed with the pensive anguish and sedated oblivion of the MoMA figures. The images visually embody a contraposition of wife Carmela and goomah Gloria; one tenaciously destined to consummate fortuitous self-fulfilment, the other a condemned victim of contorted self-loathing.

- In "Christopher" IV.3, Silvio Dante and the crew attempt to disband Native Americans protesting Columbus Day activities in New York in front of a monument to Christopher Columbus. The statue holds special sway over the Soprano crew as it stewards notions of ethnic pride, selfhood, and respect. It is an anathematic figure for the protesters who view Columbus as a slave trader and imperialist colonizer.
- In "In Camelot" V.7, Chase takes another poke at the cinema heavy bias of media critics. Christopher Moltisanti's rehab friend, J.T. Dolan, has incurred considerable debt with shark loaner Christopher. To ward off further beatings from Christopher, Dolan attempts to pawn his Emmy Award at a local pawn shop. His entreaties that the statuette is "a fuckin' Emmy. It's gold plated" are met with with mocking derision by the pawn clerk. "If it had been an Oscar maybe I could give you something. An Academy Award. But TV?" The critique is biting and ironic. Then in its fifth season, *The Sopranos* had moved television from the shadow of cinema and initiated what many have termed a new Golden Age of quality television programming.
- Phil Leotardo discusses the vicissitudes of being gay with his wife in "Cold Stones" VI.11. He scolds her that "there's nothing gay about Hell" and that brother-in-law "Vito has to be made to face his problem squarely." The predicament for Phil, stated simply, is that Vito is not a man. In the same episode, we find Carmela in Paris. As she stands before a statue of Jesus Christ she reads the inscription

Ecce Homo (behold the man). The epitaph becomes doubly and ironically cogent after the above discussion regarding Vito Spatafore. Since it is Carmela that views the statue, we may also make a connection to the painting of Jesus as a babe in his mother Mary's arms in "Amour Fou" III.12. We recall that Carmela is visiting MoMA with daughter Meadow. After a brief discussion upon the message of Giuseppe de Rivera's painting *The Mystical Marriage of St. Catherine*, Carmela warns Meadow that all men are babes, and that all women marry one. This crucial moment in the series is revisited again here as she ponders the statue of Mother and Child over the church's main altar. Does the vision of Jesus as a man signal Tony's maturity as a man? Probably not, since the spiritual truth of Jesus the child runs eternally parallel to the image of the Christ as a man. In other words, Tony the man will always harbour the unbridled and immature folly of youth. This reality is immediately confirmed by the viewer as the innocence of Carmela's awe-inspired gaze as she admires the statues in Notre Dame cathedral is contrasted sharply with a close-up of Tony's face and vulgar grunts as he is pleasured by one of the Bada Bing strippers in the very next scene.

- The title of episode VI.11, "Cold Stones," alludes to balls, a euphemism for masculine strength or guts in more prosaic terms. As Tony and Phil Leotardo meet beneath the Lou Costello monument in Paterson, New Jersey, allusions to baseball and ballparks abound. The discussion between the two gravely deliberate straight men contrasts with Costello's lighthearted role as comedic second banana. Phil accuses Tony of lacking balls for harbouring the sexually wayward Vito Spatafore. Tony refuses to wack Vito because he is a good earner and also because he has acquired a more enlightened view of Vito's sexual proclivity. Unfortunately for Vito, however, Phil possesses the requisite cold stones and waits for his opportunity to kill the disgraceful mobster. Lou Costello's bat is again the visual inspiration for the punishing pummelling of Vito with heavy lead pipes. Brother-in-law Phil sits and views the spectacle from a front-row seat.

Chapter Six

Conclusion

"American Skin."
    Bruce Springsteen

In the fairs and market places of the world, in the bustle of street vendors, sideshow barkers, public masquerade, and liturgical rites, Mikhail Bakhtin finds pockets of resilience and resistance to the traditional power bases of state, church, and family.[1] In our present media-saturated age, where the image (*imagos*) reigns supreme and word-based orders of knowledge (*logos*) have been sapped by a new communication cyberspace, collective cultural consciousness often depends upon the same right-brain pattern skills that inspired Bakhtin to find evidence of a vibrant popular culture in the occurrences of everyday life. Today, these vital street images no longer captivate the imagination but instead fill our LED screens with vicarious representations. The displayed messages are always dynamic, usually digressive, often rebarbative, and intermittently nonsensical. They proffer, nevertheless, a logic and locution that posit almost a point-for-point opposition to official high culture. The ascendance of iconic information over written words permits us to reformulate the traditional struggle between power and its disenfranchised partners as a movement from the retrofitted margins to an ever-shifting centre. Television, as the first technology to stream both words and images into the domestic and public sphere, most assuredly remains the touchstone of our contemporary fantasy structure.

A major criticism of television is that it encourages viewer passivity. Yet, in my courses of cultural criticism, I ask students to consider the alternative mores and modes of being they encounter in a program such as *The Sopranos* with a view towards understanding the adage that culture follows power, and that power is a multifarious cultural representation replete with preferred images and historical pre- and post-rhetoric. They are encouraged to discover canonical monuments while deconstructing current discourses of representation, communication, and, ultimately, knowledge. Towards this end, I have found the *The Sopranos* an essential component of my study of alternative cultures in our own period. Alan Sepinwall terms the present television moment "a revolution," with the small screen reaching "its full potential."[2] This revolution caused an explosion that was both artistic and technical. As writers began to flex their muscles in the newly hatched age of the *auteur*,[3] creative freedom edged beyond the bounds of convention, and the traditional television machine evolved to accommodate their spiralling expectations. DVDs, DVRs, on-demand cable, Netflix, YouTube, online streaming, big screens, projection TVs, plasma, 3D, Blu-Ray, all contributed to the pleasurable experience of watching the startlingly consistent high-quality television programming. The internet and the immediacy of blogging fostered a new intimacy between widely dispersed viewers. The tech-crazed audience reviewed, commented, critiqued, blogged, recapped, and speculated upon roguish themes intricately interlaced scenes, and equally variegated dialogue. Production staff felt simultaneously liberated and engaged; the audience revelled in the newly hatched zeitgeist.

HBO blazed the trail. The Premium Network began broadcasting sports and rose to prominence when it broadcast the *Thrilla in Manilla* in 1975.Though sport remains the station's anchor, its acclaimed and smartly marketed dramas have become its inspired centrepiece. Its programs boast a faithful community of viewers who are both captivated by the original content on display and captured by the destabilizing social paradigms that these programs promote and explore. Transgressive mores, audience objections, and unsolicited suggestions are openly discussed on the HBO website where viewers are invited to join the interactive community of like-minded intellectuals, pseudo- and non-, who regularly express their disdain or delight to a character's latest wisecrack. Ironic, savvy, knowing, the site promotes populism at is best, with a liberal dose of product marketing. It is precisely this sort of reflexivity and self-promotion, sprinkled with a heavy dose of fiery provocation that stoked the postmodern discourse of *The Sopranos* and of future HBO programs.

The Sopranos ushered in post-ethnic American television and introduced viewers to many of their shared pent-up social frustrations and unspeakable common foibles regarding sex, violence, and, above all, ethnic mythology. As Toby Miller states, the series "engages so many key themes of US culture: the quotidian mundanity of family life; irresolvable discrepancies between ideology and reality; hypermasculine white violence; ethnic stereotypes; state and corporate corruption; and mendacity as a way of life."[4] To this impressive list I would add antiracism, existentialism, art appreciation, postfeminism, and explorations into notions of postethnicity. In an industry traditionally organized around the production of easily repeatable and cloneable genre pieces, David Chase birthed an enterprise of multilayered entertainment firmly grounded within paradigms of author and ambience, popular and avant-garde, historical and contemporary, repetition and difference. Given that the series became and remained a critical, popular, and commercial success, he could promiscuously dispatch any cheap formulaic implications of political correctness and ethnic super sensibility with a smartly written quip and temptingly controversial storyline. Rich in detail, visually appealing, thematically inventive, *The Sopranos* redefined the gangster genre and, because of its luxuriant production values, shortened the distance between television and cinema screens.

It also spawned and influenced an efflorescence of television dramas, including *Oz* (1997–2002); *Sex and the City* (1998–2003); *Six Feet Under* (2001–5); *The Wire* (2002–8); *The Shield* (2002–8); *Lost* (2004–10); *Deadwood* (2004–6); *24* (2001–10); *Battlestar Galactica* (2004–); *Friday Night Lights* (2006–); *Mad Men* (2007–); and *Breaking Bad* (2008–13). These dramas represent a veritable Golden Age of television. They have continued the transcendent debate on the essence and fibre of America as it plodded through the final gasps of the second millennium and trudged into the unexplored waters of the third.

The *Sopranos* imprimatur continues into the new century and takes the avid fan from the low counties of New Orleans (*Treme* [2010–]), to the high tides of Atlantic City (*Boardwalk Empire* [2010–]), documentaries that explore the underbelly of unspoken vexation (*The Big Picture: Rethinking Dyslexia* [2012]; *The Latino List* [2012]; *Vito* [2011]; *Mea Maxima Culpa: Silence in the House of God* [2012]), to the profanely liberating exploration of contemporary idiosyncrasies (*The Boring Life of Jacqueline*, *Girls* [2012–]; *Enlightened* [2011–]), HBO has continued to transform the material conditions of spectatorship by inviting its viewers to engage in critical reflections on questions of iconography and image construction while championing inspired narrative construction. Indeed, the nature of fiction itself has spiralled into the television "psycho-sphere" by the two redoubling heroes of HBO's latest pioneering spine-chiller *True Detectives* (2014–). These programs contribute to our shared model of the multicultural nation, at once urban, lusty, rural, and pristine. They bespeak a subsidized sense of belonging to a massive social enterprise laced with the identifying optics of ethnic, social, sexual, and sometimes just plain weird, multiple and enfolded personal spaces. There seems to be something for everyone. No one is left stranded between the cultural gaps. It's called America. The game seems fixed in advance. David Chase advanced that game to a place where insults are tolerated, where a genuine inter-ethnic mosaic exists that is neither self-loathing nor self-projecting. It simply is. *The Sopranos* revelled in the complex and controversial. It refused to be ambivalent, demure, or vapid. Its resonating storylines and characterizations laid the template for the relevant storytelling that ensued and that grounded competitive individuality and personal responsibility in national terms. No room for self-denial, self-pity, or group specificity. Survival in America is not just wishful thinking based on ethnic, group, or political affiliation. It is instead the unflinching belief in the indiscriminate mix of self-initiative, individual esthetic, and intellectual forms played upon the background of inevitable cultural pluralism. "*He* is an American," wrote J. Hector St. John de Crèvecoeur, "who, leaving behind him all his ancient prejudices and manners, receives new ones from the new mode of life he has embraced, the new government he obeys, and the new rank he holds."[5]

HBO once boasted that it was not TV. By the time *The Sopranos* ended its run, television itself had been changed to respect the level of artistry of HBO programming. New shows sought to maintain a multiplication of authorial perspectives that engage viewers in maturational questions of national reflexivity. The contemporary television fan is not a distracted consumer. Educated and matured by the gaze of *The Sopranos*, they no longer settle for generic indeterminacy but enjoy the high prestige cinematic conceits of popular high quality programs that run counter to the hegemony of self-destructing reality television. Active viewers demand active programming. Though these programs may expose issues that the traditionally stereotyped generation of passive viewers preferred to hide, they no doubt promote radical change because of their unpredictability. Of course, all this is underwritten by corporate politics and bottom-line profits. Yet one could argue that never has so much corporate television money been spent so well.

The Sopranos remains the most financially successful cable television series in history. It has been regaled as perhaps the greatest television series of all times and received sixty major awards and 231 nominations for awards between 1999 and 2007. The program won twenty-one Emmy Awards in 111 nominations. It was nominated for the Primetime Emmy Award for Outstanding Drama Series in every eligible year and won in 2004 (as the first series on a cable network) and 2007. It also won five Golden Globe Awards in twenty-three nominations, including a win for Best Television Series – Drama for its first season in 2000. The series was honoured with two consecutive George Foster Peabody Awards in 2000 and 2001, and also won several major guild awards (Directors [1], Producers [2], Writers [3], and Actors [4]) in addition to numerous other awards. Because of the show's long hiatuses between seasons, it eventually lost eligibility for further awards. James Gandolfini and Edie Falco received the most nominations and wins of the show's cast members. These included three Emmy wins each. Series creator David Chase received numerous awards as director and producer, while winning three Emmys for writing.

Unquestionable quality, upbeat style, irreverent themes, David Chase subverted staid television structures in favour of a discourse that privileges active vision, super verbal acuity, detailed depiction, and post-viewing contemplation as a means of active intellectual viewer involvement. As Brian L. Ott has argued, "Popular television enhances viewers' lives beyond its obvious capacity to inform, educate, and entertain."[6] Of course, not all viewers came along for the ride. But such a view tends to trivialize the art, leaving the series on the margins of the social canvas. Chase understood this sort of voyeurism as both a contemporary malaise and a source for commercial success. He was not just looking for a story. Passivity be damned, he was fabricating a viewing experience, seeking to take a hold of the minds of acolytes willing to travel the road, to wait days anticipating the opening shot of the next episode, to participate in the playful voyages inside the recurring leitmotifs, to bemoan the final revelatory lyrics and closing credits. He formed an emotional attachment with his consumers, had a hold on his customers. Essentially, *The Sopranos* was an education in television business economics whose port of call permitted a vision of contemporary society as it had never been seen on television. This is the key to making sense of the all-encompassing outreach of *The Sopranos* machine. Chase knew all the tricks, but was his own toughest customer. Beyond the guerilla-style marketing campaigns and spin-offs, Chase kept the show clever and simple. End of story.

Fortunately, *The Sopranos* aesthetic uniqueness has become an enduring legacy of innovative story and mesmerizing points of view. Its mixture of narrative ellipsis and thematic synthesis, mise-en-scène and mis-en-abîme strategies gave its viewers the pleasures of intense self-gratifying interaction with the series. Whether enticed by the mobster mystique, deliberate violence, domestic infidelities, or just the voyeurism of living in contemporary America, viewers suffered little ennui in following a series that offered both cathartic release and discriminating social critique. *The Sopranos* aficionados actually watch television. And here is my point entirely. Rather than making an audience, David Chase attracted viewers. In a medium that defines itself within the delicate but deciding balance of supply and demand, it is the ideal viewer of *The Sopranos* who demanded more, and David Chase obligingly, intelligently, artistically, shrewdly, and sagely delivered.

Notes

Introduction

1 See Allan Bloom, *The Closing of the American Mind* (New York: Simon and Schuster), 344.
2 Life, indeed, goes on and on for Tony as his ultimate imago as proud loving father and boastful ruthless gangster is successfully forged in the crucible of the final scene of the final episode of the series. Tony is shot in extreme camera close-up, his face filling the screen. He is mammoth and forever relentless. It is what it is, or as he often bleats: "I'm a man, you're a woman. End of story."
3 *Slate* is a daily updated online magazine created in 1996 that covers current affairs, including politics, arts and culture, sports, and news. It is ad-supported and is available free of charge. The magazine invited a quartet of psychiatrists and like-minded professionals to review each episode of *The Sopranos*. Glen O. Gabbard, MD, a professor of psychiatry at Baylor College of Medicine and author of *The Psychology of The Sopranos*; Philip A. Ringstrom, PhD, PsyD, a senior faculty member at the Institute of Contemporary Psychoanalysis in Los Angeles; Joel Whitebook, PhD, a faculty member of the Columbia Center for Psychoanalytic Training and Research; Margaret Crastnopol, PhD, is on the faculty of the Northwest Center for Psychoanalysis. All are practising therapists. Daniel Menaker is the author of *The Treatment*, a novel about therapy, and is executive editor at HarperCollins. Judith Shulevitz writes the "Close Reader" column for *The New York Times Book Review*. Jodi Kantor is *Slate's* New York editor. It is available at http://www.slate.com/
4 American and Canadian newspapers reviewed each episode on a weekly basis. Of special note was New Jersey's *The Star-Ledger* whose television

reviewer Alan Sepinwall wrote a weekly episode recap and review. After *The Sopranos* ended, David Chase granted his only interview to Sepinwall.

5 Quoted in Alan Sepinwall, *The Revolution Was Televised: The Cops, Crooks, Slingers, and Slayers Who Changed TV Drama Forever* (New York: Simon and Schuster, 2013), 38.
6 From IMDb, *The Internet Movie Database*, Biography for David Chase, retrieved 18 Januaary 2010 from http://www.imdb.com/name/nm0153740/bio
7 For a discussion of David Chase as an innovator, see Roberta Pearson, "Cult Television as Digital Television's Cutting Edge," in James Bennett and Niki Strange, eds., *Television as Digital Media* (Durham, NC: Duke University Press), 105–31.
8 Chase quoted in Sepinwall, *The Revolution Was Televised*, 48.
9 Chase quoted in Brett Martin, *Difficult Men: Behind the Scenes of a Creative Revolution: From The Sopranos and The Wire to Mad Men and Breaking Bad* (New York: The Penguin Press, 2013), 37.
10 Columbus Citizens Foundation protested the invitation of members of *The Sopranos* cast by Mayor Michael Bloomberg to participate in the annual New York Columbus Day parade. "The Columbus Citizens Foundation has the full support of The National Italian American Foundation (NIAF), the national organization for Italian Americans that is based in Washington, DC. NIAF firmly believes that any member of *The Sopranos* should not be invited to the Columbus Day Parade because the program perpetuates a negative and inaccurate image of Italian Americans. NIAF is committed to promoting the best of Italian American culture and heritage. As a result, NIAF is profoundly disappointed with Mayor Bloomberg's poor choice of invitees. Why would Mayor Bloomberg invite *The Sopranos* cast members to this important event rather than any one of the thousands of successful Italian Americans who project a positive image?" Retrieved 23 December 2013 from http://www.italystl.com/ra/756.htm
11 The subtitle of the volume *The Sopranos and Philosophy: I Kill Therefore I Am* cleverly situates the essays in the philosophical genre while drawing attention to the fact that violence emerges as a crucial element in the development of story in the television series. See Richard Greene and Peter Vernezze, eds., *The Sopranos and Philosophy: I Kill Therefore I Am* (Chicago: Carus Publishing Company, 2004).
12 "Sympathy for the Devil" is the title of a fascinating essay by Noel Carroll that explores the morbid infatuation and pro-attitude of viewers with Tony Soprano. See Greene and Vernezze, eds., *The Sopranos and Philosophy*, 121–36.

13 Tony Soprano acts alongside a long revered list of loners that inhabit the American collective imagination. The fact that he is a third-generation Italian immigrant epitomizes the fundamental theory of upward mobility as a pan-american virtue not restricted to the indigenous power elite, as had been the case before Mario Puzo reinvented the American dream with Don Corleone. For Thomas J. Ferraro: "All we need to call to mind is the best-known literary figure of the twentieth century in America, F. Scott Fitzgerald's Jay Gatsby, to remember that the great American tragedy is that of a self-willed orphan turned self-made gangster, the doomed pretender to the upper-class throne. The orphaned fighter and rebel, no longer bound by apron strings of any domestic ambition of a familiar sort, disowned by his birth family if ever he had one and is disinterested in lording over a new one, is the quintessential figure of the American imagination, a figure that was nowhere more powerfully at work than in the genre of the gangster film as we knew it before Puzo. Whatever their personal ethnic markings, the gangsters of the 1930s and 1940s – Irishman James Cagney, Edward G. Robinson of Jewish stock, the omni-cultural Paul Muni – epitomized the central American myth of competitive individualism." See Thomas J.Ferraro, *Feeling Italian: The Art of Ethnicity in America* (New York: New York University Press, 2005), 221.
14 Quoted in Martin, *Difficult Men*, 65.
15 Chase reveled in the commercial and critical success of his series. As Brett Martin comments, "All of this, Chase had achieved on his own terms and in the very system that had caused him so much shame all those years. What could be more in the rock'n'roll, maverick spirit of what directors like Coppola and Scorsese had done to the big Hollywood studios in the seventies? Stick it to the bastards in their own house, right under their noses, and make them thank you for it." *Difficult Men*, 156.

1. Inner Sanctums

1 The notion of an ideal or model consumer of an artwork as developed by Umberto Eco is a response to the crisis of representation in postmodern literature and art. A model reader, as Eco terms him/her, activates an innovative reading or interpretation of a work by searching for connections between the spectrum of fragments offered by the text, thereby implicitly acknowledging the inexhaustibility of any work of art. See Umberto Eco, *The Role of the Reader* (Indiana: Indiana University Press, 1979). For further readings on the aesthetic response of readers, see Wolfgang Iser, *The Implied Reader* (Baltimore: Johns Hopkins University Press, 1974), and Iser,

The Act of Reading (Baltimore: Johns Hopkins University Press, 1978). Iser tags his model, or implied, reader as ideal and states: "The ideal reader, unlike the contemporary reader, is a purely fictional being; he has no basis in reality, and it is this very fact that makes him so useful: as a fictional being, he can close the gaps that constantly appear in any analysis of literary effects and responses." See *The Implied Reader*, 29.

2 Quoted in Alan Sepinwall, *The Revolution Was Televised: The Cops, Crooks, Slingers, and Slayers Who Changed TV Drama Forever* (New York: Simon and Schuster, 2013), 47. Chase left many storylines without resolution, including Dr. Melfi's refusal to sic Tony on her rapist, Carmela and Furio's nipped romance, Tony's expected confrontation with Furio. The most enduring, and maddening for Chase, was the public's fascination for the missing Russian in "Pine Barrens" III.11.

3 In 1938 Frank Sinatra was arrested in New Jersey facing the outdated charge of seduction, allegedly committed under the promise of marriage. The complaint was filed by Toni Della Penta, embittered because of Sinatra's lack of attention after her miscarriage. The complaint was later withdrawn when it was discovered that Della Penta was still legally married to another man. The mug shot of Sinatra as prisoner No. 42799 became a pop poster staple.

4 An abundance of literature is available on the topic of interart comparisons. Because this section uses this critical vantage as a method, I include a list of seminal works. Aristotle, *De Anima II*, trans. W.W. Hett (Cambridge, MA: Harvard University Press, 1957); Leonardo Da Vinci, *Paragone: Poetry and Painting*, ed. A. Phillip McMahon (Princeton: Princeton Umiversity Press, 1956); Leon Battista Alberti, *On Painting*, trans. John R. Spencer (New Haven: Yale University Press, 1966); G.E. Lessing, *Laocoon: An Essay upon the Limits of Poetry and Painting*, trans. Ellen Frothingham (New York: Farrar, Straus and Giroux, 1969). A few contemporary commentators include Norman Bryson, *Vision and Painting: The Logic of the Gaze* (New Haven: Yale University Press, 1983); David Freedberg, *The Power of Images* (Chicago: Chicago University Press, 1989); Rudulph Arnheim, *Visual Thinking* (Berkeley: California University Press, 1969); Claude Gandelman, *Reading Pictures, Viewing Texts* (Bloomington: Indiana University Press, 1991); Anne Hollander, *Moving Pictures* (Cambridge, MA: Harvard University Press, 1991); Murray Krieger, *Ekphrasis: The Illusion of the Natural Sign* (Baltimore: Johns Hopkins University Press, 1992); Peter Brunette and David Wills, eds., *Deconstruction and the Visual Arts: Art, Media, Architecture* (Cambridge: Cambridge University Press, 1994); W.J.T. Mitchell, *Picture Theory* (Chicago: Chicago University Press, 1994); Alberto Manguel, *Reading Pictures* (Toronto: Vintage, 2002).

5 David Johansson, "Homeward Bound: Those Sopranos Titles Come Heavy," in David Lavery, ed., *Reading The Sopranos* (New York: I.B. Tauris, 2006), 27–38; and Lance Strate, "No(rth Jersey) Sense of Place; The Cultural Geography (and Media Ecology) of The Sopranos," in David Lavery, ed. *This Thing of Ours: Investigating The Sopranos* (New York: Columbia University Press, 2002), 178–94.
6 For Walter Benjamin, "the technique of reproduction detaches the reproduced objet from tradition." See "The Work of Art in the Age of Mechanical Reproduction," in *Illuminations,* ed. Hannah Arendt, trans. Harry Zohn (New York: Schocken Books, 1969), 221.
7 Francis Bacon (1909–1922) produced haunting portraits that featured tortured and distorted visions of raw humanity.
8 Ur is a prefix, a combining form that denotes the primal stage of a historical or cultural entity. It means original and as such indicates a possible archetype.
9 Medusa was a mythological sorceress, one of the Gorgons who were three in number, including Stheno and Euryale. She had a head of snakes instead of hair. Her most powerful weapon was her image. Any man that looked at her was immediately turned to stone. She is the potent prototype for the female that fixes a man's gaze thereby stilling him. She paralyzes action and thought. Her serpentine locks lend to popular aesthetic images of castration and weakness, as well as political emblems of the Other.
10 Tony is actually referring to the Rorschach technique, named after Hermann Rorschach, but also known as the inkblot test. A patient's interpretation of inkblots is used to create a psychological profile. The test displays emotional disorders and underlying personality characteristics. It is interesting that Tony uses the painting as an inkblot test and misinterprets what he sees. The viewer is also introduced to Tony's often humorous misappropriation and mispronunciation of words.
11 I am referring to the final extended black screen that ends the series. More on this point later.
12 I am referring to the final scenes of *The Godfather* where the staccato juxtaposition of sacred and profane imagery creates a powerful collage of mobster justice.
13 It is interesting that in "Mayham" VI.3 it is once again Meadow's voice calling out "Don't go, Daddy" and the gentle wafting of trees that re-establishes Tony's humanity and brings him back from the brink of death.
14 I am reminded of Don Corleone's similar view on familial obligations that extend throughout one's life. He reminds singer Johnny Fontane, "A man who is not a father to his children can never be a real man." Mario Puzo, *The Godfather* (1969; reprint, New York: New American Library, 2002), 37.

15 "Our reality is created through our fictions; to be conscious of these fictions is to gain creative access to, and participation in, the poetics or making of our psyche or soul-life." John Hillman, *Healing Fiction* (New York: Station Hill Press, 1983), ix.
16 The first two seasons of *The Sopranos* were screened in their entirety, along with *The Public Enemy, Mean Streets*, and Laurel and Hardy's *Saps at Sea*, at the Museum of Modern Art in February 2001. The series was titled *Selected by David Chase*. Peter Bogdanovich, the MoMA curator, sponsored the event and eventually had the television series installed in the museum's permanent collection. It was a particularly proud moment for Chase. *The Sopranos* had been elevated into the pantheon of films that he so revered.
17 While Tony surprisingly quotes a well-known citation from Nicolò Machiavelli's *The Prince* published in 1519, he is probably unaware of Machiavelli's *Art of War* written in 1520.
18 The malapropism refers to Francisco Goya (1746–1828), whose sunny and bright paintings of the Spanish court eventually gave way to dark and haunting portraits of vacuous insanity.
19 The slang sense of the word to signify intense desire or addiction probably arose from an earlier use of Jones as a street synonym for heroin. Father Intintola, we recall, confesses to Carmela that he has a Jones for her baked ziti in "College" I.5.
20 *The Sopranos* house is located on 14 Aspen Drive, North Caldwell, NJ 07006.The house sits on 1.46 acres. Rumour has it that houses in this posh suburban community are worth $2 to $3 million. Exterior shots were filmed on location but the interior was recreated at Silvercup Studios in Queens, New York. The real owner of the home, Victor Recchia, sells a $699 CD-ROM containing the floor plans.
21 Both books are by Allen Rucker, *The Sopranos Family Cookbook* (New York: Warner Books, 2002) and *The Sopranos: A Family History* (New York: New American Library, 2000).
22 The painting is by Jacopo Carucci (1494–1557), also known as Jacopo da Pontormo, a Mannerist painter from the Florentine school. *The Visitation of the Virgin and St. Elizabeth* was painted between 1514 and 1516. The figures in the painting are balanced, colourful, expressively elongated. The two central figures, a pregnant Virgin Mary and her aged, equally pregnant cousin St. Elizabeth, are painted in profile and gracefully intertwine their arms to form a central lozenge shape. Their intimacy is measured by their touching bellies that carry both the Messenger, St. John the Baptist, and the Saviour, Jesus Christ. The two other figures are stolid and seem to be

looking directly at the viewer outside the frame. They express no emotion and stand guard and/or witness to the central event being depicted. In typical Pontormo style, the figures seem to float in a nondescript background that nevertheless reveal Renaissance-style porticos on the left and a flat though layered wall with steps. Two miniscule figures can be seen on the lower right. One is sitting, the other exits a portico. They represent humanity as it bears witness to the scene of universal revelation that plays before them. Notably, one of the figures is a possible self-portrait of the artist. The painting now adorns a small chapel in the church of Pieve di San Michele in Carmignano, just west of Florence.

23 The feminine subterfuge that subtends the series begins with the title of the series itself, *The Sopranos*, a reference to female opera singers. Singing is a euphemism for ratting or informing on fellow law breakers. The undermining motif continues in the overarching musical narrative that plays during the opening credits. "Woke Up This Morning (Chosen One Mix)" by Alabama 3, is a song about female empowerment, not virulent mobsters. A3's songwriter and lead singer Robert Spragg wrote the song after reading about a housewife who had shot her husband after years of abuse. These messages undermine the expected masculinity of Tony and present the viewer with a sweetly subliminal and twisted entry into the anticipated stereotypical world of the mob.

24 *The Public Enemy* is a 1931 crime film starring James Cagney. It is interesting that Cagney was able to shed his gentile and effeminate dancer image to don the tough guy mask that would make him famous. In an HBO interview Chase states: "When I was a little kid I was greatly traumatized by this movie *The Public Enemy* ... and I thought that movie was great. And ever since then I've just been totally into it." An HBO Interview with David Chase, retrieved 22 May 2001 from http://www.hbo.com/sopranos/insidersguide/interviews/davidchaseint.shtml

25 Neil Postman, *The Disappearance of Childhood* (New York: Vintage, 1982), 93.

26 Nelson Goodman argues that visual representations possess a characteristic that language does not. Images are dense. Every mark in a painting leads to another relation for meaning, to concepts that lead outside the visual work. See David Summers, "Real Metaphor: Towards a Redefinition of the 'Conceptual' Image," in *Visual Theory: Painting and Interpretation*, ed. Norman Bryson, Michael Ann Holly, and Keith Moxey (London: Polity Press, 1991),236.

27 In *The Sexuality of Christ in Renaissance Art and in Modern Oblivion* (New York: Pantheon, 1983), Leo Steinberg argues that viewers of a painting often block or screen those images that are uncomfortable for them as

when viewing, in Steinberg's argument, the depictions of Christ's penis in paintings.
28 Jacques Lacan, *The Language of the Self: The Function of Language in Psychoanalysis*, trans. Anthony Wilden (New York: Dell Publishing, 1968).
29 Varying degrees of reality and truth are conveyed by mirrors. A sixteenth-century Spanish saying extolls, "The mirror is the Devil's ass," indicating the mirror's self-absorbing charms. See Jurgis Baltrusaitis, *El Espejo* (Madrid: Miraguano, 1988).
30 Citing Sigmund Freud, Alberto Manguel states, "In order to know objectively who we are, we must see ourselves outside ourselves, in something that holds our image but is not part of us, discovering the internal in the external, as Narcissus did when he fell in love with his image in the pool." See Manguel, *Reading Pictures*, 163. Compare Freud's lecture "Anxiety and Instinctual Life," in Sigmund Freud, *New Introductory Lectures on Psychoanalysis*, ed. James Strachey and Angela Richards, trans. James Strachey (London: The Hogarth Press, 1964).
31 We also recall one of the most horrifically memorable scenes of *The Godfather*. When movie magnate Jack Woltz refuses to bend to the will of Don Corleone, his prized thoroughbred Khartoum's severed head is placed alongside him in bed. The bloody spectacle agitates a sense of lost love and affection that never graced the sexual relations with his many juvenile sex conquests.
32 We recall Tony's attraction/repulsion to darkness throughout the series but especially his attraction to the barn door ("Meadowlands" I.4), and cut to black of the series' last scene. In these instances, the viewer sees through Tony's eyes and is allowed to penetrate the recesses of his dark side.

2. When I Grow Up I Want to Be an American

1 The line echoes the anguished lament of Marty Piletti in the film *Marty* (1955), "I'm just a fat little man, a fat ugly man," a retort to his badgering mother's harangue about getting married. At film's end, the enlightened and determined bachelor has found his mate in Clara, a match for his own lonely heart. He reiterates the sentiment, but with more assured levity: "You don't like her, my mother don't like her, she's a dog, and I'm a fat, ugly man. Well, all I know I had a good time last night. If we have enough good times together, I'm gonna get down on my knees and I'm gonna beg that girl to marry me."
2 In Greek mythology, Medea was a priestess of Hecate and skilled in black magic. She was the wife of Jason and accompanied him in his adventures

with the Argonauts. Jason eventually divorced Medea and married Glauce, the daughter of the king of Corinth. In revenge, Medea sent the couple a wedding gift of magic ointment that burned both Glauce and her father Creon to death. As a final act of vengeance towards Jason, she killed their two children.

3 David Chase admits that he never expected, or wanted, the story to move beyond its pilot. He would have been content with a successful pilot, been told there was no money for a series, then settle to complete the arc of his idea in a feature movie. That story first came to mind in the 1980s. It would have dealt with Tony's uncle and mother conspiring to kill him, with Tony eventually smothering his mother with a pillow. That the film-length notion became an ever-expanding universe that necessitated additional hours of television rendered him reflexively pessimistic. He scrapped the pillow-smothering ending in favour of a laughing Livia's portentous smirk.

4 For an engaging discussion of the television medium, see John Carey, *What Good Are the Arts?* (London: Faber and Faber, 2005); Mark Jancovich and James Lyon, eds., *Quality Popular Television: Cult TV, The Industry and Fans* (London: BFI Publishing, 2003); Robert J. Thompson, *Television's Second Golden Age: From Hill Street Blues to ER* (New York: Continuum, 1996); J. Christopher Donahue, "What's Right with Television," *America* 171, no. 10 (8 October 1994): 25; Jeffrey Mortimer, "How TV Violence Hits Kids," *The Education Digest* 6, no. 2 (October 1994): 16–19.

5 Quoted in Dawn Airey, "RTS Huw Wheldon Memorial Lecture" (lecture presented at the Royal Television Society, London, UK, 2004).

6 In 1933 the Hollywood Production Code prohibited the specific connection between organized crime and selected ethnic groups in order to avoid fostering bigotry and hatred among peoples of differing national origins in the United States. With the demise of the studio system in the 1950s, the Hays Code, as it was known, lost power over the content of film production. Subsequently, ethic labelling became the norm.

7 Stephen Marche, "How *Jersey Shore* Transformed America," *Esquire* 8 (September 2011), retrieved 19 April 2012 from http://www.esquire.com/features/thousand-words-on-culture/jersey-shore-stereotypes-0510. Studies abound on the subject of media stereotypes, interesting contributions to the argument are Courtney von Hippel, Cindy Wiryakusuma, Jessica Bowden, and Megan Shochet, "Stereotype Threat and Female Communication Styles," *Personality and Social Psychology Bulletin* 37 (2011): 1312–24; Giorgio Bertellini, "Black Hands and White Hearts: Italian Immigrants as 'Urban Racial Types' in Early American Film Culture," *Urban History* 31, no. 3 (2004): 375–99; "Hollywood vs. Italians," *The Italic Way* 27 (1997). The

Media Awareness Network (http://www.mediasmarts.ca) offers current and relevant information, resource material, and discussions concerning media issues.

8 See Richard Gambino, "The Crisis of Italian American Identity," *Beyond The Godfather*, ed. A. Kenneth Ciongoli and Jay Prine (Hanover: University Press of New England, 1997), 269–88, for a discussion of the inaccurate and inauthentic myths harboured by I-Ams and the surreal cultural reality these myths engender.

9 Three major Italian American fraternal and service organizations – Order Sons of Italy in America, Unico National, and National Italian American Foundation – have active anti-defamation arms. Net-based organizations include Annotico Report, the Italian-American Discussion Network, and ItalianAware.

10 Michael Fischer, "Ethnicity and the Post-Modern Arts of Memory," in *Writing Culture: The Poetics and Politics of Ethnography*, ed. James Clifford and George E. Marcus (Berkeley: California University Press, 1986), 195.

11 The sensibilities of the audience had changed and reflected a shift in the mores of the nation. Cops and robbers drama no longer worked. For Chase, "The object of all these shows in the past had always been the protagonist pays for his sins. Crime doesn't pay. Well, that's false. Crime does pay. Having done the show for all that time, I knew that crime paid." Quoted in Brett Martin, *Difficult Men: Behind the Scenes of a Creative Revolution: From The Sopranos and The Wire to Mad Men and Breaking Bad* (New York: The Penguin Press, 2013), 287.

12 Tony Soprano spawned a coterie of television characters that populated the suddenly raw American landscape. "Man Beset of Man Harried" is how Brett Martin terms the typology of the television male hero of end-of-millennium America in his book *Difficult Men*. These are characters in search of a personality (to paraphrase Pirandello's play *Six Characters in Search of an Author* [1921]), men who succumb to their testosterone-fuelled ambition, unbothered by the requisites of untethered consumerism. The characters are deeply flawed but supremely committed; they are as smart and agile as they are gullible and dispirited. Their numbers include Cedric Daniels of *The Wire* (2002–8), Vic Mackey of *The Shield* (2002–8), Al Swearengen of *Deadwood* (2004–8), Tommy Gavin of *Rescue Me* (2004–11), *Dexter's* (2006–) inimitable Dexter Morgan, Dan Draper of *Mad Men* (2007–), and Walter White of *Breaking Bad* (2008–13).

13 See my article, "Tu vu' fare l'italiano, ma sci 'nnate 'n America, Argentina, Canada …," *VIA: Voices in Italian Americana* 13, no. 1 (2002): 36–44.

14 The existential query is at the heart of all the characters but none more so than for Tony. He reaches the apex of his inquiry when he imagines what Chase terms the "alternate universes" of his coma dream. Interestingly, "the sequence was inspired by Chase's longtime friend John Patterson, who directed many episodes of the series before dying of cancer in 2005. At one point in his cancer fight, Patterson found himself in a hospital, muttering the same words – 'Who am I? Where am I going?' – that Chase would put into the mouths of both Tony in his hospital bed and Kevin Finnerty in the alternate reality. 'The way my mind worked,' Chase says, 'I wondered what he was seeing when he said that ... The line between dreaming and reality, and death and sleep and all that – I'm into that whole thing.'" Quoted in Sepinwall, *The Revolution Was Televised*, 56–7.

15 Anthony E. Rotundo, "Wonderbread and Stugots: Italian American Manhood and *The Sopranos*," in Regina Barreca, ed., *A Sitdown with the Sopranos* (New York: Palgrave Macmillan, 2002), 47–74. Rotundo goes on to comment, "Organized crime, then, had a purity about it, a refusal to compromise, that made it visible – even riveting – for the Italian American majority that rejected its rapacity, its illegality, its apparent un-Americanism" (48).

16 Mario Puzo, *The Godfather* (1969; reprint, New York: New American Library, 2002), 29.

17 *Cafone*, the proper spelling of the word, is a derogatory term first used by the Bourbon rulers of Naples in the 1600s to identify peasants who normally used rope, instead of belts, to hold up their pants. The term is a conflation of the words peasants *con la fune* meaning literally peasants *with a rope*. Hence, any peasant was eventually referred to as a *cafone*.

18 In *The Godfather Part II*, Peter Clemenza gives a young Vito Corleone a satchel of guns for safe keeping while his own apartment is searched by the police.

19 The social structures and agricultural organization that shaped the related values of what came to be known as "amoral familism" have been revisited, enforced, and debunked ever since Edward C. Banfield, in his ground breaking study *The Moral Basis of a Backward Society* (New York: The Free Press, 1958), first proposed the definition. Banfield suggested that the dominant ethos of southern Italian communities "maximized the material, short-term advantage of the nuclear family" (85) and posited a social system completely lacking in moral sanctions outside the parameters of self-serving familial needs. This sort of convenient definition helped explain the rise of the Mafia in North America. Subsequent studies have focused on the realistic conditions and the conceptual apparatus of southern Italy, and have presented a more convincing analysis of the disparate nature of

its anthropology. See, for example, Sydel F. Silverman, "Agricultural Organization, Social Structure, and Values in Italy: Amoral Familism Reconsidered," *American Anthropologist* 70, no. 1 (2009): 1–20; Stephen Steinberg, *The Ethnic Myth: Race, Ethnicity, and Class in America* (Boston: Beacon Press, 1981); Luigi Barzini, *From Caesar to the Mafia* (New York: Library Press, 1971); Renza Del Carria, *Proletari Senza Rivoluzione: Storia delle Classi Subalterne del 1869 al 1950* (Milan: Oriente, 1970).

20 See Rotundo "Wonderbread and Stugots; Italian American Manhood and *The Sopranos,*" 48.

21 Noteworthy examples of novels that describe the generational shift of values and appropriation of American ways are plentiful. Notable writers include Pietro Di Donato, *Christ in Concrete* (New York: Penguin Putnam, 1993); Rocco Fumento, *Trees of Dark Reflection* (New York: Knopf, 1962); Mario Puzo, *The Fortunate Pilgrim* (New York: Lancer Books, 1964). Third- and fourth-generation writers write to rediscover their ethnic roots: Lou D'Angelo, *What the Ancients Said* (Garden City, NY: Doubleday, 1971); Joseph Papaleo, *All the Comforts* (New York: Little Brown, 1967). For a more complete list and commentary on these and other writers, see Mangione's chapter on I-Am writers in Jerry Mangione and Ben Morreale, *La Storia* (New York: Harper Perennial, 1993).

22 The escape from poverty, superstition, and disease gave immigrants a thirst for opportunity that was infinitely greater and even more important, at times, than the font of their hard won fortune. In *La Storia*, Jerry Mangione writes, "For some, it seemed that self-esteem could be recovered only through a life of crime that might bring enough wealth and power to show Americans how important the immigrant's offspring had become" (223).

23 Janus was the Roman god of beginnings and ends, stasis and transitions. He is typically depicted as having two faces on his head, each facing different directions.

24 For Jerry Mangione, "We were becoming American by learning to be ashamed of our parents." See Mangione and Morreale, *La Storia*, 222.

25 Ibid., 219–20.

26 For Richard Gambino, I-Ams are trapped within their own distorted realities: "First, Italian Americans are largely in a surrealistic limbo regarding their identity. This is so partly because a people's identity needs to be expressed in the arts and reflected in the social sciences to be adequately realized. Second, wildly successful inauthentic myths of Italian Americans have come to serve as a substitute among Italian Americans for an authentic, developed identity. Thus, Italian Americans are left in a quandary

about their ethnic experience." See "The Crisis of Italian American Identity," in *Beyond The Godfather*, ed. Ciongoli and Parini, 270.
27 Interestingly, the spark that inflames Dr. Melfi's public tirade against her own therapist, Dr. Eliot Kupferburg, also occurs during a dinner, this time, however, amongst her trusted colleagues. Dr. Kupferburg instigates her ire by intimating her patient's name then further exacerbates the argument by discussing an article that indicates that therapy helps sociopaths become better criminals. A colleague's remark about the wine having a "big nose" (a euphemism for a grand bouquet) accentuates the series' insistence that stereotypes function at all levels of society.
28 Christopher Kocela, "From Columbus to Gary Cooper: Mourning the Lost White Father in *The Sopranos*," in *This Thing of Ours*, ed. Lavery, 104–17, states: "Gary Cooper takes on a kind of ghostly existence in *The Sopranos*, paradoxically present through remarks about his absence, frequently referred to but seen only once (and that in a dream)" (108).
29 These are sentiments (excluding the reference to mobsters) propounded by the philosopher Paul Tillich in his book, *The Courage To Be* (New Haven: Yale University Press, 1952), esp. chap. 4.
30 Named after its founder, Italian-American immigrant Ettore Boiardi, the Chef Boyardee Company began the production of canned pasta in the United States in the 1920s.
31 Chase often railed against those who bombasted self-deprecating rhetoric in their attempts to stall the series' production: "How can these people cling to their victimnood so much? These mingy little barbers. Italians are very successful people. Why is it so important that they stay a beaten, oppressed, suffering minority? It makes me sick. I remember thinking, 'I will shoot this show in my living room if I have to. But will keep on shooting it. And we'll keep portraying these people as they are, and we're not going to change one lick of hair one iota to suit anybody. I will do it in my living room for $10 an episode, but I won't stop.'" Quoted in Martin, *Difficult Men*, 157.
32 A fictional character and star of the sitcom *All in the Family* (1971–9) and *Archie Bunker's Place* (1979–83). An icon of television culture, Archie was a blue-collar, reactionary, bigoted commentator on issues contemporary to the times. His character became a social sounding board for contentious political issues.
33 Michael Fischer, "Ethnicity and the Post-Modern Arts of Memory," in *Writing Culture: The Poetics and Politics of Ethnography*, ed. James Clifford and George E. Marcus (Berkeley: California University Press, 1986), 201.
34 Werner Sollors employs these terms to discuss the harried nature of interpretation and criticism in "A Critique of Pure Pluralism" in *Reconstructing*

American Literary History, ed. Sacvan Bercovitch (Cambridge, MA: Harvard University Press, 1986), 250–79.
35 Michael Flamini, "Pa Cent'Anni, Dr. Melfi: Psychotherapy in the Italian American Community," in *A Sitdown with the Sopranos*, ed. Regina Barreca (New York: Palgrave Macmillan, 2002), 127.

3. God Help the Beast in Me

1 For a discussion of these principles, see the work of Leonard Schlain, including *The Alphabet Versus the Goddess: The Conflict Between Word and Image* (New York: Penguin Group, 1998); *Sex, Time and Power: How Women's Sexuality Shaped Human* Evolution (New York: Penguin Books, 2003); *Finding Balance: Reconciling the Masculine/Feminine in Contemporary Art and Culture* (Houston: Houston Center for Contemporary Craft, 2006).
2 Leonardo Sciascia, a Sicilian writer defiantly resisting the violent maelstrom of organized crime, wrote novels describing the treacherous relations between individuals and the state. In *The Day of the Owl* (New York: New York Review of Books, 1961), Sciascia wrote about the Sicilian underworld. In a particularly telling description of social reality, he divides Sicilian men into popularly held categories: men (*uomini*) of which there are very few; the half men (*mezz'uomini*) who are directionless, the little men (*ominici*) who aimlessly mimic the gestures of men; the cuckholds (*cornuti*), and the duck-like (*quaquaraquà*) who normally wallow in the mud.
3 When Christopher and Georgie are charged to dig up Emil Kolar in order to move his corpse, the physically repulsed diggers note that the fast-decomposing body has grown hair and fingernails. "Look at those fingernails!" Georgie exclaims. To which Christopher derisorily replies, "Oh fuck, they're like a woman's!'" ("The Legend of Tennessee Moltisanti" I.8).
4 See Schlain, *The Alphabet Versus the Goddess*, especially chap. 1.
5 The dynamics of the psyche and the dynamic of opposites are touchstones of Jungian theory. See Carl Gustav Jung, *Man and His Symbols* (New York: Random House, 1968).
6 *Men Are from Mars, Women Are from Venus* (Toronto: HarperCollins, 1992) is the title of a self-help book by John Gray that discusses human gender issues based on the differences between the sexes. It spawned an industry of self-help books that explored social relations.
7 For an excellent discussion of the possible reconfiguration of the human mind and crucial insights into the human sexual condition, see Shlain, *Sex, Time and Power*.
8 See Fred L. Gardaphé, *From Wiseguys to Wise Men: The Gangster and Italian American Masculinities* (New York: Routledge, 2006), xvii.

9 An old Italian proverb states that priests never stop being priests, and Mafiosi never cease to be Mafiosi. The importance of blood symbolism in both callings is an interesting aside as both professions require the drinking/spilling of the blood of others as proof of acquired consanguinity. In both instances, too, men are born again, literally receiving two baptisms, one of water and the other of fire.
10 In *The Psychology of The Sopranos* (New York: Basic Books, 2002), Glen O. Gabbard speaks of Tony as both fatherless and motherless in the chapter "Medea, Oedipus and Other Family Myths," 99–124.
11 The brooding, painfully introverted, supremely reluctant Don is a variegated template for the figure of Tony Soprano. Michael's heroic attempts to rehabilitate himself, to win the trust and affection of those he loves is fraught with the self-righteous angst that similarly fuels Tony's unstoppable drive towards the role of charismatic master manipulator.
12 The dysfunctional dynamics between mother, son, uncle, and dead father is reminiscent of Shakespeare's Hamlet and is treated by Gabbard in *The Psychology of The Sopranos*: "Like Claudius in Hamlet, Uncle Junior moves in on Livia after the death of his brother and, in his platonic way, relates to her as though she is his wife. Tony, like Hamlet, deeply resents him for taking that position with his mother. Junior, on the other hand, redirects any rivalry with his brother that he may have once had toward his nephew" (118).
13 Tony's obsession with muscle mass and strength is constant throughout the series but made relevant is several episodes, including Episode 71 "Live Free or Die" in Season VI, which features close-ups of bulging biceps and body builders. His unsolicited provocation and beating of his much younger and muscled bodyguard and driver Perry Annunziata, serves to assuage his ego and display external virility to his underlings but costs him physically. Interestingly, this is also the episode in which Vito Spatafore's gay proclivities is openly vented. This unexpected shock wave simultaneously undermines and inflames everyone's already fragile male ego.
14 Guy Corneau, *Absent Fathers, Lost Sons: The Search for Masculine Identity* (Boston: Shambhala Publications, 1991), 137.
15 I am reminded of another literary knight, Italo Calvino's tale of *The Non Existent Knight* (Toronto: Vintage Books, 2009), in which an empty suit of armour executes the duties and protocols of knighthood. The empty armour affirms itself as participant in the dynamic of chivalry code in spite of its own knowledge of vacuous non-being.
16 Again, an Italo Calvino short story, "The Spiral," in *Cosmicomics*, trans. William Weaver (New York: Harcourt Brace Jovanovich, 1968), reminds this reader of the male necessity of secreting a hard shell exterior to protect a gelatinous and vulnerable interior.

17 The caged inner beast that gnaws at the frail and fragile underpinnings of Tony's outward bravado is eloquently expressed by Nick Lowe's lyrics in "The Beast in Me" (1994).
18 For a discussion of authoritarian order and its reliance upon unsatisfied sexual longing, see Wilhelm Reich, *The Mass Psychology of Fascism* (New York: Farrar, Straus, 1976.)
19 All the men in *The Sopranos* belong to a brotherhood, legal or illegal, that denotes the ideals and practices considered suitable for manhood. Their cultural inheritance and social environment determine their individual pursuits. FBI agents form the basis for seignorial jurisdiction. Members of the mob supplant nobility as an expedient. Both follow codes, both rely upon each other for their existence. Consequently, a buffer must remain between them for legitimacy. When Agent Harris is placed on the Terrorism Squad and sent to the Middle East, he longs for the old neighbourhood, a Sartriale panino, and Tony Soprano. When Salvatore "Big Pussy" Bonpensiero realizes he will no longer be a part of the Mafia, he fears engulfment and loss of self. His anxiety leads him to create a healing fiction as an FBI agent. He must be reminded repeatedly by Agent Skip Lipari that he is "a cooperating witness, you wear a wire, that's what you do." And, "You're not an FBI employee, Sal." But "Big Pussy" cannot fathom the nothingness of not belonging, so Agent Lipari insists: "Sal, you are gonna help us build a case against Tony Soprano. And then you're gonna go do your time for sellin' heroin. And then you get out and start a new life. It's a good thing" ("Knight in White Satin Armor" II.12). All these men wish to be knights, they crave determinacy, and they want to belong to a clan. Their anxiety is their finitude; their spectre is the fear of not belonging to a personal hell.
20 A.J.'s heredity is a plagued and vexing bequest. Subject to the same emotional patterns as his father, Tony himself regrets his biomedical endowment. In "Walk Like a Man" VI.17, he vents his deep sorrow to Dr. Melfi: "It's in his blood, this miserable fuckin' existence. My rotten fuckin' putrid genes have infected my kid's soul. That's my gift to my son."
21 For a valuable discussion on the hero archetype, see Otto Rank, Lord Fitzroy Richard Somerset Raglan, and Alan Dundes, *In Quest of the Hero* (Princeton: Princeton University Press, 1990). This comprehensive study includes the seminal works of the authors, with an introduction by Robert A. Segal.
22 Victor Turner, *The Ritual Process: Structure and Anti-Structure* (New York: Aldine de Gruyter, 1969), 28.
23 It is interesting that A.J. uses the term mummy to describe his great-uncle ("I'm gonna put a bullet in his fuckin' mummy head. I promise," "Join the

Club" VI.2). The derogatory moniker recalls the excerpt from "The Western Lands" by William Burroughs, *The Western Lands: A Novel* (New York: Viking Press, 1987). The passage is read by William Burroughs himself to the background music "Seven Souls" by the group Material. The poem has been called a twentieth-century version of Dante Alighieri's *Inferno*. Rather than prophesizing a return to God, Burroughs lampoons religion by using Egyptian rituals and philosophy to describe scenes of morbid destruction while on a voyage to the Promised Land. The words of the opening sequence of Season VI are supposedly prophetic as they are visually linked to characters in the series. A scene of diabolical A.J. taking a picture of himself with his cell phone is accompanied with the words: "Number five is Ka, the Double, most closely associated with the subject. The Ka, which usually reaches adolescence at the time of bodily death, is the only reliable guide through the Land of the Dead to the western Lands." A.J.'s bodily death ends his adolescence, while Ka remains the living spirit of the ritual symbolism of his act.
24 See Turner, *The Ritual Process*, 97.
25 At the beginning of *The Godfather*, Michael Corleone is dressed in full Marine uniform. His mode of dress, unusual for a Corleone wedding, distinguishes him from family and guests. No respectable son would offer such an affront to his family, especially since his joining the Marines ran counter to the family's wishes. The semiotic valence of the military uniform, coupled with the unconventionality of arriving with an American girlfriend, set Michael apart both visually and ideologically. His flippant remark, "That's my family, Kay. It's not me," separates him from his gene pool and culture, a wish he partially fulfills by eventually marrying Kay.
26 In "Walk Like a Man" VI.17, Tony gives Christopher advice about grilling steaks: "The steak's done. It keeps cookin' even if it's off the flame; the juices." In an episode where Tony consoles his son that everyone "gets the blues" and chides Christopher for "not having balls," the metaphor of stewing in one's own juices aptly describes the existential dilemmas of both aberrant sons.
27 In "Isabella" I.12, a drug-numbed Tony imagines himself a babe suckling at the breast of a loving mother. This is the same episode of his mother's failed assassination attempt on his life.
28 Beyond the title of a Stevie Nicks song recorded by Fleetwood Mac and released in 1975, Rhiannon is the name of a blond goddess of Welsh origin. Her mythical attributes are disputed; however, she is generally considered beautiful and gracious. Later emanations depict her as being dark. A.J. is immediately drawn to her calm haunting fragility. The lyrics of the Nicks'

song "Dreams unwind/ Love's a state of mind," provide an appropriate coda to their evolving relationship.
29 The Rocky Balboa figure is a semiotic path rich with notions of American saga, selfless heroism, and individuality that run contrary to the self-involved bravado of the young Soprano.
30 See Fred L. Gardaphé, *From Wiseguys to Wise Men*, 20.
31 Paulie's self-centred view of the world excludes the fact that the world is only a potential and not present when one is not present to observe it. All of the world's events are potentially present but not actually seen or felt unless one sees or feel. But there is also a reality of the mind, an *in here* that may or may not correspond to the world *out there* (though it may be closer to that reality because it is my reality). But what if there existed a third reality, a quantum field where objects follow laws that are outright paradoxical. This way of seeing is termed the superposition principle by physicists. Erwin Schroedinger speculated that quantum wave functions, or quiffs, can be added together but they can be in two or more places at the same time. "When two systems of which we know the states by their respective representatives, enter into temporary physical interaction due to known forces between them, and when after a time of mutual influence the systems separate again, then they can no longer be described in the same way as before, viz. by endowing each with a representative of its own. I would not call that the ONE but rather THE characteristic trait of quantum mechanics, the one that enforces its entire departure from classical ideas of thought." E. Schroedinger, "Discussions of Probability Relations between Separated Systems," *Cambridge Philosophical Society Proceedings* 31 (1935): 555, quoted in Fred Alan Wolf, *Taking the Quantum Leap* (New York: Harper and Row, 1989), 189.
32 Since, indeed, "everythang is everythang," even Barone Sanitation routes can become Cinelli Routes ... end of story.
33 The ground for thinking in opposites is the psychic differentiation between masculine and feminine traits. In *Healing Fiction* (New York: Station Hill Press, 1983), James Hillman notes, "Psychic hermaphroditism holds juxtapositions without feeling them as oppositions ... Hermaphroditus presents an image in which what is natural is the unnatural, a primordial image of *contra naturam*" (102).
34 Loose lips are a common theme and an anathema in the series. A metaphor for blabber mouth, Tony recognizes the rat-informer Fabian Petrullo in "College" I.5, because of the misshapen lips on his sculpture of Ronald Regan. The very name of the family, Soprano, alludes to Tony's singing, a euphemism for talking, to a psychiatrist. Phone conversations, wire taps, whispered directives,

coded messages, and third-party interlocutors all reflect the maniacal necessity for utmost secrecy and unspoken words, hence tightly pursed lips.
35 Plato, *The Republic*, trans. R.E. Allen (New Haven: Yale University Press, 2006).
36 See Jackson Katz, *The Macho Paradox* (Chicago: Sourcebooks, 2006), for an expanded discussion of this topic.
37 Avi Santo, "Fat Fuck! Why Don't You Take a Look in the Mirror? Weight, Body Image, and Masculinity in *The Sopranos*," in *This Thing of Ours: Investigating The Sopranos*, ed. David Lavery (New York: Columbia University Press, 2002), 72–94, see esp. 73.
38 We recall the particularly moving occasion when he plaintively asks his uncle Junior, "Don't you love me?" The docile and humbling query is shrouded in tears, heartfelt angst, visible pain, but no vocal response from the stoically conditioned and silent uncle ("Where's Johnny" V.3).
39 I disagree with Alan Sepinwall's conclusion that there is no resolution to the characters' existential being in the world when he states:

> Tony's lack of forward progress wasn't a case of a TV show refusing to change because it would disrupt a successful formula, but an expression of what seemed to be the show's deeply cynical take on humanity ... Time and again throughout the series, characters were presented with the choice between what is right and what is easy ... they inevitably took the easy choice ... They might pretend to change ... but pretending was all it was ... When Tony survives being shot by a senile, confused Uncle Junior ... [he] vows to be a better, more patient person. But the demands of his job, and his own deep-seated emotional issues, bring back the same ol' Tony in short order. (*The Revolution Was Televised*, 49)

A basic tenant of narrative is that events must evince a change in the state of characters otherwise there is no story, no plot. While characters in the series may choose to remain the same, the fact that they have made a choice moves them closer to their core. In essence, they change towards themselves and reveal their true nature. Sepinwall seems to think that only a movement towards a predetermined and morally inspired text provides progress, while history has always proved that such certainties are ephemeral at best. Chase best sums the tone of the series:

> I believe people have said that the whole theme of *The Sopranos* was that change is impossible ... that was never the theme of *The Sopranos*. That was never what I meant to say or meant to imply. Of course change isn't impossible. It's very, very difficult. It's very rare ... My view of it is people do their best. They just muddle through ... And

there's nothing guiding us, and we know it, and we feel it, and we feel that lack, and don't know what to do. I think the overall feeling of the show, the thing about life isn't that it's good or bad, but that it's sad. There's a lot of sadness in *The Sopranos*. People want to cry, and don't, or can't. (Quoted in Sepinwall, *The Revolution Was Televised*, 52)

40 I believe the best way to understand the anatomy of Tony is by reprising Northrup Frye's discussion of a heroic human situation. When a character has made a choice towards destiny, that choice is often heroic and may be traced back to Adam. "Adam ... is in a heroic human situation: he is on top of the wheel of fortune, with the destiny of the gods almost within his reach. He forfeits that destiny in a way which suggests moral responsibility to some and a conspiracy of fate to others. What he does is to exchange a fortune of unlimited freedom for the fate involved in the consequences of the act of exchange, just as, for a man who deliberately jumps off a precipice, the law of gravitation acts as fate for the brief remainder of his life." Frye goes on to speak of the ontological and psychological consequences of this initial choice when, years later, one becomes conscious of its ultimate ramifications. "The discovery or *anagnorisis* which comes at the end of the tragic plot is not simply the knowledge by the hero of what has happened to him ... but the recognition of the determined shape of the life he has created for himself, with an implicit comparison with the uncreated potential life he has forsaken. Frye, *Anatomy of Criticism: Four Essays* (Princeton: Princeton University Press, 1957), 212.

4. Two Tonys: Drawing Conclusions from Mediated Mob Images

1 The song "The Beast in Me," lyrics by Nick Lowe, closes the pilot episode of *The Sopranos* thereby exacting a biting commentary of Tony's hurtful and malignant personality. The song "I'm Not Like Everybody Else" by the Kinks reinforces the notion at the end of "Cold Cuts" V.10. Incapable of taking pride in his sister Janice's relative newfound calm, a hideously meddling and jealous older brother draws out her venom by instigating a futile argument.
2 Niccolò Machiavelli writes: "From this arises an argument: whether it is better to be loved than to be feared, or the contrary. I reply that one should like to be both one and the other; but since it is difficult to joint them together, it is much safer to be feared than to be loved when one of the two must be lacking." See *The Prince*, trans. Peter Bondanella and Mark Musa (Oxford: Oxford University Press, 1998), 56.

Notes to pages 164–9

3 See Peter Bondanella, *Hollywood Italians: Dagos, Palookas, Romeos, Wise Guys, and Sopranos* (New York: Continuum, 2004) for an exhaustive overview of the gangsters, lovers, prizefighters, comedians, and so forth that populate the world of media Italians.
4 Ibid., 297.
5 The term *guido* originated as a demeaning term for young male I-Ams adorned in muscle shirts, gold chains, unbuttoned dress shirts, and pompadours. Usually associated with East Coast I-Ams, the term *gino* is prevalent in the Mid-West and Canada. Female equivalents are *guidette* and *gina*, respectively.
6 John. T. Waisanen, *Thinking Geometrically: Re-Visioning Space for a Multimodal World* (New York: Peter Lang, 2002).
7 Linda Hutcheon, *A Poetics of Postmodernisn: History, Theory, Fiction* (Cambridge: University Printing House, 1988), 60.
8 Robert Ludlum, *The Bourne Identity* (New York: Richard Marek, 1980).
9 See Dana Polan, *The Sopranos* (Durham, NC: Duke University Press, 2009), 135.
10 Charles Newman, *The Post-Modern Aura: The Act of Fiction in and Age of Inflation* (Evanston, IL: Northwestern University Press, 1985), 52. Michel Foucault also speaks of "discontinuous systematization" in *The Archeology of Knowledge and the Discourse of Language*, trans. A.M. Sheridan Smith (New York: Pantheon, 1972), 201. For a comprehensive discussion of the fundamental questions surrounding postmodernism, see Thomas Docherty, ed., *Postmodernism: A Reader* (New York: Columbia University Press, 1993).
11 The most studied of these reactions occurs in "Live Free or Die" VI.6 when Tony feels he must dissuade any notion of physical or mental weakness that has installed itself in the crew in the wake of his extended coma. He chooses to prove his virility and reasserts his power over the crew by initiating a fight with his younger, stronger, behemoth driver. The public display dissipates any doubt his crew may have harboured regarding his physical condition or mental state, but it costs him private, physical pain.
12 This rapacious mob refrain has spawned a coterie of self-help books extolling the positive qualities of gangster-style business. Among them, *Nothing Personal, It's Just Business: A Street Smart Guide for New Managers and CEO's* by Louis Gonzales (Bloomington: Author House, 2006). The oft-quoted mob mantra designed to place distance between an individual and his actions has been taken out of context and devalues the original intent of Michael Corleone's use of the phrase. When Tom Hagen attempts to calm the future Don's vengeful rant against Sollozzo and McCluskey by telling him, "You

shouldn't let that broken jaw influence you ... McCluskey is a stupid man and it was business, not personal," Michael reminds him that when people are affected by an action, that action and its alternatives must be weighed as pre-eminently personal. "Tom, don't let anybody kid you. It's all personal, every bit of business. Every piece of shit every man has to eat every day of his life is personal. They call it business, OK. But it's personal as hell. You know where I learned that from? The Don. My old man. The Godfather. If a bolt of lightning hit a friend of his, the old man would take it personal. He took my going into the Marines personal. That's what makes him great. The Great Don. He takes everything personal. Like God." Mario Puzo, *The Godfather* (1969; reprint, New York: New American Library, 2002), 147.

13 If Tony were to simply acknowledge any of his acts, he would be caught up in the Hegelian conundrum of recognizing that action is the finality of possibility. When something is, it is such and nothing else. The act ceases to be something that is presumed or pretended but a performance that either is or is nothing. G.W.F. Hegel, *The Phenomenology of the Mind*, trans. J.B. Baillie (London: Harper and Row, 1967).

14 Noel Carroll, "Sympathy for the Devil," in *The Sopranos and Philosophy*, ed. Richard Green and Peter Vernezze (Chicago: Open Court Publishing, 2004), 125.

15 "The Minister's Black Veil" is a short story written by Nathaniel Hawthorne that appeared in the volume *Twice-Told Tales* in 1836. In this didactic allegorical tale, Hawthorne explores themes of sin and repentance, of public and private morality. The Reverend Hooper's mysterious self-veiling forces the townspeople to uncomfortably face their own invisible veils and the often tragic truth of humanity's double nature.

16 In this sense, television can function like a therapist. It can provide strategies for coping with the psychological challenges of our age of informationalism. As a mode of public discourse in "the same way that writing (not mailing) an angry letter to an ex-lover can help resolve his/her feelings of anger, watching television can help one resolve feelings of discomfort about the social world." See Brian L. Ott, *The Small Screen: How Television Equips Us to Live in the Information Age* (Boston: Blackwell Publishing, 2007), x.

17 We recall that in "D-Girl" II.7, Livia Soprano provides a questioning A.J. the mysteries of life ending with the phrase, "In the end, you die in your own arms."

18 Masada is the site of an ancient fortification in the Southern District of Israel. The Hassidic Jew in *The Sopranos* is referring to the siege of Masada by Roman troops in 72 BC. The Roman legion, led by Lucius Flavius Silva,

surrounded Masada and isolated the 960 inhabitants for one year. When the Romans eventually entered the fortress, they found the inhabitants had committed a mass suicide rather than capitulate to the Romans. Documentation of the events is sketchy at best as the legend of Masada has become the source of myth and popular lore.

19 Chase quoted in Alan Sepinwall, *The Revolution Was Televised: The Cops, Crooks, Slingers, and Slayers Who Changed TV Drama Forever* (New York: Simon and Schuster, 2013), 56.

20 The terminology is Noam Chomsky's, "The United States and the 'Challenge of Relativity,'" in *Human Rights Fifty Years On: A Reappraisal*, ed. Tony Evans (Manchester: Manchester University Press, 1998), 8.

21 The allegory of Plato's Cave is presented in *The Republic*. It describes a group of prisoners who are chained to the floor of a cave. They stare at a blank wall upon which shadows are projected by slaves moving statues before a fire. The shadows are as close as these prisoners get to perceiving reality. The allegory theorizes an intellectual construct that in turn posits an ethical concept. The courage to confront reality and affirm one's self in an act of self-knowledge is a central position in the structure of being. To remain in the dark, to reside forever bound in the cave is to remain forever without a personally defined destiny.

22 The mythological figure of the snake-tressed Medusa had the power to change anyone that looked directly at her into stone. Psychoanalytic interpretations place her at the centre of the son's need to behead the mother archetype in order to avoid the regressive tendency to submit to maternal power thereby thwarting emotional relationships with other women. In literature, the Medusa figure is a graphic symbol of female sexual energy and power. Able to still men with her stare, in word and image studies, she represents anticipated muteness, the disruption of male action (time) by female description (space).

23 The mobster's linguistic reality is a miasma of malapropisms, shielded truths, and outright lies. A few memorable examples include Hesh Rabkin's repartee with Massive Genius in "A Hit Is a Hit" I.10. Concerning music copyright, Hesh boasts: "Back then we were makin' all the rules, makin' and breakin' them as we went along." Massive Genius corrects the sly swindler: "You mean rapin' and pilligin'." Massive Genius continues his legal posturing by stating, "It's reparations that I seek." To which a lucid Tony aptly retorts, "Why don't we call it for what it is – a shakedown." The linguistic gymnastics continue as Massive Genius asks Hesh, "So you bought horses with your royalties. And Little Jimmy's royalties, whatever became of those?" This time it is Silvio Dante's turn to play the game of innuendo: "He bought horse." Tony's "we had coffee" is also reminiscent of

Tony Manero's desire to "go for coffee" with heart-throb Stephanie Mangano in *Saturday Night Fever* (1977). She reads through the sexual innuendo of the euphemism and suggests a less potent and risky tea.

24 For a discussion of these issues with respect to left- and right-brain activity, see Leonard Shlain, *Sex, Time and Power* (New York: Viking Penguin, 2003), esp. chap. 2.

25 Tigers abound in *The Sopranos*. Adriana La Cerva is depicted as a sexy feline who often sports tiger patterns as clothing. A prowling tiger statue sits on the Soprano's mantle; a tiger graces Tony's right shoulder; Tigers is the name of his high school football team; and the animal's image is painted on the wall of Holsten's Diner in the final episode. Tigers are an apt symbol for Tony. A menacing and fearful animal, it is an apex predator, an obligate carnivore.

26 Alan Sepinwall agrees: "Tony was not only a bad guy, but an increasingly unapologetic one as the series aged. Where previous dramas had humanized edgy characters over time, *The Sopranos* did the opposite." *The Revolution Was Televised*, 48.

27 As Tony rifles through the jukebox, the camera focuses on the song titles. Interestingly, the song by Journey, "Don't Stop Believin'" is the penultimate title seen on screen. It is my contention that Tony did not choose this song as many commentators have suggested, but instead makes the more logical, sequential choice of selecting the last song the viewer is shown. Life may or may not "go on and on" for Tony, but that choice is not his prerogative. The decision to end or not end the series was made by David Chase, as was the choice of song chosen to close the series in its enigmatic darkness. The song chosen by Tony is "I've Gotta Be Me" by Tony Bennett, flip side "A Lonely Place." Both titles express the real sentiments of Tony while at Holsten's Diner. Both songs have yet to play and be heard.

28 "Writing is the most primordial 'activity' of differentiation ... it inaugurates language, bestows consciousness, institutes being." See Vincent B. Leitch, *Deconstructive Criticism: An Advanced Introduction* (New York: Columbia University Press, 1983), for a discussion of *ecriture* (writing and logocentrism) and *phone* (voice and phonocentrism).

29 The comment is by David Simon, creator of the TV series *The Wire*, a series that displays similar tragic undertones that explored the idiosyncratic psychologies of modern America. Quoted in Brett Martin, *Difficult Men: Behind the Scenes of a Creative Revolution: From The Sopranos and The Wire to Mad Men and Breaking Bad* (New York: The Penguin Press, 2013), 87.

30 Ibid., 289.

31 Chase had wished the black screen to run through the entire credit time with no music or credits at all. Just darkness. Social, cultural, historical,

and religious commentary concerning the lightness/darkness binary opposition abound and it is not my intention to provide an exegetic encyclopedia of allegorical differences between the light of day and the horrors of the night. On the other hand, I have discussed the duplicitous nature of Tony and have shed light upon the beast that resides within the cavelike darkness of his soul.

In the 1946 film version of the classic fairy tale *Beauty and the Beast* by Jean Cocteau, a loveable beast resides in a secluded castle. On the back of the beast's chair, in Latin, are the words: All men are beasts when they don't have love. Tony Soprano is such a beast. As viewers, we are allowed to make contact with him and survive the meeting. Tony is not so fortunate. On the symbolic level, the absence of a protective and loving mother has been substituted with an encapsulating masculine code. On the textual level, Tony's manic scrutinizing of his face in a mirror corresponds to a haptic scanning of his features in search of a vital text to rationalize his nefarious choices.

In his work *Miroir du Monde* (Paris 1587), Joseph de Chesnes wrote that God had created the world and that world was a text that man could read as if looking into a mirror. "If man wishes to see himself/If he wishes to gaze upon the greatness of his soul/He must cast his eye upon this mirror of the world," quoted in Alberto Manguel, *Reading Pictures, Viewing Texts* (Bloomington: Indiana University Press, 1991), 170. We have already briefly discussed mirrors as a *memento mori/memento vitae* motif in the series. No man can recognize his face or see the world in a dark mirror. Darkness is the opposite of light. Warmth, love, grace, all emanate from the all-embracing and illuminating love of God. The Prince of darkness rules the nether world of cold, hateful, and graceless lightlessness.

The darkness that envelops the series at its end has sparked enduring debate concerning the possible death of Tony. This abrupt "cut to black," however, is only relatively foreboding since it is reminiscent of many other instances of darkness descending around Tony throughout the series but especially in the final episode of Season I. The chiaroscuro effect is apparent from the opening shot of the episode. The capos are meeting in the back room of Satriale's Pork Store. From here the story moves to darkened elevators, Livia Soprano roaming the night in a nebulous haze of memory loss, Tony and FBI Chief Frank Cubitoso in a boarded room listening to shrouded conversations, the backroom of the Bada Bing, subdued shadows and hushed tones in the Soprano master bedroom, Father Phil Intintola's confessional pew.

The most memorable dark scene occurs at the end of the episode and effectively closes the season. Tony has just expedited some family business. His immediate enemies are either dead or have been jailed. At the moment that Tony seems to have reached a threshold of meaning, the lights go out. At this particular moment that he has achieved lucid insight concerning the malicious turpitude of his closest relatives, darkness envelops him. A storm breaks. As he enters Dr. Melfi's evacuated office, a power failure momentarily dims the lights, surrounding his figure in distressing darkness. Foreboding thunder sounds. Tony is alone. He has lost a vital psychogenic lifeline and appears helpless and forlorn. His voyage into the light of consciousness has abruptly halted. Fortunately, he has his family. But it, too, is buffeted by the tempest. A crystallization of the forces of denial and negation pummel him both physically and spiritually. The darkness is fraught with fear, but on this night he finds respite in the familiar warmth of Artie Bucco's restaurant, a safe haven in the storm. In the darkened restaurant, both his families find momentary peace and uneasy tranquillity.

These moments of darkness are gaze-directing threshold moments for Tony. Rather than providing illuminating exits, they further embroil him in wanton corruption. Especially relevant for Tony, the events parse further entry into the role of psychopathic dark knight. At series' end, he essentially becomes a one-man mob, the charismatic leader of a dwindling collective.

5. An Appendix of Verbal Bits and Bytes

1 See Brett Martin, *The Sopranos: The Complete Book* (New York: Melcher Media, Time Inc. Home Entertainment, 2007), 161.
2 In *The Role of The Reader: Explorations in the Semiotics of Texts* (Bloomington: Indiana University Press, 1979), Umberto Eco speaks of "the basic story stuff" of narrative structures. For Eco, the *fabula* (story) of a narrative "need not necessarily be a sequence of human actions (physical or not), but can also concern a temporal transformation of ideas or a series of events concerning inanimate objects" (27).
3 In *The Role of the Reader*, Umberto Eco analyzes the iterative narrative schemes inserted into a text that allow the reader (in our case both reader and viewer) to move beyond what is read or seen and create interpretations based on one's own knowledge of the material presented. At these moments the reader "walks, so to speak, outside the text, in order to gather intertextual support" for his/her hypotheses (32).

4 Originally published in 1676, the work was "Translated by a Painter" and "Printed for J. Osborn, at the Golden Ball at Paternoster Row, 1743."

6. Conclusion

1 Mikhail Bakhtin, *Rabelais and His World*, trans. Helene Isowlsky (Bloomington: Indiana University Press, 1984).
2 Alan Sepinwall, introduction to *The Revolution Was Televised: The Cops, Crooks, Slingers, and Slayers Who Changed TV Drama Forever* (New York: Simon and Schuster, 2013), 1–6.
3 Brett Martin sums the burgeoning importance of writers by citing the appearance of writer Stephen J. Cannell's "bumper" or snippet of video that appeared on screen after the credits of his shows. "It depicted the man himself, bearded, impressively coiffed, and usually puffing on a pipe, at his typewriter at the final moments of finishing a script. He would pound out a final few characters – no doubt a last-minute plot twist or crucial piece of character nuance – and then confidently rip the page from its carriage and fling it across the room, where upon it morphed into animation, fluttered onto the top of a manuscript, and settled into a royal, curved 'C.'" This supremely narcissistic gesture was a visual cue that times had indeed changed. "What's more, though he was a savvy, in some ways revolutionary, businessman, making a fortune by essentially starting his own studio and thus owning all his shows, Cannell's bumper specifically insisted on his role, first and foremost, as a writer." See *Difficult Men: Behind the Scenes of a Creative Revolution: From The Sopranos and The Wire to Mad Men and Breaking Bad* (New York: The Penguin Press, 2013), 41.
4 Toby Miller, *Television Studies: The Basics* (New York: Routledge, 2010), 98.
5 J. Hector St. John de Crèvecoeur, *Letters from an American Farmer* (1782; reprint, New York: Albert and Charles Boni, 1925), 54–5.
6 Brian L. Ott, *The Small Screen: How Television Equips Us to Live in the Information Age* (Boston: Blackwell Publishing, 2007), x.

Suggested Readings

General Texts

Alba, Richard. *Italian Americans: Into the Twilight of Ethnicity*. Upper Saddle River, NJ: Prentice Hall, 1985.
Alberti, Leon Battista. *On Painting*. Translated by John R. Spencer. New Haven: Yale University Press, 1966.
Allen, Dennis W. "Making Over Masculinity: A Queer 'I' for the Straight Guy." *Genders* 44. Retrieved 19 June 2008 from http://www.genders.org/g44/g44_allen.html
Amfitheatrof, Erik. *The Children of Columbus: An Informal History of the Italians in the New World*. Boston: Little, Brown, 1973.
Aristotle. *De Anima II*. Translated by W.W. Hett. Cambridge, MA: Harvard University Press, 1957.
Arnheim, Rudolf. *Visual Thinking*. Berkeley: California University Press, 1969.
Bakhtin, Mikhail. *Rabelais and His World*. Translated by Helene Isowlsky. Bloomington: Indiana Univeristy Press, 1984.
Baltrusaitis, Jurgis. *El Espejo*. Madrid: Miraguano, 1988.
Banfield, Edward C. *The Moral Basis of a Backward Society*. New York: The Free Press, 1958.
Barthes, Roland. *Mythologies*. London: Paladin, 1973.
Barthes, Roland. *The Pleasure of the Text*. Translated by Richard Miller. New York: Hill and Wang, 1975.
Barzini, Luigi. *From Caesar to the Mafia*. New York: The Library Press, 1971.
Benhabib, Seyla. *The Claims of Culture: Equality and Diversity in the Global Era*. Princeton: Princeton University Press, 2002.
Benjamin, Walter. "The Work of Art in the Age of Mechanical Reproduction." In *Illuminations*. Edited by Hannah Arendt. Translated by Harry Zohn, 217–52. New York: Schocken Books, 1969.

Benjamin, Walter. *Reflections*. New York: Harcourt Brace Jovanovich, 1978.
Bertellini, Giorgio. "Black Hands and White Hearts: Italian Immigrants as 'Urban Racial Types' in 'Early American Film Culture.'" *Urban History* 31, no. 3 (2004): 375–99.
Bloom, Allan. *The Closing of the American Mind*. New York: Simon and Schuster, 1987.
Bondanella, Peter. *Hollywood Italians: Dagos, Palookas, Romeos, Wise Guys, and Sopranos*. New York: Continuum, 2004.
Bordon, Susan. *The Male Body*. New York: Farrar, Straus and Giroux, 1999.
Brunette, Peter, and David Wills, eds. *Deconstruction and the Visual Arts: Art, Media, Architecture*. Cambridge: Cambridge University Press, 1994.
Bryson, Norman. *Vision and Painting: The Logic of the Gaze*. New Haven: Yale University Press, 1983.
Burroughs, William. *The Western Lands: A Novel*. New York: Viking Press, 1987.
Butler, Judith. *Gender Trouble: Feminism and the Subversion of Identity*. New York: Routledge, 1990.
Butler, Judith. *Undoing Gender*. New York: Routledge, 2004.
Calvino, Italo. *The Nonexistent Knight and The Cloven Viscount*. New York: Harcourt, Brace and Co., 1977. Originally *Il cavaliere inesistente*. Turin: Einaudi, 1959.
Calvino, Italo. "The Spiral." In *Cosmicomics*. Translated by William Weaver, 141–53. New York: Harcourt Brace Jovanovich, 1968. Originally *La spirale*. Turin: Einaudi, 1965.
Castaneda, Carlos. *The Teachings of Don Juan: A Yaqui Way of Knowledge*. New York: Washington Square Press, 1968.
Chomsky, Noam. "The United States and the 'Challenge of Relativity.'" In Tony Evans, ed., *Human Rights Fifty Years On: A Reappraisal*, 24–57. Manchester: Manchester University Press, 1998.
Ciongoli, A. Kenneth, and Parini, Jay, eds. *Beyond The Godfather: Italian American Writers on the Real Italian American Experience*. Hanover: University Press of New England, 1997.
Corneau, Guy. *Absent Fathers, Lost Sons: The Search for Masculine Identity*. Boston: Shambhala Publications, 1991.
Cosco, Joseph P. *Imagining Italians: The Clash of Romance and Race in American Perceptions, 1880–1910*. Albany: State University of New York Press, 2003.
D'Angelo, Lou. *What the Ancients Said*. Garden City, NY: Doubleday, 1971.
Da Vinci, Leonardo. *Paragone: Poetry and Painting*. Edited by A. Phillip McMahon. Princeton: Princeton University Press, 1956.

Dal Cerro, William. "Hollywood versus Italians: Them – 400, Us – 50." *The Italic Way* 27 (1997): 10–11. Retrieved 22 March 2011 from http://italic.org/ItalicWay/editions/ItalicWay1997XXVII.pdf

de Crèvecoeur, J. Hector St. John. *Letters from an American Farmer*. 1798. Reprint, New York: Albert and Charles Boni, 1925.

Del Carria, Renza. *Proletari Senza Rivoluzione: Storia delle Classi Subalterne del 1869 al 1950*. Milan: Oriente, 1970.

Dickie, John. *Cosa Nostra: A History of the Sicilian Mafia*. London: Hodder and Stoughton, 2004.

Di Donato, Pietro. *Christ in Concrete*. New York: Penguin Putnam, 1993.

Dines, Gail, and Jean M. Humez, eds. *Gender, Race and Class in Media: A Text-Reader*. Thousand Oaks, CA: Sage Publications, 1995.

Docherty, Thomas. *Postmodernism: A Reader*. New York: Columbia University Press, 193.

Eco, Umberto. *The Role of the Reader: Explorations in the Semiotics of Texts*. Bloomington: Indiana University Press, 1979.

Eco, Umberto. *Travels in Hyperreality*. Translated by William Weaver. London: Picador, 1987.

Elkins, James. *The Object Stares Back: On the Nature of Seeing*. New York: Simon and Schuster, 1996.

Ferraro, Thomas J. *Feeling Italian: The Art of Ethnicity in America*. New York: New York University Press, 2005.

Fields, Ingrid Walker. "Family Values and Feudal Codes: The Social Politics of America's Twenty-First Century Gangster." *Journal of Popular Culture* 37, no. 4 (2004): 611–33.

Fischer, Michael. "Ethnicity and the Post-Modern Arts of Memory." *Writing Culture: The Poetics and Politics of Ethnography*. Edited by James Clifford and George E. Marcus. Berkeley: California University Press, 1986.

Flamini, Michael. "Pa Cent'Anni, Dr. Melfi: Psychotherapy in the Italian American Community." *A Sitdown with The Sopranos*. Edited by Regina Barreca, 113–27. New York: Palgrave McMilllan, 2002.

Foucault, Michel. *The Archeology of Knowledge and the Discourse of Language*. Translated by A.M. Sheridan Smith. New York: Pantheon, 1972.

Freedberg, David. *The Power of Images*. Chicago: Chicago University Press, 1989.

Freud, Sigmund. *New Introductory Lectures on Psychoanalysis*. Translated by James Strachey. Edited by James Strachey and Angela Richards. London: The Hogarth Press, 1964.

Frye, Northrop. *Anatomy of Criticism: Four Essays*. Princeton: Princeton University Press, 1957.

Fumento, Rocco. *Trees of Dark Reflection*. New York: Knopf, 1962.

Gage, Nicholas. *Mafia, U.S.A.* Chicago: Playboy Press, 1972.

Gambino, Richard. "The Crisis of Italian American Identity." In A. Kenneth Ciongoli and Jay Parini, eds., *Beyond The Godfather: Italian American Writers on the Real Italian American Experience*, 269–88. Hanover: University Press of New England, 1997.

Gandelman, Claude. *Reading Pictures, Viewing Texts*. Bloomington: Indiana University Press, 1991.

Gardiner, Judith Kegan. "Masculinity, the Teening of America, and Empathic Targeting." *Signs* 25, no. 4 (2000): 1257–61.

Gombrich, Ernst. *Art and Illusion: A Study in the Psychology of Pictorial Representation*. Princeton: Princeton Univrsity Press, 1960.

Gombrich, Ernst. *The Image and the Eye*. Ithaca, NY: Cornell University Press, 1982.

Goodman, Nelson. *Of Mind and Other Matters*. Cambridge, MA: Harvard University Press, 1984.

Gardaphé, Fred L. *From Wiseguys to Wise Men: The Gangster and Italian American Masculinities*. New York: Routledge, 2006.

Gray, John. *Men Are from Mars, Women Are from Venus*. Toronto: HarperCollins, 1992.

Greene, Richard, and Peter Vernezze, eds. *The Sopranos and Philosophy: I Kill Therefore I Am*. Chicago: Carus Publishing Company, 2004.

Hawthorne, Nathaniel. "The Minister's Black Veil." *Twice-Told Tales*. Boston: Houghton, Mifflin, 1900.

Heller, Dana. "Taking the Nation 'From Drab to Fab': Queer Eye for the Straight Guy." *Feminist Media Studies* 4, no. 3 (2004): 347–50.

Heller, Dana, ed. *The Great American Makeover: Television, History, Nation*. New York: Palgrave Macmillan, 2006.

Hegel, G.W.F. *The Phenomenology of the Mind*. Translated by J.B. Baillie. London: Harper and Row, 1967.

Hillman, James. *Healing Fiction*. New York: Station Hill Press, 1983.

Hollander, Anne. *Moving Pictures*. Cambridge, MA: Harvard University Press, 1991.

Hutcheon, Linda. *A Poetics of Postmodernisn: History, Theory, Fiction*. Cambridge: University Printing House, 1988.

Iser, Wolfgang. *The Implied Reader: Patterns of Communication in Prose Fiction from Bunyan to Beckett*. Baltimore: Johns Hopkins University Press, 1974.

Jung, Carl Gustav. *Man and His Symbols*. New York: Random House, 1968.

Jung, Carl Gustav. *Modern Man in Search of a Soul*. London: Routledge, 2005.

Jung, Carl Gustav. *The Undiscovered Self: The Problem of the Individual in Modern Society*. Princeton: Princeton University Press, 2006.

Katz, Jackson. *The Macho Paradox: Why Some Men Hunt Women and How All Men Can Help*. Chicago: Sourcebooks, 2006.

Krieger, Murray. *Ekphrasis: The Illusion of the Natural Sign*. Baltimore: Johns Hopkins University Press, 1992.
Lacan, Jacques. *The Language of the Self: The Function of Language in Psychoanalysis*. Translated by Anthony Wilden. New York: Dell Publishing, 1968.
Lakoff, Robin Tolmach. *Talking Power: The Politics of Language in Our Lives*. New York: Basic Books, 1990.
Laing, R.D. *The Divided Self*. New York: Pantheon, 1965.
Laing, R.D. *Self and Others*. New York: Pantheon, 1968.
Laing, R.D. *The Politics of the Family*. Toronto: Hunter Rose, 1969.
Leitch, Vincent B. *Deconstructive Criticism: An Advanced Introduction*. New York: Columbia University Press, 1983.
Lessing, G.E. *Laocoon: An Essay upon the Limits of Poetry and Painting*. Translated by Ellen Frothingham. New York: Farrar, Straus and Giroux, 1969.
Ludlum, Robert. *The Bourne Identity*. Westport, CT: Richard Marek, 1980.
Machiavelli, Nicolò. *The Prince*. Translated by Peter Bondanella. Oxford: Oxford University Press, 1998.
Mangione, Jerry, and Ben Morreale. *La Storia: Five Centuries of the Italian American Experience*. New York: Harper Perennial, 1993.
Manguel, Alberto. *Reading Pictures*. Toronto: Vintage, 2002.
McCarty, John. *Bullets over Hollywood: The American Gangster Picture from the Silents to The Sopranos*. Cambridge, MA: Da Capo Press, 2004.
McKay, Keith. *Robert De Niro: The Hero behind the Masks*. New York: St. Martin's Press, 1986.
Miller, Toby. *Television Studies: The Basics*. New York: Routeledge, 2010.
Mitchell, W.J.T. *Picture Theory*. Chicago: Chicago University Press, 1994.
Newman, Charles. *The Post-Modern Aura: The Act of Fiction in an Age of Inflation*. Evanston, IL: Northwestern University Press, 1985.
Nietzsche, Friedrich. *Beyond Good and Evil: Prelude to a Philosophy of the Future*. Translated by Helen Zimmern. Mineola, NY: Dover Publications, 1997.
Nietzsche, Friedrich. *Thus Spoke Zarathustra*. Translated by Thomas Common. Blacksbug, VA: Wilder Publications, 2009.
Ong, Walter J. *The Presence of the Word*. Minneapolis: MinnesotaUniversity Press, 1967.
Panella, Vincent. *The Other Side: Growing up Italian in America*. Garden City, NY: Doubleday, 1979.
Papaleo, Joseph. *All the Comforts*. New York: Little, Brown, 1967.
Pattie, David. "Mobbed Up: The Sopranos and the Modern Gangster Film." In David Lavery, ed., *This Thing of Ours: Investigating The Sopranos*, 125–45. New York: Columbia University Press, 2002.
Piles de, Roger. *The Principles of Painting*. Translated by a Painter in 1676 and Printed for J. Osborn, at the Golden Ball at Paternoster Row, 1743.

Plato. *The Republic*. Translated by R.E. Allen. New Haven: Yale Univrsity Press, 2006.
Plummer, David. *One of the Boys: Masculinity, Homophobia, and Modern Manhood*. New York: Haworth, 1999.
Postman, Neil. *The Disappearance of Childhood*. New York: Vintage Books, 1982.
Puzo, Mario. *The Fortunate Pilgrim*. New York: Lancer Books, 1964.
Puzo, Mario. *The Godfather*. 1969. Reprint, New York: New American Library, 2002.
Rank, Otto, Lord Raglan, and Dundes Alan. *In Quest of the Hero*. New Jersey: Princeton University Press, 1990.
Reich, Wilhelm. *The Mass Psychology of Fascism*. New York: Farrar, Straus, 1976.
Renga, Dana, ed. *Mafia Movies: A Reader*. Toronto: Toronto University Press, 2011.
Ricci, Franco. "Tu vu' fare l'italiano, ma sci nnate 'n America, Argentina, Canada." *VIA: Voices in Italian Americana* 13, no. 1 (2002): 36–44.
Sciascia, Leonardo. *The Day of the Owl*. New York: New York Review of Books, 1961.
Shlain, Leonard. *The Alphabet versus the Goddess: The Conflict between Word and Image*. New York: Penguin Group, 1998.
Shlain, Leonard. *Sex, Time and Power: How Women's Sexuality Shaped Human Evolution*. New York: Penguin Books, 2003.
Silver, Alain, and James Ursini, eds. *Gangster Film Reader*. New Jersey: Limelight Editions, 2007.
Silverman, Sydel F. "Agricultural Organization, Social Structure, and Values in Italy: Amoral Familism Reconsidered." *American Anthropologist* 70, no. 1 (2009): 1–20.
Sollors, Werner. "A Critique of Pure Pluralism." In Sacvan Bercovitch, ed., *Reconstructing American Literary History*, 250–79. Cambridge, MA: Harvard University Press, 1986.
Speranza, Gino. *Race or Nation: A Conflict of Divided Loyalties*. Indianapolis: Bobbs Merrill, 1923.
Steinberg, Leo. *The Sexuality of Christ in Renaissance Art and in Modern Oblivion*. New York: Pantheon, 1983.
Steinberg, Stephen. *The Ethnic Myth: Race, Ethnicity, and Class in America*. Boston: Beacon Press, 1981.
Summers, David. "Real Metaphor: Towards a Redefinition of the 'Conceptual' Image." In Norman Bryson, Michael Ann Holly, and Keith Moxey, eds., *Visual Theory: Painting and Interpretation*, 231–59. London: Polity Press, 1991.
Tillich, Paul. *The Courage to Be*. New Haven: Yale University Press, 1952.

von Hippel, Courtney, Cindy Wiryakusuma, Jessica Bowden, et al. "Stereotype Threat and Female Communication Styles." *Personality and Social Psychology Bulletin* 37 (2011): 1312–24.
Waisanen, John T. *Thinking Geometrically: Re-Visioning Space for a Multimodal World.* New York: Peter Lang, 2002.
Walsh, Clare. *Gender and Discourse: Language and Power in Politics, the Church and Organizations.* Toronto: Pearson Education, 2001.
Wilson, Bill. *The Search for Bill Wilson.* Minnesota: Hazelden, 2000.
Wister, Owen. *The Virginian: A Horseman of the Plains.* New York: Macmillan.
Wolf, Fred Alan. *Taking the Quantum Leap: The New Physics for Non-Scientists.* New York: Harper and Row, 1989.
Yaquinto, Marilyn. *Pump'em Full of Lead.* New York: Twayne, 1998.

Television Texts

Airey, Dawn. "RTS Huw Wheldon Memorial Lecture." Lecture presented at the Royal Television Society, London, UK, 2004.
Arnheim, Rudolph. *Film as Art.* London: Faber and Faber, 1969.
Buonanno, Milly. *The Age of Television: Experiences and Theories.* Bristol: Intellect, 2008.
Carey, John. *What Good Are the Arts?* London: Faber and Faber, 2005.
Carter, Bill. "A New Report Becomes a Weapon in Debate on Censoring TV Violence." *The New York Times,* 7 February 1996, C11, C16.
Diamant, Anita. "Media Violence." *Parents,* October (1994): 40–1.
Donahue, J. Christopher. "What's Right with Television." *America* 171, no. 10 (8 October 1994): 25.
Friedman, Wayne. "Full Frontal Television." *MediaPost's TVWatch* I (2009): 2.
Guttman, Monika. "A Kinder, Gentler Hollywood." *U.S. News & World Report,* 9 May 1994, 39–46.
Jancovich, Mark, and James Lyons, eds. *Quality Popular Television: Cult TV, the Industry and Fans.* London: BFI Publishing, 2003.
Marche, Stephen. "How Jersey Shore Transformed America." *Esquire,* 8 September 2011. Retrieved 22 April 2012 from http://www.esquire.com/features/thousand-words-on-culture/jersey-shore-stereotypes-0510
Martin, Brett. *Difficult Men: Behind The Scenes of a Creative Revolution: From The Sopranos and The Wire to Mad Men and Breaking Bad.* New York: The Penguin Press, 2013.
Miller, Toby. *Television Studies: The Basics.* New York: Routledge, 2010.
Mortimer, Jeffery. "How TV Violence Hits Kids." *Education Digest* (October 1994): 16–19.
Neifert, Marianne. "TV: How Much Is Too Much?" *McCall's Magazine* (June 1995): 52.

Ott, Brian L. *The Small Screen: How Television Equips Us to Live in the Information Age.* Boston: Blackwell Publishing, 2007.

Ott, Brian L. *It's Not TV: Watching TV in the Post-Television Era.* New York: Routledge, 2008.

Rich, Frank. "The Idiot Chip." *The New York Times,* 10 February 1996, 23.

Selznick, Barbara J. *Global Television: Co-producing Culture.* Philadelphia: Temple University Press, 2008.

Sepinwall, Alan. *The Revolution Was Televised: The Cops, Crooks, Slingers, and Slayers Who Changed TV Drama Forever.* New York: Simon and Schuster, 2012.

Seppa, Nathan. "TV Displays Violence without the Mess." *APA Monitor* (April 1996): 1–2.

Stempel, Tom. *Storytellers to the Nation: A History of American Television Writing.* New York: Continuum, 1992.

Thompson, Robert J. *Television's Second Golden Age: From Hill Street Blues to ER.* New York: Continuum, 1996.

Zoglin, Richard. "Chips Ahoy." *Time Magazine,* 19 February 1996, 58–61.

Soprano Texts

This listing does not include the myriad of newspaper and magazine articles that accompanied the series during its television tenure unless pertinent and compelling.

Barreca, Regina, ed. *A Sitdown with the Sopranos: Watching Italian American Culture on TV's Most Talked-About Series.* New York: Palgrave Macmillan, 2002.

Bishop, David. *Bright Lights, Baked Ziti: The Unofficial, Unauthorized Guide to The Sopranos.* London: Virgin Books, 2001.

Brownfield, Paul. "Call It Must-Buy TV: At the Home of *The Sopranos.*" *Los Angeles Times,* 25 February 2001, 8.

Buckley, William F. "The Sopranos Underside." *National Review* (April 2001): 58–9.

Chase, David. *The Sopranos: Selected Scripts for Three Seasons.* New York: Warner Books, 2002.

Chris, Seay. *The Gospel According to Tony Soprano.* New York: Punguin Putnam, 2002.

Errico, Marcus. "'Sopranos' Columbus Controversey." *E! Online,* 10 october 2002. Retrieved 14 August 2005 from http://ca.eonline.com/news/43997/sopranos-columbus-controversy

Gabbard, Glen O. *The Psychology of The Sopranos: Love, Death, Desire, and Betrayal in America's Favorite Gangster Family.* New York: Basic Books, 2002.

Gonzales, Louis. *Nothing Personal, It's Just Business: A Street Smart Guide for New Managers and CEO's*. Bloomington: Author House, 2006.
Greene, Richard, and Peter Vernezze, eds. *The Sopranos and Philosophy: I Kill Therefore I Am*. Chicago: Open Court, 2004.
Jaramillo, Deborah L. "The Family Racket: AOL Time Warner, HBO, The Sopranos, and the Construction of a Quality Brand." *Journal of Communication Inquiry* 26, no. 1 (2002): 59–75.
Johansson, David. "Homeward Bound: Those Sopranos Titles Come Heavy." In David Lavery, ed., *Reading The Sopranos*, 27–38. New York: I.B. Tauris, 2006.
Kocela, Christopher. "From Columbus to Gary Cooper: Mourning the Lost White Father in *The Sopranos*." In David Lavery, ed., *This Thing of Ours: Investigating The Sopranos*, 104–17. New York: Columbia University Press, 2002.
Lavery, David, ed. *This Thing of Ours: Investigating The Sopranos*. New York: Columbia University Press, 2002.
Lavery, David. "The Sopranos." In Glen Creber, ed., *50 Key Television Programmes*, 188–92. London: Arnold, 2004.
Lavery, David, ed. *Reading The Sopranos: Hit TV from HBO*. New York: I.B. Raurias, 2006.
Leverette, Marc, Brian L. Ott, and Cara Louise Buckley, eds. *It's Not TV: Watching HBO in the Post-Television Era*. New York: Routledge, 2008.
Martin, Brett. *The Sopranos: The Complete Book*. New York: Melcher Media, Time Inc. Home Entertainment, 2007.
Mattessi, Peter. "The Strong, Silent Type: Psychoanalysis in *The Sopranos*." *Metro Magazine* 138 (2003): 136–8.
New York Times on *The Sopranos*, The. New York: Ibooks, 2000.
Pearson, Roberta. "Cult Television as Digital Television's Cutting Edge." In James Bennett and Niki Strange, eds., *Television as Digital Media*, 105–31. Durham, NC: Duke University Press.
"Peter Bogdanovich Interviews David Chase." *The Sopranos: The Complete First Season*. DVD. NY: HBO-Time-Warner Prod., 2000.
Polan, Dana. *The Sopranos*. Durham, NC: Duke University Press, 2009.
Remnick, David. "Is This the End of Rico? With *The Sopranos* the Mob Genre Is on the Brink." *New Yorker*, 2 April 2001, 38–44.
Roman, Steven A., ed. *The New York Times on The Sopranos*. New York: Simon and Schuster, 2002.
Rotundo, Anthony E. "Wonderbread and Stugots: Italian American Manhood and *The Sopranos*." In Regina Barreca, ed., *A Sitdown with The Sopranos*, 47–74. New York: Palgrave McMilllan, 2002.
Rucker, Allen. *The Sopranos Family Cookbook: As Compiled by Artie Bucco*. New York: Warner, 2002.

Rucker, Allen. *The Sopranos: A Family History, Updated for the 4th Season*. New York: New American Library, 2003.

Rucker, Allen. *Entertaining with the Sopranos: As Compiled by Carmela Soprano*. New York: Warner Books, 2006.

Sepinwall, Alan. *Sopranos Rewind. The Star-Ledger*. Available at http://www.nj.com/starledger/

Simon, David. *Tony Soprano's America: The Criminal Side of the American Dream*. Boulder: Westview Press, 2002.

Strate, Lance. "No(rth Jersey) Sense of Place: The Cultural Geography (and Media Ecology) of *The Sopranos*." In David Lavery, ed., *This Thing of Ours: Investigating The Sopranos*, 178–94. New York: Columbia University Press, 2002.

Yacowar, Maurice. *The Sopranos on the Couch: Analyzing Television's Greatest Series*. New York: Continuum, 2002.

Episodes Index

"A Hit Is a Hit," 6, 64, 93, 106, 112, 184, 216, 217, 223, 289n23
"All Due Respect," 74, 75, 76, 172, 177, 204, 250
"All Happy Families," 70, 216, 245, 246
"Amour Fou," 47, 49, 137, 162, 164, 240, 258, 259
"Another Toothpick," 218, 238
"Army of One, The," 30, 59, 100, 210, 215

"Big Girls Don't Cry," 44, 45, 120, 147, 149, 214, 256, 257
"Blue Comet, The," 20, 71, 87, 177, 189, 190, 192, 212, 223, 255
"Boca," 130, 151, 153, 168, 204, 221, 236
"Bust Out," 59, 99, 173, 225, 233, 237

"Calling All Cars," 7, 77, 165, 189, 216
"Chasing It," 140
"Christopher," 7, 110, 111, 113, 226, 241, 258
"Cold Stones," 90, 106, 157, 168, 217, 222, 253, 258, 259

"College," 41, 96, 99, 169, 230, 256, 272n19, 282n34
"Commendatori," 89, 106, 165, 214, 218

"D-Girl," 15, 141, 149, 221, 288n17
"Denial, Anger, Acceptance," 39, 173
"Do Not Resuscitate," 36
"Down Neck," 44, 45, 69, 79, 126

"Eloise," 218, 227, 231, 243
"Employee of the Month," 47, 116, 184
"Everybody Hurts," 50, 64, 142, 168, 173, 204, 242

"Fleshy Part of the Thigh," 144, 145, 177, 207, 228, 251, 252
"For All Debts Public and Private," 35, 118, 127, 210, 221, 240, 241
"Fortunate Son," 46, 126, 127, 128, 159, 221, 238
"46 Long," 79, 96, 107, 168, 209, 224
"From Where to Eternity," 41, 54, 90, 160, 230, 233, 257

"Full Leather Jacket," 45, 95
"Funhouse," 41, 70, 143, 158, 175, 237

"Guy Walks into a Psychiatrist's Office," 32, 40, 214, 217, 218

"Happy Wanderer, The," 44, 61, 214
"House Arrest," 26, 207, 213, 215, 221, 225

"I Dream of Jeannie Cusamano," 41, 62, 236, 250
"In Camelot," 26, 34, 72, 132, 208, 210, 222, 258
"Isabella," 8, 30, 69, 79, 88, 141, 208, 210, 236, 250, 283n27

"Johnny Cakes," 90, 139, 157, 208, 228, 253
"Join the Club," 8, 80, 90, 207

"Kaisha," 140, 208, 216, 219, 233, 253, 255
"Kennedy and Heidi," 41, 150, 158, 168, 187, 214, 217, 255
"Knight in White Satin Armor," 88, 226, 231, 233, 237, 282n19

"Legend of Tennessee Moltisanti," 77, 96, 103, 105, 107, 146, 149, 213, 220, 280n3
"Live Free or Die," 8, 101, 147, 281n13, 287n11
"Long Term Parking," 40, 41, 248
"Luxury Lounge," 191, 222, 223, 228

"Made in America," 7, 63, 104, 142, 143, 212, 214, 220, 255, 256
"Marco Polo," 93, 205, 246

"Mayham," 8, 158, 207, 219, 271n13
"Meadowlands," 22, 37, 39, 139, 204, 210, 274n32
"Members Only," 35, 79, 211, 250
"Mergers and Acquisitions," 222, 231, 242
"Moe n' Joe," 208, 216
"Mr. and Mrs. John Sacrimoni Request," 8, 151, 219, 222
"Mr. Ruggierio's Neighborhood," 40, 61

"No-Show," 216, 226, 229, 241
"Nobody Knows Anything," 58, 90, 164, 225

"Pax Soprana," 121, 175, 224
"Pie-O-My," 29, 30, 36, 71, 72–4, 204, 242
"Pine Barrens," 41, 47, 207, 215, 257, 270n2
"Proshai, Livushka," 9, 45, 54, 172, 204, 210, 215, 218, 221, 226, 238

"Ride, The," 63, 106, 144, 164, 257

"Second Coming, The," 141, 191, 229, 255
"Second Opinion," 32, 49, 51, 180, 221, 226, 231
"Sentimental Education," 232
"Soprano Home Movies," 172, 254
"Sopranos, The," 35, 58, 62, 90, 135, 153, 183, 186
"Stage 5," 7, 211, 228, 229
"Strong Silent Type, The," 73, 176, 243

"Telltale Moozadell," 218, 239, 240
"Test Dream, The," 39, 68, 135, 179, 227, 247

"Toodle-Fucking-oo," 7, 96
"To Save Us All from Satan's
  Power," 240
"Two Tonys," 73, 128

"Unidentified Black
  Males," 101, 154
"University," 71, 151, 238, 239

"Walk Like a Man," 133, 138, 207,
  232, 254, 282n29, 283n26
"Watching Too Much Television,"
  216, 242
"Where's Johnny?" 128, 244, 245,
  285n38
"Whitecaps," 29, 40, 51, 100, 243
"Whoever Did This," 36, 208, 239, 243

Name Index

Adam, 52, 218, 240, 286n40
al-Qaeda, 256
Annunziata, Perry, 8, 281n13
Alcinder, Lew (Kareem Abdul-Jabbar), 221
Alighieri, Dante, 230
Adams, Kay, 139, 283n25
Aprile, Jackie, 38, 103,
Aprile, Jackie Jr., 100, 103, 210, 215, 218, 240
Aprile, Kelly, 100
Aprile, Richie, 36, 86, 103, 233, 237
Aprile, Rosalie, 30, 90, 212
Aristotle, 13, 270n4
Astaire, Fred, 65
Augustine of Hippo, Saint, 123

Bacal, Lauren, 222
Baccilieri, Bobby "Baccalà" Jr., 111, 156, 212, 216, 218, 238, 246, 253, 255
Bada Bing, 19, 23, 25, 29, 35, 53, 60–4, 69–71, 76, 144, 153, 168, 180, 205, 210, 238, 257, 259, 291n31
Balboa, Rocky, 142, 163, 284n29
Bandello, Rico, 163, 238
Barbarino, Vinnie, 132, 163

Barnes, Fred, 230, 232
Barthes, Roland, 3, 295
Bartoli, Celia, 47
Batali, Mario, 242
Beach Boys, The, 78
Beatles, The, 77
Benjamin, Walter, 28, 271n6
Bertolucci, Bernardo, 9
Bevilaqua, Matthew, 41, 225, 237
Blake, William, 22
Blanca, Selgado, 139–40, 207, 253, 254
Bloom, Allan, 5, 267n1
Bloom, Jill, 229
Bloomberg, Michael, 268n10
Blundetto, Anthony "Tony B", 73–5, 152, 175, 243, 246, 249
Bocelli, Andrea, 106
Bogart, Humphrey, 65
Bonanno, Joseph, 110
Bonasera, Amerigo, 93
Bonpensiero, Salvatore "Big Pussy," 9, 41, 70, 103, 147, 156, 175, 210, 213, 217, 218, 221, 224, 225, 237, 240, 256, 282n19
Bourne, Jason, 167
Boyles, T.C., 224

Bradley, Marion Zimmer, 229, 231
Brown, Dan, 229
Bucco, Artie, 26, 50, 92, 105, 106, 153, 168, 173, 174, 191, 203, 223, 228, 244, 292n31
Bucco, Charmaine, 92, 153
Bunker, Archie, 117, 185, 279n32
Buonarotti, Michelangelo, 103, 109
Burroughs, Edgar Rice, 224
Bush, George W., 232

Cabot, John, 110
Cabrini, St. Frances Xavier, 110
Cagney, James, 16, 58, 65, 269n13, 273n24
Camonte, Tony, 160, 163
Capra, Frank, 18
Carradine, David, 251
Carroll, Noel, 171, 268n12, 288n14
Carrucci, Jacopo "Pontormo," 55, 272n22
Caruso, Enrico, 249
Castaneda, Carlos, 214, 224
Cavett, Dick, 255
Centanni Meat Market, 23, 64
Cestone, Gigi, 151
Chamberlain, Wilt "The Stilt," 221
Charlie (of *Mean Streets*), 132
Chase, David, x, 4, 8–14, 20–21, 23–8, 39, 46, 52–3, 57, 64, 75, 78, 80, 84–7, 94–7, 107–14, 117–18, 137, 140, 144, 146–7, 164–5, 175–6, 181, 193–7, 200–1, 212, 222, 223, 224, 225, 227, 234–5, 258, 262–5, 268n4, 268n6, 268n7, 268n8, 268n9, 269n15, 270n2, 272n16, 273n24, 275n3, 276n11, 277n14, 279n31, 285n39, 289n19, 290n27, 290n31
Churchill, Winston, 242
Ciccerone Waldrup, Deborah, 87

Cifaretto, Ralph, 29, 30, 36, 63, 71, 73–4, 103, 151, 176, 208, 238, 239, 240, 242, 243
Clark, Higgins, 226
Coleman, Ronald, 237
Colson, Charles, 228
Columbus, Christopher, 7, 110–15, 118, 226, 241, 258, 268n10, 279n28
Cooper, Gary, 16, 90, 114–15, 150, 173, 279n28
Confucius, 120
Coppola, Francis Ford, 18, 25, 239, 269n15
Corleone, Don Vito, 86, 120, 133, 164, 269n13, 271n14, 274n31, 277n18
Corleone, Michael, 76, 97, 127, 133, 136, 169, 227, 247, 281n11, 283n25, 287n12
Corneau, Guy, 128–9, 281n14
Corzine, Jon, 222
Costello, Lou, 256–7, 259
Crowe, Russell, 238
Cubitoso, Frank, 87–8, 210, 291n31
Cuomo, Mario, 81, 99
Cusamano, Dr. Bruce, 92–3, 96, 105–6, 184, 216
Cusamano, Joan, 53, 95

Dante, Silvio, 7, 56, 71, 76, 111, 113–18, 143, 172, 176, 196, 208, 212, 223, 226, 229, 236, 258, 290n23
Da Rimini, Francesca, 230
Da Verrucchio, Paolo, 230
Da Vinci, Leonardo, 211, 239
David, Larry, 244
Davis, Sammy Jr., 65, 204
De Crèvecoeur, J. Hector St. John, 263, 293n5
De Niro, Robert, 96
De Piles, Roger, 22, 201

Name Index 311

De Rivera, Giuseppe, 48, 259
Detrolio, Finn, 101–3, 105, 155, 245
Devon, 26, 203, 204
Dickens, Charles, 17
Dickinson, Angie, 221
Diddley, Bo, 64
DiMeo crime syndicate, 165
Dostoyevsky, Fyodor, 226
Douglas, Kirk, 238

Eliot, George, 17
Eve, 122

Fegoli, Russ, 93–5
Feldman, Warren, 228
Fellini, Federico, 13, 18, 246
Felstein, Fran, 34, 72, 208
Fields, W.C., 65, 240, 248
Finnerty, Albert, 80, 143, 173, 277n14
Flammer, Rhiannon, 141–2, 214, 283n28
Flaubert, Gustave, 230, 232
Flintstone, Fred, 60
Frankenstein, 38, 39, 247
Frazier, Charles, 232
Freud, Sigmund, 19, 175, 274n30
Fried, Dr. Ira, 240
Frost, Robert, 215

Gadarphé, Fred, 142, 280n8, 284n30
Gaeta, Peter "Beansie," 36, 44, 45, 211, 237, 257
Gambino, Carlo, 110
Gambino, Richard, 107, 276n8, 278n26
Gamiello, Dominic "Fat Dom," 219
Garepe, Angelo, 74
Geary, Pat, 71
Gervasi, Carlo, 219
Genco Oil, 64

Giacomelli, Geminiano, 48, 257
Giannini, Amadeo, 110
Gigli, Begniamino, 65
Girls Against Boys, 206
Giuliani, Rudolph, 81
Giunta, Furio, 106, 112–13, 218, 231, 240, 242, 243, 257, 270
Gleason, Jackie, 245
Goddard, Jean-Luc, 13
Golding, William, 232
Gombrich, E.H., 196
Golden, Arthur, 229, 233
Graham, Robert, 43
Graham Bell, Alexander, 109
Grafton, Sue, 230, 233
Grasso, Frank, 87, 96, 109
Gualtieri, Donatucci "Dottie," 144–5, 252
Gualtieri, Marianucci "Nucci," 144–6, 252
Gualtieri, Paulie "Walnuts," 6, 41, 56, 63, 74–5, 87, 96, 106–7, 118, 144–5, 151, 176, 207, 211, 212, 213, 218, 223, 225, 237, 240, 251, 252, 256, 257, 284n31
Gurian, Michael, 229

Hagen, Tom, 71, 287n12
Harpo, 247
Harris, Dwight, 7, 26, 30, 86, 213, 250, 256
Hauser, Coach Don, 153, 221
Hawthorne, Nathaniel, 169, 171, 175, 189, 224, 230, 288n15
Hepburn, Katherine, 255
Hitler, 15, 113
Hockney, David, 38
Holbrook, Hal, 145
Holm, Celeste, 237

Holsten's Diner, 67, 189, 194, 290n25, 290n27
Hopkins, Anthony, 230

Imperioli, Michael, 147, 196
Intintola, Father Phil, 62, 96, 105, 111, 230, 272n19, 291n31
Ishiguro, Kazuo, 230

Jackson, Andrew, 70
Jackson, Jesse, 81
Jesus Christ, 62, 100, 109, 117, 137, 219, 240, 257–9, 272n22
John XXIII, Pope, 53
Jung, Carl Gustav, 27, 122, 280n5

Kane, Marshall Will, 16
Kahlo, Frida, 245
Kakuk, Bela, 246
Kennedy, John F., 53
King Arthur, 128–9, 131, 230, 231
Kingsolver, Barbara, 231
Kinks, The, 160, 247, 286n1
Kirilenko, Svetlana, 29
Klee, Paul, 38
Klimt, Gustav, 32
Kolar, Emil, 64–5, 147, 280n3
Kubrick, Stanley, 13

Lacan, Jacques, 68
La Cerva, Adriana, 41, 70–1, 130, 146, 148, 149–50, 152, 216, 217, 241, 242, 246, 248–9, 255, 290n25
La Manna, Michele "Feech," 176, 246
La Paz, Valentina, 26, 29, 73, 208, 222, 231, 248
La Penna, Jason, 107–8, 117
La Penna, Richard, 96–7, 106, 108, 116–17, 241
Lallo-Murphy, Professor, 110–14

Lanza, Mario, 249
Laural and Hardy, 65
Lector, Hannibal, 185
Lee, Spike, 64
Leotardo, Phil, 7, 75, 151, 157, 171, 189, 211, 223, 229, 252, 253, 256, 258, 259
Lipari, Skip, 218, 221, 282n19
Loeb, Lisa, 206
Lofgren, Nils, 51
Lucania, Salvatore (Charlie Lucky Luciano), 10
Lucchese, Gaetano, 110
Ludlum, Robert, 167, 287n8
Lund, Ilsa, 254
Lupertazzi, Carmine, 35, 63, 103, 127, 203, 211, 227, 241, 243
Lupertazzi, Carmine "Little" Jr., 74, 203, 205, 246
Lynch, David, 67

Machiavelli, Nicolò, 48, 162, 178, 224, 272n17, 286n2
Malanga, Gennaro "Little Pussy," 35, 251
Malloy, Terry, 80
Manero, Tony, 132, 163
Mangione, Jerry, 104, 278n21, 278n22, 278n24
Mann, Thomas, 227
Mansfield, Jane, 238
Marche, Stephen, 83, 275n7
Marquez, Joe, 213
Martin, Brett, 21, 196, 268n9, 269n15, 276n11, 276n12, 290n29, 292n1, 293n3
Martin, Dean, 65, 204, 240
Mass, Peter, 227
Massive Genius, 112–13, 289n23

Name Index 313

McCluskey, Sargeant Mark, 247, 287n12
McCourt, Frank, 225
Medusa, 35–6, 122, 153, 180, 186, 271n9, 289n22
Melfi, Dr. Jennifer, 6, 8, 15, 19, 23, 32–3, 35, 37–9, 41–52, 56, 59, 61–2, 67, 70–1, 75–6, 78–80, 90, 93, 96, 105–9, 116–18, 126–8, 132, 138, 143–4, 153, 164, 168, 170, 172–7, 180–8, 190–4, 203, 204, 209, 214, 215, 216, 217, 224, 225, 235, 241, 244, 253, 256, 257, 258, 270n2, 279n27, 280n35, 282n20, 292n31
Melville, Herman, 227
Meucci, Antonio, 109
Migliaccio, Eduardo, 77
Miller, Arthur, 224
Miller, Toby, 262, 293n4
Millio, Rusty, 74
Molinaro, Coach, 135, 188, 247
Moltisanti, Christopher, 6, 9, 26, 27, 35, 39, 41, 48, 50, 63–5, 70–1, 106, 113, 118, 144, 146–53, 160–3, 186, 191, 199, 207, 208, 210, 212, 213, 214, 215, 217, 219, 220, 222, 227, 229, 240, 241, 242, 243, 246, 248, 249, 250, 254, 255, 257, 258, 280n3, 283n26
Monroe, Marilyn, 29, 65
Moonspell, 206
Musto, Vic, 231, 233

Natanuf, 206
Newman, Charles, 167, 287n10
Nozick, Robert, 225

Obama, Barack, 81

Palmice, Mikey, 39, 40
Pandora, 122

Parisi, Pasquale "Patsy," 40, 61, 90, 217
Parisi, Phillip "Philly Spoons," 61
Peltsin, Irina, 29, 38, 225, 226
Peparelli, Joe "Peeps," 74
Percival, 128–31, 144
Pesci, Joe, 9, 147
Petrullio, Fabian "Febby," 41, 170, 256
Picasso, Pablo, 26, 203, 204, 207
Pie-O-My, 29, 30, 36, 71–4, 204, 242
Piletti, Marty, 132, 163, 274n1
Polanski, Roman, 13, 18
Pontecorvo, Gene, 211, 218
Postman, Neil, 58, 273n25
Powers, Tom, 165, 238
Profaci, Giueppe, 110

Rabkin, Hesh, 64, 112–3, 132, 289
Reginal G., 145
Rickles, Don, 65
Rivera, Geraldo, 229
Robinson, Edward G., 65
Rogers, Ginger, 65
Romano, Ray, 163, 241
Rommel, General Erwin, 75–6, 177
Rotundo, E. Anthony, 92, 277n15, 278n20
Rubble, Barney, 60

Sacco, Nicola, 110
Sacrimoni, Johnny "Sack," 75, 102, 151, 159, 211, 219, 228, 239, 242, 243, 250, 252, 253
Salierno Mason, Alane, 160
Safier, Manny, 229
Samenov, Stanton E., 191–2
Sanseverino, Robyn, 87
Satriale, Francis, 126, 127

Name Index

Satriale's Pork Store, 7, 23, 26, 53, 60, 63, 64, 87, 93, 111–12, 147, 196, 205, 211, 212, 213, 217, 219, 291
Savalas, Telly, 65
Scatino, Dave, 105, 106, 173–4
Scorsese, Martin, 9, 18, 25, 147, 269n15
Sepinwall, Alan, 261, 268n4, 268n5, 268n8, 270n2, 277n14, 285n39, 289n19, 290n26, 293n2
Serling, Rod, 20
Sharpton, Al, 81
Sheehy, Gail, 226
Schroedinger, Erwin, 145, 252, 284n31
Signori, Chucky, 41, 217
Sinatra, Frank, 25, 61, 65, 110, 204, 238, 270n3
Sollozzo, Virgil "The Turk," 247, 287n12
Soprano, Anthony Junior (A.J.), 31, 58–60, 99, 103, 109–10, 118, 131, 132–44, 149, 151, 168, 188, 191, 192, 203, 204, 206, 207, 208, 210, 214, 215, 217, 220, 221, 226, 227, 232, 233, 242, 243, 245, 246, 251, 253, 254, 255, 257, 282n20, 282n23, 283n23, 283n28, 288n17
Soprano, Barbara, 98, 185
Soprano, Carmela, 6, 29–30, 32, 39–40, 48–52, 52–4, 57–8, 68, 70–1, 90, 93–6, 99, 105–6, 109–10, 118, 127, 130, 135, 142–3, 154, 163, 172, 175, 177, 179–80, 188, 194, 196, 207, 212, 214, 215, 216, 217, 218, 219, 221, 222, 225, 226, 227, 228, 229–34, 236, 237, 239, 240, 241, 242, 243, 245, 246, 247, 248, 253, 255, 256, 258, 259, 270, 272

Soprano, Corrado "Uncle Junior," 6, 9, 30, 31, 35, 39, 70, 80, 88, 101, 134, 135, 151, 152–4, 169, 176, 207, 211, 212, 215, 221, 222, 236, 238, 239, 242, 244, 245, 246, 250, 251, 252, 253, 281n12, 285n38, 285n39
Soprano, Giovanni Francis "Johnny Boy," 43, 44, 126, 221
Soprano, Janice, 6, 7, 32, 40, 98, 171–2, 185, 214, 216, 233–4, 237, 238, 244, 246, 247, 256, 286
Soprano, Livia, 6, 30–2, 34, 40, 46, 53, 78, 79–80, 86, 88, 98, 126, 133, 163, 172, 204, 208, 210, 214, 215, 226, 236, 238, 250, 275, 281, 288, 291
Soprano, Meadow Mariangela, 31, 39, 48, 53, 58–9, 62, 67, 71, 87, 95-96, 99–105, 110, 130, 155, 170–1, 179, 188, 194, 206, 207, 208, 214, 215, 216, 218, 219, 222, 226, 227, 231, 236, 239, 240, 241, 245, 259, 271
Soprano, Tony, x, 6, 7, 11, 14, 18, 20, 21, 22, 31–3, 43, 55–7, 60, 62, 66, 77–8, 82, 92, 96, 101, 106, 125–6, 130, 132, 136, 138, 142, 148–50, 153, 160, 163–4, 166–8, 179–80, 190–1, 193, 194, 199, 210, 213, 215, 218, 231, 234, 257, 268n12, 269n13, 276n12, 281n11, 282n19, 291n31
Spatafore, Vito, 61, 102, 140, 147, 154–8, 188, 208, 219, 222, 228, 253, 258–9, 282n13
Spatafore, Vito Jr., 140
Springsteen, Bruce, 260
Steely Dan, 87
Steinberg, Leo, 67, 273n27, 278n19
Stendhal, 226
Strasser, Heinrik, 254
Stooges, The Three, 65

Stuck Mojo, 206
Sugarcult, 207

Tannenbaum, Noah, 218, 239
Temptations, The, 237
Tiamat, 122
Tippy, 72, 208
Tracey, Spencer, 238
Trillo, Gloria, 29–30, 48–51, 70, 73, 105, 163, 168, 218, 239, 240, 257–8
Trollope, Anthony, 17
Tzu, Sun, 49, 178, 224, 226

Under Armor Boyz, 207

Valacci, Joe, 227
Valli, Frankie (and The Four Seasons), 115, 120

Vanzetti, Bartolomeo, 110
Virgin Mary, 55, 63, 144, 215, 257, 267, 272n22
Veblen, Thorstein, 231

Waisanen, J.T., 166, 287n6
Watson, Emma, 230
Wayne, John, 65
Wegler, Robert, 232, 233
Wegman, William, 26, 208
Williams, Montel, 241
Wills, Charles, 243
Wilson, Bill, 227

Yockelson, Samuel, 191–2

Zucca, Annalisa, 106

Subject Index

anima, 32, 122–3, 126, 182,
animus, 99, 122–3, 126

cowboy, 15–16, 71, 86, 147, 149

ethnicity, 5, 7–8, 19, 23, 65, 77–8, 80, 97, 110, 113, 119, 124, 132, 155, 198, 275n6; and culture, 14, 17, 53–4, 61, 97–8, 107, 119; and identity, 80–8, 94–6, 105, 116–18, 146, 157, 184, 241, 258, 269n13; post-, 19, 65, 89–90, 91–3, 103, 113–15, 118, 225, 262–3; and stereotypes, 11, 53, 82–4, 105–6, 111, 160, 163, 181, 194, 205, 213, 262

eye, 65–76, 79; active, 36, 181, 185, 200, 210, 232, 247, 291n31; inner, 75, 126, 169, 174–5; gaze of, 36, 55; monocular, 71, 235; *trompe l'oile*, 205

eye-candy, 29

eyewitness, 75, 220

gangster, 6, 11, 17, 42, 49, 52, 90–3, 107, 137, 158, 186, 220, 262, 267n2, 269n13, 287n3, 287n12; Black, 112; film, 9, 14, 86, 146, 149;

gangsterism, 61, 69, 89, 124, 135, 150, 156; I-Am, 84, 96

HBO, 3–4, 10–11, 21, 196, 261–3, 273n24

heraldic crest, 56–9, 74, 133, 164, 254

homosexuality, 61, 140, 147, 156, 188, 222

identity: divided, 102, 212; ethnic, 80, 84, 105, 117–18, 146, 278n26; feminine, 7; group, 91; I-Am, 5; masculine, 34, 125–7, 128, 138, 154; Mafia, 11, 152; public, 4, 6–7, 19, 26, 66, 73, 82–3, 89, 91, 132, 136, 146, 151, 165, 172; self, 19–20, 37, 103, 114, 124, 127–9, 154, 184, 191; unstable, 7–8, 74, 80, 81, 84–5, 90, 107, 140, 144, 155–7, 166, 244, 254

images, 25, 28, 50, 56, 123, 141, 200; art, 22, 50; and word, 28, 185, 200–2, 234–5, 260; composite, 198; death, 230; fear of, 153; glass, 62; graphic, 25–6, 59, 60, 61, 63, 66, 143, 150, 190–4, 224; media, 253;

memory, 47, 72; of legs, 35; of Tony, 38; painted, 41–2, 57, 70, 76, 205, 218; photo, 53; public, 65, 76, 152; screen, 5, 24, 59, 254; stereotypical, 80, 83, 90, 164, 183; subliminal, 182; video, 53
imagos, 193, 260
irony, 18, 20, 65, 104, 111, 114, 118, 127, 166, 218, 245, 253, 255
Italian-American (I-Am), 4, 7–8, 10, 25, 26, 43, 61, 64, 87, 89–90, 92–3, 105–19, 125, 132, 139, 184, 187, 198, 203, 227, 276n8; myths, 106–7, 278n26; stereotypes, 5–6, 14, 53, 80–5, 95–7, 107–12, 115–19, 163–65, 287n5; writers, 278n21

legs, 29, 33–9, 44–5, 51, 63, 138, 181, 239; of statues, 33, 35, 44, 138
logos, 14, 193, 260

Mafia, 4, 11, 44, 65, 84, 97, 99, 104, 106, 107, 108, 110, 121, 136, 137, 173, 178, 184, 211, 212, 243, 277n19, 282n19; code, 146, 150, 182–3; initiation, 124; movies, 138
masculinity, 34, 126, 128–30; code, 128, 144, 151, 158; constructing, 154; hyper, 148; mob, 28; public, 126, 129, 157, 273n23; wounded, 52, 125, 134–6, 158
memory, 18, 40, 42, 46, 63, 66, 71–2, 80, 127, 136, 161, 167, 180, 191, 205, 209, 211, 226, 228, 240, 244, 245, 251, 291n31

mirrors, 9, 11, 29, 35, 46, 47, 50–1, 66, 69, 73–5, 78–9, 126, 157, 171, 173, 274n29, 292n31

Native Americans, 7, 110, 258

omertà, 6, 55–6, 129–30, 151, 182–3, 207, 221, 256
open-ended, 18, 24–5, 198, 202, 203
Other, 4, 8, 72, 85, 91, 153, 179; controlling, 98; ethnic, 105; false, 84, 104, 166; feminine, 122; Lacanian, 68–9; self-effacing, 36, 50

Rat Pack, 204, 244,
rites of passage, 55, 124, 134, 260; for A.J., 134–40; for Christopher, 39, 215; for Michael Corleone, 127; for Paulie, 257; for Tony, 79, 130, 228; for Vito, 157
ritual, 17, 20, 55–6, 91, 124–5, 177, 179, 183, 193, 283n23; and initiation, 131, 138–42

self: divided, 20, 36, 74, 80, 130, 165, 168, 170–7; ethnic, 85, 89, 111; false, 34, 47, 49, 80, 148, 151, 191; feminine, 56; inner, 27, 33, 42, 66, 76, 102; loss of, 282n19; masculine, 129, 154; objectified, 69
self-affirmation, 44, 50, 99, 114, 117, 125, 134, 140, 152, 155, 157–8, 177, 241, 258
self-consciousness, 14, 14, 20, 26, 33, 81, 200, 235
self-destruction, 255
self-effacement, 36, 72, 79, 83, 93, 95, 98, 117, 128, 131, 140, 144, 146–7, 149, 163, 194, 207, 253, 263, 279n31

selfhood, 6–8, 20, 66, 85, 122, 124–5, 133, 149, 155, 164–5, 167, 191, 258, 278n22

self-identity, 19, 32, 35, 41, 68, 69, 71, 73–6, 103–4, 163, 184–5, 212

self-knowledge, 62, 79, 150, 188, 209, 223, 289n21

self-sacrifice, 156

statues, 19, 23, 25, 30, 32–8, 42–52, 76, 138, 162, 170, 180–2, 188, 233, 256; green statue, 32–4, 42–3, 47, 52, 138, 182, 188, 256–9, 289n21, 290n25

virago, 34–5, 38, 47, 138, 170, 180, 182, 258

water, 39–41, 115, 141, 214, 247, 281n9

words, active, 121; and feminine, 121; and images, 19, 29, 188, 200–2, 213, 260; written, 149, 190–3, 200, 212, 215

Title Index

AB Attack (fitness magazine), 228
Abelard and Heloise (collection of twelfth-century love letters), 230, 232
A Christmas Carol (1938 film), 247
America's Most Wanted (1988–2011 television series), 82
Anarchy, State, and Utopia (1974 novel by Robert Nozick), 225
Annapolis (2006 film), 255
Art of War (sixth-century text by Sun Tzu), 48, 178, 224, 226,
Audubon Society Encyclopedia of North American Birds, The (1995 by John Terres), 224

Battlestar Galatica (2004– television series), 262
Bible, 230, 240
Bob Villa Home Improvement Shows (1979–89, 1990–2005, 2005–7 television series), 244
Born Again (1976 novel by Charles Colson), 228
"Big Girls Don't Cry" (1962 song by The Four Seasons), 120
Big Picture: Rethinking Dyslexia, The (2012 documentary), 262

Billy Bud (1888–1924 novella by Herman Melville), 227
Bitchin' Kitchen (2010– television cooking series), 83
Boardwalk Empire (2010– television series), 262
Boring Life of Jacqueline, The (2012 television series)
Breaking Bad (2008–13 television series), 262

C Is for Corpse (1986 mystery novel by Sue Grafton), 230, 233
Casablanca (1942 film), 253
Champagne for Caesar (1950 film), 237
Chicken Soup for the Soul (1993 book series), 225
Chinatown (1974 film), 247
Cleaver (fictional film by Christopher Moltisanti), 146, 148, 229
COPS (1989 television series), 82
Crime and Punishment (1866 novel by Fyodor Dostoyevsky), 226
CSI (2000– television series), 82
Cul-de-Sac (1996 film), 13
Curb Your Enthusiasm (1999– television series), 83, 244

"Dawn (Go Away)" (1963 song by The Four Seasons), 115
Dead Presidents (1995 film), 147
Deadwood (2004–6 television series), 262
Death in Venice (1912 novella by Thomas Mann), 227
Death of a Salesman (1949 play by Arthur Miller), 224
Dementia 13 (1963 film), 239
Devil at Four O'Clock (1961 film), 238
Dick Cavett Show, The (1968–75 television talk show), 255
"Dirty Work" (1972 song by Steely Dan), 87
Divine Comedy, The (1308–21 poem by Dante Alighieri), 230
Do the Right Thing (1989 film), 64
"Don't Stop Believin'" (1981 song by Journey), 189
Dr. Strangelove (1964 film), 26, 208
Dragnet (1951–9 television series), 82

Enlightened (2011– television series), 262
Entourage (2004–11 television series), 83
Everybody Loves Raymond (1996–2005 television series), 82, 163, 241

Fit for Life (1985 self-help book by H. Diamond), 225
Frankenstein (1931 film), 39, 247
Frida (2002 film), 245
Friday Night Lights (2006– television series), 262

Girls (2012– television series), 262
Girls Against Boys (female hard-core band), 206

Gladiator (2000 film), 238
Godfather, The (1972 film), 9, 11, 39, 64, 71, 86, 93, 108, 112, 114, 120, 133, 136, 138, 139, 147, 160, 163, 164, 165, 210, 214, 227, 247, 256, 271n12, 271n14, 274n31, 277n18, 279n26, 283n25, 288n12
Godfather Part II, The (1974 film), 71, 76, 95, 97, 277n18
Goodfellas (1990 film), 9, 108, 147, 164
Grandma Memory Book, The (Livia Soprano's diary), 226
Great Caruso, The (1951 film), 248
Growing Up Gotti (2004–5 television series), 83

Harvey Birdman (2001–7 cartoon series), 60
Healthy Living (self-help medical magazine), 224
Help Me Help My Child (1991 self-help book by Jill Bloom), 229
High Noon (1952 film), 9, 16, 247
History Channel, The (television channel), 9, 75, 175, 176, 235, 236, 237, 242, 253, 255
Honeymooners, The (1955–6), 245
How to Clean Practically Anything (1994 Consumer Reports paperback), 229
How to Marry a Millionaire (1953 film), 243

I'll Fly Away (1991–3 television series), 12
"I'm Not Like Everybody Else" (1966 song by The Kinks), 160, 247, 286n1
Imitation of Life (1959 film), 253
It's a Gift (1934 film), 239, 248
It's a Wonderful Life (1946 film), 240

Title Index

"I've Gotta Be Me" (1968 song by Sammy Davis Jr.), 189

Jersey Couture (2010–12 television series), 83
Jersey Shore (2009–12 television series), 83
Jerseylicious (2010– television series), 83

Kolchak: The Night Stalker (1974–5 television series), 12
Kung Fu (1972–5 television series), 251

La Dolce Vita (1960 film), 246
Last Tango in Paris (1972 film), 9
Last Time I Saw Paris, The (1954 film), 243
Latino List, The (2012 documentary), 262
Le Rouge et le Noir (1830 novel by Stendhal), 226
Little Caesar (1931 film), 163
Little Rascals, The (1922–4 television series and movie), 243
Lord of the Flies (1954 novel by William Golding), 232
Lost (2004–10 television series), 262

Madame Bovary (1856 novel by Gustave Flaubert), 230, 232
Mad Men (2007– television series), 262
Magnum P.I. (1980–8 television series), 241
Mario Eats Italy (2001–3 cooking series), 242
Marty (1955 film), 132, 163, 274n1

Mea Maxima Culpa: Silence in the House of God (2012 documentary), 262
Mean Streets (1973 film), 132, 272n16
Memoirs of a Geisha (1997 novel by Arthur Golden), 229, 233
Mists of Avalon, The (1983 novel by Marion Zimmer Bradley), 229, 231
Montel Williams Show, The (1991–2008 television show), 241
Mystical Marriage of St. Catherine, The (1503 painting), 48, 259

Natanuf (female pop-rap duo), 206
Northern Exposure (1990–5 television series), 12
Not Fade Away (2012 film), 21

On the Waterfront (1954 film), 80
Oz (1997–2002 television series), 262

Passages: Predictable Crises of Adult Life (1984 self-help book by Gail Sheehy), 226
Paths of Glory (1957 film), 250
People's History of the United States, A (1980 book by Howard Zinn), 226
Prince of Tides, The (1991 film), 244
Public Enemy, The (1931 film) 3, 9, 16, 58, 165, 238, 272n16, 273n24

Reader's Digest (1922 general interest magazine), 228
Rebel-in-Chief: Inside the Bold and Controversial Presidency of George W. Bush (2006 biography by Fred Barnes), 230, 232
Rebel Without a Cause (1955 film), 149, 214

Remains of the Day, The (1989 novel by Kazuo Ishiguro; 1993 film), 230
Rio Bravo (1959 film), 9, 240
Riven Rock (1998 novel by T.C. Boyles), 224
Rockford Files, The (1974–80 television series), 12
Rocky (1976 film), 163

Sands of Iwo Jima (1949 film), 216
Saturday Night Fever (1977 film), 132, 163
Scarface (1932 film), 160, 163
Search for Bill W., The (2000 novel by Mel B.), 227
Seinfeld (1989–98 television series), 83
Sex and the City (1998–2003 television series), 262
Shield, The (2002–8 television series), 262
Six Feet Under (2001–5 television series), 262
60 Minutes (1968– television newsmagazine), 247
Spartacus (1960 film), 238
Sposa son disprezzata (1734 opera aria), 48, 257
Star-Ledger, The (newspaper), 220, 221, 222, 223, 267n4
"Stopping by Woods on a Snowy Evening" (1922 poem by Robert Frost), 215
Stuck Mojo (heavy metal rock band), 206
"Surfin' USA" (1963 song by The Beach Boys), 78

Theory of the Leisure Class, The (1899 economic treatise by Thorstein Veblen), 231
30 Rock (2006–13 television series), 83

"This Magic Moment" (1969 song by Jay and the Americans), 189
"Those Were the Days" (1968 song by Mary Hopkin), 189
Three Amigos, The (1986 film), 249
Thrilla in Manilla (1975 televised boxing match), 261
'Tis (1999 memoir by Frank McCourt), 225
Treme (2010– television series), 262
True Detective (2014– television series), 263
Twilight Zone, The (1959–64 television series), 20–1

Untouchables, The (1959–63 television series), 82

Valacci Papers, The (1968 novel by Peter Maas), 227
Virginian, The (1929 film), 16
Virginian: A Horseman of the Plains, The (1902 novel by Owen Wister), 16
Visitation of the Virgin and St. Elizabeth (1528 painting), 55, 272n22
Vito (2012 documentary), 262

Welcome Back, Kotter (1975–9 television series), 82, 132, 163
Who Wants to Be a Millionaire (1999–2002 game show), 242
"Who Will You Run To?" (1987 song by Heart), 189
Wire, The (2002–8 television series), 262
Wise Guide to Wise Guys (fictional Mafia work by fictional author Manny Safier), 229
Wonder of Boys, The (2006 self-help book by Michael Gurian), 229

www.ingramcontent.com/pod-product-compliance
Lightning Source LLC
Chambersburg PA
CBHW030304080526
44584CB00012B/429